A note about this combined book

Thank you for purchasing the *Adobe Photoshop Elements 6 and Adobe Premiere Elements 4 Classroom in a Book Collection*. By combining two books in one, you'll get the opportunity to learn two exciting applications in the same book.

The *Adobe Photoshop Elements 6 Classroom in a Book* is in the front of this combined volume. The index for the *Adobe Photoshop Elements 6 Classroom in a Book* immediately follows the text, and begins on Page 366.

Immediately following is the *Adobe Premiere Elements 4 Classroom in a Book*, beginning after Page 372 of the previous book. Note that this book's pages are numbered separately, and its index begins on Page 292 in the very back of the book.

A note about the DVD

The lesson files for both books are included on a single DVD-ROM.

Lesson files for the *Adobe Photoshop Elements 6 Classroom in a Book* are in a folder called "Adobe Photoshop Elements 6.0."

Some lessons in the *Adobe Photoshop Elements 6 Classroom in a Book* refer to files on an accompanying CD-ROM. Those files are all on the single Windows DVD-ROM in the back of this book.

Lesson files for *Adobe Premiere Elements 4 Classroom in a Book* are in a folder named "Adobe Premiere Elements 4.0."

ADOBE®
Photoshop®
Elements 6

CLASSROOM IN A BOOK®

Lesson files . . . and so much more

The *Adobe Photoshop Elements 6.0 Classroom in a Book* CD includes the lesson files that you'll need to complete the exercises in this book, as well as other content to help you learn more about Adobe Photoshop Elements and use it with greater efficiency and ease. The diagram below represents the contents of the CD, which should help you locate the files you need.

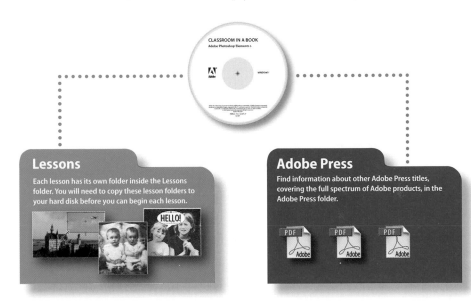

Lessons

Each lesson has its own folder inside the Lessons folder. You will need to copy these lesson folders to your hard disk before you can begin each lesson.

Adobe Press

Find information about other Adobe Press titles, covering the full spectrum of Adobe products, in the Adobe Press folder.

Contents

Getting Started

1   A Quick Tour of Photoshop Elements

2   Basic Organizing

3 Advanced Organizing

4 Creating Projects

5 Printing, Sharing, and Exporting

6 Adjusting Color in Images

7   Fixing Exposure Problems

8   Repairing and Retouching Images

9 **Working with Text**

10 **Combining Multiple Images**

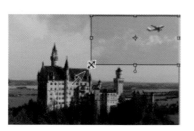

11   Advanced Editing Techniques

Getting Started

Adobe® Photoshop® Elements 6.0 delivers image-editing tools that balance power and versatility with ease of use. Photoshop Elements 6.0 is ideal for home users, hobbyists, business users, and professional photographers—anyone who wants to produce good-looking pictures and sophisticated graphics for the Web and for print.

If you've used earlier versions of Photoshop Elements, you'll find that this Classroom in a Book® teaches many advanced skills and describes innovative features that Adobe Systems has introduced in this version. If you're new to Adobe Photoshop Elements 6.0, you'll learn the fundamental concepts and techniques that help you master the application.

About Classroom in a Book

Adobe Photoshop Elements 6.0 Classroom in a Book is part of the official training series for Adobe graphics and publishing software developed by Adobe product experts. Each lesson in this book is made up of a series of self-paced projects that give you hands-on experience using Photoshop Elements 6.0.

The *Adobe Photoshop Elements 6.0 Classroom in a Book* includes a CD attached to the inside back cover of this book. On the CD you'll find all the image files used for the lessons in this book, along with additional learning resources.

Prerequisites

Before you begin working on the lessons in this book, make sure that you and your computer are ready.

Requirements on your computer

You'll need about 400 MB of free space on your hard disk for the lesson files and the work files you'll create. The lesson files necessary for your work in this book are on the CD attached to the inside back cover of this book.

Required skills

The lessons in the *Adobe Photoshop Elements 6.0 Classroom in a Book* assume that you have a working knowledge of your computer and its operating system. This book does not teach the most basic and generic computer skills. If you can answer yes to the following questions, then you're probably well qualified to start working on the projects in these lessons. Most users should work on the lessons in the order in which they occur in the book.

• Do you know how to use the Microsoft Windows Start button and the Windows Taskbar? Can you open menus and submenus, and choose items from those menus?

• Do you know how to use My Computer, Windows Explorer, or Internet Explorer to find items stored in folders on your computer or browse the Internet?

• Are you comfortable using the mouse to move the cursor, select items, drag, and deselect? Have you used context menus, which open when you right-click items?

• When you have two or more open applications, do you know how to switch from one to another? Do you know how to switch to the Windows Desktop?

• Do you know how to open, close, and minimize individual windows? Can you move them to different locations on your screen? Can you resize a window by dragging?

• Can you scroll (vertically and horizontally) within a window to see contents that may not be visible in the displayed area?

• Are you familiar with the menus across the top of an application and how to use those menus?

• Have you used dialog boxes, such as the Print dialog box? Do you know how to click arrow icons to open a menu within a dialog box?

• Can you open, save, and close a file? Are you familiar with word processing tasks, such as typing, selecting words, backspacing, deleting, copying, pasting, and changing text?

• Do you know how to open and find information in Microsoft Windows Help?

If there are gaps in your mastery of these skills, see the Microsoft documentation for your version of Windows. Or, ask a computer-savvy friend or instructor for help.

Installing Adobe Photoshop Elements 6.0

You must purchase the Adobe Photoshop Elements 6.0 software separately and install it on a computer running Windows Vista® or Windows® XP. For system requirements and complete instructions on installing the software, see the Photoshop Elements 6.0 application CD and documentation.

Copying the Classroom in a Book files

The CD attached to the inside back cover of this book includes a Lessons folder containing all the electronic files for the lessons in this book. During the lessons, you will organize these files using a catalog that is an essential part of many projects in this book. Keep all the lesson files on your computer until after you have finished all the lessons.

Note: *The files on the CD are practice files, provided for your personal use in these lessons. You are not authorized to use these files commercially, or to publish or distribute them in any form without written permission from Adobe Systems, Inc. and the individual photographers who took the pictures, or other copyright holders.*

Copying the Lessons files from the CD

1   Insert the *Adobe Photoshop Elements 6.0 Classroom in a Book* CD into your CD-ROM drive. If a message appears asking what you want Windows to do, select Open folder to view files using Windows Explorer, and click OK.

If no message appears, open My Computer and double-click the CD icon to open it.

2   Locate the Lessons folder on the CD and copy it to the My Documents folder on your computer.

3   When your computer finishes copying the Lessons folder, remove the CD from your CD-ROM drive and put it away.

Go to the procedure on the next page before you start the lessons.

Creating a work folder

You'll now create a folder where you can save all of your work as you complete the lessons in this book. You'll use this folder in many of the lessons.

1   In Windows Explorer, open the Lessons folder that you copied to the My Documents folder on your hard disk.

2   In the Lessons folder, choose File > New > Folder. A new folder is created in the Lessons folder. Type **My CIB Work** to name the folder.

Creating a catalog

You'll use a catalog to organize the image files for the lessons in this book. This will keep all your images together in one easy-to-access location. You'll use the process of importing files into a catalog whenever you need to import images into Photoshop Elements from your digital camera, or import images already stored on your hard drive.

1   Start Adobe Photoshop Elements 6.0. In the Photoshop Elements Welcome Screen, click Organize in the row of shortcut buttons across the lower part of the Welcome Screen. This starts Photoshop Elements in the Organizer mode. If Photoshop Elements opens without first displaying the Welcome Screen, click the Welcome Screen button (⌂) located to the left in the menu bar to display the Welcome Screen.

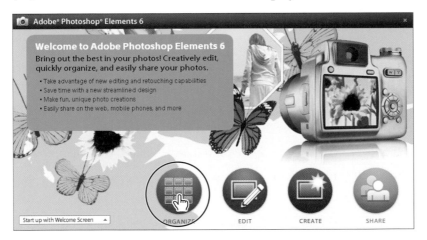

Note: If this is the first time you have started the Organizer, an alert message may appear asking if you would like to specify the location of photos. Click No if this alert message appears.

2   In Photoshop Elements 6.0 (Organizer), choose File > Catalog.

3   In the Catalog Manager dialog box, click New.

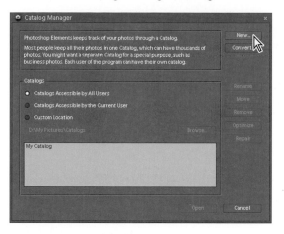

Note: Do not change the location where the Catalog file is stored.

4   In the Enter a name for the new catalog dialog box, type **CIB Catalog** as file name, deselect the Import free music into this catalog option, and then click OK.

5   In the Organizer, choose File > Get Photos and Videos > From Files and Folders. In the Get Photos from Files and Folders dialog box, open the My Documents folder. Click only once to select the Lessons folder that you copied from the CD. Do not double-click, as you do not want to open the Lessons folder.

6   Set the following options in the Get Photos from Files and Folders dialog box:

•   Confirm that the Get Photos from Subfolders checkbox is selected in the list of options above the Get Photos button.

•   Deselect the Automatically Fix Red Eyes and the Automatically Suggest Photo Stacks options. These are great options that you will learn more about as you work through the lessons, but we won't use them just yet. *(See illustration on the next page.)*

7 Click the Get Photos button. A window will open showing the photos being imported.

8 The Import Attached Keyword Tags dialog box opens. Click the Select All button, and then click the OK button.

The images you are bringing into the catalog contain additional information, known as keyword tags, which will help you organize those images as you proceed through the book. We've added these keyword tags to help make it easier to work with the lessons in this book. You'll learn all about keyword tags in Lessons 2 and 3. After the image files are imported into the catalog, the imported keyword tags are available in the Keyword Tags palette. The keyword tags will be referenced in the lessons throughout this book.

9   Photoshop Elements may display a dialog box informing you that the only items displayed in the Organizer are those you just imported. If an alert is displayed, click OK to close this dialog box.

10   Click OK to close any other alert dialog box. The imported files are displayed in the Photo Browser. Use the scrollbar at the right side to browse through the images.

11   Click the Show All button above the Photo Browser.

Reconnecting missing files to a catalog

After images are added to a catalog, Adobe Photoshop Elements expects them to remain in the same location. If you move the Lessons folder or any of the files after you have created the catalog, Adobe Photoshop Elements may no longer be able to find the files. In this case, a file-missing icon (📷) on top of the image thumbnail in the Photo Browser will alert you. If there are no files missing, you can now go on to the first lesson.

Note: To avoid missing files in your catalog, use the File > Move, File > Rename, and Edit > Delete From Catalog commands in Photoshop Elements to move, rename, or delete them.

If Photoshop Elements alerts you that it cannot find an image file, you will need to carry out the following procedure to reconnect the file to your catalog.

1   Choose File > Reconnect > All Missing Files. If the message "There are no files to reconnect" appears, click OK, then skip the rest of this procedure.

2 If a message "Searching for missing files" appears, click the Browse button. The Reconnect Missing Files dialog box opens.

3 In the Browse tab on the right side of the Reconnect Missing Files dialog box, navigate to and open the moved folder.

4 Continuing to work in the Browse tab, locate and click once to select the folder that has the same name as the folder listed underneath the image thumbnail. The folder name is listed on the left side of the Reconnect Missing Files dialog box, directly under the image thumbnail.

5 After you select the appropriate folder and the correct thumbnail picture appears in the right side of the dialog box, click the Reconnect button.

6 Repeat steps 4 and 5, continuing to select the appropriate folders and clicking the Reconnect button as you find matching files. When all the files are reconnected, click the Close button.

You can now use the Photoshop Elements Organizer to select and open files in the Photoshop Elements Editor.

Note: This procedure also eliminates error messages regarding missing files when you work with Creations, or print from the Organizer.

Additional resources

Adobe Photoshop Elements 6.0 Classroom in a Book is not meant to replace documentation that comes with the program, nor is it designed to be a comprehensive reference for every feature in Photoshop Elements 6.0. For additional information about program features, refer to any of these resources:

• Photoshop Elements Help, which is built into the Adobe Photoshop Elements 6.0 application. You can view it by choosing Help > Photoshop Elements Help.

• You can also choose Help > Online Support or Help > Online Learning Resources for access to the support pages or links to additional learning resources on the Adobe Web site (www.adobe.com). Both of these options require that you have Internet access.

• The Adobe Photoshop Elements 6.0 Getting Started Guide, which is included either in the box with your copy of Adobe Photoshop Elements, or on the installation CD for the application software in PDF format. If you don't already have Adobe Reader (or if you don't have the latest version of Adobe Reader, formerly called Acrobat Reader) installed on your computer, you can download a free copy from the Adobe Web site (www.adobe.com).

Adobe Certification

The Adobe Training and Certification Programs are designed to help Adobe customers improve and promote their product-proficiency skills. The Adobe Certified Expert (ACE) program is designed to recognize the high-level skills of expert users. Adobe Certified Training Providers (ACTP) use only Adobe Certified Experts to teach Adobe software classes. Available in either ACTP classrooms or on-site, the ACE program is the best way to master Adobe products. For Adobe Certified Training Programs information, visit the Partnering with Adobe Web site at http://partners.adobe.com.

1 A Quick Tour of Photoshop Elements

This lesson introduces the tools and the interface of Adobe Photoshop Elements 6.0. Further lessons in this book provide more in-depth exercises and specific details as to how you can take advantage of the tools.

This lesson provides an overview of the concepts and procedures involved with capturing and editing digital images using Photoshop Elements. If you prefer to skip this overview, you can jump right into working with digital images in Lesson 2. However, we encourage you to review this lesson before you get too far along in the book.

In this lesson, you will learn how to do the following:

- Work with the Organizer and the Editor.
- Attach media.
- Use the Photo Downloader.
- Review and Compare Photos.
- Send Photos in e-mail.
- Use Help and the How To palette.

How Photoshop Elements works

About workspaces

Photoshop Elements has two primary workspaces: the Organizer for finding, organizing and sharing photos and media files, and the Editor for creating, editing and fixing your images.

When a photo is selected in the Organizer, clicking the Editor button (▨) located near the top right corner of the Organizer window, and then choosing Quick Fix, Full Edit, or Guided Edit from the menu, opens the selected photo in the Editor workspace. In the Editor, clicking the Organizer button (▦▦) located near the top right corner of the Editor window opens the Organizer workspace.

Use the buttons at the top of the work area to switch between the Organizer (shown in the background in the above illustration) and the Editor (shown in the foreground in the above illustration).

💡 *Once both the Organizer and the Editor are open in Photoshop Elements, you can also move between the two workspaces by clicking the corresponding button in the Windows task bar at the bottom of the screen.*

The Organizer workspace

The Organizer lets you find, organize and share your photos and media files in the Photo Browser. It can display a single photo or media file, or display thumbnails of all the photos and media files in your catalog. If you prefer viewing your photos and media files by date, the Organizer has a Date View workspace that lets you work with your files in a calendar format.

The Photo Browser lists all the photos and cataloged assets in one comprehensive window that you can easily browse through. It can show previews of files stored remotely, such as on a CD.

In the Organize panel of the Task pane, organize your photos by using keyword tags and by placing them in albums.

The Fix panel of the Task pane offers tools for the most common photographic editing tasks, such as color correction and red eye removal. For more complex editing tasks, selecting Quick Fix, Full Edit, or Guided Edit switches to the Editor workspace.

Use the Create panel of the Task pane to create projects such as greeting cards or slide shows, and use the tools in the Share panel to share your files with others.

The Editor workspace

The Editor lets you focus on creating and editing images. Depending on your needs, you can choose between the Full Edit workspace with tools to correct color, create special effects, or enhance photos, the Quick Fix workspace with simple tools and commands to quickly fix common problems, and the Guided Edit workspace with step-by-step instructions for common editing tasks.

If you are new to digital imaging, Quick Fix or Guided Edit is a good place to start fixing photos.

If you've previously worked with image editing software, you'll find that the Full Edit workspace provides a more flexible and powerful image editing environment. This function has lighting and color correction commands, tools to fix image imperfections, selection tools, text editing tools and painting tools. You can arrange the Full Edit workspace to best suit your needs by moving, hiding and showing palettes, arranging palettes in the Palette Bin, zooming in or out of a photo, scrolling to a different area of the document window and creating multiple windows and views.

The Full Edit workspace.

Using the Palette Bin

The Palette Bin of the Full Edit workspace provides a convenient location to store and manage the palettes you use for editing images. By default, only the Effects and Layers palettes are placed in the Palette Bin. Other palettes that you open (using the Window menu) are positioned in the work area. These are known as floating palettes. You can change which palettes float and which are stored in the Palette Bin.

To add floating palettes to the Palette Bin

1 *Choose Window > [palette name] to open the palette you want to place in the Palette Bin.*

2 *Drag the palette by its tab to the Palette Bin. The tab contains the palette name. To reposition the palette without placing it in the Palette Bin, drag the palette by the bar across the top of the palette.*

You can also choose the Place in Palette Bin when Closed option from the palette menu, and then close the palette window.

To remove palettes from the Palette Bin or close palettes:

1 *Drag a palette out of the Palette Bin by clicking and dragging the title bar that lists the name of the palette.*

2 *Click the palette menu and deselect Place in Palette Bin when Closed option.*

3 *To close a palette, choose Window > [palette name], or click the close box (✖) in the top right corner of a floating palette. Palettes that display a check mark adjacent to their name in the Window menu are visible; selecting a palette name that includes a check mark causes the palette window to close.*

To adjust palette sizes in the Palette Bin

Adjust the height of palettes by doing either or both of the following:

- Click the triangle to the left of the palette bin to adjust the palette bin width.
- Click and drag the separator bars between palettes up or down to adjust the height of a palette.

Workflow

The fundamental workflow for Adobe Photoshop Elements is to:

• Capture images and media into the Organizer from a digital camera, scanner, or digital video camera.

• Organize images and media—including applying keyword tags—using the Organizer.

• Edit images and media by color correcting or adding text, using the Editor.

• Share images and media by e-mailing, using a sharing service, or burning to CD/DVD ROM.

Attaching media

Importing digital files directly into Photoshop Elements is easy.

Getting photos

To view and organize your photos in Photoshop Elements, you first need to bring them into the application. You can get photos into Photoshop Elements in several ways:

• Bring photos from your camera or card reader directly into the Photoshop Elements Organizer using Adobe Photo Downloader. Getting photos directly will save you time and enable you to quickly start working with your photos.

- Use the software that came with your digital camera to download pictures to your computer, and then bring them into Photoshop Elements using the From Files and Folders command. If you prefer to work with other software to import your files to your computer, you'll need to disable Adobe Photo Downloader to use the other software. To disable the Adobe Photo Downloader, click its icon (▣) in the system tray or task bar, and then choose Disable. Only do this if you plan to use other software to bring images onto your computer.

- If your camera or card reader displays as a drive, e.g., in My Computer, you can drag the files to a folder on your hard drive, and then bring them into Photoshop Elements using the From Files and Folders command.

In most cases, you'll need to install software drivers that came with your camera before you can download pictures to your computer. You may also need to set up the Photoshop Elements Camera or Card Reader Preferences. See "Getting photos" in Lesson 2, "Basic Organizing."

Creating a new catalog

You organize your photographs in catalogs, which manage the image files on your computer but are independent of the photo files themselves. Along with digital photographs, you can include in a catalog video and audio files, scans, PDF documents, and other personal creations. A single catalog can efficiently handle thousands of files, but you can also create separate catalogs for different types of work.

1 Start Photoshop Elements, either by double-clicking the shortcut on your desktop or by choosing Start > All Programs > Adobe Photoshop Elements 6.0.

2 Do one of the following:

- If the Welcome Screen appears, click Organize in the row of shortcut buttons across the lower part of the Welcome Screen. Wait until the Organizer has finished opening.

- If Photoshop Elements 6.0 (Editor) opens without first displaying the Welcome Screen, click the Welcome Screen button (⌂) located to the left in the menu bar to display the Welcome Screen, and then click Organize. Or, click the Organizer button (▦) located to the right in the menu bar. Wait until the Organizer has finished opening.

- If Photoshop Elements 6.0 (Organizer) opens, you are ready to continue with step 3.

3 In Organizer mode, choose File > Catalog.

4   In the Catalog Manager dialog box, click New.

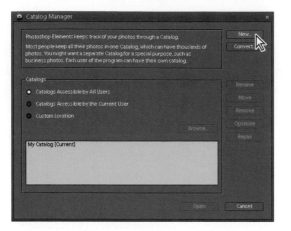

5   In the Enter a name for the new catalog dialog box, type **Lesson1** as file name, deselect the Import free music into this catalog option, and then click OK.

Now you have a special catalog that you'll use just for this lesson. All you need is some pictures to put in it.

Using the Adobe Photo Downloader

For the rest of this lesson you will need to import images into the Organizer. If you have a digital camera and images of your own, follow the steps in the next section. Otherwise, skip to the section, "To get photos from files and folders."

Getting photos from a digital camera or card reader

You can import files from your camera directly into Photoshop Elements.

1   Connect your camera or card reader to your computer. For instructions on connecting your device, see the documentation that came with it.

2   Do the following:

• If the Windows Auto Play dialog box appears, click Cancel.

• If the Photo Downloader dialog box appears automatically, continue with step 3.

• If the Photo Downloader dialog box does not appear automatically, choose File > Get Photos and Videos > From Camera or Card Reader.

3   Under Source in the Photo Downloader dialog box, choose the name of the connected camera or card reader from the Get Photos from menu.

4   Under Import Settings, accept the folder location listed next to Location, or click Browse to choose a new location for the files.

5   Next to Create Subfolder(s), choose one of the date formats if you want the photos to be stored in a folder whose name includes the date the photos were imported or taken. You can also choose Custom Name to create a folder using a name you type in the text box, or choose None if you don't want to create any subfolder. Your selection is reflected in the pathname displayed next to Location.

6 Choose Do not rename files from the Rename Files menu, and from the Delete Options menu choose After Copying, Do Not Delete Originals. If selected, deselect the Automatic Download check box.

You will learn more about customizing import settings and the advanced features of the Adobe Photo Downloader in Lessons 2 and 3.

7 Click the Get Photos button.

The photos are copied from the camera to the specified folder location.

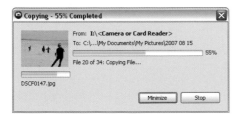

8 If the Files Successfully Copied dialog box appears, click OK.

The Getting Photos dialog box appears and the photos are imported into Photoshop Elements.

If the imported photos contain keyword metadata, the Import Attached Keyword Tags dialog box appears. Select the keyword tags you want to import. The keyword tags you select are added to the Keyword Tags palette when the photos are imported. If a keyword tag has an asterisk (*), you already have a keyword tag of the same name in your catalog and that keyword tag is attached to the photos.

9   Click OK to close any other alert dialog box.

The imported photos appear in the Photo Browser.

About keyword tags

Keyword tags are personalized labels, such as "Vacation" or "Beach," that you attach
to photos, video clips, audio clips and other creations in the Photo Browser to easily
organize and find them. When you use keyword tags, there's no need to manually
organize your photos in subject-specific folders or rename files with content-specific
names. Instead, you simply attach one or more keyword tags to each photo. You can
then easily retrieve the photos you want by clicking the appropriate keyword tags in
the Keyword Tags palette.

For example, you can create a keyword tag called "Christine" and attach it to every
photo featuring your sister, Christine. You can then instantly find all the photos with
the Christine keyword tag by clicking the Find box next to the Christine keyword
tag in the Keyword Tags palette, regardless of where the photos are stored on your
computer.

You can create keyword tags using any labels you want. For instance, you can create
keyword tags for individual people, places and events in your life. You can attach
multiple keyword tags to your photos. When photos have multiple keyword tags,
you can easily run a search on a combination of keyword tags to find a particular
person at a particular place or event. For example, you can search for all "Christine"
keyword tags and all "John" keyword tags to find all pictures of Christine with
her husband, John. Or search for all "Christine" keyword tags and all "California"
keyword tags to find all the pictures of Christine vacationing in California.

Use keyword tags to organize and find photos by their content. You specify names
for your keyword tags and choose the photos that fall into those categories. See
Lessons 2 and 3 for more information on keyword tags.

The control bar, which contains buttons for playing, rotating and zooming disappears from view when you don't move the mouse for a couple of seconds.

3   To make the control bar reappear, move the mouse.

💡 *When you view images in full screen, you can quickly assign a rating. On the right end of the control bar, click a star to apply a rating. You can also apply the rating using the shortcut keys, 1 (for 1 star) through 5 (for 5 stars).*

4   Press the Esc key on your keyboard to return to the Organizer.

5   Click the Display button (■), and then choose Compare Photos Side by Side to display two photos simultaneously. Side by Side View is useful when you need to focus on details and differences between photos. You can select two or more photos to compare. When you click the Next Photo button (●) in the control bar, the selected image changes to the next image in your catalog. By default, image # 1 (on the left or top) is selected. To select image #2 instead, click it.

Note: The selected image has a blue border. If you have the filmstrip showing, you can click any image in the filmstrip to view it in place of the selected image.

Use Side by Side View to analyze composition and details.

You can switch between views by clicking the Full Screen View button (■) or the Side by Side View button (■■) in the control bar. While in either view, you can right-click an image and access further options from the context menu. You can, for example, mark an image for printing, fix red eye, add a photo to an album, and delete or apply keyword tags.

6 Press the Esc key on your keyboard to return to the Organizer.

💡 *Choose the photos to be compared in the Organizer by holding the Ctrl key and selecting the images. Then, choose View > Compare Photos Side by Side.*

Choosing files

To select more than one photo in the Photo Browser, hold down the Ctrl key and click the photos you want to select. Holding down the Ctrl key enables you to select multiple, non-consecutive files. To select photos that are in consecutive order, click the first photo, and then hold down the Shift key and click the last photo you want. All the photos between the first and last photos will be selected as well.

Sharing photos in e-mail

Have you ever had to wait long time for an incoming e-mail to download, and then find that the e-mail contained only a single photograph in an unnecessarily high resolution? You can avoid imposing this inconvenience on others by using the Organizer e-mail function, which creates a version of the image that is optimized specifically for sending via e-mail.

1 In the Photo Browser, select the photo (or photos) you'd like to send in an e-mail.

2 In the Share panel of the Task pane, click the E-mail Attachments button.

Note: *When you use this function for the first time, you are asked to select the e-mail service you want to use. You can later review or change your settings under Edit > Preferences > Sharing.*

3 (Optional) Drag photos from the Photo Browser to add to your selection.

4 Select Very Small (320 x 240 px) from the Maximum Photo Size menu and adjust the image quality using the Quality slider (the higher the quality the larger the file size and the longer the download time). The resulting file size and download time for a typical 56 Kbps dial-up modem are estimated and displayed for your reference. When done, click Next.

5   Under Message, select and delete the "Here are the photos…." text and type a message of your own.

6   Next to Select Recipients, click the Edit Contact Book button (⬚). In the Contact Book dialog box, click the New Contact button (⬚). In the New Contact dialog box, type in the name (or a nickname—our example uses Mom) of the person to whom you want to send the picture, and that person's e-mail address. Click OK to close the New Contact dialog box and click OK again to close the Contact Book dialog box.

7   Under Select Recipients, click the check box next to Mom to select it, and then click Next.

Your default e-mail application immediately creates an e-mail message. You can edit the message and Subject line to say what you want. When you are finished and ready to send the e-mail, then either make sure that you are connected to the Internet and click Send if you want to send an actual e-mail, or close the message without saving or sending it.

8 Switch back to Photoshop Elements (Organizer).

Using Help

Help is available in several ways, each one useful to you for different circumstances:

Help in the application The complete documentation for using Adobe Photoshop Elements is available as Help in the application, which is HTML content you access through your default browser, such as Internet Explorer. Help in the application provides easy access to summarized information on common tasks and concepts. Help in the application can be especially useful if you are new to Photoshop Elements or if you aren't connected to the Internet.

LiveDocs Help on the Web This is the most comprehensive and up-to-date version of Photoshop Elements Help. It is the recommended choice if you have an active Internet connection.

Note: You do not need to be connected to the Internet to view Help in the application. However, with an active Internet connection, clicking the "This page on the Web" link on any page in the application's Help opens the corresponding page in LiveDocs.

Help PDF Help is also available as a PDF that is optimized for printing; just go to http://www.adobe.com/go/learn_pse_printpdf to download the PDF document.

Note: The Help PDF file is about 36 MBytes in size and may take a considerable time to download when using a slow Internet connection.

Links in the application Within the Photoshop Elements application there are links to additional help topics, such as the "Tell me more" link at the bottom of the panel in each guided task.

Navigating Help in the application

Choose Help > Photoshop Elements Help, or press the F1 key. Your default Web browser will open and display the starting page of the Adobe Photoshop Help in the application. Do any of the following:

• Select Contents in the top left corner of the window. Click a topic heading in the table of content on the left side of the window. Click the plus sign (+) to the left of a topic heading to see its sub-topics. Select a topic or sub-topic to display its content on the right side of the window.

• Select Contents in the top left corner of the window. Click on a letter to display index entries starting with that letter. Click the plus sign (+) to the left of an index header or click the index header to see its entries. Click the index entry to display its content on the right side of the window.

• Select Search in the top left corner of the window. Enter a search term, and then click Search. When the search has finished, click a search result in the list on the left side of the window to display its content on the right side of the window.

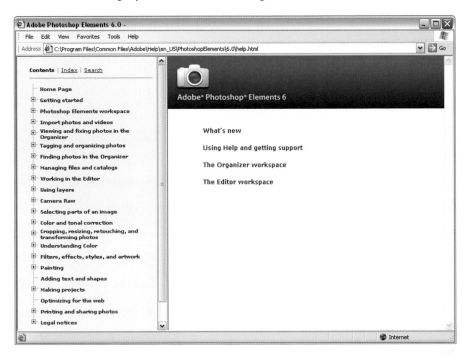

Search tips

Adobe Help Search works by searching the entire Help text for topics that contain all the words typed in the Search box. These tips can help you improve your search results in Help:

• If you search using a phrase, such as "shape tool," put quotation marks around the phrase. The search returns only those topics containing that specific phrase.

• Make sure that the search terms are spelled correctly.

• If a search term doesn't yield results, try using a synonym, such as "photo" instead of "picture."

Accessing LiveDocs Help on the Web

LiveDocs Help on the Web contains the most up-to-date version of Photoshop Elements Help. In addition, it enables you to search across multiple applications.

1   To access Photoshop Elements' LiveDocs Help on the Web, part of the Adobe Help Resource Center, do any of the following:

•   Click the "This page on the Web" link, located at the bottom of any topic page in Adobe Help in the application.

•   In your Web browser, open the Adobe Help Resource Center at http://www.adobe. com/support/documentation. Select Photoshop Elements from the list of products, and then click Go. On the Photoshop Elements resources page, click the LiveDocs link.

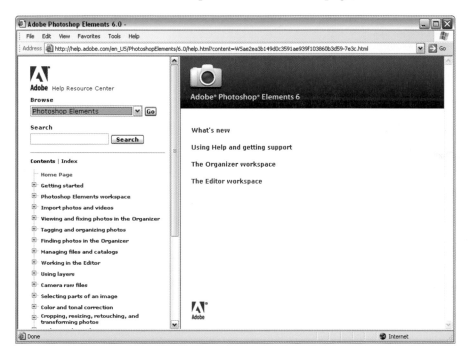

2   To switch to LiveDocs Help for a different product, select that product from the list under Browse, and then click Go.

3   To search for a topic, enter the search term under Search, and then click Search. To search across all products, select Search all products on the LiveDocs Search Results page, enter the search term, and then click Go.

Links to help in the application

There are some links to additional help within the Photoshop Elements application. Clicking these links will take you to the corresponding topic in either Help in the application or LiveDocs Help on the Web.

Hot-linked tips

Hot-linked tips are available throughout Adobe Photoshop Elements. These tips display information in the form of a typical tip balloon, or they will link you to the appropriate topic in the help file.

You've reached the end of the first lesson. Now that you understand how to get photos and the essentials of the Photoshop Elements interface, you are ready to start organizing and editing photos—which you'll do in the next lessons.

Review

▶ **Review questions**

1   What are the primary workspaces in Adobe Photoshop Elements 6.0?

2   Define the fundamental workflow.

3   What is the function of a catalog?

4   What are keyword tags?

5   How can you select multiple thumbnail images in the Photo Browser?

▶ **Review answers**

1   Photoshop Elements has two main workspaces: the Organizer workspace for finding, organizing and sharing photos and media files, and the Editor workspace for creating, editing and fixing your images. You can use the buttons on the top of the work area to switch between the Organizer and the Editor.

2   The fundamental workflow in Adobe Photoshop Elements involves:

   a   Capturing media into the Organizer from a digital camera, scanner, digital video camera, or an image created from scratch in the editing component.

   b   Categorize the media in the Organizer using the tag assignment features.

   c   Edit the media by color correcting or adding text, using the Editor.

   d   Share the media by e-mailing, using a sharing service or burning to CD/ DVD ROM.

3   You organize your photographs in catalogs that manage the image files on your computer but are independent of the photo files themselves. Along with digital photographs, you can include video and audio files, scans, PDF documents, and your personal creations in a catalog. A single catalog can efficiently handle thousands of photos, but to better manage your image files you can also create separate catalogs for different types of work.

4   Keyword tags are personalized labels such as "House" or "Beach" that you attach to photos, creations, and video or audio clips in the Photo Browser so that you can easily organize and find them.

5   To select more than one photo in the Photo Browser, hold down the Ctrl key and click the photos you want to select. Holding down the Ctrl key enables you to select multiple, non-consecutive files. To select photos that are in consecutive order, click the first photo, hold down the Shift key, and then click the last photo you want. All the photos between the first and last photos will be selected as well.

2 | Basic Organizing

After capturing your memories with your digital camera, you'll want to store and organize your pictures on your computer. This lesson gets you started with the essential skills you'll need to import and track your images.

In this lesson, you will learn how to do the following:

- Open Adobe Photoshop Elements 6.0 in Organizer mode.

- Create a catalog of your images.

- Import images into a catalog from a digital camera or from folders on your computer.

- Change the display of thumbnails in your Photo Browser.

- Create, organize, and apply tags to images.

Photoshop Elements 6.0 for Windows includes two primary parts: the Editor and the Organizer. Together they work hand-in-hand to help you find, share, and make corrections to your photographs and images.

Before you start working in Adobe Photoshop Elements 6.0, make sure that you have installed the software on your computer from the application CD. See "Installing Adobe Photoshop Elements 6.0" on page 3.

Also make sure that you have correctly copied the Lessons folder from the CD in the back of this book onto your computer's hard disk. See "Copying the Classroom in a Book files" on page 3.

Most people need between one and two hours to complete all the projects in this lesson.

Getting started

In this lesson, you're going to work primarily in the Organizer component of Photoshop Elements.

1   Start Photoshop Elements, either by double-clicking the shortcut on your desktop, or by choosing Start > All Programs > Adobe Photoshop Elements 6.0.

2   Do one of the following:

• If the Welcome Screen appears, click Organize in the row of shortcut buttons across the lower part of the Welcome Screen.

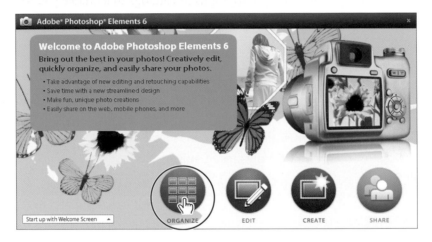

• If Photoshop Elements 6.0 (Editor) opens without first displaying the Welcome Screen, click the Welcome Screen button (⌂) located to the left in the menu bar to display the Welcome Screen, and then click Organize. Or, click the Organizer button (▦) located to the right in the menu bar. Then, wait until the Organizer has finished opening.

• If Photoshop Elements 6.0 (Organizer) opens, you don't have to do anything more and are all set to start with this lesson.

 From the menu located in the lower left corner of the Welcome Screen, you can choose to either display the Welcome Screen next time you start Photoshop Elements, or not to display the Welcome Screen and instead open directly in the Editor or Organizer.

Getting photos

The Organizer component of Photoshop Elements gives you a working area where you can efficiently organize, sort, and perform basic editing of your pictures. When you want to print your photographs or send them with an e-mail, having the images collected in the Organizer is an essential step in the process, as you'll see later in this lesson.

Creating a new catalog

Photoshop Elements organizes your photographs in catalogs that enable you to manage the image files on your computer. Catalogs are independent of the photo files themselves. You can include video and audio files along with digital photographs and scans in your catalogs. A single catalog can efficiently handle thousands of photos, but you can also create separate catalogs for different types of work. You'll create a new catalog now so that you won't confuse the practice files for this lesson with the other lesson files for this book.

Note: In this book, the forward arrow character (>) is used to refer to commands and submenus found in the menus at the top of the application window, for example, File, Edit, and so forth.

1   In Photoshop Elements 6.0 (Organizer), choose File > Catalog.

2   In the Catalog Manager dialog box, click New.

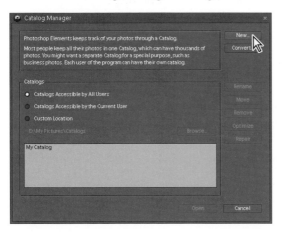

3   In the Enter a name for the new catalog dialog box, type **Lesson2** as file name, deselect the Import free music into this catalog option, and then click OK.

You will use this catalog to import—by various methods—the images for this lesson.

Dragging photos from Windows Explorer

This method of adding photographs to an Organizer catalog, using the familiar drag-and-drop technique, couldn't be easier or more intuitive.

1   Minimize the Organizer by clicking the Minimize button (⬚) towards the right end of the menu bar, or by clicking the Organizer application button on the Windows taskbar.

2   Open My Computer by whatever method you usually use, such as double-clicking an icon on the desktop, using the Start menu, or using Windows Explorer.

3   Navigate through the folder structure to find and open the Lesson02 folder you copied to your hard disk (see "Copying the Classroom in a Book files" on page 3). You'll see three folders inside the Lesson02 folder: BATCH1, BATCH2, and BATCH3.

4   Drag and hold the BATCH1 folder icon over the Organizer application button on the Windows taskbar.

5 Wait until the Organizer becomes the foreground application, and then drag and release the pointer with the BATCH1 folder icon in the Organizer application window.

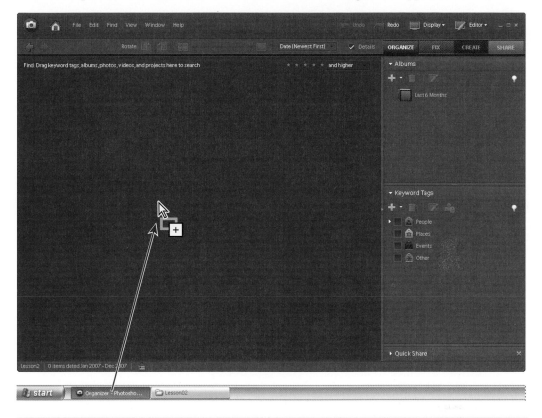

If you can arrange the Windows Explorer window and the Organizer application window on your screen so that you can see both windows at the same time, you can also drag and drop the folder icon (or individual files) directly from the Windows Explorer window onto the Organizer application window.

The Organizer will briefly display a dialog box while searching inside the BATCH1 folder for files to import.

Because the files found in the BATCH1 folder have keyword tags applied to them to help keep them organized, the Import Attached Keyword Tags dialog box will open.

6   In the Import Attached Keyword Tags dialog box, click Select All, and then click OK.

You will briefly see the Getting Photos dialog box while the Organizer is importing the image files from the BATCH1 folder.

7   If a message appears telling you that only the newly imported items will be visible in the main window of the catalog, click OK.

![Adobe Photoshop Elements dialog]
Adobe Photoshop Elements

The only items in the main window are those you just imported. To see the rest of the Catalog, click Show All.

Don't Show Again

OK

💡 *If you don't want to see this message each time you import new items, select Don't Show Again before clicking OK. To have it show again, click Reset All Warning Dialogs in the General section of the Preferences dialog box.*

8 Click the Maximize button (▣) towards the right end of the menu bar in the Organizer window. This causes the window to expand and cover the entire screen.

In the Photo Browser, you can now see thumbnails of the four images you've added to your Lesson2 catalog. Don't drag the other two batches into the Organizer because you're going to use different methods of adding them to your catalog.

💡 *The timeline above the Photo Browser that you might be familiar with from earlier versions of Photoshop Elements, is now hidden by default. To toggle the visibility of the timeline, choose Window > Timeline. To customize the amount of information displayed in the Photo Browser, select or deselect View > Details. With View > Details selected, you can additionally select or deselect View > Show File Names, or View > Show Grid Lines. Another option is to select or deselect View > Show Borders around Thumbnails.*

Getting photos from specific locations

A second technique for adding items to your catalog is to use a menu command instead of having to resize and arrange windows on the desktop.

1	Choose File > Get Photos and Videos > From Files and Folders.

2	In the Get Photos from Files and Folders dialog box, navigate to the Lesson02 folder and open the BATCH2 folder.

3	One by one, hover (don't click!) with the pointer over each of the four image files inside the BATCH2 folder. You'll see additional information about the image next to the pointer, and a thumbnail image is displayed in the Preview area.

4	If selected, deselect the Automatically Fix Red Eyes and the Automatically Suggest Photo Stacks check boxes.

5	Press Ctrl+A, or drag-select the four images in the BATCH2 folder, and then click the Get Photos button.

💡 *Select a folder icon in the Get Photos from Files and Folders dialog box, and then click Get Photos to import all items within that folder (and its subfolders if the Get Photos From Subfolders check box is selected).*

6	In the Import Attached Keyword Tags dialog box, notice that the keyword tag "Lesson 2" from the new batch of images will, if selected, map to the existing keyword tag in the catalog (from the import of the images in the first batch). Click the Advanced button in the lower left corner of the dialog box. Here you could assign a new name to keyword tags found in the imported items, or map them to other existing keyword tags in the catalog. But for now, leave things unchanged and just click the Reset to Basic button.

7   Click Select All, and then click OK. To close any other alert dialog box, click OK.

8   Click the Show All button above the Photo Browser to see all eight images.

9   To rotate the last image of the second batch, named 02_08.jpg, click to select it, and then click the Rotate Left button (⬐) above the Photo Browser.

Automatically Fixing Red Eyes

The term "red eye" refers to the often-observed phenomenon in photos taken with a flash, where the subject's irises are red instead of black. This is caused by the flash reflecting off the back of the eye.

While none of the images in this lesson require red eye correction, when needed you can quickly remove red eye automatically while importing images into the Photo Browser. To remove red eye automatically, select the Automatically Fix Red Eyes check box in the Get Photos from Files and Folders dialog box.

Additional ways to fix red eye will be discussed in lessons 3 and 6.

Searching for photos to add

This method is probably the one you'll want to use if you're not sure where in your folder structure you've stashed photographs and other resources over the years. Ordinarily, you might run this search on your entire hard disk or for the whole My Documents folder. For this demonstration, you'll limit your search area to a very restricted part of the folder organization on your computer.

1   In the Organizer, choose File > Get Photos and Videos > By Searching.

2   Under Search Options in the Get Photos By Searching for Folders dialog box, choose Browse from the Look In menu.

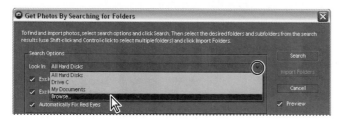

3   In the Browse For Folder dialog box, click to select the Lesson02 folder, and then click OK.

4   Under Search Options in the Get Photos By Searching for Folders dialog box, deselect the Automatically Fix Red Eyes check box, if not already deselected.

5   Click the Search button located in the upper right corner of the dialog box.

6   Under Search Results, click to select only the BATCH3 folder, and then click the Import Folders button.

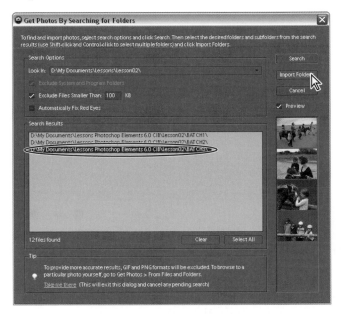

7   In the Import Attached Keyword Tags dialog box, click Select All, and then click OK. Click OK to close any other alert dialog box. In the Organizer, examine the newly imported items, and then click the Show All button above the Photo Browser to see all 12 images now in your Lesson2 catalog.

Importing from a digital camera

This exercise is optional and requires that you have an available digital camera or memory card from your camera with pictures on it. You can either perform this procedure now, or skip to the Viewing photo thumbnails section later in this lesson.

1   Connect your digital camera or the card reader for your digital camera to your computer, following the equipment manufacturer's instructions.

2   Do the following:

• If the Windows Auto Play dialog box appears, click Cancel.

• If the Photo Downloader dialog box appears automatically, continue with step 3.

• If the Photo Downloader dialog box does not appear automatically, choose File > Get Photos and Videos > From Camera or Card Reader.

💡 *You can also launch the Adobe Photo Downloader by double-clicking its icon (🖼) in the system tray in the lower right corner of your screen.*

3   Under Source in the Photo Downloader dialog box, choose from the Get Photos from menu the name of the connected camera or card reader.

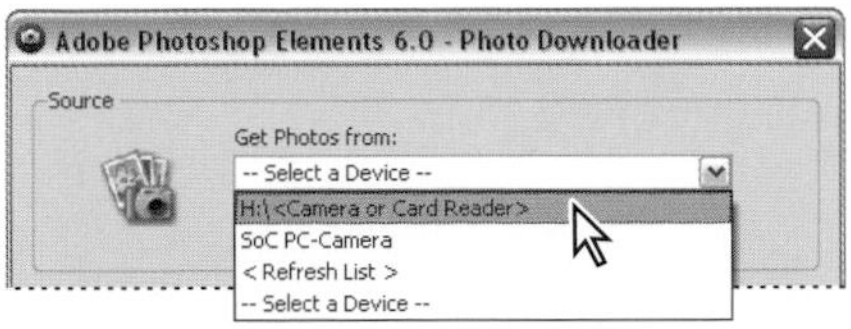

4   Under Import Settings, accept the folder location listed next to Location, or click Browse to choose a new location for the files.

5   Next to Create Subfolder(s), choose Today's Date (yyyy mm dd) as folder name format from the menu. Your selection is reflected in the pathname displayed next to Location.

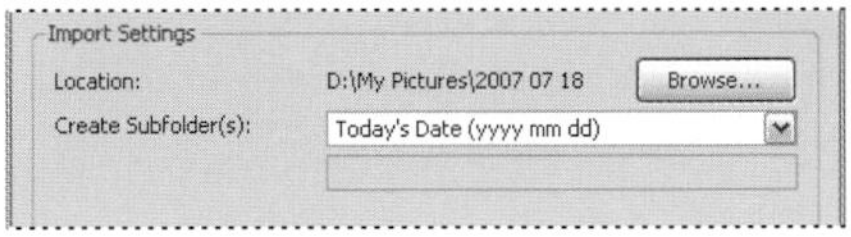

6   Choose Do not rename files from the Rename Files menu, and from the Delete Options menu choose After Copying, Do Not Delete Originals. If selected, deselect the Automatic Download check box.

7   Click the Advanced Dialog button.

Thumbnail images of the photos in your camera's memory card appear in the Advanced Dialog of the Photo Downloader.

8   (Optional) Click the check box (removing the green check mark), to remove photos from the import list. Unselected images are not imported.

Note: If you choose to delete the originals after copying under Advanced Options, only images actually imported will be deleted from the camera.

9   (Optional) Select one or more photos to rotate. Click the Rotate Left button or the Rotate Right button located in the lower left corner of the dialog box:

10   Under Advanced Options, if selected, deselect the three check boxes for Automatically Fix Red Eyes, Automatically Suggest Photo Stacks, and Make 'Group Custom Name' as a Tag. Then, click Get Photos.

The selected photos are copied from the camera to the specified folder on your hard disk.

11 If the Files Successfully Copied dialog box appears, click OK.

The Getting Photos dialog box appears and the photos are imported into Photoshop Elements.

12 Click OK to close any other alert dialog box.

The imported photos appear in the Photo Browser, already rotated where specified.

Using watched folders

Watched folders are folders on your computer that automatically alert Photoshop Elements when a new photo is saved or added to the folder. By default, the My Pictures folder is watched, but you can add additional folders to the list. New images added to these folders can be automatically added to the Organizer.

You can set up watched folders in two ways. You can choose to have new photos that are detected in a watched folder automatically added to your catalog, or you can opt to be asked before photos are added. When you choose this option, the message "New files have been found in Watched Folders" appears when new photos are detected. Just click Yes to add the photos to your catalog, or click No to skip them.

Now you'll add a folder to the watched folders list.

1   Choose File > Watch Folders.

2   Under Folders to Watch in the Watch Folders dialog box, click Add, and then browse to the Lesson02 folder.

3   Select the Lesson02 folder, and then click OK.

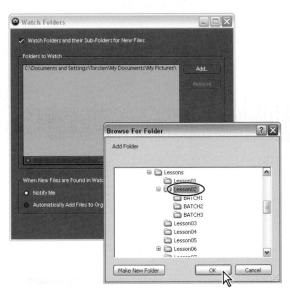

The folder name appears in the Folders to Watch list. To delete a folder name from that list, select its name, and then click Remove.

4   Keep the Notify Me option selected, and then click OK to close the Watch Folders dialog box.

Note: *In Lesson 3, which talks about advanced organizing, you will find more ways of getting pictures.*

Viewing photo thumbnails in the Organizer

There are several ways to view your Organizer catalog. While some display preferences let you change the display to meet your needs, other options can make it easier to work with items in the Organizer.

Using Photo Browser view

Up to this point, you've been working in the default Photo Browser view, the Thumbnail View. The Organizer also has other options for displaying images.

1   Click the Display button (🖥) near the upper right corner of the Organizer window, and then choose Import Batch from the menu to see the thumbnails organized by their separate import sessions.

Notice the bar and film canister icons (🎞) separating each row of thumbnails.

2   Try the following:

• Click the separator bar between two batches (reading "Imported from hard disk on ...") to select the thumbnails of all images imported in that session.

• Change the thumbnail size by dragging the slider above the Photo Browser.

- Choose Window > Timeline if the timeline is not currently visible above the Photo Browser. Click one of the three bars in the timeline to jump to the first image imported in that session.

The view switches to the first image in that batch, the date for that image flashes off and on, and a green border temporarily surrounds the image.

3   Before you continue, reduce the thumbnail size if necessary, making it small enough so that you can see all the images in your catalog.

4   Using the Display menu that you used in Step 1, select Folder Location to see the thumbnails organized according to the folders in which they are stored on your computer.

5   Repeat the same steps you performed in Step 2.

6   Select one of the bars in the timeline above the Photo Browser to jump to the photographs taken at the selected point in the timeline.

Note: To display the file name of individual images in the Browser View, make sure View > Details is selected, and then choose View > Show File Names.

Using Date View

Particularly if you are working with a collection of pictures that span a number of years, Date View is a great way to organize your images.

1   Click the Display button (▬) near the upper right corner of the Organizer window, and then choose Date View from the menu.

2   Select the Year option under the calendar display (bottom center left), if it is not already selected. Use the right and left arrows on either side of the year heading in the calendar to go to 2007, if it is not already selected.

3   Select June 30 on the 2007 calendar.

A preview of the first photograph taken on June 30, 2007, appears on the right.

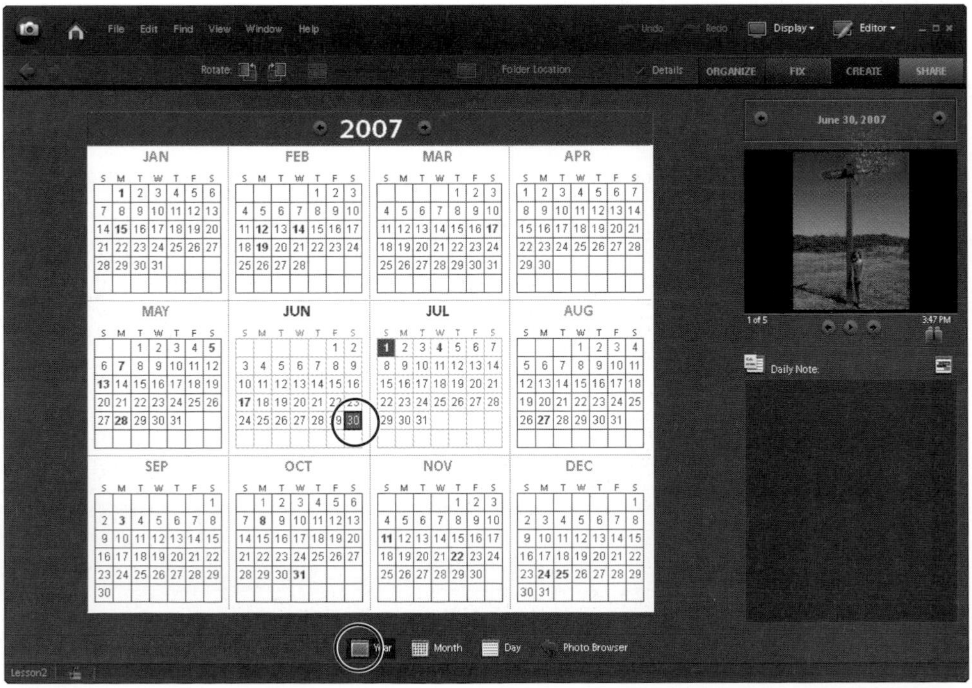

4 Under the thumbnail image on the right side of the Organizer window, click the Next Item On Selected Day button (●) repeatedly to see the other photographs taken on the same day.

💡 *You can also click the Start Automatic Sequencing button (●) to view all photos of the selected day as a slide show.*

5 Under the thumbnail image to the right, click the Find this photo in the Photo Browser button (🔍) to switch to the Photo Browser with the current photo highlighted.

6 In the Photo Browser, click the Back to previous view button (◀) near the upper left corner of the Organizer window to return to the Date View.

7 Select the Month option under the calendar display.

8 Using the date at the top of the calendar, click the word June, and then choose July from the menu of months that appears. You can use this method to quickly jump to a specific month. In this case a simple click on the Next Month button would have done the trick as well.

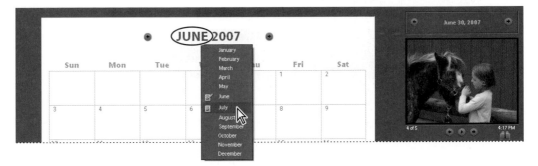

9 Click in the Daily Note area (bottom right) and type **A grand day out** to add a note to the date.

Now that you know how to locate your images in Date View, you can reset the Organizer to your preferred settings whenever you want to. For these lessons, you'll go back to Photo Browser rather than Date View.

Working with star ratings and keyword tags

Most of us find it challenging to organize our files and folders efficiently. Forgetting which pictures were stored in what folder is easy, and it's tedious to have to open and examine the contents of numerous folders looking for images or files.

The good news is that such searches are a thing of the past. You saw earlier how you can use the Search feature in the Organizer to find and import files from multiple locations on your computer. The next set of topics will show you how a little time invested in applying star ratings and keyword tags can streamline the process of sorting through your pictures, regardless of where the image files are stored.

Applying keyword tags and rating photos

Keyword tags and keyword tag categories are search criteria that you apply to images. You can also rate photos—applying one to five stars— and choose to display items based on their assigned rating. In this example, you'll apply a rating and a couple of keyword tags from the default set to one of the images you imported into your catalog.

1   Click the Display button (▦), and then choose Thumbnail View from the menu.

2   In the Photo Browser, hover (don't click yet!) with the pointer over the stars underneath a thumbnail image of your choice. When the number of yellow stars you'd like to assign to this image is selected, click to apply that rating.

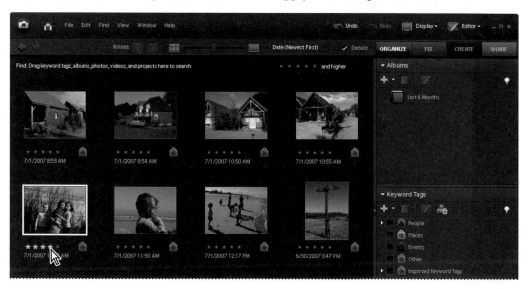

Using Star rating and the Hidden tags

Star rating—Use *Star rating* to rank you photos. You can attach only one star rating value per photo. If you assign 5 stars to a photo that already has 4 stars assigned, the 5 stars replace the 4 stars.

Hidden—The *Hidden tag* hides photos in the Photo Browser, unless you select the Hidden tag as search criteria. Use the Hidden tag, for example, to hide items that you want to keep, but generally don't want to see.

—From Photoshop Elements Help

3   Find images based on their assigned rating using the stars and the menu located above the Photo Browser.

4   Click the Show All button.

5   Under Keyword Tags in the Organize panel, click the arrow next to the People category to expand it so that you can see the Family and Friends sub-categories.

6   Drag the Family sub-category tag to the thumbnail showing the four children at the beach.

7   Allow the cursor to rest for a few seconds over the keyword tag icons under each thumbnail image until a tip appears, identifying the keyword tags that are applied to the image.

Creating new categories and sub-categories

You can add or delete new keyword tag categories and sub-categories to meet your needs.

1   Under Keyword Tags in the Organize pane, click the Create New button (✛) and choose New Category from the menu.

2   In the Create Category dialog box, type **Nature**, and select the flower symbol under Category Icon. You may have to scroll to the right to see the flower symbol. Click OK.

3   Under Keyword Tags, click to select the People category, and then click the Create New button (✛) and choose New Sub-Category.

4   In the Create Sub-Category dialog box, type **Kids** in the Sub-Category Name field. Make sure that People is shown in the Parent Category or Sub-Category field, and then click OK.

The new keyword tag category and sub-category become part of this catalog.

Applying and editing category assignments

You can add keyword tags to several files at once, and—or course—remove keyword tag assignments.

1   In the Photo Browser, click to select a picture with a child. Then, press and hold the Ctrl key and click all other kid pictures to select them, too. You should have multiple pictures selected.

2   Drag the Kids keyword tag to either one of the selected kid thumbnails. When you release the pointer, the keyword tag is applied to all selected pictures.

3   Keeping the same images selected, drag the Nature keyword tag to one of the unselected images. The keyword tag is applied to just this picture. Selecting the thumbnail or deselecting the other thumbnails is not necessary.

4   Select the image with the four children at the beach—the one with the Family sub-category keyword tag applied. Then, choose Window > Properties to open the Properties palette.

💡 *You can also show or hide the Properties panel by holding down the Alt key, and then pressing the Enter key.*

5 Select the Keyword Tags tab (🏷) in the Properties palette to see which keyword tags are applied to this image.

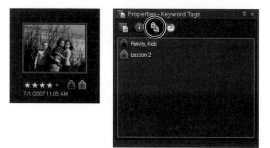

6 Remove the Family keyword tag from the image by doing one of the following:

• Right-click the blue keyword tag image underneath the thumbnail in the Photo Browser, and then choose Remove Family sub-category Keyword Tag from the menu.

• Right-click the thumbnail image and choose Remove Keyword Tag > Family from the context menu.

• In the Properties palette, right-click the Family, Kids listing, and then choose Remove Family sub-category Keyword Tag from the menu.

7 Close the Properties palette by clicking the Close button (✖) in the upper right corner of the palette, or by choosing Window > Properties again.

Creating and applying new keyword tags

In the previous topic, you created new keyword tag categories and subcategories. In this topic, you'll create a new keyword tag and specify its location.

1 Under Keyword Tags in the Organize panel, click the Create New button (+) and choose New Keyword Tag from the menu. The Create Keyword Tag dialog box appears.

2 In the Create Keyword Tag dialog box, choose Family (under People) for category and type **Lilly** for Name, and then click OK.

3 Drag the picture from the previous exercise, the four children at the beach, to the Lilly keyword tag under Keyword Tags. The image becomes the tag icon because it's the first image to get this tag. You will adjust the tag icon in the next steps, before applying the new keyword tag to additional photos.

4 Under Keyword Tags in the Organize panel, select the Lilly keyword tag, and then click the Edit button ( ) above the list of keyword tags. Or, right-click the Lilly keyword tag, and then choose Edit Lilly keyword tag from the context menu.

5 In the Edit Keyword Tag dialog box, click the Edit Icon button to open the Edit Keyword Tag Icon dialog box.

6 In the Edit Keyword Tag Icon dialog box, drag the corners of the boundary in the thumbnail so that it surrounds just the face of the girl with the flowers in the center of the photo.

7 Click OK to close the dialog box and click OK again to close the Edit Keyword Tag dialog box.

You can later update the keyword tag icon when you find another photo that you think works better as keyword tag icon.

8 Drag the Lilly keyword tag to the picture of Lilly on the pony next to her mother. The Lilly keyword tag is now applied to two images.

Converting keyword tags and categories

Changing the hierarchy of categories and keyword tags, and promoting or demoting them whenever you like is easy. Doing this does not remove the keyword tags or categories from the images to which you've assigned them.

1   Click the empty Find box next to the Kids sub-category. A binoculars icon (🔍) appears in the Find box to remind you that it is selected. Only the thumbnails tagged with the Kids keyword tag are displayed in the Photo Browser.

2   Click the Show All button above the Photo Browser to see all images.

3   Under the People category, right-click the Kids sub-category and choose Edit Kids sub-category from the context menu.

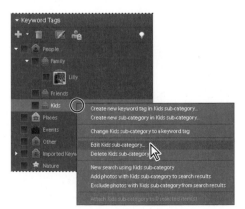

4 In the Edit Sub-Category dialog box, select None (Convert to Category) from the Parent Category or Sub-Category menu, and then click OK.

Now Kids is no longer a sub-category under People but a category on its own. Its icon has been inherited from its former parent category.

5 (Optional) Select a different category icon by choosing Edit Kids category.

6 Click the empty Find box next to the Kids category. Notice that the selection of images tagged with the Kids tag did not change. Click the Show All button.

7 Under Keyword Tags, drag the Kids category to the People category.

Now the Kids category appears as a sub-category under People. Because it's no longer a category, it has the generic sub-category icon.

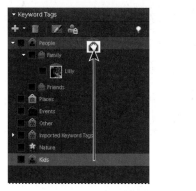

8 Click the empty Find box next to the Kids sub-category. Notice that the selection of images tagged with the Kids tag did not change. Click the Show All button.

9 Under the Family category, right-click the Kids sub-category and choose Change Kids sub-category to a keyword tag from the context menu.

10 Under Keyword Tags, right-click the Kids keyword tag and choose Edit Kids keyword tag from the context menu. In the Edit Keyword Tag dialog box, click the Edit Icon button. In the Edit Keyword Tag Icon dialog box, select a different image for this tag by clicking on the arrows under the thumbnail image.

11 Click OK to close the Edit Keyword Tag Icon dialog box and click OK again to close the Edit Keyword Tag dialog box.

Applying more keyword tags to images

There are a few simple ways to automatically tag multiple images, as well as manual methods you can use for applying custom tags.

1   Click the Display button (▣) near the upper right corner of the Organizer window, and then choose Folder Location from the menu.

2   Click the Instant Keyword Tag icon on the right end of the separator bar above the thumbnails of BATCH1. That way you can quickly apply the same keyword tag to all items in that group.

3   In the Create and Apply New Keyword Tag dialog box, choose Other in the Category menu, leaving BATCH1 for Name, and then click OK.

4   Repeat Steps 2 and 3 for the other folder groups, BATCH2 and BATCH3.

5   Switch back to Thumbnail View, using the same menu you used in Step 1.

6   Click and drag to apply the Nature keyword tag to any image you'd like to see in that category.

7 (Optional) Create and apply any other keyword tags or categories you might want. For example, you could create a keyword tag in the Places category, naming it after the location where the pictures have been taken.

Creating a keyword tag for working files

You can create a keyword tag to apply to the files you create and save in the Organizer, as you work through the book.

1 Open the Photoshop Elements Organizer. If Show All appears above the Browser View, click it.

2 Under Keyword Tags in the Organize panel, click the Create New button, and then choose New Category from the menu.

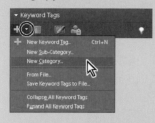

3 In the Create Category dialog box, type **Work Files** *as the Category name and select one of the Category icons. You can scroll to the right to see other icons. Click OK.*

4 Apply this keyword tag to all the files you create while working through the lessons in this book.

Automatically finding faces for tagging

When you use the Find Faces for Tagging command, Photoshop Elements isolates and displays faces in photos so that you can quickly tag them. This makes it easy to tag faces of friends or family members. Thumbnails of individual faces appear in the Face Tagging dialog box, where you can apply existing tags or create and apply new tags. As you apply tags to faces in the Face Tagging dialog box, Photoshop Elements removes those faces, making it easier to find and tag the remaining faces. You can select Show Already Tagged Faces if you want the faces to remain after you tag them.

1   Choose Edit > Select All to select all of the photos in the Photo Browser section of the Organizer.

2   Choose Find > Find Faces for Tagging.

Photoshop Elements processes the photos and searches for faces. Thumbnails of the faces display in the Face Tagging dialog box.

*A. Select to show faces already tagged or deselect to hide those faces. **B**. Keyword tags.*
*C. Recently used keyword tags. **D**. Full context image of the most recently selected face.*

Note: *If you press Ctrl as you choose Find > Find Faces for Tagging, Photoshop Elements will produce more accurate results (for example, it will find more faces in the background of a busy photo), but it will take longer for the faces to appear. You can select your preferred*

searching method as default under Face Tagging in the Keyword Tags and Albums section
of the Preferences dialog box (Edit > Preferences > Keyword Tags and Albums).

3   In the Face Tagging dialog box, drag the Lilly keyword tag onto a face (Lilly wears
the red helmet), or drag a face onto the Lilly keyword tag. You can apply other tags
in the same manner, and apply keyword tags to a selection of multiple images. Once
tagged, a face disappears from the display.

4   Select the Show Already Tagged Faces option to show the already tagged faces.

5   Click Done.

You'll use keyword tags throughout this book as a way to locate and organize lesson
files.

Using keyword tags to find pictures

Why create and apply all these keyword tags? Because they make it amazingly simple to
find your pictures.

1   In the Organizer, click the empty Find box next to the Kids keyword tag. A
binoculars icon appears in the Find box to remind you that it is selected. Only the
thumbnails tagged with the Kids keyword tag are displayed. *(See illustration on next*
page.)

2   Leave the Kids keyword tag selected. Click the Find box for the BATCH2 keyword tag. Only four thumbnails appear: those tagged with both the Kids and the BATCH2 keyword tags.

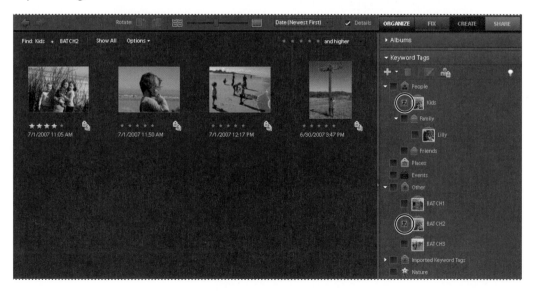

3   From the Options menu above the Photo Browser, select Show close match results. The thumbnails display changes, also showing images that are tagged with some but not all of the selected keyword tags. These *close matches* are identified by a check mark in the upper left corner of the thumbnail images.

4   Click Show All to display all images.

Congratulations! You've finished the lesson, and we're hoping that you feel pretty good about your accomplishment.

In this lesson, you've imported files into the Organizer using various techniques and you've used several ways to view your Organizer catalog. You've also created, edited, and applied keyword tags to individual photographs so that they'll be easy to find in future work sessions.

Review

Review questions

1   How do you open the Organizer component of Adobe Photoshop Elements?

2   Name three methods to import photos located on your computer hard disk into your Organizer catalog.

3   What are "watched folders"?

4   Explain the difference between Photo Brower view and Date view in the Organizer.

▶ **Review answers**

1   There are several ways to open the Organizer. Click Organize in the row of shortcut buttons across the lower part of the Welcome Screen when you start Photoshop Elements. Or, if the Photoshop Elements Editor is already open, click the Organizer button located to the right in the menu bar. If you always want to open Photoshop Elements in the Organizer, use the Start Up In menu in the lower left corner of the Welcome Screen to choose the Organizer.

2   This lesson demonstrated three different methods to import the three batches of photos into the Organizer:

• Use the drag-and-drop technique to add photographs from a Windows Explorer window into the Organizer catalog.

• Choose File > Get Photos and Videos > From Files and Folders, and then navigate to the folder containing your photos. You can select those images you want to add to your catalog.

• Choose File > Get Photos and Videos > By Searching, and then select the folder on the hard disk containing your photos for Look In. This method can collect all images in that folder and its subfolders.

3   Watched folders are folders on your computer that automatically alert Photoshop Elements when a new photo is saved or added to the folder. By default, the My Pictures folder is watched, and you can add additional folders to the list. New images added to these folders can be automatically added to the Organizer.

4   The default Photo Browser view of the Organizer lets you browse thumbnail images of your photos sorted by chronologic order, folder location, or import batches. In Date view you can quickly find photos taken on a particular day, month, or year.

3 | Advanced Organizing

Working with hundreds or thousands of images can be a daunting task. But rest assured, Photoshop Elements 6.0 comes to the rescue with advanced organizing options that not only get the job done but in fact make the work quite enjoyable.

In this lesson, you will learn how to do the following:

- Use advanced import options in the Photo Downloader.
- Acquire still frames from a video.
- Import pictures from a PDF document.
- Import pictures from a scanner.
- Use Version sets and Stacks to organize photos.
- Place and find photos by location using a Yahoo Map.
- Utilize other methods to find photos.
- Create Albums and Smart Albums.

Before you begin, make sure that you have correctly copied the Lessons folder from the CD in the back of this book onto your computer's hard disk. See "Copying the Classroom in a Book files" on page 3.

Getting started

In this lesson, you're going to work primarily in the Organizer component of Photoshop Elements. You will only briefly switch to the Full Edit component to import photos from a video and a PDF document. You'll also create a new catalog to manage the image files for this lesson.

1 Start Photoshop Elements, either by double-clicking the shortcut on your desktop or by choosing Start > Programs > Adobe Photoshop Elements 6.0.

2 Do one of the following:

• If the Welcome Screen appears, click Organize in the row of shortcut buttons across the lower part of the Welcome Screen.

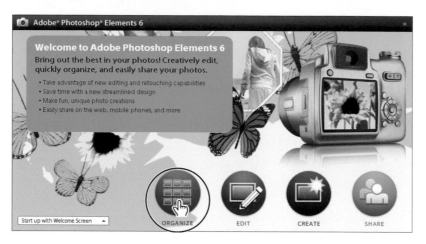

• If Photoshop Elements 6.0 (Editor) opens without first displaying the Welcome Screen, click the Welcome Screen button (⌂) located to the left in the menu bar to display the Welcome Screen, and then click Organize. Or, click the Organizer button (▦) located to the right in the menu bar. Then, wait until the Organizer has finished opening.

• If Photoshop Elements 6.0 (Organizer) opens, continue with step 3.

3 In the Organizer, choose File > Catalog.

4 In the Catalog Manager dialog box, click New.

5 In the Enter a name for the new catalog dialog box, type **Lesson3** as file name, deselect the Import free music into this catalog option, and then click OK.

Now you have a special catalog that you'll use just for this lesson. All you need is some pictures to put in it.

Advanced Import Options

In Lesson 2 you've learned how to import photos into the Organizer and how then to apply tags to organize them. Here you will find out how some options already available during the import process can make organizing your pictures even easier. You will also learn how to import photos from other sources, namely capturing a frame from a movie, extracting images embedded in a PDF document, and acquiring an image from a scanner.

Photo Downloader options

If you have an available digital camera or memory card from your camera with pictures on it, you can step through this exercise using your own pictures. For best results, you should have several batches of pictures taken at different times on a single day. Alternatively, you can simply follow the process by studying the illustrations provided, without actually performing the exercise yourself.

1   Connect your digital camera or the card reader for your digital camera to your computer, following the manufacturer's instructions for your camera.

2   Do the following:

• If the Windows Auto Play dialog box appears, click Cancel.

• If the Photo Downloader dialog box appears automatically, continue with step 3.

• If the Photo Downloader dialog box does not appear automatically, choose File > Get Photos and Videos > From Camera or Card Reader.

3   If the Photo Downloader dialog box opens in the Advanced mode, click the Standard Dialog button located near the lower left corner of the dialog box. Under Source in the standard mode Photo Downloader dialog box, choose from the Get Photos from menu the name of the connected camera or card reader.

4   Under Import Settings, accept the folder location listed next to Location, or click Browse to choose a new location for the files.

5   Without making any other changes to the settings, click the Advanced Dialog button in the lower left corner of the dialog box.

Thumbnail images of all photos on your camera or card reader appear in the Advanced dialog box. You also have access to several options not available in the Standard dialog box.

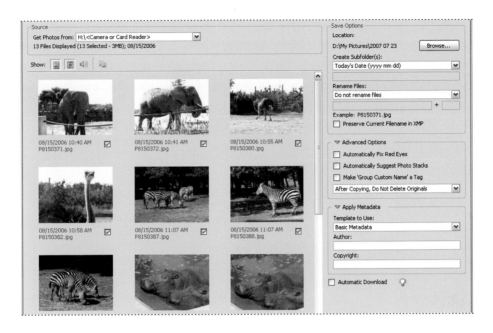

6   Under Save Options, choose Custom Groups (Advanced) from the Create
Subfolder(s) menu. Your selection is reflected in the pathname displayed next to
Location.

The thumbnail images on the left side of the dialog box are divided into groups, based
on the time and date the photos were taken.

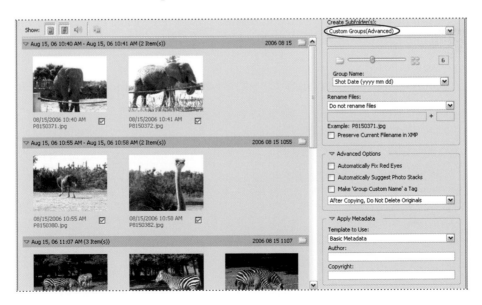

7 Use the slider under the Create Subfolder(s) menu to adjust the granularity of the subdivision to suit your needs. Move the slider to the left to generate fewer groups (or subfolders), or move the slider to the right to generate more groups. Scroll down the list of thumbnail images to review the grouping of the images. The number of groups chosen is displayed in the box to the right of the slider.

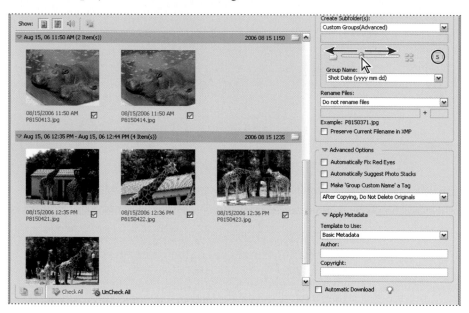

💡 *You can increase or decrease the number of groups one by one by typing Control-Shift-M or Control-Shift-L respectively on your keyboard.*

8 Choose Shot Date (yyyy mm dd) + Custom Name from the Group Name menu.

9   On the right end of the separator bar above the thumbnails of the first group, click the Custom Name field and type **Elephant** into the text box that appears.

10   Repeat step 9 for all other groups in the thumbnail list, giving each group a distinct name (in this example, that could be **Ostrich**, **Zebra**, **Hippo**, and **Giraffe**).

11   Under Advanced Options, select the Make 'Group Custom Name' a Tag check box. This will automatically create appropriate tags and apply them to the pictures when imported in the Organizer. If they are selected, deselect the check boxes for Automatically Fix Red Eyes and the Automatically Suggest Photo Stacks.

12   Click Get Photos.

The photos are copied from the camera to the specified group folder locations.

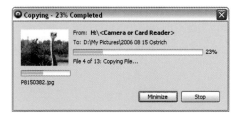

13 If the Files Successfully Copied dialog box appears, click OK.

The Getting Photos dialog box appears and the photos are imported into Photoshop Elements. The tags for the groups are created and applied, and the imported photos appear in the Photo Browser.

Other options available in the Advanced Photo Download dialog box include picking and choosing which files to import, rotating images, applying red eye fix, suggesting photo stacks, and adding metadata like name and copyright information. The more of these options you can take advantage of when importing files into the Organizer, the less work you will have later on to manage and organize your files, and the easier it will be to find a specific photo again months or even years after it has been imported. Later in this lesson, you'll hear more about organizing your photos. But first, you'll learn about other options to import images into your catalog.

Acquiring still frames from a video

You can capture frames from your digital videos if they are saved in a file format that Photoshop Elements can open, including AVI, MPG, MPEG, WMV, ASF, and MLV. To capture frames from video, you'll need to open the Editor.

1 If you have any image selected in the Organizer from the previous exercise, choose Edit > Deselect.

2 Click the Editor button (🖉) located near the top right corner of the Organizer window, and then choose Full Edit from the menu. Wait until the Editor has finished opening.

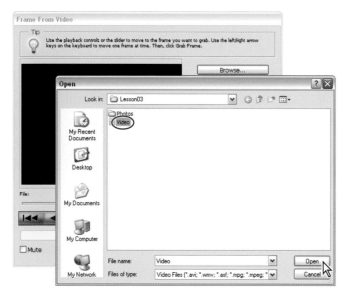

3 In the Editor, choose File > Import > Frame From Video.

4 In the Frame From Video dialog box, click the Browse button. In the Open dialog box, navigate to the Lesson03 folder and select the file Video.avi, and then click Open.

5 To start the video, click the Play button (▶). Click the Pause button (⏸) after about 4 seconds, and then use the arrow keys on your keyboard to move forward or backward one frame at a time until you find a frame you would like to capture.

Note: Some video formats don't support rewinding or fast-forwarding. In these cases, the Rewind (⏪) and Fast Forward (⏩) buttons are dimmed.

6   To get a frame of the video as a still image, click the Grab Frame button or press the spacebar when the frame is visible on the screen.

7   (Optional) You can move forward and backward in the video to capture additional frames.

8   When you have all the frames you want, click Done.

Depending on your video footage, you might notice artifacts in the still image resulting from the fact that a video picture consists of two interlaced half-pictures. The odd-numbered scanlines of the image, also called odd fields, constitute one half-picture, and the even-numbered scanlines, the even fields, the other. Since the two half-pictures of the video were recorded at slightly different times, the captured still image might look distorted.

You can remedy this problem by using Photoshop Elements' De-Interlace filter. With the De-Interlace filter you can remove either the odd or even fields in a video image and replace the discarded lines by duplication or interpolation from the remaining lines.

9   With the captured still image selected in the Editor, choose Filter > Video > De-Interlace. In the De-Interlace dialog box, choose either Odd Fields or Even Fields under Eliminate and either Duplication or Interpolation under Create New Fields by, and then click OK. Which combination of options to choose for best results depends on the actual image at hand.

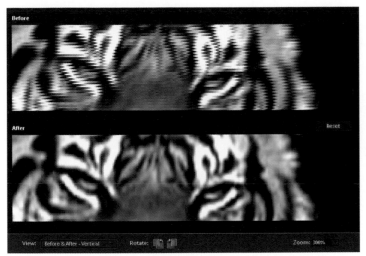

A still frame picture captured from video footage, before and after the De-Interlace filter has been applied (image detail at 300% magnification).

10 Save your work in the My CIB Work folder, and then close the image window in the Editor.

Importing from a PDF document

Photoshop Elements enables you to import whole pages or just selected images from a PDF document.

1 In the Editor, choose File > Open.

2 In the Open dialog box, navigate to the Lesson03 folder and select the file PDF_File.pdf, and then click Open.

Note: If you can't see the file PDF_File.pdf, make sure you have either All Formats or Photoshop PDF (*.PDF, *.PDP) selected in the Files of type menu.

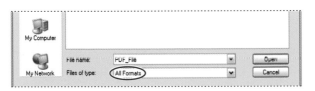

In the Import PDF dialog box, you can choose to import entire pages, or just the images from the PDF file. If your PDF file contains multiple pages, you can control-click the page thumbnail images to select just the pages you want to import. Likewise, you can selectively import one or more images from the PDF file. Pages are rasterized according to your choice of images size, resolution, and color mode. The result will be an image of each page, similar to an image acquired by scanning in a document.

3   Under Select in the Import PDF dialog box, choose Images.

4   Select Fit Page from the Thumbnail Size menu to see the preview images as large as possible. Use the scrollbar on the right to scroll down to the last image.

5   Click to select the image you want to import. Optionally, control-click any additional images you want to import at the same time. Then, click OK.
Each selected image opens in its own document window in the Editor, ready for further processing.

6   For each imported image choose File > Save As, navigate to the My CIB Work folder, and save the file with a descriptive name in Photoshop (*.PSD,*.PDD) file format. Select the Include in the Organizer option before you click Save, if you want to add the files to your catalog.

Scanning images

This exercise is optional and requires that you have an available scanner.

Note: Photoshop Elements 6.0 allows you to scan images using a video input source like a web camera attached to your computer.

1   To prepare for acquiring images from a scanner, choose Edit > Preferences > Scanner, and then do the following:

•   If you have more than one scanner or an additional video input source installed, make sure that the correct scanner is selected in the Scanner menu.

•   Either leave unchanged the default settings for Save As (jpeg), and Quality (6 Medium), or if you want different settings, change them now.

•   Deselect the Automatically Fix Red Eyes check box. You will learn in Lesson 8, "Repairing and Retouching Images," how to fix red eye in the Organizer.

•   If you want to change the location to which the scanned files will be saved, click Browse. Then, find and select the folder you want to use.

•   Click OK to close the Preferences dialog box.

2   Place the picture or document you want to scan in the scanner bed and make sure your scanner is turned on.

3   If the scan dialog box does not appear automatically, go to the Organizer and choose File > Get Photos and Videos > From Scanner.

4   In the scan dialog box, click the Preview button and examine the resulting image.

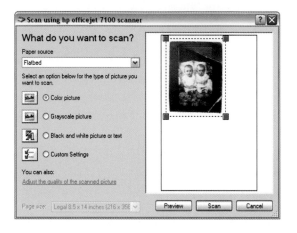

Note: The general appearance of the dialog box and the options available for your scanner may vary from those shown in the illustrations.

5   (Optional) If you want to make adjustments, change the settings as preferred.

6   Click Scan.

When the scan is complete, the image thumbnail appears in the Organizer.

7   Click Back to All Images to see your entire catalog.

When you scan several photographs together, Photoshop Elements can automatically crop the scan into individual photos and straighten them. For more information on the Divide Scanned Photos feature, see Photoshop Elements Help.

Organizing photos

Organizing files and folders efficiently can be challenging. It's easy to forget which pictures are stored in what folder, and having to open and examine the content of numerous folders to look for files or images can be time consuming and tedious.

With the Organizer, such searches are now a thing of the past. The next set of topics will show you how investing a little time in organizing your pictures can streamline the process of sorting through your image files, regardless of where they are stored.

Working with Version sets

A version set groups one original photo and edited versions of the original. Version sets make it easy to find both the edited versions of an image and the original, because they are visually stacked together instead of scattered throughout the Photo Browser.

Now you'll use Auto Smart Fix to edit an image in the organizer and create a version set. To start off, you'll clear all the images you might have added to the catalog since the beginning of this lesson.

1 With the Lesson3.psa catalog open in the Organizer, if you see the Show All button above the Photo Browser, click it. Choose Edit > Select All, and then choose Edit > Delete from Catalog. If available in the Confirm Deletion from Catalog dialog box, select the Delete all photos in collapsed stacks and the Delete all items in collapsed version sets option, and then click OK.

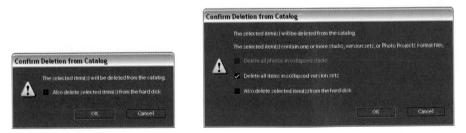

2 Choose File > Get Photos and Videos > From Files and Folders.

3 In the Get Photos from Files and Folders dialog box, navigate to the Lesson03 folder and select the Photos folder. Select the Get Photos From Subfolders check box. If selected, deselect the Automatically Fix Red Eyes and the Automatically Suggest Photo Stacks check boxes, and then click Get Photos.

4   In the Import Attached Tags dialog box, click Select All, and then click OK. Click OK to close any other alert dialog box. Click the Show All button above the Photo Browser.

You can now see the thumbnails of the images you added to your Lesson 3 catalog in the Photo Browser.

5   Under Keyword Tags, click the triangle next to Imported Keyword Tags to see the newly added keyword tags.

6   In the Photo Browser, select the first photo of the Elephant, taken at 10:40 am, and then choose Edit > Auto Smart Fix. The Auto Smart Fix command corrects the overall color balance and improves shadow and highlight detail, if necessary. The edited copy of the photo is automatically grouped with the original photo in a version set.

Version sets are identified by a version set icon in the upper right corner of an image.

Note: If you edit a photo in the Organizer, a version set is automatically created for you. If you edit the photo in the Editor and choose File > Save As, you can select the Save in Version Set with Original option to put the photo and its edited copy together in a version set.

7   Click the expand button on the right side of the thumbnail image, to see the original and edited images in a version set.

8   To see only the topmost photo in a version set, click the collapse button on the right side of the last thumbnail image in the version set, or right-click any of the thumbnail images in the expanded view of the version set, and then choose Version Set > Collapse Items in Version Set from the context menu. Notice the other commands available from the same context menu—as well as from the Edit menu—such as converting all images in a version set into individual photos in the catalog (Version Set > Convert Version Set to Individual Items).

Note: If you edit a photo that's already in a version set, the edited copy is placed at the top of the existing version set. To specify a different photo as the topmost, select it in the expanded view of the version set, and then choose Edit > Version Set > Set as Top Item.

About stacks

You can create stacks to visually group a set of similar photos together, making them easy to manage. Stacks are useful for keeping multiple photos of the same subject in one place, and they reduce clutter in the Photo Browser.

For instance, you can create a stack to group together multiple photos of your family taken with the same pose, or for photos taken at a sports event using your camera's burst mode or auto-bracket feature. Generally, when you take photos this way, you end up with many variations of the same photo, but you only want the best one to appear in the Photo Browser. Stacking the photos lets you easily access them all in one place instead of having them scattered across rows of thumbnails.

1   Click the empty Find box next to the Zebra tag in the Imported Tags category.

2   To marquee-select all images, click below the first thumbnail image and drag to the top and right. When you release the pointer, all images within the selection box are selected.

3   Choose Edit > Stack > Stack Selected Photos.

All the Zebra photos are now grouped in a stack. You can expand and collapse stacks in the Photo Browser the same way you expand and collapse version sets.

*Stacks are identified by a stack icon
in the upper right corner of an image.*

4　Click the Show All button above the Photo Browser, and then click the empty Find boxes next to the Hippo and the Ostrich tags in the Imported Tags category.

5　Choose Edit > Select All, and then choose Edit > Stack > Automatically Suggest Photo Stacks.

The Automatically Suggest Photo Stacks dialog box appears. The two photos of the hippopotamus have been successfully placed in a group already, but the ostrich photos will need to be grouped manually.

6 In the Automatically Suggest Photo Stacks dialog box, scroll down to the bottom of the thumbnail list. Click the photo of the ostrich in the last group and drag it up to place it in one group with the other ostrich photo.

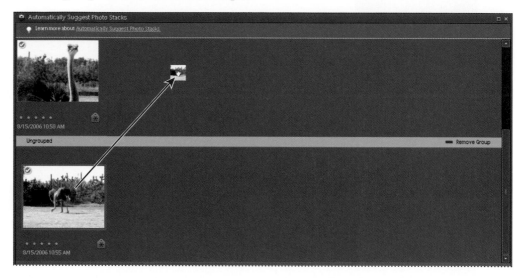

7 To split one group into two, position the cursor between two images of the first group and when the cursor changes to the scissors icon, click to split the group.

8 To exclude all photos in a group from being stacked, click the Remove Group button. Or, select individual photos, and then click the Remove Selected Photo(s) button in the lower left corner of the dialog box.

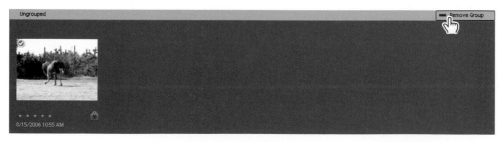

9 If you change your mind about photos excluded from being stacked, make sure the Show Removed Photos check box at the bottom of the dialog box is selected. Then, drag the thumbnail image from the removed photos bin to add it to a group in the main thumbnail area.

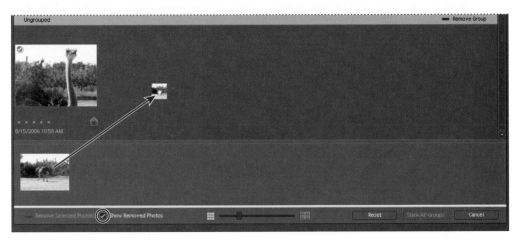

10 When done, click Stack All Groups to close the Automatically Suggest Photo Stacks dialog box and to stack the photos in each group. Click Show All in the Photo Browser.

Stacks are identified by a stack icon in the upper right corner of an image.

Note: *If you edit a photo that's already in a stack, the photo and its edited copy are put in a version set that is nested in the original stack.*

Tips for working with stacks

Keep these points in mind when working with stacks:

• By default, the newest photo is placed on top of the stack. As you create the stack, you can specify a new top photo by right-clicking that photo and using the context menus.

• Combining two or more stacks merges them to form one new stack. The original stacks are not preserved. The newest photo is placed on top of the stack.

• Many actions applied to a stack, such as editing, e-mailing, and printing, are applied to the topmost item only. To apply an action to all photos in a stack, reveal the stacked photos or unstack the photos.

• If you apply a keyword tag to a collapsed stack, the keyword tag is applied to all items in the stack. When you run a search on the keyword tag, the top photo with the stack icon appears in the search results. If you want to apply a keyword tag to only one photo in a stack, reveal that photo in the stack, and then apply the keyword tag.

• You can access stack commands by right-clicking or by using the Edit menu.

Creating Albums

Another way of grouping photos is to organize them in albums. Think of a Photoshop Elements Album as being the equivalent of a physical photo album. You can, for example, create a new album for a special occasion like a wedding, or to collect images you want to use in a project such as a slideshow. Then, you add pictures to the album the same way you would associate pictures with keyword tags. The main difference between albums and keyword tags is that in albums you can arrange the photos into any order you want. Smart albums are a special sort of album. They contain photos matching a search criteria rather than being manually assembled. You'll learn more about smart albums later in this lesson under "Viewing and finding photos."

1   If necessary, click the triangle next to Albums in the Organize bin to expand the palette.

2   To create a new album, click the Create New button (✚) under Albums in the Organize bin, and then choose New Album from the menu.

3   In the Create Album dialog box, type **Animals** for Name, and then click OK.

4   Ctrl-click to select two or three photos in the Photo Browser, and then drag the group onto the Animals album icon.

Note: If you add a collapsed version set or a collapsed stack to an album, only the topmost picture of the version set or stack will be visible in the album. To add a different picture to the album, first expand the version set or stack.

5 To see the content of an album, click the album icon, or drag and drop the album icon onto the Find bar above the Photo Browser. Notice the number in the top left corner of each photo, representing its order in the album.

Note: You can only view one album at a time.

6 To change the order in an album, select one or more photos in the Photo Browser, and then drag the selection to its new position. The photos are reordered when you release the pointer.

7 (Optional) To remove a picture from an album, right-click the picture in the album view, and then choose Remove from Album > *[album name]* from the menu.

8 Click Show All above the Browser View to see all photos in your catalog.

💡 *You can group related albums in an album group—similar to grouping keyword tags in categories. You can change an album's properties and icon by clicking the Edit album button—similar to using the Edit keyword tag button for keyword tags.*

9　To delete an album, right-click its icon in the Albums palette, and then choose
Delete *[album name]* album from the menu.

10　Click OK in the Confirm Album Deletion dialog box.

*Note: Deleting an album does not delete any photos from your catalog. Albums store only
references to the actual photos.*

The Map View

In the Map view of the Organizer, you can arrange photos by geographic location. You
can drag photos from the Photo Browser directly to a location on the map. In the Map
view, you can then search for and view photos in specific geographic locations.

1　In the Organizer, right-click the thumbnail image of the elephant, and then choose
Place on Map from the context menu.

2　In the Photo Location on Map dialog box, type **1 Zoo Road, San Francisco, CA** in
the text box, and then click Find.

Note: You must have an active Internet connection to use this feature.

3 In the Look Up Address dialog box, click OK to confirm 1 Zoo Rd San Francisco, CA, 94132-1027 US.

4 In the Map view that opens to the left of the Browser view you can use the Hand tool to drag the map in any direction. The red pin indicates the location for your photo.

5 Select Hybrid from the menu in the bottom right corner of the Map view.

6 Use the Zoom In tool and the Hand tool in combination to magnify the view on the San Francisco Zoological Gardens. Use the Move tool to reposition the red pin to exactly where you want it to appear on the map. *(See illustration on next page.)*

7 To place additional photos on the map, drag them from the Photo Browser to the Map view. If you get too close to an existing pin, the photos will be grouped under one pin location—this may or may not be what you want.

💡 *You can drag a keyword tag (e.g. a keyword tag in the Places category) to the Map view to position all photos tagged with this keyword tag on the map.*

8 Select the Limit Search to Map Area check box in the lower left corner of the Map View. Only photos mapped to the currently visible map area are displayed in the Browser View.

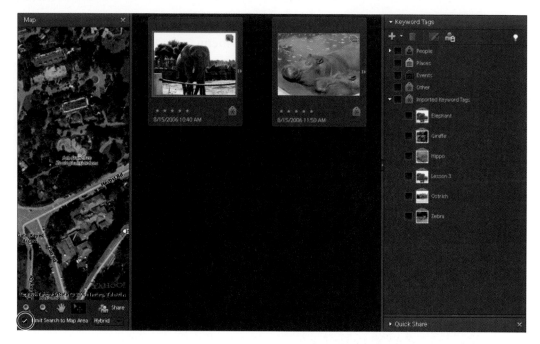

9 To hide the Map view, click the Close button (✖) in the upper right corner of the Map View. Click the Show All button above the Photo Browser. Right-click the thumbnail image of the first elephant, and then choose Show on Map from the context menu. The Map view will open, displaying the location to which the photo was mapped.

10 Hide the Map view.

This concludes the section on organizing your photos. You've learned about version sets and stacks, how to group photos in albums, and how to arrange photos by their geographic location using the Map view. In the next section, you will learn how you can find photos in your catalog even if not much time was spent on properly organizing them.

Viewing and finding photos

In the Organizer, Photoshop Elements lets you find photos using several methods:

*   **Timeline**—If necessary, choose Window > Timeline to display the timeline above the Browser View. Then, click a month or set a range to find photos and media files chronologically by date, or by import batch or folder location.

*   **Find bar**—Drag and drop a photo, keyword tag, creation, or album onto the find bar to locate matching or similar photos and media files.

*   **Find menu**—Use the commands in this menu to find photos by date, caption or note, file name, history, media type, metadata, or color similarity. Commands are also available for finding photos and media files that have unknown dates, are untagged, or are not in any album.

Finding photos by visual similarity

You can search for photos containing similar images, color, or general appearance.

1   In the Organizer, choose Edit > Select All. Choose Edit > Stack > Unstack Photos, and then choose Edit > Version Set > Revert to Original. Click OK to close any alert dialog box that might appear.

2   Choose Edit > Deselect. Then, drag the first image with the zebras to the find bar.

Photos are displayed in decreasing order of similarity in visual appearance. A similarity percentage appears in the bottom left corner of each image.

3   Click the Show All button.

Finding photos using details and metadata

You can search for your images by file details or metadata. Searching by metadata is useful when you want to search using multiple criteria at once. For example, if you want to find all photos captured on a certain date that are marked with a specific keyword tag, you can search using both capture date and keyword tags in the Find by Details (Metadata) dialog box.

Searchable metadata includes file name, file type, keyword tags, albums, notes, author, map location, and capture date, as well as camera model, shutter speed, and F-stop—to name just a few of the many available search criteria.

Here you will search for photos taken near a specific location using the Find by Details (Metadata) dialog box.

1   Choose Find > By Details (Metadata) in the Organizer to display the Find by Details (Metadata) dialog box.

2   Under Search Criteria, click the first menu, and then use the scrollbar to scroll down towards the end of the list. While scrolling, notice the many options available as search criteria. Some meta data is generated automatically for each picture, some is added and available only when you spend time organizing your catalog. For this exercise, choose the last entry in the list, Map Location.

3   From the menu next to Map Location, choose Within.

4   Click the magnifying glass button to open the Photo location on Map dialog box. In the Photo location on Map dialog box, enter **1 Zoo Road, San Francisco, CA** as address, and then click Find. Click OK to close the Photo location on Map dialog box.

5   In the Find by Details (Metadata) dialog box, enter **1** as distance and choose Miles from the last menu.

Note: To include other metadata values in your search, click the plus (+) sign and specify new values using the menus that appear. To remove metadata from your search, click the minus (-) sign along the right side of the metadata you want to remove. If you specify more than one search criteria, click the appropriate radio button to search for files matching any or all of the search criteria.

6   If selected, deselect the Save this Search Criteria as Smart Album check box. You'll learn about smart albums in the last part of this lesson. Then, click the Search button. All images that match the specified criteria are displayed.

7   (Optional) To modify the search, click Options in the find bar, and then choose Modify Search Criteria from the menu. This will open the Find by Details (Metadata) dialog box with the current search criteria entered. Make your changes, and then click Search to display your new results in the Photo Browser.

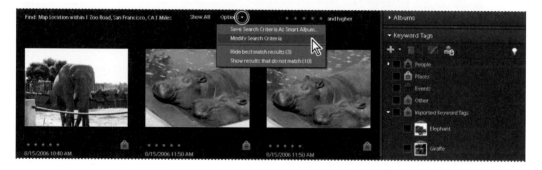

8   Click the Show All button in the find bar.

Viewing and managing files by folder location

The Folder Location view in the Organizer splits the Photo Browser into three sections: a folder hierarchy panel on the left, an image thumbnail panel in the center, and the Palette Bin on the right. From this view you can manage your folders, add files to your catalog, automatically tag files using their folder name as the keyword tag, and add or remove folders from Watched Folder status.

By default, the left panel displays all the folders on your hard disk, and the center panel displays only the thumbnails of the managed files in the selected folder. Folders containing managed files have a Managed folder icon (🗐). Watched folders have a Watched folder icon (🗐).

1   Click the Display button (🖳) near the upper right corner of the Organizer window, and then choose Folder Location from the menu.

The folder hierarchy appears on the left side of the Photo Browser and the image thumbnails appear in the center.

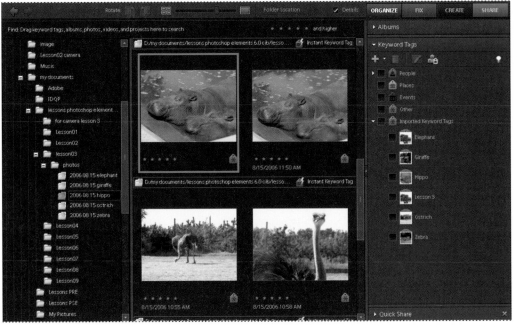

The contents of a selected folder are displayed when using Folder Location view.

Note: *You can change the default view for each panel by choosing Edit > Preferences > Folder Location View and selecting the options you want.*

2   Do one of the following to specify which files appear in the center panel:

• To view only the managed files in the selected folder, right-click in the left panel and deselect Show All Files.

- To view all your managed files in the center panel grouped by folder location, right-click in the left panel and select Show All Files.

- If you want to search all your managed files while in Folder Location view, select Show All Files.

- To find the folder location of a file, click the file's thumbnail in the center panel. The file's folder is highlighted in the left panel.

- To find files in a specific folder, click the folder in the left panel. Thumbnails for the files in that folder appear in the center panel, grouped under the folder name.

- To instantly tag files by their folder locations, click the Instant Keyword Tag icon in the center panel on the right side of the window. In the Create and Apply New Keyword Tag dialog box you can attach keyword tags simultaneously to all images in that folder.

3   To manage files and folders, select a folder and do any of the following:

- To move a file to a different folder, drag the file's thumbnail from the center panel to a folder in the left panel.

- To view the folder in Windows Explorer, right-click in the left panel and choose Reveal in Explorer.

- To add or remove the folder from watched-folder status, right-click in the left panel and choose Add to Watched Folders or Remove from Watched Folders.

- To add a file in the folder to your catalog, right-click in the left panel and choose Add Unmanaged Files to Catalog.

- To rename the folder, right-click in the left panel and choose Rename Folder. Then, type a new name.

- To delete the folder, right-click in the left panel and choose Delete Folder.

4   Click the Display button (■), and then choose Thumbnail View from the menu.

Working with smart albums

Smart albums, like albums, contain photos of your choosing. However, instead of manually selecting individual photos as for albums, you only need to specify search criteria to create a smart album. Once you set the criteria for a smart album, any photo in a catalog that matches the criteria will appear automatically in that smart album. As you add new photos to the catalog, those photos matching smart album criteria will appear automatically in that smart album. Smart Albums keep themselves up-to-date.

1   To set up search criteria for a new smart album, choose Find > Find by Details (Metadata). In the Find by Details (Metadata) dialog box, select the search criteria for the smart album. Click the plus sign (+) to add a criterion, click the minus sign (-) to remove a criterion.

2   If necessary, select the Save this Search Criteria as Smart Album. Enter **My first smart album** as name, and then click Search.

3   To display the photos in a smart album in the Photo Browser, select the smart album from the Albums palette.

Note: You cannot change the order of photos in a smart album, as you can for an album. Nor can you add photos to a smart album by dragging them onto the album's icon; you need to modify the album's search criteria to change the content of a smart album. The content of a smart album may change over time even without modifying the search criteria if photos matching the search criteria are added or removed from the catalog; e.g. a smart album may contain photos captured within the last six months from today's date.

4 To change the name of a smart album, do the following:

• Select the smart album from the Albums palette.

• Click the Edit button (⬛) in the Albums palette.

• Enter a new name in the Edit Smart Album dialog box, and then click OK.

5 To change the search criteria of a smart album, do the following:

• Select the smart album from the Albums palette.

• Click Options in the find bar, and then choose Modify Search Criteria from the menu.

6 Modify the search criteria in the Find by Details (Metadata) dialog box, and select to save it as smart album. Provide a new name for the smart album, and then click Search.

Note: You can save the modified search criteria using the same name, but this is not recommended. A second smart album with the same name will be created, rather than the first smart album being overwritten. A dialog box will alert you about the duplicate file name. Click OK if you want to create a second smart album with the same name anyway.

7 To delete the smart album, right-click its icon in the Albums palette, and then choose Delete *[smart album name]* album from the menu. Click OK to confirm.

Congratulations! You've reached the end of Lesson 3. In this lesson, you've learned about advanced import options in the Photo Downloader, how to acquire still frames from a video, and how to import images from a PDF file or by using a scanner. You've organized images in version sets, stacks and albums, placed photos on a map, and learned some advanced methods to find and manage photos in your catalog.

You can review and test your command of the concepts and techniques presented in this lesson by working through the following questions and answers.

Review

▶ Review questions

1 How can you automatically create and apply tags to images while importing them from a digital camera or card reader?

2 What does the Photoshop Elements De-Interlace filter do?

3 What does the Auto Smart Fix command do?

4 What are Version Sets and Stacks?

5 What is the main difference between grouping pictures using tags and grouping them in an album?

▶ Review answers

1 In the Advanced Photo Downloader dialog box, select Custom Groups (Advanced) from the Create Subfolder(s) menu. Next, select an option including Custom Name from the Group Name menu. Enter a Group Name in the Custom Name field of the separator bar in thumbnail view. Finally, select the Make 'Group Name' as a Tag check box before clicking Get Photos.

2 The Photoshop Elements De-Interlace filter can improve the appearance of still frame images acquired from a video. Depending on your video footage, you might notice artifacts in the still image, caused by the fact that a video picture consists of two interlaced half-pictures. With the De-Interlace filter you can remove either the odd or even fields in a video image and replace the discarded lines by duplication or interpolation from the remaining lines.

3 The Auto Smart Fix command corrects the overall color balance and improves shadow and highlight detail, if necessary. When invoked from within the Organizer, the Auto Smart Fix command groups the edited copy of the photo automatically with the original photo in a version set.

4 A version set groups one original photo and its edited versions. Stacks are used to group a set of similar photos, like multiple photos of your family taken with the same pose, or photos taken at a sports event using your camera's burst mode or auto-bracket feature. A version set can be nested inside a stack: if you edit a photo that's already in a stack, the photo and its edited copy are put in a version set that is nested in the original stack.

5   The main difference between albums and keyword tags is that in albums you can arrange the photos into any order you want.

4 Creating Projects

You can quickly and easily create original and interesting projects from your photos by using templates with different themes for online galleries, photo collages, greeting cards, CD/DVD labels, slide shows, flipbooks, and so on.

Such projects enable you to combine images, text, animations, music, and narration to design unique multimedia creations that are fun to produce. Whether it's sharing your photos online, presenting a slide show, personalizing a CD or DVD label, designing a very special greeting card for your family or friends, or even printing your own coffee table book. Adobe Photoshop Elements enables you to unleash your creativity. This lesson concentrates on the design of creations, while in Lesson 5 you will learn different ways to share them.

In this lesson, you'll do the following:

- Create a greeting card.
- Present your photos in an Online gallery.
- Animate your photos in a Slideshow.

Before you begin, make sure that you have correctly copied the Lessons folder from the CD in the back of this book onto your computer's hard disk. See "Copying the Classroom in a Book files" on page 3.

Getting started

While working on the projects in this lesson, you'll use the CIB Catalog you created in the "Getting Started" section at the beginning of this book. To use the CIB Catalog, follow these steps:

1 Start Photoshop Elements, and in the Welcome Screen, click the Organize button. Then, wait until the Organizer has finished opening.

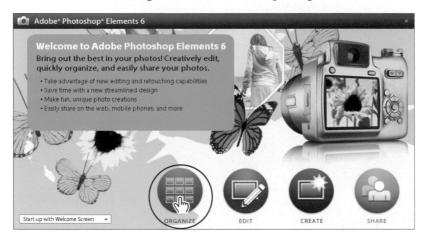

2 Choose File > Catalog.

3 In the Catalog Manager dialog box, select the CIB Catalog under Catalogs, and then click Open.

If you do not see the CIB Catalog file, review the procedures found in "Getting Started." See "Copying the Lessons files from the CD" on page 3, and "Creating a catalog" on page 4.

Creating a Greeting Card

Eye-catching greeting cards are a sure way to impress family and friends, and a really attractive card can spend many months on someone's mantelpiece, or even get framed and displayed with pride.

The Greeting Card Editor in Adobe Photoshop Elements offers you a variety of templates to create attractive cards with ease and efficiency. You can include one or more photos on each page of a greeting card that can be printed on your home printer, ordered online, or sent via e-mail.

This lesson will enable you to experience how easy it is to choose a format and theme and present a photo in a creative and professional looking manner. When you're finished, you'll have transformed your photo into a delightful greeting card.

1   In the Organizer, use the Keyword Tags palette to find the portrait of a little girl, tagged with Lesson 4, named 4_Pauline.jpg.

2   Click to select the purple Create tab in the Task pane.

3   In the Create panel of the Task pane, choose Greeting Card from the More Options menu.

4   In the New Greeting Card dialog box, under Choose a Theme, scroll down and select Wedding Classic, the third theme from last, showing grey torn paper with white flowers along the bottom. Under Choose a Layout, select the middle layout in the second row, a portrait format rectangle on an angle. Select the Auto-Fill with Project Bin Photos option and deselect Include Captions. Then, click Done.

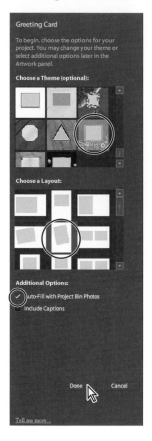

5   You'll see a preview of your greeting card in the Editor panel, with a bounding box around the photo you have chosen. You can move, rotate and resize the photo if you wish. To resize the picture, position the pointer over a handle in the corner of the bounding box—the pointer turns into a double arrow—and drag to change the size. When dragging the bounding box, the image is scaled proportionally by default. Click and drag the photo if you want to reposition it on the greeting card.

6 When done resizing and repositioning the photo, click the green Commit button
(✔) at the bottom of the bounding box to commit the changes.

That was quick! Composing your photo with an appropriate theme and layout can make
a really distinctive card.

When the Move tool is selected, you can use the arrow keys on your keyboard to move the elements of a selected layer in small increments instead of dragging them using your pointer. Similarly, you can use the arrow keys to move a selection when a selection tool is active.

7   Choose File > Save. In the Save As dialog box, navigate to the My CIB Work folder and name the file **4_Greeting_Card.psd**. Make sure that the Include in the Organizer option is selected. Click Save.

8   Choose File > Close. Be certain not to save any changes to the original photo.

Congratulations, you've finished your first creation. Now you've experienced how quickly you can get attractive results using pre-designed styles. Look for yourself, there is an abundance of styles and templates to choose from to best suit your creative projects. In Lesson 5 you will learn more about printing, sharing and exporting from the Organizer.

Working with multiple pages

Photoshop Elements enables you to create multi-page layouts. This comes in handy for any multi-page Creations—photo albums for example—where you want consistency of layout from page to page. Under Edit you have the choice of adding blank pages or using the same layout. The example shown below uses the Wedding Classic theme as background, but with a different layout from that used for the greeting card.

Presenting your photos in a Photo gallery

The next project is an online presentation of your photos. Web galleries come in a variety of layouts and designs, and are optimized for viewing images on a web page. For this project you will work on an imaginary birth announcement using an animated template.

The Online Gallery wizard will guide you through the process of adding photos, applying web page layouts and background styles, writing captions, previewing in the Browser, and sharing the files. The Online Gallery wizard only lets you arrange photos, not edit them.

Using the Online Gallery Wizard

1 Switch back to the Organizer and select the last three images from the Lesson 4 folder, 4_Gallery1.jpg, 4_Gallery2.jpg, and 4_Gallery3. jpg.

2 Select the Create panel of the Task pane, and then click Online Gallery. Under Items, only the selected three images are displayed. Then, click Next.

💡 *You can arrange the order of the photo thumbnails on the left side of the wizard. To move a thumbnail, drag a thumbnail between the other thumbnails.*

3   Choose Animated from the Select a Category menu. Under Select a Template, click the first template—featuring a baby on a blue background. Then, click Next.

💡 *The design thumbnails change according to the type of gallery you choose. For example, the Interactive gallery offers different design thumbnails than the Animated or the Web galleries.*

4   A preview of the animation you are creating will be visible in the lower part of the dialog box. *(See illustration on next page.)* At the end of the animation, the first photo included in the template will be displayed. The other pictures can be seen by clicking the previous and next buttons under the picture.

5   With your first picture visible on the right, type **Finally - here she is!** in the Title text box under Customize. Then, type **We are so proud and delighted...** in the subtitle text box and your e-mail address in the E-Mail Address text box. Click the Refresh button to see your changes applied.

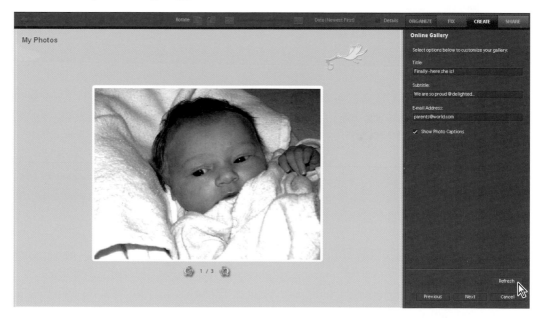

6   Your captions, which are now part of the animation, are featured prominently at the upper left of your photos. Click Next.

7   Type **Birth Announcement** in the Gallery Name box, and then click the Browse button next to Save To.

8   In the Browse For Folder dialog box, select the My CIB Work folder, and then click OK to close the Browse For Folder dialog box.

9   In the Create panel, click Next. Under Share this gallery to, you have the choice between Photoshop Showcase, My FTP, or CD/DVD. For now just click Done. The preview will automatically close and you will see your saved project in the Organizer window.

Previewing in Internet Explorer

1   Switch to Internet Explorer (or your favorite Web browser).

2   Choose File > Open, and then click Browse in the Open dialog box.

3   In the Windows Internet Explorer dialog box, navigate to the My CIB Work folder. Within that folder, open the Birth Announcement folder.

4   Select the index.htm file and click Open.

5   Click OK to close the Open dialog box. Internet Explorer will open and display the animated photo gallery you just created. When done playing the animation, close your Web browser window.

Note: To be able to view the animation, you might have to install Adobe Flash Player ActiveX Control in your Web browser.

As you've just seen, with the help of the Online Gallery wizard you don't have to be a Web expert—or cause yourself a headache with a lengthy creation process—to present your images online in a professional looking manner. You will learn more about sharing your projects in Lesson 5.

Animating your photos in a slideshow

Creating slide shows is a popular feature of Photoshop Elements. It's a fun way to share your images because you can choose from an array of formats, transitions, and graphics, as well as having the option to add captions and even sound or narration.

Using the Slideshow Editor

1   Switch back to the Organizer, and select the six photos with the four girls sitting on a wall. These pictures, tagged with Lesson 4, are named 4_Slideshow1.jpg through 4_Slideshow6.jpg.

2   Select the Create panel of the Task pane, and then click the Slide Show button.

3   In the Slide Show Preference dialog box, choose 3 sec for Static Duration, Dissolve as Transition, and 2 sec for the Transition Duration. Deselect the Include Photo Captions as Text option and select Landscape Photos next to Crop to Fit Slide. You can leave the other settings unchanged. *(See illustration on next page.)* Click OK and your project will automatically open in the Slide Show Editor window.

4   Click the Play button (▶) located below the preview panel, or press the spacebar to start the slide show. Although you'll see the four girls and their changing visual expressions during the presentation of those six images, the transition from one picture to the next seems too fast and needs to be adjusted.

Add Music and Narration to a slide show

Sound adds yet another dimension to the animation of your images and complements your work. You can add an ambitious, full-scale soundtrack or simply record narration. You can import music from your Photoshop Elements catalog or from any location on your computer. In the Slide Show dialog box, click Add Media, and then navigate to the place where your music files are located.

In the Add Audio dialog box, you can listen to a clip before adding it by selecting the clip and clicking Play. To align the pace of the slide show with the music, select Fit Slides To Audio (the length of each slide is updated in the film strip). You can also drag the audio file to begin playing on a specific slide.

You can record voice narration to a slide if you have a microphone attached to your computer. You can also attach the narration to the photo as an audio caption. You'll find the narration button in the Extras palette of the Slide Show dialog box,

For more information regarding adding music and narration, please consult the Photoshop Elements Help file.

Refining the Slide Show

In the next steps, you will adjust the transitions and change the order of the images.

1 From the menu in the Slide Show Editor window, choose Edit > Select All Transitions.

2 In the Properties panel, reduce the time to 1 sec under Multiple Transitions, and select Clock Wipe from the Transition menu.

3 Press the spacebar to play your slideshow, which now looks livelier with the new settings applied. But there is still room for improvements: For example, the image where two of the girls look away is not a good choice with which to start the slide show.

4 The second last picture looks like a better choice as first image of the show. Click its thumbnail, drag it to the left, and place it right in front of the first thumbnail. As a result, the first four images move back one position. To work with the thumbnail images in a larger panel, click the Quick Reorder button (⏏), located above the thumbnail images to the left. When done, click Back in the Quick Reorder panel.

Adding Extras

Now that you're happy with the picture order and transitions, let's increase the impact of the slide show by including some graphic elements. First, let's add a message with a speech bubble and text.

1 In the Slide Show Editor window, select the first thumbnail image in the row of thumbnail images near the bottom of the window.

2   Under Extras, select the graphics category, and then scroll down to Thought & Speech Bubbles. If necessary, click the triangle next to the name to show the available shapes. Click the first speech bubble icon and drag it near the first girl's head.

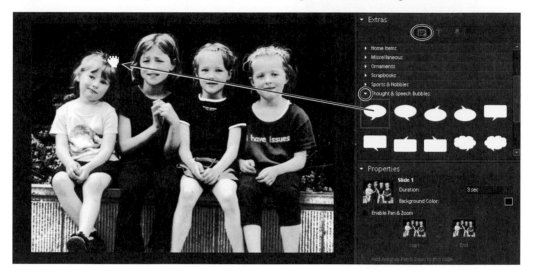

3   To change the size or shape of the bubble, position the pointer over one of the six handles located at the corners and sides of the bounding box, and when the pointer turns into a double arrow, drag to reduce the size or change the shape of the bubble. Try to size and shape the bubble as show in the illustration below. If necessary, click and drag the bubble to reposition it on the image.

4 Under Extras, select the type category, and then locate the second T in the third row, a thin, black letter that represents the font Myriad Pro Condensed.

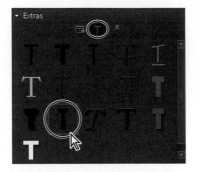

5 Drag the T onto the speech bubble in the Editor panel.

6 Click the Edit Text button in the Properties panel and type HELLO! in the Edit Text dialog box that appears. Then click OK.

7 Click and drag the text box to center the text in the speech bubble.

8 Now the first slide has a prominent message, but there is so much more you could do. Explore on your own! For example, add items to the last image from Costumes in the graphics category, to finish off your presentation with some fun touches.

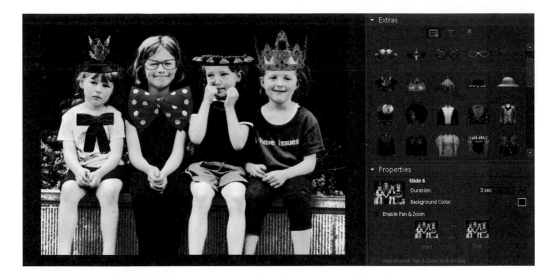

9   When done, choose File > Save As, and type **4_Slideshow_work** as name in the Adobe Photoshop Elements dialog box. Then click Save.

Done! You've completed this lesson and have learned about some fun features. There are, as mentioned before, many more exciting templates to choose from and great projects ahead of you to be created.

Review

▶ Review questions

1 How do you create a photo project such as an online gallery, greeting card, or slide show?

2 How can you resize and reposition a photo when creating a greeting card?

3 What is an online gallery?

4 How can you change the order of your slides in a slide show?

▶ Review answers

1 To create a project in the Organizer, select an option in the Create panel of the Task pane, which then guides you through the creation process, offering several choices to personalize your project, such as specifying a template, layout, theme, and more.

2 Once you've selected a theme and a layout for the greeting card and clicked Done, an edit window opens with a bounding box around your photo. You can resize the photo by placing the pointer over a handle in the corners or the bounding box and dragging it to the desired position. When resizing a bounding box, the image is scaled proportionally by default. Click and drag the photo to reposition it.

3 An online gallery is a dynamic presentation of your images, which you can burn onto a CD, upload to Adobe Photoshop Services, or post to your Web site. You don't need to know anything about HTML programming to create a photo gallery—the Online Gallery wizard provides you with a wide variety of gallery styles from which you can select, and guides you through every step of the project.

4 One way to reorganize the order of slides is to click the thumbnail in your project bin, and then drag it to the right or left, until you've found the correct spot. You can also reorder your slides by clicking the Quick Reorder button, which is located above the thumbnail images to the left.

5 | Printing, Sharing, and Exporting

In the previous lessons you've learned how to import and organize your photos and how to combine text and images to design stunning Creations. Naturally, you'd like to have printed copies of your favorite pictures and share your files with your friends and family.

In this lesson, you'll learn how to do the following:

- Print photos on your home printer.
- Order professionally printed photos online.
- Share photos in e-mail.
- Create a quick share flow.
- Use an online sharing service.
- Burn photos to CD or DVD.
- Export images for Web use.

Before you begin, make sure that you have correctly copied the Lessons folder from the CD in the back of this book onto your computer's hard disk. See "Copying the Classroom in a Book files" on page 3.

Getting started

For this lesson, you can use either a catalog you have created with your own pictures or the CIB Catalog you created at the start of the book. To use the CIB Catalog, follow these steps:

1 Start Photoshop Elements. In the Welcome Screen, click Organize in the row of shortcut buttons across the lower part of the Welcome Screen. If the CIB Catalog is open, skip to "About printing" on the next page. If the CIB Catalog is not open, complete the following steps.

2   Choose File > Catalog.

3   In the Catalog Manager dialog box, select the CIB Catalog under Catalogs, and then click Open.

If you do not see the CIB Catalog file, review the procedures found in "Getting Started." See "Copying the Lessons files from the CD" on page 3, and "Creating a catalog" on page 4.

About printing

Photoshop Elements provides several options for printing your photos. You can have photos professionally printed by online providers through Adobe Photoshop Services, or you can print your photos on your home printer. You can print individual photos, contact sheets (thumbnails of each selected photo), picture packages (a page of one or more photos printed at various sizes), or labels (arranging the photos on a grid for printing on commercially available label paper). Finally, you can print creations you've made in Photoshop Elements, such as photo albums, greeting cards, and calendars.

Printing individual photos

The Organizer helps you reduce waste of expensive photographic paper. You can print single or multiple images on the same page, arranging them on the paper in the sizes you want.

1   In the Organizer, select your favorite thumbnails. Click one thumbnail to select it, and then hold down Ctrl and click several others images you want to print.

2   Choose File > Print.

3   In the Print Photos dialog box, make the following adjustments:

• Under Select Printer, select an available printer.

• Under Select Type of Print, choose Individual Prints.

• Under Select Print Size and Options, select 3.5" x 5".

If a warning appears about print resolution, click OK to close it. Some of the sample files are provided at a low resolution, which is why you might get this warning.

• If selected, deselect the One Photo Per Page check box.

4 (Optional) Do any of the following:

• On the left side of the dialog box, select one of the thumbnails, and then click the Remove button (➖) at the bottom of the thumbnails column to remove that image from the set that will be printed.

• Click the Add button (➕) under the column of thumbnails. Select the Entire Catalog option, and then click the check box of any image that you want to add to the set to be printed. Click Done.

• If you have more pictures selected than fit on one page, click the arrows under the Print Preview in the middle of the dialog box, to see the other pages that will be printed.

Note: You can select only images that are part of the current catalog. If you want to add other pictures to the printing batch, you must first add them to the catalog, using one of the methods described earlier in this lesson.

5 Do one of the following:

• Click Cancel to close the dialog box without printing. This is recommended if you want to save your ink and paper for your own images.

• Click Print to actually print the pictures.

Printing a contact sheet

Contact sheets let you easily preview groups of images by displaying a series of thumbnail images on a single page.

1   In the Photo Browser, select one or more photos.

2   Choose File > Print.

Note: If you don't select specific photos before choosing Print, Photoshop Elements asks whether you want to print all photos in the Photo Browser.

3   In the Print Photos dialog box, choose a printer from the Select Printer menu.

4   Choose Contact Sheet from the Select Type of Print menu. The preview layout automatically uses all photos listed on the left side of the Print Photos dialog box. To remove a photo, select its thumbnail and click the Remove button.

5   For Columns, type **4** to specify the number of columns in the layout. You can specify between 1 and 9 columns.

The thumbnail size and number of rows are adjusted according to your choice. If the number of photos listed in the Print Photos dialog box exceeds the capacity of a single page, more pages are added to accommodate them.

6   To add text labels below each thumbnail, select any of the following:

• Date, to print the date embedded in the image.

• Caption, to print the caption text embedded in the file's metadata.

• Filename, to print the image file name.

• Page Numbers, to print page numbers at the bottom of each page (this option is only available if multiple contact sheets are printed).

Note: Words in the text label may be truncated, depending on the page setup and layout.

7   Click Print to print, or click Cancel.

Printing a Picture Package

Picture Package lets you place multiple copies of one or more photos on a single printed page. You can choose from a variety of size and placement options to customize your package layout.

1 Select one or more pictures from the browser, and then choose File > Print.

2 In the Print Photos dialog box, choose a printer from the Select Printer menu.

3 Choose Picture Package from the Select Type of Print menu. If a Printing Warning dialog box cautioning against enlarging pictures appears, click OK. You will print multiple smaller pictures.

4 Choose a layout from the Select a Layout menu, and select the Fill Page With First Photo check box.

Note: The options available under the Select a Layout menu depend on the paper size selected in the printer preferences. To change the printer preferences, click the button next to the Select Printer menu.

5 (Optional) Choose Icicles (or another border of your preference) from the Select a Frame menu. You can select only one border for the picture package.

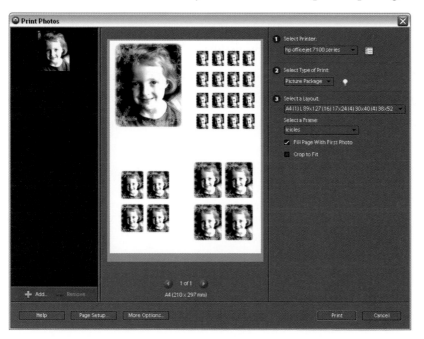

💡 *To print the images listed in the dialog box on separate pages, click the Fill Page with First Photo option. You can use the Navigation buttons below the layout preview to view each layout.*

Note: Depending on the layout you choose, the images are oriented to produce the optimum coverage of the printable area. This feature is automatic and cannot be overridden. You cannot rotate the images placed in the layout.

6   To crop photos so they fit the layout size perfectly, click Crop to Fit.

Note: If you want to add a photo to your picture package layout and it's not listed in the Print Photos dialog box, click the Add button and use the Add Photos dialog box to select the photos you want. Click Done to add the selected photos to the list in the Print Photos dialog box. To replace a photo in the layout, drag an image from the left side of the Print Photos dialog box over an image in the layout preview and release the mouse button.

7   Click Print to print the package on your computer, or click Cancel.

Ordering professionally printed photos online

If you want highest quality prints of your photos—for your own enjoyment or to share with others—you can order professionally printed photos online. In this exercise you will learn how to order individual prints from the Organizer (a service available in the US, Canada, and Japan).

Note: You must have an active Internet connection to order prints online.

1   In the Organizer, select one or more pictures you would like to have professionally printed.

2   If the Quick Share palette is not already open in the Organize bin, choose Window > Quick Share to open it.

3   Drag the selected photos from the Browser view onto the words *Drag photos here to create an order* in the Quick Share palette.

The New Order Prints Recipient dialog box appears.

4   In the New Order Prints Recipient dialog box, enter all required information for the person to receive the printed photos. For this exercise, you can enter your own name, address, and home phone number (and select the This is my home address check box). Or, if you want to import contact information from an existing contact book entry, click the Choose Existing Contact button, select a contact from the list, and then click OK to close the Contact Book dialog box.

5   Click OK to close the New Order Prints Recipient dialog box.

A new target entry appears in the Quick Share palette. If you selected the This is my home address check box in the New Order Prints Recipient dialog box in step 4, you'll see a home icon next to the name of the target entry. The number in brackets next to the name indicates the number of selected photos for this print order.

6   In the Quick Share palette, double-click the name of the new target entry to open the Order Prints for *your name* dialog box. Do any of the following:

- Use the slider to increase or decrease the thumbnail image size.

- Select one or more photos and click Remove Selected Photo(s).

- Click Remove All to remove all photos from the current order.

7 When done, click Close to close the dialog box without confirming the order yet.

8 (Optional) Drag additional photos from the Browser view onto the same target entry in the Quick Share palette:

9 In the Quick Share palette, click the Order button on the right side of the target entry.

10 In the Welcome to Adobe Photoshop Services dialog box, do one of the following:

• If you are already an Ofoto or EasyShare Gallery member, click Sign in, and then use the e-mail address and password associated with your existing online account to sign in.

• Create a new account by entering your first name, e-mail address, and a password of at least six characters. If you agree with the Terms of Service select the respective check box under Create Account, and then click Next.

11 In the Review Order dialog box, do any of the following:

• Click Change quantities or sizes to change the quantity or size of each photo in your order.

• Click Remove under a thumbnail image in the list on the left side of the dialog box to remove a print from your order.

• Review the information under Order Summary and Delivery Information.

12   When done reviewing your order, click Checkout:

13   If you wanted to proceed with an order, you would now provide your credit card details in the Billing Information dialog box and review the information under Billing Address and Order Summary. Then, starting the processing of your order—including charging your credit card!—would only be one Place Order click away. But for this exercise, click Cancel if you don't want to order any prints. In the dialog box that appears, click OK to confirm that you want to stop using this service. Right-click on the target name in the Order Prints palette, and then choose Cancel Order from the context menu. Click Yes to confirm canceling the order in the alert dialog box.

About sharing

In Lesson 1 you have learned how to use the Organizer's e-mail function, to create versions of your photos that are optimized to be sent as e-mail attachments. See "Sharing photos in e-mail" on page 26. Instead of sending photos as simple e-mail attachments, you can use the Photo Mail option to embed your photos in the body of an e-mail, using colorful custom layouts. To share items other than photos—like slide shows, photo galleries, or flipbooks—you generally have a choice of output options during the creation process.

Using Photo Mail

1   In the Organizer, select one or more photos that you would like to share via e-mail with your friends or family.

2   In the Share panel of the Task pane, click the Photo Mail button.

3   Next to Items, select the Include captions check box, and then click Next.

4   Under Message, select and delete the "Here are the photos...." text and type a message of your own.

5   Select a recipient from the list under Select Recipients. (If you didn't work through Lesson 1 and your recipient list is still empty, click the Edit Contact Book button (👤), and then create a new entry using the Contact Book dialog box).

6   Click Next.

7   In the Stationery & Layouts Wizard dialog box, select a stationery format appropriate for the selected photos: Click on a category name to show the available design choices, and then select a stationery type from the submenu. A preview of your e-mail body will appear on the right side of the dialog box.

8   Click Next Step. Customize the layout by selecting an option under Photo Size and under Layout. Click the message text to edit it. Click next to the photo (either left or right or under the photo, depending on your layout selected in step 7) to edit the caption text.

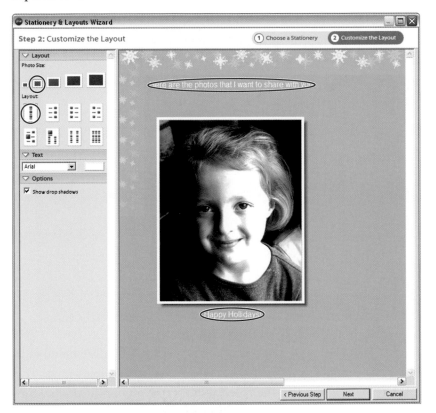

9 Click Next.

Photoshop Elements opens your default e-mail application and creates an e-mail message with your design in the body of the message. You can send Photo Mail through Outlook Express, Outlook, or Adobe E-mail Service.

10 Switch back to Photoshop Elements (Organizer).

Creating a quick share flow

If you find yourself sending the same kind of documents to the same group of people on a regular basis, then setting up a quick share target can help you automate your work considerably. For example, if you frequently (or even only occasionally) send your family an e-mail message with selected photos from each vacation, only once do you need to set up the quick share target (including information such as the mailing list and the desired image size for the photos), and then reuse these settings again and again by simply dropping photos on the quick share target.

While you can create a new order prints target by clicking the New button in the Quick Share palette, you can create a quick share target only from within the respective workflow. In the following steps you will set up a quick share target to send photos to a group of people as an e-mail attachment.

1   In the Photo Browser of the Organizer, select several photos of your choice.

2   In the Share panel of the Task pane, click the E-mail Attachments button.

3   Select Very Small (320 x 240 px) from the Maximum Photo Size menu (a good choice to keep the overall file size small if you want to send multiple images via e-mail) and adjust the image quality using the Quality slider (the higher the quality the longer the download time). The resulting file size and download time for a typical 56 Kbps dial-up modem are estimated and displayed for your reference. When done, click Next.

4   Under Message, select and delete the "Here are the photos...." text and type a message of your own.

5   Under Select Recipients, click to select the check boxes next to the recipients you want to include in this quick share target.

6   Under Save as Quick Share Flow?, select Yes, and then enter a descriptive name for this quick share target.

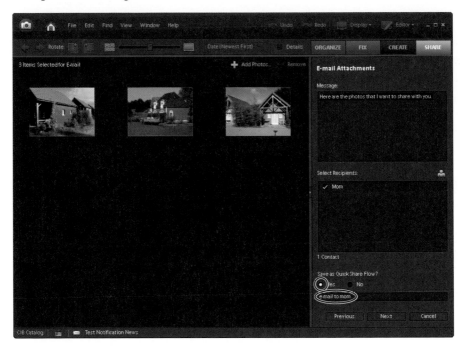

7   Click Next.

Your default e-mail application opens and creates an e-mail message with the selected photos attached in the selected image quality and size. You can further edit the message and Subject line if you want. When you are finished and ready to send the e-mail, make sure that you are connected to the Internet, either click Send if you want to send an actual e-mail, or close the message without saving or sending it.

8   Switch back to Photoshop Elements (Organizer). In the Quick Share palette, notice the new e-mail attachments quick share target. Select one or more photos in the Photo Browser and drop the selection onto this quick share target.

9 (Optional). Drop additional photos onto this quick share target. The number in brackets next to the name indicates the number of selected photos for this quick share target.

10 When done, click the E-mail button in the quick share target.

With just one click your default e-mail application opens and creates an e-mail message with the selected photos attached in the chosen image quality and size, ready to be send out.

11 Close your e-mail application, and then switch back to Photoshop Elements (Organizer).

Using an online sharing service

You can use Adobe Photoshop Services in Photoshop Elements to send images and creations to online service providers. You can also use the services to get photos.

1 In the Photo Browser of the Organizer, select the photos you wish to share.

2 In the Share panel of the Task pane, click the More Options button, and then choose Share with Kodak Easyshare Gallery from the menu to access the Kodak® EasyShare Gallery.

3 If the Welcome to Adobe Photoshop Services dialog box appears, do one of the following:

- If you are already an Ofoto or EasyShare Gallery member, click Sign in, and then use the e-mail address and password associated with your existing online account to sign in.

- Create a new account by entering your first name, e-mail address, and a password of at least six characters. If you agree with the Terms of Service, select the respective check box under Create Account, and then click Next.

Note: If you are still signed in to the Adobe Photoshop Services from the previous exercise, you don't need to sign in again. Just click Next to continue.

4 In the Share Online dialog box, click to select the Add New Address option.

5 In the Add Address dialog box, complete the address information for the person with whom you will share the photos, and then click Next.

6 In the Share Online dialog box, select the newly added address book check box. Under Message, type **Photos** in the subject field and type **Enjoy!** in the message field. Then, click Next.

Your photos are being uploaded.

7 In the Share Online Confirmation dialog box, click Done. Or, click Order Prints if you want to purchase prints of your photos, and then follow the on-screen directions.

An e-mail will be sent to the recipient you've specified in step 6, containing a Web link where the photos can be viewed online in a slide show.

About exporting

Even though there are a variety of ways to share your photos and creations using commands in Photoshop Elements, there may be situations where you want to export a copy of your files to use in another program. In the Organizer, you can move or copy your files to a CD or DVD. In the Editor, you can export you photos optimized for use in a Web design application.

Burning photos to CD or DVD

Use the Make a CD/DVD command in the Organizer to copy a set of photos to a CD or DVD. For instance, you might want to give your photos to a friend, or backup only selected images. Or, use the Copy/Move to Removable Disk to copy or move photos to any storage device—including hard disk, USB stick, network drive, or CD/DVD writer—attached to your computer.

Note: To make a full or incremental backup of your entire catalog, use the Backup Catalog to CD, DVD or Hard Drive command.

1   Make sure you have a CD or DVD drive with writable media connected to your computer.

2   In the Photo Browser, select the items you want to burn to a CD or DVD.

3   Choose File > Make a CD/DVD.

If you haven't selected any files, you'll see a dialog box giving you the option of selecting all files in the Photo Browser.

4   In the Make a CD/DVD dialog box, select a destination drive, and then click OK to actually copy your files to a writable CD or DVD. Or, click Cancel to exit the Make a CD/DVD dialog box without copying any files.

5   In the Photo Browser, select the items you want to copy or move.

6   Choose File > Copy/Move to Removable Disk.

The Copy/Move to Removable Disk wizard appears.

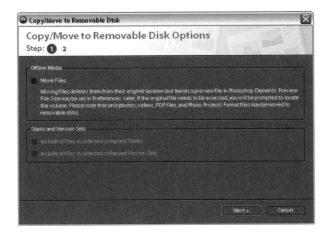

7   If selected, deselect the Move Files check box under Offline Media.

Note: Choosing the Move Files option deletes the original files from your hard disk after they are copied to the new location, keeping only a smaller low-resolution proxy file in the catalog. This is useful if you want to save hard disk space on your computer and only need to access the original files occasionally.

8   Under Stacks and Version Sets, you have the choice to copy/move only the first file or all files in a stack or version set. These options are dimmed, if you don't have any stacks or version sets in your selection of photos.

9   Click Next.

10   Select a destination drive in the Destination Settings dialog box. If you want to specify a subfolder on the destination drive as target location, click Browse, and then select the folder in the Browse For Folder dialog box.

11   Click Done to actually copy your files to the target location. Or, click Cancel to exit the Copy/Move to Removable Disk wizard without copying or moving any files.

Using the File > Export > As New File(s) command enables you to export photos not only in the original file format, but also in JPEG, PNG, TIFF, or PSD file format, along with options for images size, location, and custom file name.

Saving copies of the images for Web use

Your final task in this lesson is to convert a file to JPEG format so it can be shared on
a Web page. The JPEG file format reduces the file size and can be displayed by Web
browsers such as Internet Explorer, which makes it an efficient file format for Web use.
If your file contains multiple layers, the conversion to the JPEG file format will flatten
them into one inseparable layer.

Here, you'll use the Save for Web feature, which enables you to tweak the export settings
while comparing the original image file with the proposed Web version of the image.

1   In the Photo Browser, select a photo you want to save for Web use.

2   Click the Editor button (🖉) located near the top right corner of the Organizer
window, and then choose Quick Fix, Full Edit, or Guided Edit from the menu. Or, click
the Quick Fix, Full Edit, or Guided Edit button in the Fix panel of the Task pane.

3   Wait until the Editor workspace has loaded, and then choose File > Save for Web.

4   In the Save For Web dialog box, choose Fit on Screen from the Zoom menu in the
lower left corner of the dialog box.

Note: *When previewing images using Save for Web, you can use the Zoom tool (🔍) in the
upper left corner of the dialog box to zoom in, or zoom out by holding down Alt key when*

clicking. When zoomed in, use the Hand tool ( ) to drag both images at once, so that you see the same details in both views.

5   Under the two views of the image, notice the file-size information. The image on the left displays the file size of the original document.

6   On the right side of the dialog box, select JPEG Medium in the Preset menu. Notice the change in file size for the JPEG image on the right side of the dialog box.

7   Under New Size, select Constrain Proportions and type **300** in the Width field. Because you selected Constrain Proportions, the Height automatically changes to keep the image proportional.

8   In the New Size section of the Save for Web dialog box, click the Apply button. Again notice the change in the file size displayed beneath the JPEG view of the image. If necessary, choose Fit on Screen from the Zoom menu.

Note: *If you need to reduce the file size even more, you can select JPEG Low, which reduces the file size by discarding more image data and further compressing the image. You can select intermediate levels between these options by changing the Quality value, either by typing a different number or by clicking the arrow and dragging the slider.*

9   Click OK and in the Save Optimized As dialog box, navigate to the My CIB Work folder and add **_Work** to the end of the file name. Click Save.

Converting the files to the JPEG format reduces the file size by using JPEG compression and discarding some of the data, based upon the setting you select.

10   Back in the Editor, choose File > Close without saving any changes.

Congratulations! You've completed this lesson and should now have a good understanding of the basics of printing, sharing, and exporting.

In this lesson, you have seen how to set up single or multiple images for printing on your home printer and how to order professionally printed photos online. You've learned how to share photos using Photo Mail or an online sharing service and you've seen how a quick share flow can automate tasks you perform frequently. Finally, you've exported photos for backup purpose and for Web use.

Review

▶ **Review questions**

1   How do you print multiple images on a single sheet of paper?

2   What is Photo Mail?

3   What is a quick share flow?

4   What command can you use to backup all photos in your catalog to a CD or DVD?

5   Is the Save for Web command also available in Quick Fix mode?

▶ **Review answers**

1   All multi-photo printing with Photoshop Elements is done in the Organizer, although you can also start the process in the Editor. You start by selecting the photo or photos you want to print and choosing File > Print. Then, deselect the One Photo Per Page check box.

2   Instead of sending photos as simple e-mail attachments, you can use the Photo Mail option to embed your photos in the body of an e-mail, using colorful custom layouts. You can send Photo Mail through Outlook Express, Outlook, or Adobe E-mail Service.

3   A quick share flow can help you automate tasks you perform frequently. Save your settings as a quick share target from within the respective workflow—for example, when sending photos to a group of people as an e-mail attachment—and then perform the same task again by dropping photos onto the quick share target in the Quick Share palette.

4   In the Organizer, choose File > Backup Catalog. After the first full backup, you can choose to perform only an incremental backup. To copy or move only selected files in your catalog, use the File > Copy/Move Offline command.

5   Yes, the Save for Web command is available in all three modes of the Editor, Quick Fix, Full Edit, and Guided Edit.

6 Adjusting Color in Images

Color casts, or unwanted imbalances in the color of an image, can be caused by the light source, incorrect camera exposure settings, or other issues relating to the input device. Photoshop Elements provides several tools for fixing color problems in your photos. You can also use these tools creatively to vary the color of an object in a picture.

In this lesson, you will learn how to do the following:

- Correct color problems in Guided Edit mode.

- Auto-correct images in either Quick Fix or Full Edit mode.

- Use individual automatic options to improve images.

- Adjust skin tones.

- Correct an image using Smart Fix.

- Apply the Color Variations feature to shift color balance.

- Removing red eyes in the Editor.

- Make and save selection areas for future use.

- Apply color adjustments to a selected image area.

- Troubleshoot common problems when printing color pictures.

- Work with color management.

This lesson shows you many different ways to change the color balance in your pictures, beginning with the one-step correction features. From there, you'll discover advanced features and adjustment techniques that can be mastered easily.

Most people need at least an hour and a half to complete the work in this lesson. Several different projects are involved and you can do them all in one session or in several sessions.

In this lesson, you will use the CIB Catalog you created earlier in the "Getting Started" section at the beginning of this book. If the CIB Catalog is not currently open in the Organizer, choose File > Catalog, and then select and open the CIB Catalog.

This lesson focuses primarily on the Editor and also builds on the skills and concepts covered in earlier lessons.

Before you begin, make sure that you have correctly copied the Lessons folder from the CD in the back of this book onto your computer's hard disk. See "Copying the Classroom in a Book files" on page 3.

Note: As you gain advanced skills in Photoshop Elements 6.0, you may require additional information about issues and problems. For help with common problems you might have when completing lessons in this book, see "Why won't Photoshop Elements do what I tell it to do?" later in this lesson.

Getting started

Before you start working, take a few moments to make sure that your work area and palettes are set up to match the illustrations in this section.

1   Start Photoshop Elements in Full Edit mode by selecting Edit in the Photoshop Elements Welcome Screen. If the Organizer is already open, click the Editor button (📝) located near the top right corner of the Organizer window, and then choose Full Edit from the menu.

2   In Full Edit, use the Window menu to make the Tools palette, Palette Bin, and Project Bin visible. In both Full Edit and Quick Fix modes, you can expand collapsed palettes in the Palette Bin by clicking the arrow beside the palette name on the palette title bar.

Note: For instructions on how to add or remove palettes from the Full Edit Palette Bin, see "Using the Palette Bin" in Lesson 1, "A Quick Tour of Photoshop Elements." You cannot add or remove palettes in Quick Fix mode.

In this lesson, you will be using the Editor in Full Edit mode, Quick Fix mode, and Guided Edit mode.

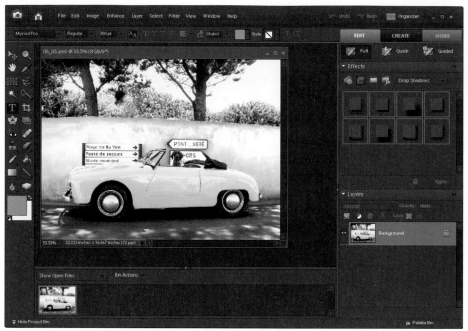

Editor workspace in Full Edit mode.

Editor workspace in Quick Fix mode.

Editor workspace in Guided Edit mode.

Fixing photographs automatically

You may have noticed that not all the photographs used for the lessons in this book are of professional quality. Many of the pictures were selected to illustrate typical challenges that people might face when attempting to make the most of their photographs.

Batch-processing multiple files

Photoshop Elements can fix multiple photographs in batch mode. In this section, you'll apply automatic fixes to all the image files used in this lesson. You'll save those fixed files as copies of the originals so that you can compare the results at the end of each project.

1   In the Editor, choose File > Process Multiple Files. The Process Multiple Files dialog box opens.

2   In the Process Multiple Files dialog box, set the source and destination folders as follows:

• Choose Folder from the Process Files From menu.

• Under Source, click the Browse button. Find and select the Lesson06 folder in the Lessons folder. Click OK to close the Browse for Folder dialog box.

• Under Destination, click Browse. Then, find and select the My CIB Work folder that you created at the start of the book. Click OK to close the Browse for Folder dialog box.

3   Under File Naming, select Rename Files. Select Document Name in the first field, and type **_Autofix** in the second field. This adds the appendix "_Autofix" to the existing document name as the files are saved in the My CIB Work folder.

4   Under Quick Fix on the right side of the dialog box, select all four options: Auto Levels, Auto Contrast, Auto Color, and Sharpen.

5   Review all selections in the dialog box, comparing them to the following illustration. Make sure that the Resize Images and the Convert Files to options are not selected.

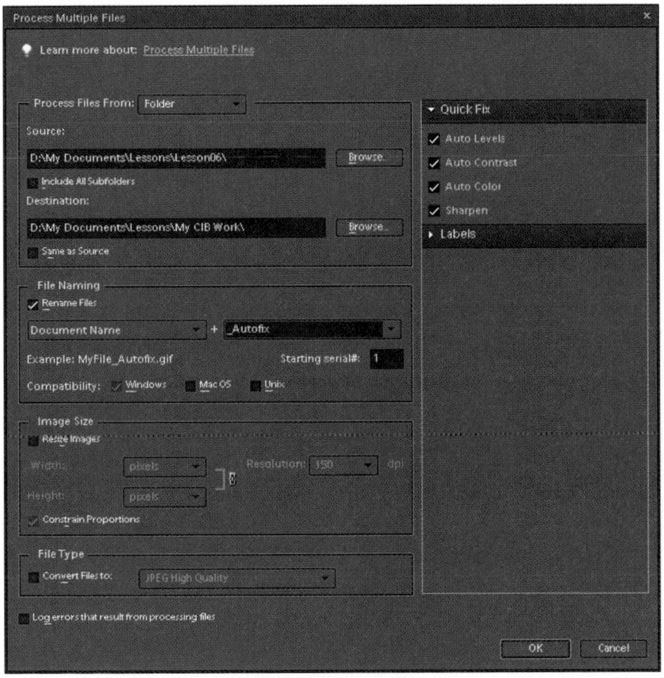

Note: While performing the next step, if an error message appears saying that some files couldn't be processed, ignore it. This might be caused by a hidden file that is not an image, so it has no effect on the success of your project. If an error message appears saying that files are missing, that means that the Lessons folder has been moved or was not expanded

correctly. See "Copying the Classroom in a Book files" on page 3 and redo that procedure, following the instructions exactly.

6   When you are sure that all selections are correct, click OK.

Photoshop Elements goes to work, automatically opening and closing image windows. All you need to do is sit back and wait for the process to finish.

Note: You can use Windows Explorer to see the images fixed by Quick Fix or, after adding them to your catalog as explained in the next section, in the Photo Browser of Photoshop Elements. For more information on the Photo Browser, see Photoshop Elements Help.

Adding the corrected files to the Organizer

The Save, Save As, and Save Optimized As dialog boxes all have an Include in Organizer option that is selected by default. When you use the Process Multiple Files feature, this option isn't part of the process, so you must add the files to the Organizer manually.

1   In the Editor, click the Organizer button (⬛) to open the Organizer workspace.

2   In the Organizer, choose File > Get Photos and Videos > From Files and Folders.

3   In the dialog box that appears, locate and open the My CIB Work folder.

4   Ctrl-click or drag-select all five _Autofix files.

5   Select Automatically Fix Red Eyes, deselect Automatically Suggest Photo Stacks, and then click Get Photos.

6   The Import Attached Keyword Tags dialog box opens. Click OK without selecting any keyword tags, as you'll be adding keyword tags manually in the next few steps.

7   If the Auto Red Eye Fix Complete dialog box appears, click OK.

8   If a message appears reminding you that only the new photos will appear, click OK. The Organizer displays the newly added image thumbnails.

9   Choose Edit > Select All, or press Ctrl+A.

10   If necessary, click the triangle next to Imported Keyword Tags in the Keyword Tags palette to show the imported keyword tags. Scroll down to find the Lesson 6 keyword tag. Then, drag the Lesson 6 keyword tag to any of the selected image thumbnails to apply it to all selected images.

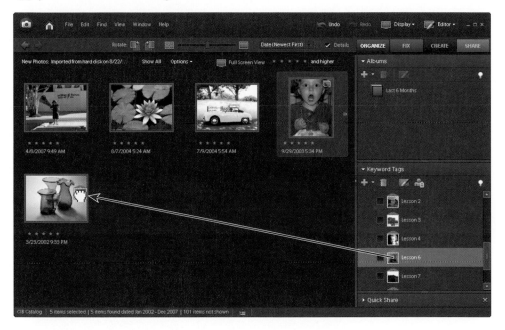

11   Click the Show All button above the Photo Browser.

Now you are ready to discover other methods for correcting color.

Using Guided Edit for editing

If you are new to digital photography, Guided Edit is the place to start for fixing common image problems. But by using the Guided Edit mode, even more experienced users can pick up some tricks, or just enjoy the simplicity of working in that mode.

Removing a color cast using Guided Edit

One of the images in the Lesson 6 folder, the picture of three vases, has a very obvious color cast. The picture was taken indoors with inadequate lighting. You will remove that color cast using the Guided Edit mode of the Editor.

1   If the Organizer is not currently active, switch to it now.

2   In the Keyword Tags palette, click the Find box next to the Lesson 6 keyword tag.

3   Select the original picture of the three vases, 06_01.jpg, to make it active. Pay attention not to confuse the original file with the file 06_01_Autofix.jpg, where color correction—among other things—has already been applied.

Note: To show the file names in the Photo Browser, choose View > Show File Names.

4   Click the Editor button (![icon]) located near the top right corner of the Organizer window, and then choose Guided Edit from the menu.

5   Wait until the Editor workspace has loaded with the image of the three vases open in Guided Edit mode.

6   If necessary, click the triangle next to Color Correction under What would you like to do. Then, click to select Remove a Color Cast in the group of Color Correction tasks.

7 Click the button near the bottom of the Guided Edit panel to select Before & After - Horizontal as display mode.

8 Read the instructions under Correct Color Cast. Then, using the Color Cast Eyedropper tool, click near the top left corner of the Before image to remove the color cast. Notice the change in the After image.

9 (Optional) If you are not satisfied with the result, click the Undo button (⟲) next to the menu bar of the organizer window, and then click a different area in the Before image. Or, to clear the Undo/Redo history and start all over with the original version of the image, click the Reset button in the Guided Edit panel.

10 When you are satisfied with the result of the color correction in the After image, click Done near the bottom of the Guided Edit panel of the Tasks panel.

Adjusting lighting using Guided Edit

As with many images, this image has more than just one imperfection. After the color cast has been removed, the image looks as if it could benefit from some lighting adjustment.

1 If necessary, click the triangle next to Lighting and Exposure under What would you like to do. Then, click to select Lighten or Darken in the group of Lighting and Exposure tasks.

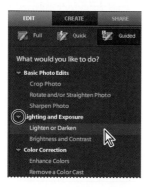

2 In the panel that appears, click the Auto button under Lighten or Darken a Photo. Notice the immediate big improvement to the image quality.

3 Use the sliders for Lighten Shadows, Darken Highlights, and Midtone Contrast to further adjust the lighting of the image. We used a value of 30 for Lighten Shadows, left the value for Darken Highlights at 0, and used a value of 32 for Midtone Contrast. Your choices may vary, based on your results from the color correction as well as your preferences for the appearance of the final image.

4 When you are satisfied with the result of the lighting adjustment in the After image, click Done near the bottom of the Guided Edit panel of the Tasks panel.

5 (Optional) Select Sharpen Photo in the group of Basic Photo Edits under What would you like to do. Click the Auto button under Sharpen Photo. Use the slider to manually adjust sharpening to your liking, and then click Done.

6 Choose File > Save As. In the Save As dialog box, navigate to and open the My CIB Work folder, leave the JPEG file format selected, name the file **06_01_Guided**, select Include in the Organizer, deselect Save in Version Set with Original, and then click Save.

7 Click OK in the JPEG Options dialog box without making any changes.

8 In the Editor, choose File > Close, and then switch back to the Organizer.

9 In the Organizer, click the Show All button above the Photo Browser, and then scroll down to find the newly added file 06_01_Guided.jpg and apply to it the Lesson 6 keyword tag.

With just a few clicks you have dramatically improved the quality of the image. To get good results using Guided Edit you don't have to have prior experience in using an image editor. Guided Edit even offers two Guided Activities—called "Touch Up Scratches, Blemishes or Tear Marks" and "Guide for Editing a Photo"—taking you step-by-step in the recommended order through several image editing tasks to get professional results. When you are ready to move on to the next level of photo editing there is Quick Fix, which you will use in the next exercise.

Using Quick Fix for editing

Quick Fix conveniently assembles many of the basic photo fixing tools in Photoshop Elements. If one control doesn't work for your image, click the Reset button and try another one. You can also adjust your image using the slider controls, whether you've used the Quick Fix feature or not.

Applying individual automatic adjustments

When you apply automatic fixes to images using the Process Multiple Files dialog box, you only briefly see the before, during, and after versions of the file. In this project, you'll apply individual aspects of automatic fixing, one at a time. This is useful because it enables you to see how the different phases affect the image, and also enables you to make individual adjustments to the correction process.

Opening image files for Quick Fix editing

You'll use the same technique you learned in Lesson 2 for using the Organizer to find and open files for editing in Quick Fix mode.

1   If the Organizer is not currently active, switch to it now.

2   In the Keyword Tags palette, click the Find box next to the Lesson 6 keyword tag.

3   Select the original version of the image with three vases, 06_01.jpg.

Note: To show the file names in the Photo Browser, choose View > Show File Names.

4   Click the Editor button (📝) located near the top right corner of the Organizer window, and then choose Quick Fix from the menu.

5   From the View menu in the lower left corner of the image window, choose Before & After - Horizontal.

Note: You can change from Before & After - Horizontal to Before & After - Vertical, if you prefer that arrangement. The horizontal view shows the before and after versions of the image side by side. The vertical view shows them one above the other.

Using Smart Fix

With Photoshop Elements in Quick Fix mode, you see four palettes in the Palette Bin on the right—General Fixes, Lighting, Color, and Sharpen. In the General Fixes palette, the first option available is called Smart Fix.

Smart Fix corrects overall color balance and improves shadow and highlight detail in your image. As with other automatic fixes in Quick Fix mode, you can click the Auto button to apply these corrections automatically. You can also move the Amount slider to vary the degree of the adjustment. Or, as in the following steps, you can use a combination of both adjustments.

1   In the Palette Bin, under General Fixes, click the Auto button for Smart Fix. Notice the immediate effect on the image.

2   Now, move the Amount slider to change the adjustments of the color balance and detail in your image. You can determine which adjustment works best for you. In our example the slider is in the middle.

3   Click the Commit button (✔) in the General Fixes palette title bar to commit the changes.

Applying other automatic fixes

Additional automatic fixes are available in the Palette Bin under Lighting, Color, and Sharpen.

1   In the Palette Bin, under Lighting, click the Auto button for Levels. You may need to open a palette to see the Auto button. Depending upon the adjustment you made in Smart Fix, you may or may not see a big shift in the lighting of this image.

2   One at a time, click the Auto buttons for Contrast, Color, and Sharpen, noticing the difference in the image with each adjustment.

3   (Optional) Experiment with the adjustment sliders in each section. Click the Commit button (✔) in the respective title bar to commit the changes. Click the Reset button above the After image if you want to undo your modifications and start over again using the original version of the image.

4   When you have obtained your preferred result, choose File > Save As. In the Save As dialog box, navigate to and open the My CIB Work folder, rename the file **06_01_ Quick** and select the JPEG format. Select Include in the Organizer. If Save in Version Set with Original is selected, deselect it. Click Save.

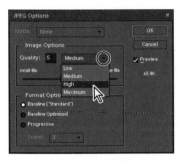

5 When the JPEG Options dialog box appears, select High from the Quality menu, and then click OK.

6 In the Editor, choose File > Close, and then switch back to the Organizer.

7 In the Organizer, find the newly added file 06_01_Quick.jpg and apply the Lesson 6 keyword tag to it.

Comparing methods of fixing color

The automatic correction features in Photoshop Elements do an excellent job of bringing out the best in most photographs. But each photograph is unique, and so are the potential problems. Some photographs don't respond well to automatic fixes and require a more hands-on approach to color correction.

Photoshop Elements offers many ways to deal with color correction. The more procedures you master, the more likely you'll be able meet the challenge of fixing a difficult photograph. In this section, you'll study three different methods for correcting a color problem, and compare the results.

Creating extra working copies of an image

You're going to compare three approaches to color correction, so you'll need three copies of the same photograph.

Note: By now, you should have mastered the procedure for using keyword tags to locate the files you need in the Organizer. From now on, the instructions for opening files will be summarized rather than explained in detail.

1   In the Organizer, use the Lesson 6 keyword tag to find the file 06_02.jpg. Pay attention not to confuse the original file with the file 06_02_Autofix.jpg.

2   Select the file 06_02.jpg in the Photo Browser, and then click the Editor button (✐) located near the top right corner of the Organizer window and choose Quick Fix from the menu.

3   In Quick Fix mode of the Editor, choose File > Duplicate. In the Duplicate Image dialog box, click OK to accept the default name, 06_02 copy.jpg.

4   Repeat Step 3 to create another duplicate, 06_02 copy 2.jpg.

Leave all three copies of the image file open for the next procedures. You can tell that the files are open because the thumbnails appear in the Project Bin at the bottom of your screen.

Automatically fixing color

At the beginning of this lesson, you applied all four Quick Fix options to each of the images used in this lesson and saved the results in a separate location. In this procedure, you'll apply just one type of Quick Fix.

1   In the Project Bin, double-click the 06_02.jpg thumbnail to make it the active file. To see the file name, hover with the pointer over the thumbnail in the Project Bin.

2   In the Color palette, click Auto to fix only the color.

Compare the Before and After views of the file.

3   Choose File > Save, saving the file in the My CIB Work folder and in JPEG format, changing the name to **06_02_Work**. Make sure Save in Version Set with Original is deselected. Click Save, leaving all other options in the Save and JPEG Options dialog box unchanged.

Adjusting the results of an automatic fix

In this procedure, you'll experiment with one of the sliders in the Quick Fix palettes.

1   In the Photo Bin, double-click the 06_02 copy thumbnail to make it the active file.

2 Click the Auto button for Color. The results are the same as you had in the previous procedure.

3 Drag the Temperature slider a small amount to the right.

This makes the image look warmer, reducing the blue and green tones while enhancing yellows, reds, and oranges.

4 Examine the results, paying particular attention to the skin tones.

5 Readjust the Temperature slider until you are satisfied with the realistic balance, achieving warm skin tones without the rest of the image getting too red. Then, click the Commit button (✔) at the top of the Color palette. In the sample shown, we moved the Temperature slider only slightly to the right.

Note: If you aren't happy with the results and want to start over, click Cancel (⊘) on the Color palette tab. If you decide to undo the color fix after you click the Commit button, click the Reset button above the image. This restores the image to its original condition.

6   Choose File > Save, saving the file in the My CIB Work folder and in JPEG format, changing the name to **06_02 copy_Work**. Notice that the Save in Version Set with Original option is not available, since the 06_02 copy.jpg file has not been added to the catalog. Click Save, leaving all other options in the Save and JPEG Options dialog boxes unchanged.

About viewing modes and image window arrangements

When you work in Quick Fix mode, only one image file appears in the work area, regardless of how many files are open. The inactive, open files appear as thumbnails in the Photo Bin but not in the work area.

When you work in Full Edit mode, other arrangements are possible. You can usually adjust the size and placement of image windows in the work area. If you can't arrange individual windows freely, your view is probably set to Maximize Mode. If opening or closing some files causes unexpected rearrangements of image windows, your view is probably set to Tile.

Maximize Mode fills the work area with the active image window, so it's the only image you can see.

Tile resizes and arranges all open images so that the image windows cover the work area. If Tile mode is active when you close an image file or open a new one, Photoshop Elements will rearrange the image windows in tile formation.

Cascade enables you to resize, arrange, or minimize files.

There are two ways to switch from one mode to another.

• Use the Window > Images menu and choose the arrangement you want: Maximize Mode, Tile, or Cascade. Or, if there is a check mark on the Maximize Mode command, choosing Maximize Mode again deactivates it and switches to the mode you were using previously.

• Select an icon on the far right end of the window title bar.

The available icons vary, depending on which viewing mode is active, and on the size of the work area on your monitor. If the work area is reduced, these icons may not appear.

A   B

A. Switch to Maximize Mode. *B. Switch to previous mode.*

For more information, see "Working in the Editor: Viewing images in the Editor" in Adobe Photoshop Elements Help.

Tweaking results from automatic fix

The top six commands in the Enhance menu apply the same changes as the Auto buttons in the Quick Fix palettes. These commands are available in both Quick Fix and Full Edit, but not in Guided Edit.

Both Quick Fix and Full Edit offer other methods of enhancing color in images. These are found in the lower half of the Enhance menu. In this procedure, you use a manual option to tweak the results produced by an automatic fix button.

1   In the Photo Bin, double-click the 06_02 copy 2 thumbnail to make it the active file.

2   In the Color palette, click Auto to apply the automatic color correction.

3   Choose Enhance > Adjust Color > Color Variations.

4   In the lower left area of the Color Variations dialog box, make sure that Midtones is selected, and that the Amount slider is approximately centered. Click the Decrease Blue thumbnail once, and then Click OK:

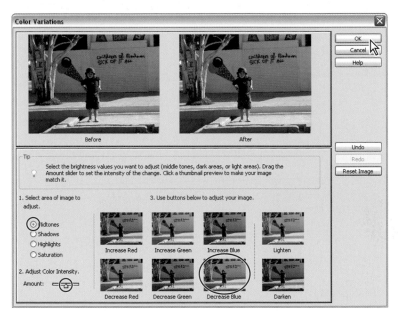

This reduces the amount of blue in the images, probably even too much. To try again, using a smaller value or a different combination of adjustments, you can undo the changes and start again. (Choose Edit > Undo Color Variations, and then try again, starting with Step 3.)

5 Choose File > Save As, and navigate to the My CIB Work folder. Rename the file **06_02 copy 2_Work**, and select the JPEG format. Click Save, leaving all other options in the Save and JPEG Options dialog boxes unchanged.

Comparing results

As you can tell by viewing the Photo Bin, all three copies of the image are open. Now you'll compare them to the autofix file you processed at the beginning of this lesson.

1 Choose File > Open. Locate and open the My CIB Work folder. Select the file 06_02_Autofix, and then click Open.

2 In the Edit panel of the Tasks pane, select the Full tab (📝) to switch to the Full Edit mode.

3 Choose Window > Images > Tile, if it's not already selected.

4 Use the Zoom tool and the Hand tool to select an area of interest in one of the images, and then choose Window > Images > Match Zoom and Windows > Images > Match Location.

5 In the toolbox, select the Zoom tool (🔍).

6 In the tool options bar, select Zoom Out.

7 Do one of the following:

• Click in the active image window until you can see the entire photo. Then, choose Window > Images > Match Zoom.

• In the tool options bar, select Zoom In. If it's not already selected, select Zoom All Windows in the tool options bar, and then click in the active image window until you can see the entire photo.

Note: At any given time there is only one active window. Look at the text in the title bars of the open image windows; the text is dimmed on all inactive image windows.

8 In the toolbox, select the Hand tool (✋).

9 In the tool options bar, select Scroll All Windows.

10 Click and drag within the active window to examine different areas of the image. Compare the four images and decide which looks best. Then, drag any corner edge of the image window to resize it so it fills the space and turn off Tile mode.

11 Choose View > Fit on Screen to enlarge the image so it fits in the window.

💡 *Press Ctrl-Tab or Ctrl-Shift-Tab to cycle through all open windows.*

Adjusting skin tones

Sometimes the combination of ambient light and surrounding color can cause skin tones in your image to be tinted with unwanted color. Photoshop Elements offers a unique solution, in both the Full Edit and Quick Fix modes (but not in Guided Edit).

To adjust color for skin tones do the following:

1 Choose Enhance > Adjust Color > Adjust Color for Skin Tone.

2 Make sure the Preview option is selected in the Adjust Color for Skin Tone dialog box. Then, with the eyedropper cursor ( ) that appears when you hover over the image in the Editor window, click an area of the kid's skin, for example on the face.

Photoshop Elements automatically adjusts the entire photo using the color of the child's skin as reference.

3 If you're unsatisfied with the correction, click on a different point in the image or move the Tan, Blush, and Temperature sliders to achieve the desired result.

While the Adjust Color for Skin Tone dialog box is open, you can switch to the Zoom tool or Hand tool in the Editor window to focus on a different area of the image. Switch back to the Eyedropper tool when you want to click another skin area in the image.

4 When you're satisfied with the skin tone, click OK to close the Adjust Color for Skin Tone dialog box, and then choose File > Close All. When asked, do not save the changes.

Working with red eye

Red eye occurs when a camera flash is reflected off the retina so that the dark center of the eye looks bright red. Photoshop Elements can automatically fix red eye when you bring photos into the Organizer. Just select Automatically Fix Red Eyes in the Get Photos dialog box when you import your photos (see the *Automatically Fixing Red Eyes* sidebar in Lesson 2). Or, you can apply the red eye fix command to images already in your catalog. In Lesson 8 you will learn how red eyes can be fixed directly in the Organizer, but here we will use the tools available in the Editor.

Using automatic Red Eye Fix in the Editor

Just as you automatically corrected color balance earlier in this lesson with Smart Fix, you can also apply an automatic red eye correction in Quick Fix mode. This method might not successfully remove red eye from all images, but Photoshop Elements provides other options.

In this procedure, you will be fixing red eyes in the Quick Fix mode of the Editor. But first, you'll use the Organizer to find the image to be fixed in your catalog.

1   In the Editor, click the Organizer button to load the Organizer workspace. If necessary, click the Show All button above the Photo Browser.

2   In the Keywords Tags palette, click the Find box next to the Lesson 6 keyword tag. For this exercise, you will be working on the uncorrected picture of the child with the red eyes, 06_03.jpg. Do not confuse this file with the version that has the autofix or auto red eye fix applied. If necessary, choose View > Show File Names.

3   In the Photo Browser, click the 06_03.jpg image to select it. Then, click the Editor button located near the top right corner of the Organizer window and choose Quick Fix from the menu that appears. Wait until the Editor has finished opening the file.

4   Select Before & After - Vertical from the View menu below the preview pane. Use the Zoom and Hand tools to focus on the eye area in the image.

5   In the Palette Bin, under General Fixes, click the Auto button next to Red Eye Fix. There is no slider available for this correction. As you can see, the Auto correction does a reasonably good job, but in this admittedly difficult case it also affects the color of the iris.

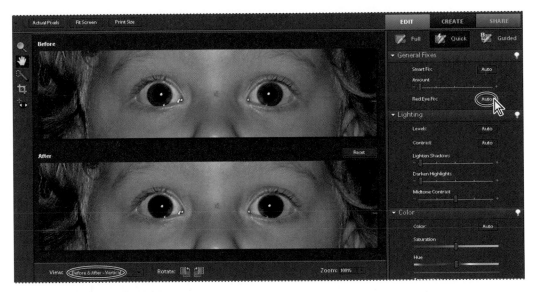

6   Click the Reset button above the edited image to revert the photo to its state before the Auto Red Eye Fix was applied.

The Auto Red Eye Fix feature works well for most images, but if you want more control in some cases, then the Red Eye Removal tool is just what you need.

Note: The Auto Red Eye Fix correction is also available as a command under the Enhance menu, along with other automatic correction controls like Auto Smart Fix, in both Quick Fix and Full Edit modes.

The Red Eye Removal tool

For those stubborn red eye problems, the Red Eye Removal tool ( ) is a simple and efficient solution. You will now learn how to customize and use the tool to fix red eye in a photo.

1   Open the file 06_03.jpg in either Quick Fix or Full Edit mode.

2   In the toolbox, select the Red Eye Removal tool (👁).

3   In the tool options bar, do one of the following:

• Click the Pupil Size menu, and then use the slider to set the value to about 25%.

• Double-click the text box next to Pupil Size, and then type **25%**, followed by Return or Enter on your keyboard.

• Hover the pointer over the Pupil Size text. When the pointer changes to the Scrubby slider icon (🖑), click and drag to the left or right to select a Pupil Size of 25%.

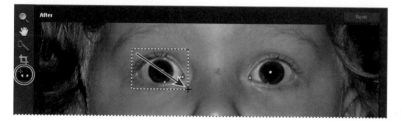

4   With the Red Eye Removal tool selected, click and drag to select a rectangular area around one eye in the After image.

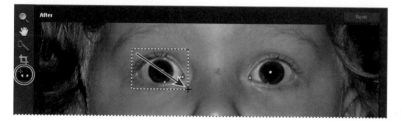

When you release the pointer, the red is removed from the eye. As an alternative to clicking and dragging to create a selection rectangle, you can click and release the pointer inside the red area of the eye.

5   With the Red Eye Removal tool still selected, click and release (don't drag!) the pointer inside the red area of the other eye.

The red is removed from the other eye.

6   (Optional) Click the Reset button, and then repeat steps 4 and 5 experimenting with other values for Pupil Size and Darken Amount in the tool options bar.

7   Choose File > Save As and navigate to the My CIB Work folder. Rename the file **06_03_Work** and select the JPEG format. If selected, deselect Save in Version Set with Original. Click Save, leaving all other options in the Save and JPEG Options dialog boxes unchanged.

8   Choose File > Close and return to the Organizer.

Making selections

Ordinarily, the entire image area can be altered by the changes you apply to an image or image layer. That's because, by default, the whole image is active. A selection is a portion of the image area that you designate as the only active area of the image. When a selection is active, any changes you apply affect only the area within the selection; the rest of the image layer is protected, or masked.

Typically, a selection marquee—a flashing border of dashed black and white lines—shows the boundaries of a selection. You can save a selection and re-use it at a later time. This can be a terrific time-saver when you need to use the selection several times.

Several tools create selections, and you'll get experience with most of them in the course of doing the lessons in this book. Selections can be geometric in shape or free form, and they can have crisp or soft edges. Selections can be created by using the mouse pointer, or by using similarities of color within the image.

Perhaps the simplest, most effective way to create a selection is to paint it on an image. This exercise focuses on the use of two selection tools in Photoshop Elements, the Selection Brush tool and the Quick Selection tool.

1   Using the Organizer, select the image of the water lily, 06_04.psd. Then, click the Editor button located near the top right corner of the Organizer window and choose Full Edit from the menu that appears. Or, use the keyboard shortcut Ctrl+I. Wait until the Editor has finished opening the file.

Notice that this file is saved as a Photoshop file and not as a JPEG file. The Photoshop file format can store additional information along with the image data. In this case, a portion of the flower has previously been selected and the selection information then saved in the file.

2   With the 06_04.psd file open in the Editor, choose Select > Load Selection. In the Load Selection dialog box, choose petals as Selection under Source. Under Operation, select New Selection, and then click OK. *(See illustration on the next page.)*

The selection information is loaded and becomes the current selection.

One petal needs to be added to make the selection of the flower complete. In the following exercise, you'll clear the current selection (the one you just loaded), use the Selection Brush tool to select just this one petal, and then reload the saved selection and add it to your new selection of the last missing petal.

3   Choose Select > Deselect to clear the current selection.

4   In the toolbox, select the Selection Brush tool (🖌), which is grouped with the Quick Selection tool.

Using the Selection Brush tool

The Selection Brush tool makes selections in two ways. You can paint over the area you want to select in Selection mode, or you can paint over areas you don't want to select using a semi-opaque overlay in Mask mode.

1   From the tool options bar, set the Selection Brush controls to the following:

• Add to selection

• 25 pixels wide

• Mode: Selection

• Hardness: 100%

2   Click and drag with the Selection Brush to paint over the large interior area of the petal in the front. Do not try to paint the edges; you will do that in the next step.

Notice that as you paint, you're actually painting with the flashing dashed line that indicates a selection. Release the mouse button to see what you've selected.

💡 *To help in making the selection, you can use the Zoom tool to magnify the area of interest in the photo.*

Now you'll reduce your brush size and paint the edges of the petal, adding them to your selection as you paint.

While you could move the Size slider to change your brush size, it's easier to use the open bracket key ([ ) to size the brush down, and the close bracket key ( ]) to size the brush up. The brush size increases or decreases in size each time you press the open or close bracket keys.

3   Press the left bracket key ([ ), to reduce the Selection Brush size to 10 pixels.

4   With the Selection Brush, paint the edges of the petal by clicking and dragging over them.

   💡 *By switching the Mode in the tool options bar from Add to selection to Subtract from selection, you can use the Selection Brush to paint out the areas that you don't want selected or only accidentally selected in your image.*

5   Continue to paint, using the brackets to change the brush size as needed, until the selection outline completely encompasses the petal.

If you found using the Selection Brush tool tedious, you'll appreciate learning about the Quick Selection tool later in this lesson. But first, you'll save the result of your hard work.

Editing a saved selection

Next you'll add your current selection to the selection that was saved with the file. You can modify saved selections by replacing, adding to, or subtracting from them.

1   With your selection still active, choose Select > Load Selection.

2   In the Load Selection dialog box, choose petals as Selection under Source. Choose Add to Selection under Operation, and then click OK.

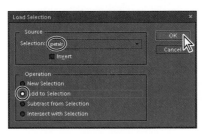

Note: The New Selection option replaces the saved selection with the current selection. Subtract from Selection subtracts the current selection from the saved selection. Intersect with Selection replaces the saved selection with the intersection between the current selection and the saved selection.

You should now see the entire water lily outlined by the flashing selection boundary.

If you've missed a spot, simply paint it in with the Selection Brush tool. If you've selected too much, switch to Subtract from selection mode in the options bar, and then paint out your mistakes.

Note: You can also modify a saved selection by loading it and using selection tools to add to it (Shift+drag) or subtract from it (Alt+drag).

3   Choose Select > Save Selection. In the Save Selection dialog box, choose petals as Selection under Selection, select Replace Selection under Operation, and then click OK.

4   Choose Select > Deselect.

Using the Quick Selection Tool

The Quick Selection tool enables you to draw, scribble, or click on the area you want to select. The mark you make doesn't need to be precise, because while you are drawing, Photoshop Elements expands the selection border based on color and texture similarity.

For this exercise, you will first select the area around the water lily, and then swap the selected and unselected areas in the photo to establish the actual selection. This technique can be a real timesaver in situations where directly selecting an object proves difficult.

1   In the toolbox, select the Quick Selection tool (✎).

2   In the tool options bar, make sure New Selection is selected. Choose a brush size from the Size menu. If you want to simply scribble over the area, you can use a larger brush. For a more precise outline, choose a smaller brush size. For this exercise, you can use the default brush size of 30 px.

3   Scribble over the area around the water lily, making sure to touch some of the yellow, green and black areas as shown in the illustration, and then release the pointer. As you draw, Photoshop elements automatically expands the selection border based on color and texture similarity.

4   Continue to scribble over or click into unselected areas around the water lily until everything but the inside of the water lily is selected.

5   Finally, turn the selection inside out by choosing Select > Inverse, thereby masking the background and selecting the flower.

Working with selections

Now that you have a flashing selection outline around the water lily, you can change the color in the selected image area.

1   With the water lily still selected, click the Quick button at the top of the Edit panel of the Task pane to switch to Quick Fix mode.

2   To make comparing easier, choose Before & After - Horizontal from the View menu below the image to the left.

3   In the Color palette on the right, click and drag the Hue slider to the left or right to change the color of the water lily.

Notice that the water lily changes color, but the background does not. This is because only pixels inside the selection change.

4   Click the Cancel button (⊘) in the Color palette to undo your changes.

You can invert the selection to apply changes to the background instead of the water lily.

5   Click the Full button at the top of the Edit panel to switch to Full Edit mode.

6   With the water lily still selected, choose Select > Inverse.

7   With the background around the water lily selected, choose Enhance > Convert to Black and White.

8   In the Convert to Black and White dialog box, choose Urban/Snapshots under Select a style.

9   (Optional) Select a different style to see the effect on the image. Use the sliders under Adjustment Intensity to vary the amount of change for red, green, blue, and contrast. Click Undo if you made changes you don't like.

10   Click OK to close the Convert to Black and White dialog box.

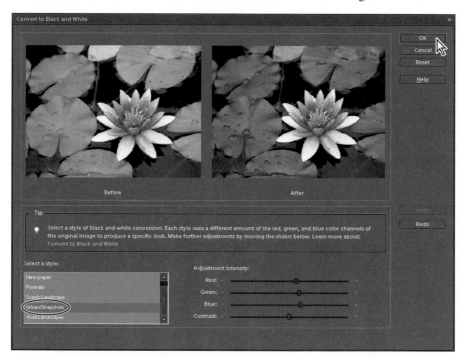

11   Choose Select > Deselect.

12   Choose File > Save As and save the file in the My CIB Work folder. For File Name, type **06_04_Work**. Make sure that the Format option is Photoshop (PSD). If Save in Version Set with Original is selected, deselect it before you click Save.

13   Choose File > Close, to close the file and switch back to the Organizer.

Congratulations, you've finished another exercise. In this exercise, you've learned how to use the Selection Brush tool and the Quick Selection tool to isolate areas of an image. You've also learned to mask out areas to which you don't want changes to be applied. And, you've learned how to add these new selections to existing, saved selections. This knowledge will be invaluable as you learn to use other selection tools.

Why won't Photoshop Elements do what I tell it to do?

In some situations, the changes you try to apply to an image may not seem to work. Or you may hear a beep sound, indicating that you're trying to do something that's not allowed. The following list offers explanations and solutions for common issues that might be blocking your progress.

Commit is required

Several tools, including the Type tool (T) require you to click the Commit button (✔) in the tool options bar before you can move on to another task. The same is true when you crop with the Crop tool or resize a layer or selection with the Move tool.

Cancel is required

The Undo command isn't available while you have uncommitted changes made with the Type tool, Move tool, or Crop tool, for example. If you want to undo such changes, click Cancel (◒) in the tool options bar instead of using the Undo command or shortcut.

Edits are restricted by an active selection

When you create a selection (using a marquee tool, the Quick Selection tool, or the Selection Brush tool, for example), you limit the active area of the image. Any edits you make will apply only within the selected area. If you try to make changes to an area outside the selection, nothing happens. If you want to deactivate a selection, choose Select > Deselect, and then you can work on any area of the image.

Edits are restricted by an active selection.

Move tool is required

If you drag a selection, the selection marquee moves, not the image within the selection marquee. If you want to move a selected part of the image or an entire layer, use the Move tool (▸₊).

Background layer is selected

Many changes cannot be applied to the Background layer. For example, you can't erase, delete, change the opacity, or drag the Background layer to a higher level in the layer stack. If you need to apply changes to the Background layer, double-click it and rename it (or accept the default name, Layer 0).

Why won't Photoshop Elements do what I tell it to do? *(cont'd)*

Active layer is hidden

In most cases, the edits you make apply to only the currently selected layer—the one highlighted in the Layers palette. If an eye icon (👁) does not appear beside that layer in the Layers palette, then the layer is hidden and you cannot edit it. Or, if the image on the selected layer is not visible because it is blocked by an opaque upper layer, you will actually be changing that layer, but you won't see the changes in the image window.

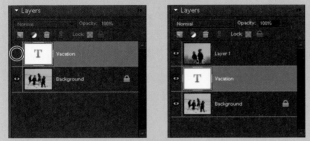

The active layer is hidden, or layer view is blocked by opaque upper layer.

Active layer is locked

If you lock a layer by selecting the layer and then selecting the Lock (🔒) in the Layers palette, the lock prevents the layer from changing. To unlock a layer, select the layer, and then select the Lock at the top of the Layers palette to remove the Lock.

Active layer is locked.

Wrong layer is selected (for editing text)

If you want to make changes to a text layer, be sure that layer is selected in the Layers palette before you start. If a non-text layer is selected when you click the Type tool in the image window, Photoshop Elements creates a new text layer instead of placing the cursor in the existing text layer.

Replacing the color of a pictured object

Photoshop Elements offers two methods of swapping color, the Color Replacement tool and the Replace Color dialog box. With the Color Replacement tool (grouped in the toolbox with the Brush tool, the Impressionist Brush tool, and the Pencil tool) you can replace specific colors in your image by painting over a targeted color—for example, a yellow flower in an image—with a different color, like red. You can also use the Color Replacement tool to correct colors.

Using the Replace Color dialog box is faster and more automatic than using the Color Replacement tool, but it doesn't work well for all types of images. This method is easiest when the color of the object you want to change is not found in other areas of the image. The photograph of a yellow car used for this exercise has very little yellow elsewhere in the image, making it a good example for this approach.

Replacing a color throughout the image

In this project, you'll change the color of a yellow car. You'll do your work on a duplicate of the Background layer, which later makes it easy to compare the finished project with the original picture.

What's nice about the Replace Color feature is that you don't have to be too meticulous when you apply it, while still producing spectacular results. You're going to do this exercise twice. First, you'll work on the entire image area. This will show you how much the color changes will affect the areas outside the car, such as the trees in the background. You will then use an area selection for the second part of this exercise.

1   Using the Organizer, find the file 06_05.psd, the picture of the yellow car, and then open it in the Editor in Full Edit mode.

2   In the Editor, choose Layer > Duplicate Layer and accept the default name. Alternatively, drag the Background layer up to the New Layer icon (⬚) in the Layers palette. By duplicating the layer, you have an original to return to if you need it.

3   With the Background copy layer still selected in the Layers palette, choose
Enhance > Adjust Color > Replace Color.

4   In the Replace Color dialog box, select Image under Selection so that you see the
color thumbnail of the car picture. Make sure that the Eyedropper tool (🖊) within the
dialog box is selected. Then, click the yellow paint area of the car.

5   Click the Selection option under the thumbnail image to see the selection, or color-
application area, indicated as white on a black background.

6   Drag the Hue slider, and optionally the Saturation and Lightness slider to change
the color of the selected area. For example, try Hue = −88 to change the yellow to pink.

7 To adjust the color-application area, start by selecting the Add to Sample eyedropper (🖊), and then click in the edit window in areas where the paint on the car still appears yellow.

8 Drag the Fuzziness slider left or right until you find an acceptable compromise between the color replacement on the car and the effect on other image areas.

9   When you are satisfied with the results, click OK to close the Replace Color dialog box.

Depending on what color and color characteristics you used to replace the yellow, you probably can see a shift in the color of the trees in the background. If this is a compromise you can live with, that's great. If not, you may need to try another technique. This is what you'll do in the next procedure.

Replacing a color in a limited area of the image

You're going to try the previous procedure again, but this time you'll limit the color change to a selected image area.

1   Choose Edit > Undo Replace Color, or select the step before Replace Color in the Undo History palette (Window > Undo History).

2   In the toolbox, select the Lasso tool (⦾) and click and drag with the pointer to draw a rough selection around the car. It's OK if some of the road and the wall in the background are included in the selection.

Note: The Lasso tool is grouped with the Magnetic Lasso tool and the Polygonal Lasso tool in the toolbox. To switch from one lasso tool to another, click the tool in the toolbox and keep the pointer pressed until a menu appears, and then choose the other tool from the menu.

3 In the tool options bar, select Subtract from selection (⬚), and then drag a shape around the yellow sticker on the windshield to remove it from the selection.

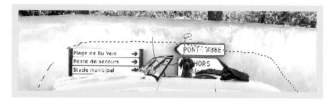

Note: Zooming in for this part of the process may be helpful. Use the slider in the Navigator palette (Window > Navigator) to zoom in so that you don't have to switch tools, or use the zoom-in keyboard shortcut, Ctrl+ = (equal sign).

4 Choose Enhance > Adjust Color > Replace Color.

5 Using the same techniques and settings you used in the previous procedure, make adjustments in the Replace Color dialog box to change the color of the car. (See "Replacing a color throughout the image," steps 4-8.)

6 When you are satisfied with the results, click OK to close the dialog box.

7   Choose Select > Deselect, or press Ctrl+D.

8   Choose File > Save As and save the file in the My CIB Work folder. For File Name, type **06_05_Work**. Make sure that the Format option is Photoshop (PSD). If Save in Version Set with Original is selected, deselect it before you click Save.

9   Choose File > Close, to close the file and return to the Organizer.

Take a bow—you've finished the five exercises in this lesson. In the last exercise, you learned how to make a selection with the Lasso tool and how to edit that selection to make it fit more closely. You then replaced one color with another using the Replace Color dialog box. In the process, you've also used the Undo History palette to step backwards to a specific point in your work.

About printing color pictures

Sometimes, pictures that look great on your computer don't turn out so well when you print them. How can you make them look as good in print as they do on screen?

Color problems can arise from a variety of sources. One may be the camera or the conditions under which a photograph was taken. If a photograph is flawed, you can usually make it better by editing it with Photoshop Elements, as you did with the images in this lesson.

There are other possible contributors to color problems. One may be your monitor, which may shift colors. You can correct that by calibrating your monitor.

Another possibility is that your color printer interprets color information differently than your computer. You can correct that by activating the appropriate type of color management.

Working with color management

Moving an image from your camera to your monitor and from there to a printer makes the image colors shift. This shift occurs because every device has a different color gamut, or range of colors that it can generate. To achieve consistent color between digital cameras, scanners, computer monitors, and printers, you need to use color management.

Color management software acts as a color interpreter, translating the image colors so that each device can reproduce them in the same way. This software knows how each device and program understands color, and adjusts colors so that those you see on your monitor are similar to the colors in your printed image. It should be noted, however, that not all colors may match exactly.

Color management is achieved through the use of profiles, or mathematical descriptions of each device's color space. If these profiles are compliant with the standards of the ICC (International Color Consortium), they help you maintain consistent color.

Photoshop Elements' color management controls are located under the Edit menu.

Setting up color management

1   In the Editor, choose Edit > Color Settings.

2   Select one of these color management options:

•   **No Color Management** uses your monitor profile as the working space. It removes any embedded profiles when opening images, and does not apply a profile when saving.

•   **Always Optimize Colors for Computer Screens** uses sRGB as the working space, preserves embedded profiles, and assigns sRGB when opening untagged files.

•   **Always Optimize for Printing** uses Adobe RGB as the working space, preserves embedded profiles, and assigns Adobe RGB when opening untagged files.

•   **Allow Me to Choose** lets you choose to assign sRGB (the default) or Adobe RGB when opening untagged files.

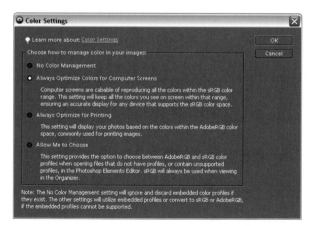

3   Click OK to close the Color Settings dialog box.

Note: When you save a file, select ICC Profile in the Save As dialog box.

Further information on color management, including monitor calibration, can be found in a series of topics in Help. To access this information, choose Help > Photoshop Elements Help and search for these subjects.

Review

▶ ## Review questions

1 What is the key difference between adjusting images in Full Edit mode, Quick Fix mode, or Guided Edit mode?

2 Can you apply automatic fixes when you are in Full Edit mode?

3 What tools can you use to fix the red-eye phenomenon created by some flash cameras?

4 What makes selections so important for adjusting color?

5 Name at least two selection tools and describe how they work.

Review answers

1 Full Edit provides a more flexible and powerful image correction environment. Full Edit has lighting and color correction commands, along with tools you'll need to fix image defects, make selections, add text, and paint on your images. Quick Fix provides access to the more basic photo fixing controls in Photoshop Elements, and enables you to make quick adjustments to your images using those controls. If you are new to digital photography, Guided Edit is the place to start for fixing common image problems. Edit capabilities are restricted or simplified. Guided Edit also offers guided activities taking you step-by-step through several image editing tasks to get professional results.

2 Yes. The Enhance menu contains commands that are equivalent to the buttons in the Quick Fix palettes: Auto Smart Fix, Auto Levels, Auto Contrast, Auto Color Correction, and Auto Red Eye Fix. The Enhance menu also provides an Adjust Smart Fix command, which opens a dialog box in which you can change the amount of automatic fixing.

3 You can choose to automatically fix red eye when importing photos into the catalog. Simply select Automatically Fix Red Eye where available in the various import dialog boxes. To fix red eye after the photos have been imported, choose Edit > Auto Red Eye Fix in the Organizer. In either the Full Edit or Quick Fix mode of the Editor, choose Enhance > Auto Red Eye Fix. Finally, the Red Eye

Removal tool located in the toolbox enables you to adjust some parameters while fixing red eye.

4   You use a selection to define an area as the only part of a layer that can be altered. The areas outside the selection are protected from change for as long as the selection is active. This aids greatly in image correction, as it enables you make different adjustments to selected portions of your image.

5   The first tool you used in this lesson to make selections is the Selection Brush tool, which works like a paintbrush. The Quick Selection tool is similar to the Selection Brush tool, but in most cases a faster, more flexible option for creating a selection. The Lasso tool creates free-form selections; you drag the Lasso tool around the area that you want to select. There are even more tools than discussed in this lesson to create selections. The Magic Wand tool selects all the areas with the same color as the color on which you click. The Rectangular Marquee tool and the Elliptical Marquee tool make selections in fixed geometric shapes when you drag them across the image. The Magnetic Lasso tool helps to draw selections along the (possibly quite irregular) edge of an object while the Polygonal Lasso tool restricts drawing to straight lines, making it the tool of choice to select regular shaped objects.

7 | Fixing Exposure Problems

You can use Photoshop Elements to fix many images that are too dark or too light and rescue some pictures that you perceive as being terribly awful, hopelessly bad, useless, and not very good either. The Automatic and Quick Fix modes with their limited options might be all you ever need to accomplish those goals. However, depending of the image, there are more sophisticated methods for even better results.

This lesson leads you through several approaches to correcting exposure problems in photographs. This aspect of image correction is often easier to deal with than you might imagine.

In this lesson, you will learn how to do the following:

- Brighten underexposed photographs.
- Correct different areas of an image individually.
- Save selection shapes to reuse in later sessions.
- Create and apply adjustment layers.
- Bring out details and colors in overexposed and faded photographs.

This lesson assumes that you are already familiar with the overall features of the Photoshop Elements work area, and recognize the two ways in which you can use Photoshop Elements: the Editor and the Organizer. If you need to learn more about these items, see Lesson 1, "A Quick Tour of Photoshop Elements" and Photoshop Elements Help. This lesson also builds on the skills and concepts covered in the earlier lessons.

Before you begin, make sure that you have correctly copied the Lessons folder from the CD in the back of this book onto your computer's hard disk. See "Copying the Classroom in a Book files" on page 3.

Getting started

While working on the projects in this lesson, you'll use the CIB Catalog you created in the "Getting Started" section at the beginning of this book. To use the CIB Catalog, follow these steps:

1   Start Photoshop Elements. In the Welcome Screen, click Organize in the row of shortcut buttons across the lower part of the Welcome Screen. If the CIB Catalog is open, skip to the next section, "Correcting images automatically as batch process." If the CIB Catalog is not open, complete the following steps.

2   Choose File > Catalog.

3   In the Catalog Manager dialog box, select the CIB Catalog under Catalogs, and then click Open.

If you do not see the CIB Catalog file, review the procedures found in "Getting Started." See "Copying the Lessons files from the CD" on page 3, and "Creating a catalog" on page 4.

Correcting images automatically as batch process

You'll start this lesson in the same way that you began your work in Lesson 6. You will process all the image files for this lesson in one session to apply automatic fixes available in Photoshop Elements. You'll save these files so that you can compare them to the files that you fix using manual techniques.

1   Start Photoshop Elements in Full Edit mode by clicking Edit in the Welcome Screen. Or, if the Organizer is already open, click the Editor button () located near the top right corner of the Organizer window, and then choose Full Edit from the menu.

2   If the Editor is already open from an earlier exercise, switch to Full Edit mode if necessary, by clicking the Full tab in the Edit pane of the Task panel.

3 Choose File > Process Multiple Files.

4 In the Process Multiple Files dialog box, do the following:

• Choose Folder from the Process Files From menu.

• Under Source, click Browse. Find and select the Lesson07 folder in the Lessons folder. Click OK to close the Browse for Folder dialog box.

• Under Destination, click Browse. Find and select the My CIB Work folder that you created at the start of the book. Click OK to close the Browse for Folder dialog box.

5 Under File Naming, select Rename Files. Select Document Name in the first field, and type _**Autofix** in the second field. This adds the appendix "_Autofix" to the existing document name as the files are saved in the My CIB Work folder.

6 Under Quick Fix on the right side of the dialog box, select all four options: Auto Levels, Auto Contrast, Auto Color, and Sharpen.

7 Review all selections in the dialog box, comparing them to the following illustration. Make sure that the Resize Images and the Convert Files to options are not selected. Then, click OK.

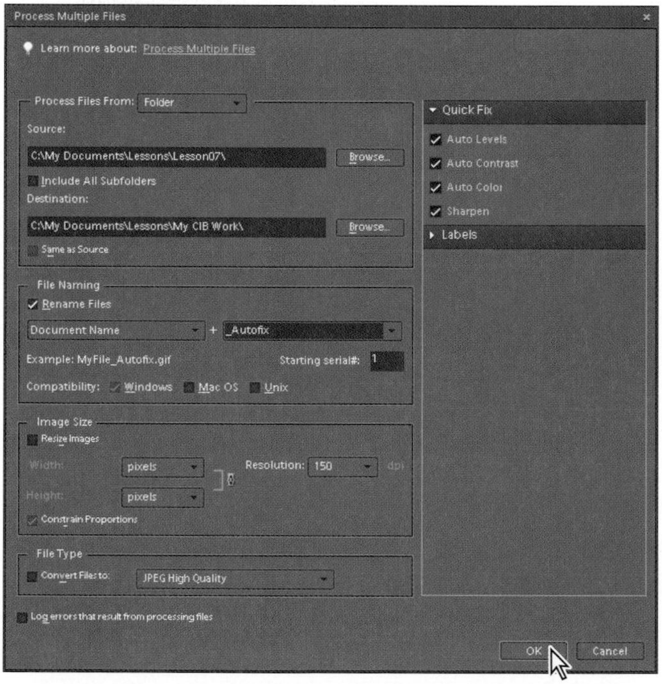

Photoshop Elements takes a few seconds to process the files. Image windows will open and close automatically as the adjustments are applied. There's nothing else you need to do. If any alerts or warnings are displayed, click OK.

At the end of this lesson, you can compare the results of this simple, automatic fixing of the images with the results from applying the manual techniques in the exercises. In many cases, the automatic method of fixing files may be sufficient to meet your needs.

Brightening an underexposed image

Slightly underexposed photographs look dingy and dull. While the auto-fix lighting feature does a terrific job of brightening up many of these photos, here you'll use different methods to adjust the exposure.

Applying the Quick Fix

1 If the Organizer is not currently active, switch to it now.

2 In the Keyword Tags palette, click the Find box next to the Lesson 7 keyword tag.

3 Click to select the file 07_01.jpg, a badly underexposed image of a woman in the countryside.

Note: To show the file names in the Photo Browser, choose View > Show File Names.

4 Click the Editor button () located near the top right corner of the Organizer window, and then choose Quick Fix from the menu.

Photoshop Elements will load the Editor workspace and open the image in Quick Fix mode.

5 Under General Fixes, click the Auto button next to Smart Fix. *(See illustration on the next page.)* Notice how the dark areas in the picture become brighter.

6   Under Lighting, make the following adjustments:

• Drag the Lighten Shadows to the right by one grey measuring bar.

• Drag the Darken Highlights slider just slightly to the right.

Of course, you can experiment with those sliders to see the range of changes you might apply to an image.

7   Click the Commit button (✔) in the Lighting palette title bar to commit the changes.

8   Choose File > Save As. In the Save As dialog box, navigate to and open the My CIB Work folder, rename the file **07_01_Quick** and select the JPEG format. If Save in Version Set with Original is selected, deselect it. Click Save. In the JPEG Options dialog box, select High from the Quality menu, and then click OK

9   Choose File > Close and return to the Organizer.

Without much effort the image has improved significantly. You'll now use other methods to adjust the lighting in the image and compare the results later on.

Employing Guided Edit

1   With the image 07_01.jpg still selected in the Photo Browser of the Organizer, click the Editor button, and then choose Guided Edit from the menu that appears. The Editor workspace will load and open the same underexposed, original photo you used in the previous exercise, but this time in Guided Edit mode.

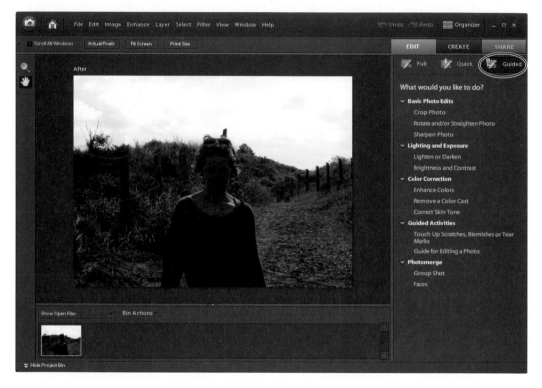

2   If necessary, click the triangle next to Lighting and Exposure under What would you like to do. Then, click to select Lighten or Darken. This opens the Lighten or Darken a Photo panel with its different options.

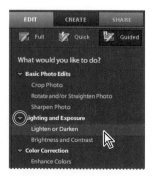

3   Click the Auto button near the top right corner of the Lighten or Darken a Photo panel. Notice that in this case the result is not quite as good as you would expect. Click the Undo button above the Edit pane, or choose Edit > Undo Auto Levels to revert the image to its original state.

4   Use the sliders to manually adjust the lighting in the image. Drag the Lighten Shadows slider to a value of 30, the Darken Highlights slider to a value of 55, and the Midtone Contrasts to a value of 25. Then, click Done.

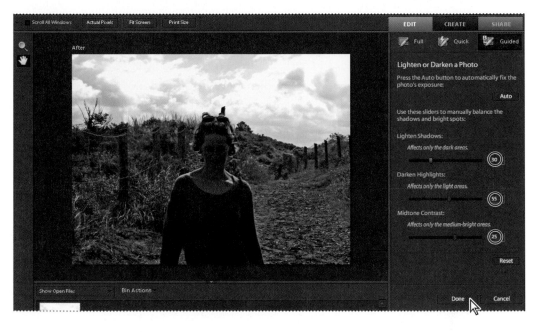

💡 *If you want to return to the original settings and start from scratch, click the Reset button.*

5   Choose File > Save As. In the Save As dialog box, navigate to and open the My CIB Work folder, rename the file **07_01_Guided** and select the JPEG format. If Save in Version Set with Original is selected, deselect it. Click Save. In the JPEG Options dialog box, select High from the Quality menu, and then click OK.

6   Choose File > Close and return to the Organizer.

Again, the image now looks considerably better than its original. However, it would be ideal if the woman and the foreground were treated differently than the background with the landscape and sky.

Fixing an image in Full Edit mode

If your photo is suffering from excessive backlighting, as is the case with our example, more elaborate methods might be necessary to achieve better results. Increasing the number of layers and applying blending modes, as well as isolating parts of the image and treating them independently, are possible in the Full Edit mode.

Adding Blending modes

To use blending modes, you need to have two or more layers. The layer mode applied to a layer can be used to affect the appearance of the image in the layer below it. As an example, if your photo is too dark, adding a duplicated layer on top and selecting Screen as layer mode might correct the problem. On the other hand, if your photo is too light, duplicating the photo layer and choosing Multiply as layer mode might be the solution.

1   With the image 07_01.jpg still selected in the Photo Browser of the Organizer, click the Editor button, and then choose Full Edit from the menu that appears. The Editor workspace will load and open the image in Full Edit mode.

2   Do only one of the following to duplicate the Background layer of the image:

•   With the Background layer selected in the Layers palette, choose Layer > Duplicate Layer, and then click OK in the Duplicate Layer dialog box, accepting the default name.

•   Right-click the Background layer in the Layers palette and choose Duplicate Layer from the context menu. Click OK in the Duplicate Layer dialog box, accepting the default name.

•   Drag and drop the Background layer on the New Layer button (▣) in the Layers palette.

The new Background copy layer is highlighted in the Layers palette, indicating that it is the selected (active) layer.

3   With the Background copy layer selected in the Layers palette, choose Screen from the layer blending mode menu. Notice how the image becomes brighter.

Note: If the layer blending mode menu is disabled, make sure that the Background copy layer, not the original Background layer, is selected in the Layers palette.

4   Choose File > Save As.

5   In the Save As dialog box, name the file **07_01_Screen** and save it in the My CIB Work folder, with Photoshop (PSD) as Format and the Layers option selected. If Save in Version Set with Original is selected, deselect it before you click Save. If the Photoshop Elements Format Options dialog box appears, keep Maximize Compatibility selected and click OK.

6   Toggle the visibility of the Background copy layer in the Layers palette to compare the original with the final image. When you've finished comparing, close the file without saving and return to the Organizer.

Here you've seen how blending modes can brighten up a dull image. However, one needs to be careful with applying blending modes over the entire image, as often it can ruin the exposure of parts of the photos that were OK to begin with. In this example, almost all details of the sky have been lost. Using layers, there are ways to obtain even better results. In the following exercises, you'll use other blending modes to correct different kinds of image problems.

Adjusting color curves

Using the Adjust Color Curves command is a great way for quickly fixing some exposure problems. You can improve color tones in a photo by adjusting highlights, midtones, and shadows in each color channel. For example, this command can fix photos with darkened images due to strong backlighting, or those that appear washed out due to harsh lighting.

In the Adjust Color Curves dialog box, you compare and choose different tonal presets represented by image thumbnails. To fine-tune the adjustment, display Advanced Options section and adjust highlights, midtone brightness and contrast, and shadows.

To preserve the original photo while experimenting, make the color curve adjustments on a duplicate layer.

—From Photoshop Elements Help

To open the Adjust Color Curves dialog box, choose Enhance > Adjust Color > Adjust Color Curves. To adjust only a specific area of the image, select it with one of the selection tools before opening the dialog box.

For of our sample image, first selecting the Lighten Shadows style preset, and then manually adjusting the highlights and shadows seems to work best.

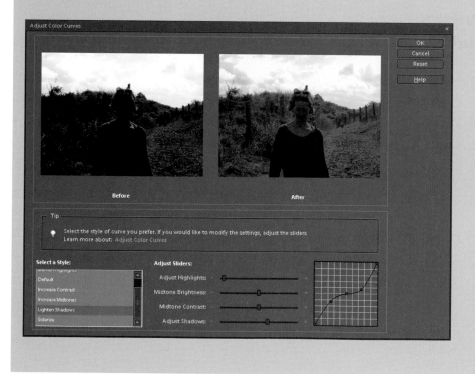

Using adjustment layers

Sometimes you need to go back and tweak your settings after the first adjustment, or even during a much later work session. Compared to image layers, adjustment layers (and fill layers) are special types of layers.

An adjustment layer is like a colored veil on top of your underlying layers. Any changes applied on an adjustment layer can be easily revised, because the pixels of the image are not permanently modified. This is an appreciable advantage, especially when you wish to apply the same changes to several images. You can either copy the adjustment layer and place it on top of the other photo, or use the Process Multiple files command (for more information please refer to Photoshop Elements Help).

Creating adjustment layers for lighting

In this next activity, we'll continue to use the same underexposed photograph to explore improving the image through the addition of an adjustment layer.

1   With the image 07_01.jpg still selected in the Photo Browser of the Organizer, click the Editor button, and then choose Full Edit from the menu that appears.

2   With the Background layer selected in the Layers palette, click the Create Adjustment Layer button (🌗.) and choose Brightness/Contrast from the menu that appears.

3   If necessary, drag the Brightness/Contrast dialog box aside so that you can also see most of the image window. Make sure the Preview box is checked. In the Brightness/Contrast dialog box, drag the sliders so that Brightness is +50 and Contrast is +10, and then click OK. *(See illustration on the next page.)*

4   Click the Create Adjustment Layer button again, but this time choose Levels (instead of Brightness/Contrast) from the menu. Levels is an effective tonal and color adjustment tool. Notice the additional layer created in the Layers palette.

5   In the Levels dialog box, drag the black, white, and gray arrows (assigned for the shadow values, middle tones and highlight values respectively) that are under the graph to the left or right until the balance of dark and light areas looks right to you. We selected values of 20, 2.0, and 190.

6   Click OK to close the Levels dialog box. The overall improvements to the image are similar to those made in Quick Fix mode.

7   Choose File > Save As. In the Save As dialog box, name the file **07_01_Adjustment** and save it in the My CIB Work folder, with Photoshop (PSD) as Format and the Layers option selected. If Save in Version Set with Original is selected, deselect it before you click Save. If the Photoshop Elements Format Options dialog box appears, keep Maximize Compatibility selected and click OK.

8   Close the file and return to the Organizer.

The beauty of adjustment layers is that you can revert to earlier settings, even in later work sessions, as long as you save the file in the Photoshop (PSD) format, preserving the layers (the default). For example, if you reopen your file and double-click the Brightness/Contrast icon in the layer thumbnail, your original settings (+50 and +10) still appear in the Brightness/Contrast dialog box, and can be further refined.

If necessary, you can even revert to the original, uncorrected image by either hiding or deleting the adjustment layers.

Correcting parts of an image

Although the adjustment layers do a fine job of bringing out the colors and details from the dark original image, the background is now too washed out. When you made corrections to the image earlier in this lesson, they applied to the entire picture. Now you will restrict the adjustments to sections of the image.

Creating a selection

In this task, you'll divide the picture into two parts: the woman in the foreground, and the background with the landscape and sky. You'll start out by selecting the silhouette of the woman in order to place it on a separate layer. This layer can then be adjusted separately from the background layer.

There are different ways of making a selection. You already used some of them in Lesson 6. The choice of tools depends largely on the picture. For our purposes here, we'll start by using the Quick Selection tool, which makes a selection based on texture similarity. By merrily scribbling inside an object the Quick Selection tool automatically determines the selection borders for you, as you will see in the following exercise.

1   With the image 07_01.jpg still selected in the Photo Browser of the Organizer, click the Editor button, and then choose Full Edit from the menu that appears.

2   In the toolbox, select the Quick Selection tool (🖊), which is grouped with the Selection Brush tool.

3   Make sure New selection is selected in the tool options bar.

4   Place the cursor at the lower center of the woman and slowly drag a line to the top of her head. Notice as you proceed how the active selection automatically expands to create a border around the silhouette of the woman. Not bad at all for a quick selection!

Next you need to refine the border a little to capture the silhouette as closely as possible. You want to deselect the triangle under the arm on the left and tighten the selection along the neck and the other arm. For this you use the Add to Selection tool (🖊) and the Subtract from selection tool (🖊), located next to the New selection button.

5 Select Subtract from selection (✎) in the options bar in order to prepare for taking away parts from the selection.

6 Draw a line over selected areas of the image background and you will see the flashing selection outline receding toward the silhouette. Reduce the Brush size as necessary—by pressing the '[' key on your keyboard—to make finer adjustments. Use the Zoom tool to zoom into the image.

7 Repeat these steps using the Add to Selection tool (✎) and the Subtract from selection tool (✎) to tighten up the selection. You should end up with a tight flashing selection outline around the silhouette of the woman in the foreground.

8 To soften the hard edges of the selection, you will smooth and feather the outline. Click Refine Edge in the tool options bar.

9 In the Refine Edge dialog box, enter **8** for Smooth and **4** pixels for the Feather, and then click OK. You can select the Zoom tool as well as the Hand tool from within the dialog box to get a better view of the details of your selection.

10 Choose Select > Save Selection. In the Save Selection dialog box, choose New from the Selection menu and type **Woman** to name the selection. Then, click OK. Saving a selection is always a good idea, because it facilitates its re-use at a later time.

Correcting overexposed areas

One of the aims in this exercise is to intensify the color and contrast in the overexposed area of the trees and sky. The woman in the foreground is already a bit darker, so you won't want to intensify this area. Your approach here is to divide and conquer—to apply different solutions to different areas of the image. Creating a copy of just the area you selected is the first step in this process. To make the job easier, let's make sure that the thumbnails are of a satisfactory size.

1   Choose Palette Options from the Layers palette menu.

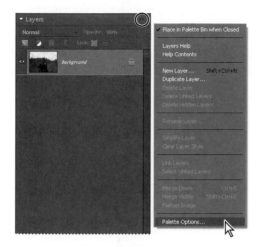

2   In the Layers Palette Options dialog box, select the medium sized thumbnail option, if it is not already selected, and then click OK.

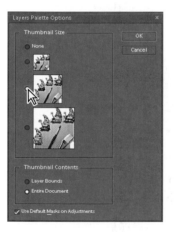

Selecting another size is OK, but do not select None. The layer thumbnail can help you visualize the layers you will work with in this project.

3   With the Zoom tool selected in the toolbox, click Fit Screen in the tool options bar so that you can see the entire image.

4   Do one of the following:

• If the selection you made in the previous topic is still active, choose Select > Inverse, and then go to Step 5.

• If the selection is not active, choose Select > Load Selection. Under Source, select Woman from the Selection menu and select the Invert option. Make sure New Selection is selected under Operation, and then click OK.

5   Choose Edit > Copy to copy the selected area.

6   Choose Edit > Paste to paste the copied area onto a new layer, Layer 1.

In the image window, the only difference you'll see is that the selection marquee has disappeared. But in the Layers palette you can see that there's a new layer.

7   In the Layers palette, select the Background layer. Choose Select > Load Selection. Under Source, select Woman from the Selection menu, but this time do not select the Invert option. Then, click OK.

8   Choose Edit > Copy.

9   With the Background layer selected in the Layers palette, choose Edit > Paste. Now you've got three layers on top of each other: Layer 1 with the landscape and sky, Layer 2 featuring the silhouette of the woman, and the Background layer with the entire photo.

10   Especially when working with multiple layers, life is made easier when you name layers descriptively. To do this, double-click the name of the layer. The pointer changes to the Type tool and a text box to type into appears. Type **Landscape** for Layer 1 and **Woman** for Layer 2.

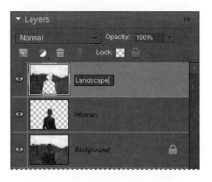

Now you can start to work on those layers individually to improve the overall photo.

Correcting underexposed areas

You can lighten the shadows of just the underexposed areas using the same techniques you used earlier on the entire image.

1   In the Layers palette, click the Woman layer to select it, and then choose Screen as the blending mode. Notice that the entire silhouette is now brighter and the details are more discernable, while the Landscape layer with the undergrowth stays exactly as before.

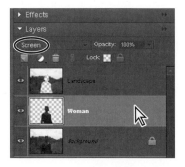

2   (Optional) Choose Enhance > Auto Sharpen.

Adding more intensity

Now that the foreground looks better, the background needs to be adjusted to appear less washed out.

1 In the Layers palette, select the Landscape layer.

2 Choose Darker Color as blending mode and notice how the background shows more detail with some clouds appearing in the sky.

3 (Optional) To further improve the appearance of the sky, copy just the sky area from the Background image into a new layer on top of the other layers. Then, change the blending mode to Multiply.

With these few adjustment to the different layers, the entire photograph now looks much more lively. There are still a lot of possibilities to continue playing around with the brightness and intensities in different areas, as well as the opacities of the layers—you will learn those techniques later in this lesson. However, this exercise has been a good start towards understanding the basic principles of separating an image into selections on different layers, and working with those layers individually.

4 When you are satisfied with the results, choose File > Save As.

5 In the Save As dialog box, name the file **07_01_Layers** and save it in the My CIB Work folder, with Photoshop (PSD) as Format and the Layers option selected. If Save in Version Set with Original is selected, deselect it before you click Save. If the Photoshop

Elements Format Options dialog box appears, keep Maximize Compatibility selected and click OK.

6   Close the file and return to the Organizer.

In Lesson 6 you learned how you can arrange the windows to best compare your results from your different methods of adjusting the image. Using this technique you might want to compare the results from working on this image before going to the next project.

Improving faded or overexposed images

In this exercise, you'll work with the scan of an old photograph that has faded badly and is in danger of being lost forever. Although it's not necessarily an award-winning shot, it could represent a treasured aspect of personal history, like our example of a beloved grandmother and her twin sister when they were babies, which you might want to preserve for future generations.

The automatic fixes you applied to a copy of this image at the beginning of this lesson (See "Correcting images automatically as batch process") improve the photograph quite a bit. In this project, you'll try to do even better using other techniques.

Creating a set of duplicate files

You're going to compare a variety of techniques during the course of this project. You'll start by creating individual files for each technique and giving them unique names. These names will help you identify the technique used to adjust each file.

1   If the Organizer is not currently active, switch to it now.

2   In the Keyword Tags palette, click the Find box next to the Lesson 7 keyword tag.

3   Click to select the file 07_02.jpg, a faded picture of the baby twins.

4   With the image 07_02.jpg selected in the Photo Browser of the Organizer, click the Editor button (📝) located near the top right corner of the Organizer window, and then choose Full Edit from the menu that appears.

The Editor workspace will load and open the image in Full Edit mode.

5   In the Editor, choose File > Duplicate. In the Duplicate Image dialog box, type **07_02_Shad_High**, and then click OK.

6   Repeat Step 5 two more times, naming the duplicate files **07_02_Bright_Con** and
07_02_Levels.

7   In the Project Bin, double-click the 07_02.jpg thumbnail to make that image active.
You can see the file names in a tool tip window when you hover the pointer over the
thumbnail images in the Project Bin.

8   Choose File > Save As. When a dialog box appears, type **07_02_Blend_Mode** as
the new file name and select Photoshop (PSD) in the Format menu. Select the My CIB
Work folder as the Save In location. If Save in Version Set with Original is selected,
deselect it before you click Save. Click OK in any dialog boxes or messages that appear,
to accept the default settings. Leave all four images open for the rest of the project.

9   Choose Window > Images > Tile.

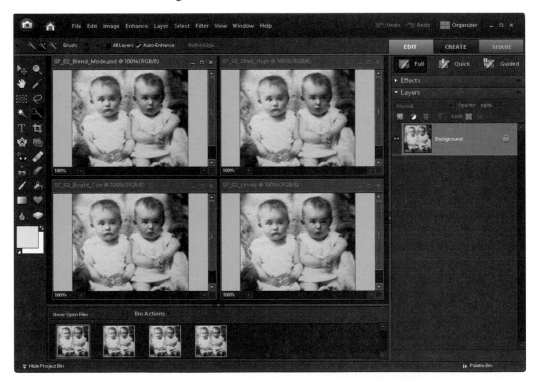

Using blending modes to fix a faded image

This technique is similar to the one you used earlier to correct an underexposed image. In this case, you'll use other blending modes to fix the exposure.

Blending modes make layers interact with the layers under them in various ways. Multiply intensifies the dark pixels in an image. Overlay tends to brighten an image. For this project, using Overlay adds clarity and brilliance without canceling out the effect of the Multiply blending mode on the underlying layers.

The stacking order of the layers makes a difference, so if you dragged one of the Multiply blending mode layers to the top of the layer stack, you'd see slightly different results.

1 Make sure that the 07_02_Blend_Mode.psd file is the active window. If necessary, double-click its thumbnail in the Project Bin to make it active.

2 Duplicate the Background layer by choosing Layer > Duplicate Layer. Click OK in the Duplicate Layer dialog box, accepting the default name, Background copy.
Leave the Background copy layer selected in the Layers palette for the next step.

3 In the Layers palette, do the following:

• Choose Multiply from the layer blending mode menu.

• Drag and drop the Background copy layer onto the New Layer icon (▣) to create a copy of the Background copy layer, named Background copy 2.

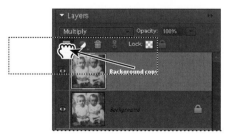

4 In the Layers palette, select the following options for the Background copy 2 layer:

• Change the layer blending mode from Multiply to Overlay.

• Set the Opacity to 50%, either by entering the value in the text field or by dragging the Opacity slider.

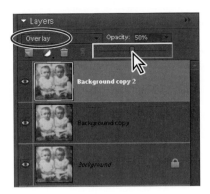

The Overlay blending mode brightens the image considerably, but the image contrast is still unimpressive.

5 (Optional) Fine-tune the results by adjusting the Opacity settings for the two background copy layers until you achieve a pleasing balance.

Note: You cannot change the Opacity of the locked Background layer.

6 Choose File > Save to save the file in the My CIB Work folder. Leave the file open.

7 If a message appears about maximizing compatibility, click OK to close it. Or, follow the instructions in the message to prevent it from appearing again.

Adjusting shadows and highlights manually

Although both auto-fixing and blending modes do a good job of correcting fading images, some of your own photos may be more challenging. You'll try three new techniques in the next three procedures.

The first technique involves making adjustments for Shadows, Highlights, and Midtone Contrast.

1 In the Project Bin, double-click the 07_02_Shad_High thumbnail image to make it the active window.

2 Choose Enhance > Adjust Lighting > Shadows/Highlights.

3 Select the Preview option in the Shadows/Highlights dialog box, if it is not already selected. If necessary, move the dialog box so that you can also see most of the 07_02_ Shad_High image window.

By default, the Lighten Shadows setting is 25%, so you'll see a difference in the image already.

4 In the Shadows/Highlights dialog box, do all the following:

• Drag the Lighten Shadows slider to 30%, or type **30**.

• Drag the Darken Highlights slider to 15%, or type **15**.

• Drag the Midtone Contrast slider to about +20%, or type **20**.

5 (Optional) Adjust the three settings as needed until you think the image is as good as it can be.

6 When done, click OK to close the Shadows/Highlights dialog box.

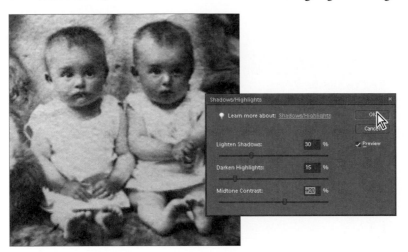

7 Choose File > Save As and save the file as 07_02_Shad_High in the My CIB Work folder, selecting JPEG as format. Click OK to accept the default settings in the JPEG Options dialog box. Leave the file open.

💡 *The adjustments you used in this technique are also available in the Lighting palette in Quick Fix mode.*

Adjusting brightness and contrast manually

The next approach you'll take for fixing exposure problems uses another dialog box, which is also available from the Enhance > Adjust Lighting menu.

1 In the Project Bin, double-click the 07_02_Bright_Con thumbnail to make it active.

2 Choose Enhance > Adjust Lighting > Brightness/Contrast.

If necessary, drag the Brightness/Contrast dialog box aside so that you can also see most of the 07_02_Bright_Con image window.

3 In the Brightness/Contrast dialog box, do all the following:

• Select Preview, if it is not already selected.

• Drag the Brightness slider to -20, or type **-20** in the text field, being careful to include the minus sign when you type. *(See illustration on the next page.)*

- Drag to set the Contrast at +40, or type **+40** in the text field.

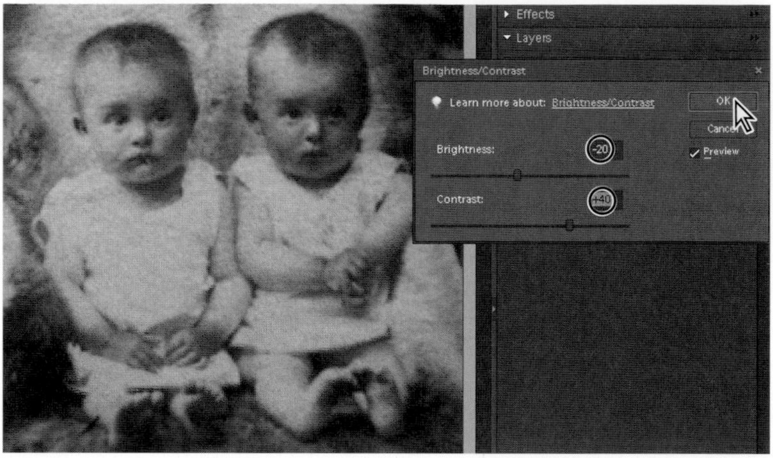

4   (Optional) Adjust the Brightness and Contrast settings until you are happy with the quality of the image.

5   Click OK to close the Brightness/Contrast dialog box.

6   Choose File > Save As and save the file as 07_02_Bright_Con in the My CIB Work folder, selecting JPEG as format. Click OK when the JPEG Options dialog box appears. Leave the file open.

Adjusting levels

Levels are the range of color values—the degree of darkness or lightness, whether the color is red, yellow, purple, or another color. In this procedure, you'll enhance the photograph by shifting the reference points for levels.

1   In the Project Bin, double-click the 07_02_Levels thumbnail image to make it the active window.

2   Choose Enhance > Adjust Lighting > Levels.

3   Select the Preview option in the Levels dialog box, if it is not already selected.

The graph represents the distribution of pixel values in the image. In this image there are no truly white pixels or truly black pixels. By dragging the sliders inward to where the pixels start to appear in the graph, you redefine what levels are calculated as dark and light. This enhances the contrast between the lightest pixels in the image and the darkest ones.

If necessary, drag the dialog box aside so that you can also see most of the image window.

4   In the Levels dialog box, do all of the following:

•   Drag the black triangle that is beneath the left side of the graph to the right and position it under the first steep spike in the graph shape. At that position, the value in the first Input Levels box is approximately 42.

•   Drag the white triangle on the right side of the graph until it reaches the edge of the final spike in the graph shape. The value of the third Input Levels box changes to approximately 225.

•   Drag the gray center triangle under the graph toward the right until the middle Input Level value is approximately 0.90. Click OK to close the Levels dialog box.

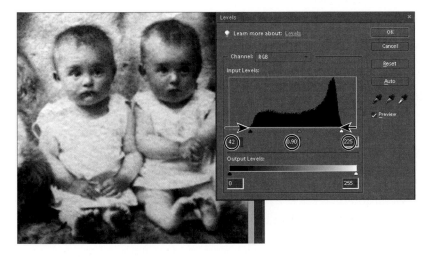

5   Choose File > Save As and save the file as 07_02_Levels in the My CIB Work folder, selecting JPEG as format. Click OK to accept the default settings in the JPEG Options dialog box. Leave the file open.

Comparing results

You can now compare the six versions of the image: the original file, these four files you have just prepared, and the one file that you auto-fixed in a batch process at the beginning of this lesson.

1   In Full Edit, choose File > Open, and then find and open the file 07_02_ Autofix.jpg in the My CIB Work folder. If you can't see the file in the Open dialog box, make sure All Formats is selected in the Files of type menu.

2   Choose File > Open, and then find and open the file 07_02.jpg in the Lesson 7 folder. If you can't see the file in the Open dialog box, make sure All Formats is selected in the Files of type menu.

3   In the Project Bin, make sure that only the six files for this project are open: 07_ 02_Blend_Mode.psd, 07_02_Shad_High.jpg, 07_02_Bright_Con.jpg, 07_02_Levels.jpg, 07_02_Autofix.jpg, and the original 07_02.jpg. Make sure, no other files are open. To see the file names displayed under the thumbnails in the Project Bin, right-click an empty area in the Project Bin, and then select Show Filenames.

4   Choose Window > Images > Tile, if it is not already selected.

5   Now you'll reduce the zoom level for all active windows. Select the Zoom tool (🔍). In the tool options bar, select Zoom Out and Zoom All Windows. Then, click in any image window until you can see a large enough image area to be able to compare the different results. Or, zoom in to focus on a detail. Select the area of interest in one window, and then choose Window > Images > Match Zoom and Windows > Images > Match Location.

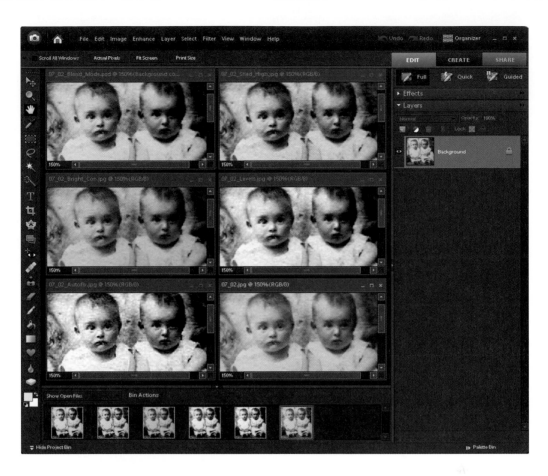

6   Compare the results and pick your favorite. The best method for fixing a file depends on the type of problem being addressed, the affected areas of the image, and how you will use the resulting image.

7   Click Window > Images > Tile again to deselect it. You won't see any difference in the arrangement of image windows, but it will stop the automatic rearrangement when you open or close other images.

8   Choose File > Close All. Save your changes if prompted to do so in My CIB Work folder and return to the Organizer.

Congratulations! You've now finished Lesson 7. In doing so, you've used various automatic and manual approaches to correct overexposed photographs and scans of faded prints. You've tried auto-fixes, blending modes, and the three dialog boxes that are available under the Enhance > Adjust Lighting menu. You know that you can apply these different adjustments either in layers, on selections, separately, or in combinations.

Review

▶ **Review questions**

1   Describe two ways to create an exact copy of an existing layer.

2   Where can you find the controls for adjusting the lighting in a photograph?

3   How do you change the arrangement of image windows in the work area?

4   What is an adjustment layer and what are its unique benefits?

▶ **Review answers**

1   Photoshop Elements must be in Full Edit mode to copy a layer. You can select the layer you want to duplicate in the Layers palette, and then choose Layer > Duplicate Layer. Alternatively, drag the layer to the New Layer button in the Layers palette. In either case, you get two identical layers, stacked one above the other.

2   You can adjust the lighting for a photo in either Full Edit, Guided Edit, or Quick Fix mode. In Full Edit, you must use the Enhance > Adjust Lighting menu to open various dialog boxes that contain the controls. Or, you can choose Enhance > Auto Levels, Enhance > Auto Contrast, or Enhance > Adjust Color > Adjust Color Curves. In the Guided Edit mode, choose Lighting and Exposure. In Quick Fix mode, you can use the Lighting palette in the Palette Bin.

3   You cannot rearrange image windows in Quick Fix and Guided Edit modes, which display only one photograph at a time. In Full Edit, there are several ways you can arrange them. One is to choose Window > Images, and select one of the choices listed there. Another method is to use the maximize or tile windows buttons in the upper right corner of each edit window. A third way is to drag the image window title bar to move an image window, and drag a corner to resize it (provided Maximize mode is not currently active).

4   An adjustment layer does not contain an image. Instead, it modifies some quality of all the layers below it in the Layer palette. For example, a Brightness/Contrast layer can alter the brightness and contrast of any underlying layers. One advantage of using an adjustment layer instead of adjusting an existing layer directly is that adjustment layers are easily reversible. You can click the eye icon for the adjustment layer to remove the effects instantly, and then restore the eye icon to apply the adjustments again. You can change a setting in the adjustment layer to zero to revert to its original condition.

8 | Repairing and Retouching Images

Images aren't always perfect. Maybe you want to clean dust and scratches off a scanned image, retouch spots and small imperfections on a person's skin, or even hide objects you don't want to appear in your photos. Or perhaps you want to restore an antique photograph.

In this lesson, you will do the following:

- Use the Straighten tool.

- Remove red eyes in the Organizer.

- Retouch wrinkles and skin flaws using the Healing Brush tool.

- Eliminate creases with the Clone Stamp tool.

- Use the Selection Brush tool.

- Mask parts of the image.

The work in this lesson should take you about one hour. The lesson includes four independent exercises, so you can do them all at once or in different work sessions. The projects vary only slightly in length and complexity.

Before you begin, make sure that you have correctly copied the Lessons folder from the CD in the back of this book onto your computer's hard disk. See "Copying the Classroom in a Book files" on page 3.

In this lesson, you will use the CIB Catalog you created earlier in the book. If necessary, open this catalog by choosing File > Catalog and selecting the CIB Catalog in the Catalog Manager dialog box.

Getting started

You can start with any of the three exercises in this lesson, because they are independent of each other in both subject matter and skill level. Some preparation is necessary, however, before you begin to open the files for this lesson.

1   Start Photoshop Elements in Full Edit mode by choosing Edit from the Welcome Screen.

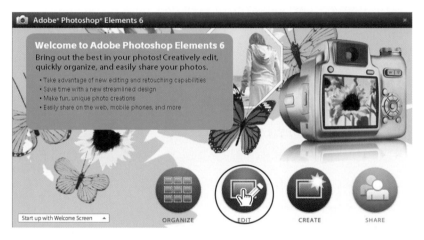

2   Make sure the Editor is in Full Edit mode by clicking the Full tab in Edit panel of the Task pane.

3   Open the Palette Bin and Project Bin, if they are not already open, by choosing Window > Palette Bin and Window > Project Bin. You should see a checkmark next to both menu commands.

4   Review the contents of the Palette Bin, making sure that the Layers palette is visible. If necessary, open this palette from the Window menu (Windows > Layers).

Note: For help with Palette Bin contents, see "Using the Palette Bin" in Lesson 1, "A Quick Tour of Photoshop Elements."

Using the Straighten tool

The Straighten tool enables you to manually specify a new straight edge, which Photoshop Elements then uses as a reference to straighten the image.

1   In the Editor, choose File > Open. In the Lesson08 folder open the file 08_01.jpg, a picture of a group of children. As is often the case when taking photos, the picture is not exactly horizontal.

2   In the toolbox, select the Straighten tool ( ).

3   With the Straighten tool, draw a line along the horizon from the top left to the right border. This represents your new straight edge.

4   When you release the pointer, Photoshop Elements straightens the image relative to the edge you've just drawn.

5   In the toolbox, select the Crop tool (🔲). Drag a cropping selection around the image, which is now displayed at an angle, being careful to not draw over the gray area around the image. Then, click the green Commit button in the lower right corner of the selection rectangle.

6   The cropped image features a straight horizon. Choose File > Save As. In the Save As dialog box, navigate to the My CIB Work folder. If selected, deselect the Save in Version Set with Original option. Choose JPEG from the Format menu, name the file **08_01_Straight.jpg**, and then click Save.

7   Click OK in the JPEG options dialog box to accept the default settings.

8   Choose File > Close to close the file.

💡 *For some images, you may want to consider using the Image > Rotate > Straighten Image or Image > Rotate > Straighten and Crop Image commands, which perform straightening functions automatically.*

Removing red eye in the Organizer

Red eye is caused by the camera's flash reflection off the subject's retina. You'll see it more often when taking pictures in a darkened room, because the subject's iris is then wide open.

While Photoshop Elements can automatically fix red eyes when you bring photos into the Organizer (see the *Automatically Fixing Red Eyes* sidebar in Lesson 2), here you'll use a command in the Organizer for fixing red eyes. Lesson 6 discusses the tools available in the Editor to fix red eye (see *Using automatic Red Eye Fix in the Editor* and *The Red Eye Removal tool* in Lesson 6).

You can remove red eye from one or more selected photos while viewing them in the Photo Browser.

1   In the Editor, click the Organizer button to load the Organizer workspace. If necessary, click the Show All button above the Photo Browser.

2   In the Keyword Tags palette, click the Find box next to the Lesson 8 keyword tag. Click to select the file 08_02.jpg, a picture of a startled child staring straight into the camera. If necessary, choose View > Show File Names.

3   In the Fix panel of the Task pane, click the Auto Red Eye Fix button. Or, if you prefer to use a menu command, choose Edit > Auto Red Eye Fix. Both commands trigger the same process.

A progress window will appear displaying the progress of the red eye fix.

When the fix is complete, an Auto Fix Red Eye dialog box may appear informing you that a version set was created. Version sets are identified by a version set icon in the upper right corner of an image. *(See illustration on the next page.)*

4 Click OK, to close the Auto Red Eye Fix Complete dialog box.

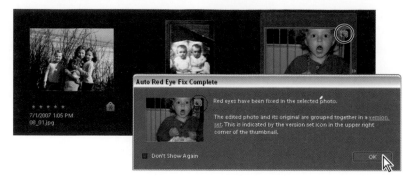

5 If not already selected, click to select the image in the Photo Browser. To view the results in the Editor, click the Editor button located near the top right corner of the Organizer window, and then choose Full Edit from the menu. Or, click the Full Edit button in the Fix panel of the Task pane.

6 In the Editor, select the Zoom tool (🔍) from the toolbox. Select Zoom In from the tool options bar, and then click to zoom in to view the results of the Auto Fix Red Eye feature. The red is now removed from the child's eyes.

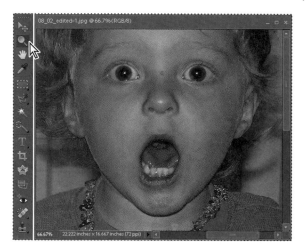

7 Choose File > Close to close the file and return to the Organizer.

Removing wrinkles and spots

Retouching photographs is both a craft and an art. In this exercise, you'll try several ways to smooth out laugh lines and wrinkles, and blend skin tones.

Preparing the file for editing

Before you actually start retouching, you'll set up the layers you need to do the work. By saving the file with a new name, you'll make it easy to identify it later as your work file.

1 Using the Organizer, find and select the file 08_03.jpg, which is tagged with the Lesson 8 keyword tag. Then, click the Editor button located near the upper right corner of the Organizer window and choose Full Edit from the menu that appears.

2 In the Layers palette of the Editor, drag the Background layer to the New Layer button (⬛) in the Layers palette to create another layer, which will be called Background copy.

3 Choose File > Save As, and then save the file in Photoshop (PSD) format as **08_03_Work** in the My CIB Work folder. If Save in Version Set with Original is selected, deselect it before you click Save. Make sure the Layers checkbox is selected.

Now you're ready to start improving the photo by creating smoother skin and natural looking skin tones using the Healing Brush tool.

Fixing Blemishes

There are three main tools in Photoshop Elements to fix flaws in your photos:

The Spot Healing brush tool

The Spot Healing Brush is the easiest way to remove wrinkles and small imperfections in your photos. You can either click once on a blemish, or click and drag to smooth it away. By blending the information of the surrounding area into the problem spot, imperfections are made indistinguishable.

The Healing Brush tool

The Healing Brush fixes large areas of imperfections when you drag over them. You need to define the part of your photo to use as source for the material you want to blend in. With this flexibility you can even remove objects from a uniform background, such as a person in a corn field.

The Clone Stamp tool

Instead of blending in the repair, the Clone Stamp tool paints with a sample of an image. You can use the Clone Stamp tool to duplicate objects, remove image imperfections, or paint over objects in your photo. This tool is useful if you wish to completely hide an object, rather than remove it by blending information over the top of it.

Using the Healing Brush tool

While using the Healing Brush tool (🖉), make sure the Background copy layer is still active.

1   Zoom in on the upper half of the photo, as you'll be retouching the skin area around the woman's eyes.

2   Select the Healing Brush tool, which is grouped with the Spot Healing Brush tool in the toolbox.

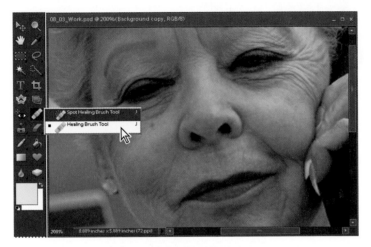

3   In the tool options bar, select the following options:

- For Brush, click the small arrow to open the palette and set the Diameter at 15 px.

- For Mode, select Normal.

- For Source, select Sampled.

- Deselect Aligned and All Layers, if they are selected.

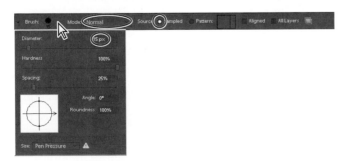

4 Alt+click with the Healing Brush tool on the woman's right cheek to establish that area as the reference texture.

Note: Until you perform this essential step, the Healing Brush tool can't work. If you switch to another tool and then back to the Healing Brush, you must repeat this step.

5 Draw a short horizontal stroke under the left eye. As you drag, it looks as if you're painting dark spots, but when you release the mouse button, the highlight color disappears and skin tones fill in the area.

Note: Be very careful to keep your brush strokes short. Longer strokes may produce unacceptable results. If that happens, choose Edit > Undo Healing Brush, or use the Undo History palette to backtrack. Or, try just clicking instead of dragging. Also, make sure that Aligned is not selected in the tool options bar.

6 Continue to use the Healing Brush to smooth the skin on the face, hands, and neck. Avoid the areas close to the eyes or near the edges of the face. Feel free to reestablish the reference texture by Alt+clicking in other parts of the face to use different skin tones.

7 Use the Undo History palette to quickly undo a series of steps. Every action you perform on the file is recorded in chronological order from top to bottom of the palette. To restore the file to an earlier state, simply select that action in the Undo History palette (Window > Undo History). If you change your mind before making any other changes, you can select a later step in the Undo History palette and restore the image to that phase of your work.

The Healing Brush tool copies texture, not color. In this case, it samples the colors from the area it brushes and arranges those colors according to the texture of the reference area (the cheek). Consequently, the Healing Brush tool appears to be smoothing the skin. So far, the results are not convincingly realistic, but you'll work on that in the next topic.

💡 *As an alternative to using the Healing Brush, use the Spot Healing Brush to remove spots and small imperfections in your photo. You can either click, or click and drag to smooth away imperfections in an area.*

Refining the healing brush results

In this next exercise, you'll use another texture tool to finish your work on this image.

1 Use the Navigator palette (Window > Navigator) to zoom in to the area of the woman's face around the eyes and mouth.

2   In the toolbox, select the Blur tool (💧). Then, set the brush diameter in the tool options bar to approximately 13 px.

3   Drag the Blur tool over the laugh lines around the eyes and mouth.

4   In the tool options bar, reduce the Blur tool brush diameter to 7 px. Drag across the lips to smooth them out, avoiding the edges.

5   Using the Healing Brush and Blur tools, continue working on the image until you have eliminated most of the lines and blended the skin tones. Use the Navigator palette to change the zoom level and shift the focus as needed.

6   In the Layers palette, change the Opacity of the Background Copy layer to about 70%, using your own judgment to set the exact percentage.

Compare your results to the original, retouched (100% Opacity), and final results illustrated below.

Note: In the Editor, you can toggle the visibility of the retouched Background copy layer to compare the original file with your edited version.

Original

Retouched (100% Opacity)

Retouched (70% Opacity)

Extensive retouching can leave skin looking artificially smooth, like molded plastic. Reducing the opacity of the retouched layer gives the skin a more realistic look by allowing some of the wrinkles on the original Background layer to show through. Although they are slightly visible, they are softened.

7   Choose File > Save to save your changes, and then close the file and return to the Organizer.

In this exercise, you learned how to set an appropriate source for the Healing Brush tool, and then use the texture of that source to repair flaws in another area of the photograph. You also used the Blur tool to smooth textures, and finished with an opacity change to create a more realistic look.

Restoring a damaged photograph

All sorts of nasty things can happen to precious old photographs—or precious new photographs, for that matter. The scanned image of an antique photograph you'll use in this project is challenging, because of a large crease in the original print, and other flaws.

With Photoshop Element tools and features, you have the power to restore this picture to a convincing simulation of its original condition. There's no magic pill that fixes significant damage in one or two keystrokes. However, for important heirloom pictures, the work is worth the effort, and we think you'll be impressed with what you can accomplish in this project.

Preparing a working copy of the image file

Your first job is to set up the file and layers for the work you'll do in this project.

1 Using the Organizer, find and select the file 08_04.psd, the scanned photo of the twin babies, tagged with the Lesson 8 keyword tag. Then, click the Editor button and choose Full Edit from the menu that appears.

2 In the Editor, choose File > Save As. In the Save As dialog box, type **08_04_Work** as the File Name and select Photoshop (PSD) as the Format. For Save In, select the My CIB Work folder. If Save in Version Set with Original is selected, deselect it before you click Save.

3 Choose Layer > Duplicate Layer and in the Duplicate Layer dialog box, click OK to accept the default name.

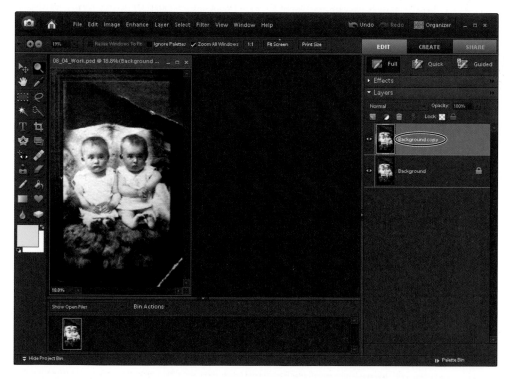

Using the Clone Stamp tool to fill in missing areas

The first thing you'll do is to eliminate the creases. The Clone Stamp tool paints with a sample of an image, which you can use to remove image imperfections, or paint over certain areas of the image, like the creases.

1 With the help of the Navigator palette or the Zoom tool, zoom in on the crease in the lower right corner.

2 In the toolbox, select the Clone Stamp tool ( ), which is grouped with the Pattern Stamp tool.

3 On the left end of the tool options bar, click the triangle and choose Reset Tool from the menu that appears.

Reset Tool reinstates the default values—Size: 21 px, Mode: Normal, Opacity: 100%, and the Aligned option is selected.

4 In the tool options bar, select from the Basic Brushes a hard, mechanical brush with the size of 48 pixels. As Mode choose Normal and set Opacity to 100%. Select Aligned.

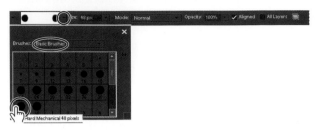

5 Move the Clone Stamp tool to the left of the crease at the bottom of the picture. Hold down the Alt key and click to set the source position. Centering the source on a horizontal line makes it easier to line up the brush for cloning. The tool duplicates the pixels at this sample point in your image as you paint.

Note: If necessary, you can reset the source by Alt+clicking again in a different location as well as click the Undo button ( ).

6 Move the brush over the damaged area so that it is centered at the same horizontal position as the source reference point. Click and drag sidewards over the crease to copy the source image onto the damaged area. As you drag, crosshairs appear, indicating where the source is—that is, the area that the Clone Stamp tool is copying. To repair the upper part of the crease, set the source position in the area above the crease and drag downwards.

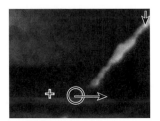

7   Continue to drag the brush over the crease-damaged area, resetting the source position if necessary, until the repair is complete.

The crosshairs follow the movement of the brush. Because you selected the Aligned option in the tool options bar, the crosshairs maintain the same distance and angle to the brush that you set when you made the first brush stroke.

8   Now, smooth out the crease in the upper right side corner. For this exercise the Healing Brush tool (✐) is the better option, because the crease is quite prominent, causing significant variations in the background color. The Healing brush with a small brush size is also the right tool to restore the defect caused by a large white speck on the ear of the baby to your right.

9   Choose File > Save to save your changes.

Using the Selection Brush tool

Next step with this project is to use the Dust & Scratches filter to remove the stray dots and frayed edges of the scanned image. This filter smoothes out the pixels in a way that puts the image just slightly out of focus. That's OK for the background, but the subject matter—the children—should be kept as detailed and as sharp as possible. To do that, you'll need to create a selection that includes only the areas you want to blur.

1   In the toolbox, select the Selection Brush tool (✐), which is grouped with the Quick Selection tool. Be careful to not select a painting brush tool by mistake.

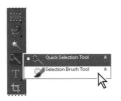

2   In the tool options bar, select a round brush shape and set the size to about 60 pixels. You may need to increase the brush size after the previous exercise.

Leave the other options at the default values: Mode should be set to Selection and Hardness should be set to 100%.

3   Drag the brush along the frayed edges of the photograph to select those areas. Then, increase or decrease the brush size as needed and continue painting the selection to include all the frayed edges and most of the background behind the children.

Note: *Don't try to be too precise; it's OK if some of your strokes go over onto the children because you'll fix that in the next topic.*

4   Choose Select > Save Selection.

5   Name the new selection **Backdrop** and click OK to close the Save Selection dialog box.

The Selection Brush tool is an intuitive way to create a complex selection. In images like this one, where there are no unique color blocks, few sharp boundaries between pictured items, and few crisp geometric shapes, the Selection Brush tool is especially useful.

Just as the Spot Healing Brush provides a quicker alternative to the Healing Brush tool, the Quick Selection Brush tool ( ) is a faster alternative to using the Selection Brush tool. The Quick Selection Brush tool automatically makes selection based on color and texture when you click or click-drag an area.

Another advantage of the Selection Brush tool is that it is very forgiving. For example, you can hold down the Alt while dragging to remove areas from a selection. Or, you can use the tool in Mask mode, which is another intuitive way of adding to the areas outside the selection, as you'll try next.

What is a mask?

A mask is the opposite of a selection. A selection is an area that you can alter; everything outside the selection is unaffected by editing changes. A mask is an area that's protected from changes, just like the solid areas of a stencil or the masking tape you'd put on window glass at home before you paint the wooden trim.

Another difference between a mask and a selection is the way Photoshop Elements presents them visually. You're familiar with the flashing line of black and white dashes that signal a selection marquee. A mask appears as a colored, semi-transparent overlay on the image. You can change the color of the mask overlay using the Overlay Color option that appears in the tool options bar when the Selection Brush tool is set to operate in Mask mode.

Refining a saved selection

As you progress through this book, you're gathering lots of experience with saving selections. In this procedure, you'll amend a saved selection and replace it with your improved version.

1   In the work area, make sure that:

• The Backdrop selection is still active in the image window. If it is not active, choose Selection > Load Selection, and choose the saved selection by name, before clicking OK.

• The Selection Brush tool (✎) is still selected in the toolbox.

2   In the tool options bar, select Mask in the Mode menu.

You now see a semi-transparent, colored overlay in the unselected areas of the image. This represents the image mask, which covers the protected areas.

3   Examine the image, looking for unmasked areas with details that should be protected, such as places where the Selection Brush strokes extended over onto the children.

Use the Navigator palette slider or Zoom tool (🔍) to adjust your view of the image, if necessary.

4   Reduce the brush size of the Selection Brush to about 30 pixels, and then use the brush to paint any areas you want to mask. Press the Alt key while painting to remove an area from the mask.

In this mode, the Selection Brush tool creates the mask rather than the selection.

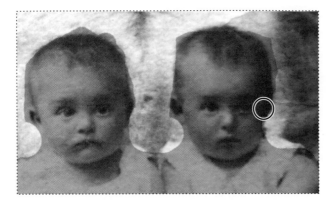

5   Switch back and forth between Selection and Mask modes, making corrections until you are satisfied with the selection—or mask for that matter.

Your goal is to mask areas that contain fine details you want to preserve.

6   Choose Select > Save Selection. In the Save Selection dialog box, choose Backdrop from the Selection menu. Then, under Operation, select Replace Selection and click OK.

7   With the Selection Brush tool still active, make sure that in the tool options bar you have Selection—not Mask—selected in the Mode menu. Keep the selection active for the next procedure.

Filtering flaws out of the backdrop area

Now that you've made your selection, you're ready to apply the filter that will soften the selected areas, reducing the tiny scratches and dust specks.

1   If the Backdrop selection is no longer active, choose Select > Load Selection and choose Backdrop before you click OK to close the dialog box.

2   Choose Filter > Noise > Dust & Scratches.

3 In the Dust & Scratches dialog box, make sure that Preview is selected, and then drag the Radius slider to 8 pixels and the Threshold slider to 10 levels. Move the dialog box so that you can see most of the image window, but do not close it yet.

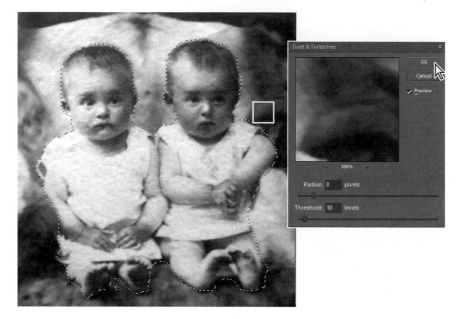

4 Examine the results in the image window. The frayed edges of the image should be repaired and the stray dust and tiny scratches eliminated. Move the cursor inside the thumbnail and drag with the hand icon to change the preview area that is displayed.

5 Make adjustments to the Radius and Threshold values until you are satisfied with the results, and then click OK to close the Dust & Scratches dialog box.

6 Choose Select > Deselect, and then choose File > Save to save your work.

The Dust & Scratches filter does a good job of clearing away spots created by flaws on the negative. However, it doesn't repair damage to the areas outside the selection.

Finishing up the project

While you could spend longer working on this picture, the quality is now acceptable for most purposes. You'll fix just a few more areas before leaving this project.

1 Double-click the Hand tool (🖐) to zoom out so that you can see the entire image. Alternatively, you can use the Navigator palette or the Zoom tool.

2   Examine the entire image, looking for dark or light flecks created by dust on the negative, especially on the dark areas of the photograph.

3   In the toolbox, select the Blur tool (⬤) and type **40 px** for Size in the tool options bar.

4   Click or drag the tool over any dust spots to blend them into the surrounding area.

5   Review all areas of the image. If you see flaws that you want to fix, make any additional repairs or corrections.

Original   *Retouched*

6   Choose File > Save, and then close the file.

Congratulations, you have finished this project. In this exercise, you've used blurring and a filter to hide spots, flecks, and texture flaws. You've also cloned one area of an image to repair an area that's been damaged. You've used the Selection Brush tool to create selections in two modes: Selection and Mask. Along the way, you've seen how to reset a tool to its default settings.

Review

▶ **Review questions**

1   What tools can you use to fix the red eye phenomenon created by some flash cameras?

2   How can you quickly undo a series of edit steps?

3   What are the similarities and differences between using the Healing Brush and the Spot Healing Brush tools to retouch photos?

4   Why is it necessary to make a selection (e.g., using the Magic Selection tool) before applying the Dust & Scratches filter to restore a damaged photograph?

5   What is the difference between a selection and a mask?

▶ **Review answers**

1   You can choose to automatically fix red eye when importing photos into the catalog. Simply select Automatically Fix Red Eye where available in the various import dialog boxes. To fix red eye after the photos have been imported, choose Edit > Auto Red Eye Fix in the Organizer. In either the Full Edit or Quick Fix mode of the Editor, choose Enhance > Auto Red Eye Fix. Finally, the Red Eye Removal tool located in the toolbox enables you to adjust some parameters while fixing red eye.

2   Use the Undo History palette to quickly undo a series of steps. Every action you perform on the file is recorded in chronological order from top to bottom of the palette. To restore the file to an earlier state, simply select that action in the Undo History palette. If you change your mind before making any other changes, you can select a later step in the Undo History palette and restore the image to that phase of your work.

3   Both tools copy from one part of an image to another. The Spot Healing Brush tool, especially with the Proximity Match option selected, enables you to remove blemishes more quickly than does the Healing Brush, because it only involves clicking and/or dragging on an imperfection to smooth it. The Healing

Brush is more customizable, but requires Alt+clicking to establish a reference texture.

4   Because the Dust & Scratches filter smoothes out pixels in an image by putting them slightly out of focus, you should create a selection that includes only the areas you need to blur. Otherwise, your subject matter won't be as detailed and sharp as possible.

5   A mask is the opposite of a selection. The selection is the area that you can alter; everything outside the selection is unaffected by editing changes. A mask is the area that's protected from changes.

Another difference between a mask and a selection is the way Photoshop Elements presents them visually. You're familiar with the flashing line of black and white dashes that signal a selection marquee. A mask appears as a colored, semi-transparent overlay on the image. You can change the color of the mask overlay using the Overlay Color option that appears in the tool options bar when the Selection Brush tool is set to operate in Mask mode.

9 Working with Text

Adding a message to your photos is yet another way to make your images and compositions more memorable and personal. Photoshop Elements provides you with tools to add crisp, flexible, and editable type to your pictures. Whether you need straightforward, classic typography or wild effects and wacky colors, it's all possible. In this lesson, you'll learn how to do the following:

- Add a border to an image by changing the canvas size.

- Format, add, and edit text.

- Manipulate text using Layer Styles.

- Warp text.

- Tile images.

- Move image layers independently.

- Hide, reveal, and delete layers.

- Transfer a layer from one image to another.

- Merge two layers into a single layer.

- Apply a type clipping mask.

Before you begin, make sure that you have correctly copied the Lessons folder from the CD in the back of this book onto your computer's hard disk. See "Copying the Classroom in a Book files" on page 3.

In this lesson, you will use the CIB Catalog you created earlier in the book. If necessary, open this catalog by choosing File > Catalog and selecting the CIB Catalog in the Catalog Manager dialog box.

Getting started

This lesson includes several projects. Each project builds on the skills learned in the previous projects. Most people need about one to two hours to complete this lesson.

This lesson assumes that you are already familiar with general features of the Photoshop Elements work area, and that you recognize the two ways in which you can use Photoshop Elements: the Editor and the Organizer. If you discover that you need more background information as you proceed, see Photoshop Elements Help, or the Tutorials available on the Welcome Screen.

Placing a text label on an image

This project involves typing, formatting, and arranging text on a photograph. The goal is to add a greeting and create a border for the photo so it can be printed and mounted in a picture frame.

The original file (left) and completed project file (right).

About Type

A font is a collection characters—letters, numerals, punctuation marks, and symbols—in a particular typeface, which share design characteristics such as size, weight, and style. A typeface family is a collection of similar fonts designed to be used together. One example is the Myriad typeface family, which is a collection of fonts in a number of styles including Regular, Bold, Italic, Condensed and other variations. Other typeface families might consist of different font style variations.

Font family
Myriad Pro
Font style
Regular, **Bold**, *Italic*, Condensed

Times New Roman
Regular, **Bold**, *Italic*

Traditionally, font sizes are measured in points, but can also be specified in millimeters or inches, as with large lettering on signs, for example. The most common formats for computer fonts are Type 1 PostScript, TrueType, and OpenType.

Each font conveys a feeling or mood. Some are playful or amusing, some are serious and businesslike, while others might convey an impression of elegance and sophistication. To get a feel for which typeface best suits your project, it's good to try out several fonts. One way to find out more about type is to go to www.adobe.com/type. Adobe Type offers more than 2,200 fonts from the world's leading type designers, which you can browse by categories such as style, use, theme, classification, and designers. This will make it easy to find the perfect font for any assignment. You can even type in your sample copy and compare different fonts.

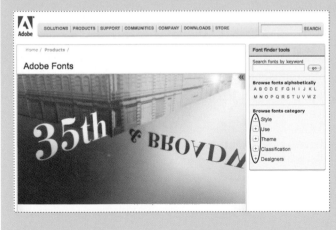

Using the Organizer to find and open tagged files

To make it easier to find the files you are now going to work with, we've tagged them with the name of the appropriate lesson.

1 Open Adobe Photoshop Elements, and choose Edit in the Welcome screen.

2 Choose File > Open, and open the file 09_01.jpg in your Lessons09 folder, a picture of a family at the beach.

3 Make sure you are working in Full Edit mode.

Adding an uneven border

In this procedure you'll enlarge the canvas—the area on which the image appears—without increasing the size of the image. The canvas size is usually the same as the image size for digital photographs, but by enlarging it you can add a border. The border area takes on the Background color, which is comparable to the paper underlying a photographic print.

You'll create this border in two phases and give it precise dimensions.

1 Choose Image > Resize > Canvas Size.

2 In the Canvas Size dialog box, complete the following steps:

• Select the Relative check box.

• For Width, type **0.5** and select inches from the menu.

- For Height type **0.5**, and select inches from the menu.

- Leave the default setting for the center square in the Anchor diagram, and White from the current Background color as the Canvas extension color.

- Click OK to close the dialog box and apply the changes. A white border now surrounds the image.

3   Now let's extend the border below the image where the greeting should go. Choose Image > Resize > Canvas Size again. Confirm that the Relative check box remains selected, and then enter the following options:

- In the Anchor diagram, select the center square in the top row.

- Confirm Width is set to 0, or enter **0** now.

- For Height, type **1**.

- Leave all other settings unchanged and click OK.

(See illustration on the next page.)

Now the border around the image has become wider at the bottom, providing a perfect stage for the text you'll add next.

Adding a text layer

With the Horizontal Type and Vertical Type tools you can place type anywhere on your image. The text you type is automatically entered on a new type layer. You can later resize the text if necessary without losing quality since the font outlines are stored as vector images.

Distinguishing between Pixels and Vectors

Computer graphics can be divided into two types: pixel-based images (bit mapped, or raster images, primarily created by cameras and scanners), and vector images (constructed with drawing programs).

Pixel-based images, like photos, are made up of pixels, or little squares (you can detect them when you zoom in). Adobe Photoshop is a widely used program that lets you manipulate pixels. To produce a medium quality print of your pictures for print, make sure that the file is at least 250 ppi (pixels per inch), while for viewing on screen, 72 ppi is fine

Vector images consist of artwork formed from paths, like a technical line drawing, the outline of a logo, or type. One big advantage of vector images is that they can be enlarged or reduced without losing detail.

In the tool options bar, which will appear once the Type tool is your active tool, you will choose formatting for the type. This includes the font family, font size, text color, paragraph style, and other text attributes.

1   In the toolbox, select the Horizontal Type tool (T).

2   In the tool options bar, select the following from the menus:

• For font family, select MyriadPro.

• For font style, select Bold.

• For font size, type **44** pt.

• Leave the default setting for the Leading (the space between two lines of text) at Auto.

• To set the text color, click the triangle beside the Color option to open the color menu palette. Then, select Pure Cyan Blue as Color.

• For paragraph alignment, select Center Text (≡).

3 Click in the frame area below the picture to set the cursor and type in all uppercase **GREETINGS FROM SANTA CRUZ.**

Note: Do not press the Enter or Return keys on the central part of your keyboard to accept text changes. When the Type tool is active, these keys add a line break in the text. To create a new line of text, press Enter.

4   Click the Commit button (✔) in the tool options bar to accept the text. Or, press Enter on the numeric keypad. Don't worry about the exact position of the text in the image or any typing errors, because you'll correct those later in this project.

(See illustration on next page.)

Notice in the Layers palette in the Palette Bin on the right of your work area, that the image is now made up of two layers: a Background, which contains the image and is locked, and the text layer, which contains the message you just typed. Most of the text layer is transparent, so only the text itself blocks your view of the Background layer.

5   Next is to center the type below the image. Select the Move tool (⤧) in the toolbox.

6   Place the cursor inside the text so that the cursor turns into a solid black arrowhead (▶) and drag the text so that it is visually centered along the lower border of the image.

Note: Adobe Photoshop Elements 6.0 also includes other tools for adding text to your images. Throughout the remainder of this lesson, the term Type tool always refers to the Horizontal Type tool, which is the default type tool.

Adding a quick border

When precision isn't important for the canvas-size enlargement, you can use the Crop tool to quickly add a border to an image.

1 Select the Zoom tool ( ) and zoom out by holding down the Alt key and clicking. The cursor will change from a magnifying glass with a plus sign ( ) to one with a minus sign ( ). If necessary, click again until you can see some of the gray pasteboard surrounding the image.

2 Select the Crop tool ( ) and drag a rectangle within the image—size doesn't matter at this point.

3 Drag the corner handles of the crop marquee outside the image area onto the pasteboard to define the size and shape of border that you want to create.

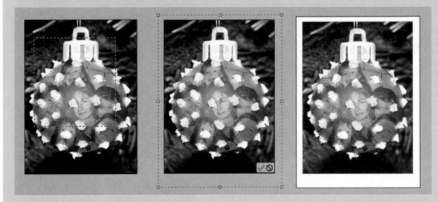

4 After you have defined the new size for the image and border, click the Commit button ( ) on the tool options bar to apply the change. Or, click the Cancel button ( ) next to the Commit button if you don't want to crop the image. The Background Color fills in the newly expanded canvas.

Editing in a text layer

Adding vector-based text is a nondestructive process, so your original image is not overwritten by the text. If you save your file in the native Photoshop (PSD) format, you can reopen it and move, edit, or delete the text layer without affecting the image.

Using the Type tool is much like typing in a word processing application. If you want to change attributes such as font style or text color, select the characters you want to change, and then adjust the settings.

1   If necessary, choose View > Zoom In to enlarge the image until you can comfortably read the text you added in the previous exercise.

2   Confirm that the text layer GREETINGS FROM SANTA CRUZ is still selected in the Layers palette and the Type tool (T) is active.

3   Click to the right of "CRUZ" and press Enter to add a line break in the text. Then type (this time in upper and lowercase) **The Evans Family,** so that the text reads: "GREETINGS FROM SANTA CRUZ
The Evans Family".
Now we want to change the font style, reduce the font size and change the color of the second line of text.

4   Move the cursor to the beginning of the second line of text. Click and drag over the text to select all the text in the second line.

5   In the tool options bar, select MyriadPro Regular and choose 30 pt as font size.

6   Click the arrow beside the Color option and select a black color swatch. When choosing your own colors, be certain to select colors that are easy to read against the background color. Press the Return key to close the Swatches palette.

Note: By clicking the Color sample instead of the arrow next to it in the tool options bar, you can open the Color Picker, which is a different way to select colors.

7   If necessary, using the Type tool, correct any typing errors you may have made. To do this:

• Click once to move the insertion point to another position within the text, or use the arrow keys to move the cursor forward or back.

• Click and drag to select multiple characters.

• Type to add text or to overwrite selected characters.

• Press Backspace or Delete to erase characters.

8   Click the Commit button (✔) in the tool options bar to accept your editing changes.

Saving your work file

In this procedure, you'll save your work file so you can review it later.

1   Choose File > Save. The Save As dialog box opens.

2   Navigate to and open the My CIB Work folder.

3   In the Save As dialog box, enter the following settings:

• As File name, type **09_01_Work**.

• As Format, confirm that Photoshop (PSD) is selected.

4   Under Save Options, confirm that the Include in the Organizer option is selected, and—if selected—deselect Save in Version Set with Original.

5   Review your settings and click the Save button. If the Photoshop Elements Format Options dialog box appears, keep Maximize Compatibility selected and click OK.

6   Choose File > Close.

Bravo, you've finished your first text project. In this section, you've formatted and edited text, and seen how layers work independently in an image. You've also enlarged the canvas size without stretching the image itself.

Overlaying text on an image

In the first project of this lesson, you've preserved the layering of the work files by saving in a file format that supports layers. This provides you with the flexibility to make changes to the images after they have been saved, without having to rebuild the image from the beginning, or modify the original image. The layers have kept the text and shapes separate from the original image.

In this project, you'll do what professional photographic studios sometimes do to protect proprietary images—stamp a copyright notice over the photo. You will apply a style to a text layer so that it looks as if the word is set on clear glass overlaid on a print of the images.

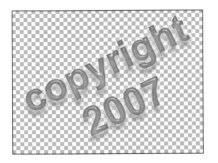

Creating a new document for the text

You'll start by preparing the text in its own file. In this procedure, you'll see a gray-and-white checkerboard pattern. This pattern indicates 100% transparency, where an area or complete layer acts like a pane of clear glass on which you can add text or graphics.

1   Make sure you're still in Full Edit mode. In the Editor, choose File > New > Blank File.

2   In the New dialog box, enter the following settings:

- For Name, type **Overlay**.

- For Width, type **600**, and select pixels.

- For Height, type **600**, and select pixels.

- For Resolution, type **72**, and select pixels/inch.

- For Color Mode, select RGB Color.

- For Background Contents, select Transparent.
- Review your settings to make sure they are correct and click OK.

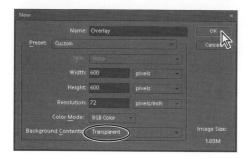

The image window shows only a checkerboard pattern. If it does not, choose Edit > Undo and repeat Step 2, being careful to select Transparent from the Background Contents menu. The pattern represents the transparent background that you selected when creating the file.

3 Select the Type tool (T), and then in the tool options bar, set the following text attributes:

- Arial as font family (a sans serif font is best for the purpose of this project)
- Bold as font style
- 120 pt as font size
- Left aligned as text alignment
- Black as text color

4 Click near the left side of the image window and type **copyright 2007**. Click the green Commit button (✔) in the tool options bar to accept the text you've typed.

5 Select the Move tool (▶⊕). Click and drag the text to center it in the image window.

6 Position the Move tool outside a corner of the text bounding box so that the cursor changes to a curved, double-ended arrow (↶), and then click and drag counter-clockwise around the center to rotate the text so it appears at a slight angle.

Note: You can also resize or reshape the text by dragging corners of the bounding box. Because Photoshop Elements text layers are vector shapes, based on mathematics rather than pixels the letter shapes remain smooth even if you drag the corners of the bounding box to enlarge the text. If you tried this with bitmap text, you'd see jagged, stair-step edges in the enlarged text.

7   Click the Commit button (✔) near the lower left corner of the selection rectangle.

Applying a Layer Style to the text layer

Next, you'll work with a Layer Style. Layer Styles are combinations of adjustments that you apply in one easy action to your text layer. Photoshop Elements gives you a wide variety of choices,

1   In the Palette Bin, locate the Effects palette. If the palette is not displayed in your work area, choose Window > Effects. If necessary, click the triangle in the upper left corner of the Effects palette to expand it.

2   At the top of the Effects palette, select Layer style (▤), and then use the scroll bar to select the second last effect, Wow Plastic.

3 If necessary, scroll down to see the end of the list of available choices, and then double-click the Wow Plastic White effect thumbnail to apply it to the selected text layer. As an alternative, you can drag the effect over your text layer image.

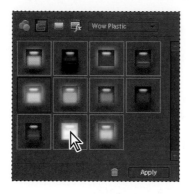

Layer Styles keep text editable. Therefore, in the Layers palette, the Copyright text layer thumbnail still displays the T icon (T) for text. Later on, if you wish to change the year of the copyright, for example, you can simply type again in the text layer—with the same Layer style already applied. Notice the Layer style icon ( ), which tells you that a layer style has been applied. Generally it's a good idea to make all text editing changes before applying styles or effects to text layers.

4 Choose File > Save to the My CIB Work folder. If the Photoshop Elements Format Options dialog box appears, keep Maximize Compatibility selected, and then click OK.

Adding the text to multiple images

Now that you've prepared the text, you'll place it onto different images you might want to mark with the copy protection message.

1 Click the Organizer (▪▪) on the shortcuts bar to switch to the Organizer.

2 On the Tags palette, click the Find boxes for Lesson 9 to help you find the images you'll use for this project.

3 Control-click to select the four images of paintings called 09_02.jpg, 09_03.jpg, 09_04.jpg, and 09_05.jpg. Then, click the Editor button (🖉) and choose Full Edit.

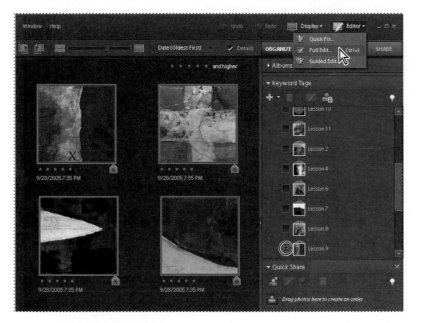

4 To view and arrange multiple windows, choose Window > Images > Tile.

💡 *To view the same section (e.g. upper left corner, center, lower right corner) of all open photos, choose Window > Images > Match Location. The view in all windows shifts to match the active (frontmost) image. The zoom level does not change.*

5 To fully view the images, select the overlay.psd and change the view from 66% (or whatever your default setting) to 30% by typing **30** into the left corner of the image.

6 With the image still active, select Window > Images > Match Zoom.

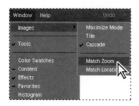

7 In the Photo Bin (the row of thumbnails across the bottom of the work area), select the Overlay.psd to make it the active file.

8   To make the overlay more transparent, reduce the opacity to 50% either by typing **50** into the box, or by dragging the upcoming slider to the left.

9   Hold down the Shift key, and then drag from the Layers palette the layer thumbnail for the Copyright 2007 text layer and drop it onto the first picture, called 09_02.jpg.

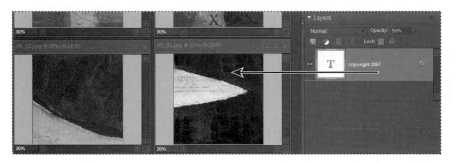

10   You can now see the image of the painting with the copyright notice as a semitransparent overlay. Repeat the previous step, dragging the text onto the two remaining images, 09_03.jpg, 09_04.jpg and 09_05.jpg. Note that you can position the bounding box with the text on each image individually.

11   In the Editor window, click to select the Overlay.psd document containing only the text. Choose File > Close. When asked to Save, click Yes, and then enter the name **Overlay**, and save the file as a Photoshop (PSD) format in the My CIB Work folder on your hard disk. If the Photoshop Elements Format Options dialog box appears, keep Maximize Compatibility selected and click OK.

12   Choose File > Close All.

Done! In this project, you've created a new Photoshop (PSD) format document without an image and added text to that document. You've copied a layer from that document to other image files by dragging it from the Layers palette to the image windows. You've used the Effects palette to apply a Layer Style to the text layer.

Using Layer Styles and distortions

In this next exercise you'll have more fun with text using type distortions and other effects. For this you will apply exciting changes, still preserving the Type layer as text.

Adding the subject text and a layer style

Your first task is to find and open the image file for this project and add the text.

1   Click the Organizer button (⚏) located near the top right corner of the Editor window to switch to the Organizer.

2   In the Keyword Tags palette, click the Find box next to the Lesson 9 keyword tag, and then click to select the file 09_06.jpg, a view of a cloudy sky.

3   Click the Editor button, and then choose Full Edit from the menu that appears.

4   In the toolbox, select the Type tool (T) and make the following selections in the tool options bar to set the text attributes:

• For the font family and style, select a bold sans serif font like Impact (as alternatives, choose Arial Bold or Arial Black).

- For the font size, type **120 pt** and press Enter to accept this setting.
- For text alignment, select Center text (≡).
- In the color palette, Set the text color to Pastel Cyan Blue.

5 Using the Type tool, click near the center of the image. In all lower upper case, type **MAYBE**.

6 Click the Commit button (✔) in the tool options bar to accept the text.

7 Choose the Move tool (▶+). Click and drag the text to center it as shown in the illustration below.

8 Open the Effects palette by clicking the little triangle next to Effects, select Layer style (■), and stay in the first category named Bevels.

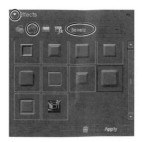

9   Select the last effect in the second row, called Simple Sharp Outer.

10   In the Layers palette, change the opacity to 75% by either typing **75**, or by dragging the slider that appears when you click the triangle next to the value.

11   Save your file into your My CIB Work folder and name it 09_06_Work. Make sure the Layers box is selected.

Warping text

Stretching and skewing text into unusual shapes is incredibly easy in Photoshop Elements. In fact, it is so easy to apply those effects that one needs to be careful not to overuse them.

1   With the Type tool still selected, click anywhere on the text "MAYBE" in the image window.

Note: Highlighting any part of the text isn't necessary, because warping applies to the entire text layer.

2   In the tool options bar, click the Create warped text button (ℒ) to open the Warp Text dialog box.

3   From the Style menu, select the Fisheye effect.

4   Confirm that Horizontal is chosen for the orientation of the effect and set the Bend value to **+80**%. Then, click OK to close the Warp Text dialog box.

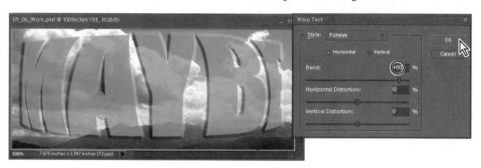

5   The text of MAYBE is still editable. You can check this out by dragging the Type tool over the word to select it, and then typing over it—just make sure the Type tool is still selected.

6   If you changed the text in the previous step, change it back to MAYBE by typing over it.

7   Choose File > Save.

Creating an unstylized copy of the text layer

For the next part of the lesson, you will experiment with an effect that needs your type layer to be simplified, meaning you cannot edit the text anymore. For this you will create two versions of the finished artwork on separate layers.

1   In the Layers palette, select the text layer. Then, click the More menu in the upper right corner of the palette. The palette menu is displayed. From the palette menu, choose Duplicate Layer. Click OK to accept the default layer name MAYBE copy.

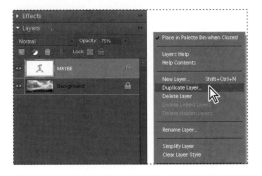

💡 *You can also drag an existing layer to the New Layer icon (🗔) in the Layers palette to create a duplicate layer.*

2   Click the eye icon (👁) to the left of the MAYBE layer. The layer becomes invisible in the image window.

3   In the Layers palette, change the opacity of the MAYBE copy layer to 100%.

4   Choose Layer > Layer Style > Clear Layer Style.

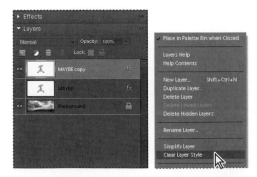

The warped text now appears again in solid white, as it did before you applied the Layer Style.

Simplifying and applying a pattern to text

You're now ready to add a different look to the copy of the text layer. Make sure that the MAYBE copy layer is selected in the Layers palette before you begin. One of the interesting things you'll do in this procedure is to lock the transparent pixels on a text layer. This enables you to do all sorts of painting on the shapes in the layer, without having to be careful about the edges.

1   In the toolbox, choose the Clone Stamp tool. In the tool options bar, choose the Pattern Stamp tool icon (🗾).

Note: You can also choose the Pattern Stamp tool by pressing and holding the Clone Stamp tool in the toolbox, and then selecting the Pattern Stamp Tool from the menu that appears.

2   In the tool options bar, select the following:

•   For Size, enter **50** px. The Size setting determines the diameter of the Pattern Stamp tool brush, and can be set by typing in a size, or by clicking the arrow to the right of the value and dragging the slider to change the size.

•   For Mode, confirm that Normal is selected.

•   For Opacity, confirm that 100% is selected.

•   Click on the triangle next to the Pattern box to open the Pattern menu. Then, choose Pink Fur as the pattern.

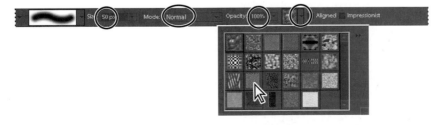

3 Click with the Pattern Stamp brush on the text. When a message appears, asking if you want to simplify the layer, click OK. After clicking OK, do not click on the text again.

4 In the Layers palette, click the Lock Transparent Pixels button to prevent changes to the transparent areas of the simplified MAYBE copy layer.

Notice that there is now a lock icon on the upper layer, reminding you that you've applied a lock.

5 Paint with the Pattern Stamp tool over the text, applying the pattern as solidly or unevenly as you like.

The pattern affects only the selected layer (the simplified text) and doesn't change any unselected layer, such as the underlying photograph. Because the transparent pixels on the upper MAYBE copy layer are locked they are also protected, so only the simplified text shapes take on the pattern.

After simplifying the text layer, as you've done here, the text can't be edited any more using the Type tool. However, you could still add the appearance of depth or other effects to the patterned text by applying a Layer Style, such as a Bevel or Inner Glow, using the Effects palette.

Hiding and revealing layers

Having placed the two design alternatives of the styled text on different layers, you can use the eye icons in the Layers palette to alternately show one of the two different designs.

1   In the Layers palette, make sure that the eye icons appear in both the Layers palette for the Background layer, and the top layer that you just painted over with the Pattern Stamp tool.

2   Click the eye icon for the top layer, MAYBE copy. This hides the layer and the eye icon is no longer displayed.

3   Click the empty box to the left of the middle MAYBE layer. This causes the eye icon to appear in the Layers palette and also displays the text layer with the warped, blue text in the document window.

The process of switching between layers enables you to quickly decide between different design solutions for a project. Once you've made up your mind, you can simply get rid of the layers you don't want.

Deleting layers and layer styles

In the next steps, you will keep just the original MAYBE text layer and remove the one with the pink fur pattern. Deleting layers that you no longer need reduces the size of your image file.

1   Delete the MAYBE copy layer by clicking the double triangles to open the Layers menu, and then selecting Delete Layer.

(See illustration on the next page.)

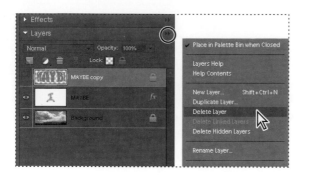

💡 *As an alternative, select Delete Hidden Layers from the Layers menu. This way you are able to remove several layers at once.*

2   In the toolbox select the Type tool (T), and then click the Create warped text button (⚓) to open the Warp Text dialog box.

3   In the Style menu, select None, and then click OK to close the Warp Text dialog box.

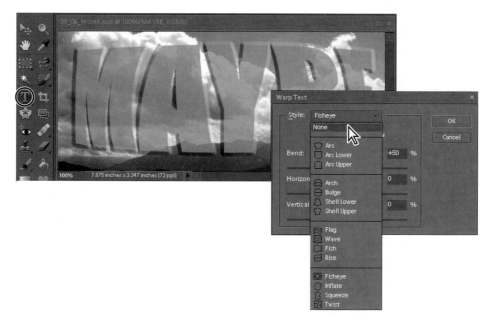

4   Now you're back to where you began before using the text warping effect. Choose File > Save and save the file as 09_Work in the My CIB Work folder. Choose Photoshop

(*.PSD, *.PDD) as file format. If Save in Version Set with Original is selected, be sure to deselect it before you click Save. If the Photoshop Elements Format Options dialog box appears, keep Maximize Compatibility selected and click OK.

5   Close your work by selecting File > Close.

In this section, you've applied a Layer Style to text and warped it, which leaves it fully editable but gives it some color and flair. Furthermore you've experimented with filling type with patterns by locking transparent pixels on a layer. Finally, you've kept two potential versions of the final art in one work file.

Working with Paragraph type

With point type, each line of type is independent—the line expands or shrinks as you edit it, but it doesn't wrap to the next line. Point type (the name derives from the fact that it is preceded by a single anchor point) is perfect for small blocks of text like headlines, logos, and headings for Web pages. Probably most of your type entries will use this mode. If you work with larger amounts of text and you want this to wrap automatically, it's best to use the paragraph type mode. By clicking and dragging the type tool you'll create a text bounding box on your image. The bounding box can be easily resized to fit your text perfectly.

Creating type masks

You can have fun with text selection borders by cutting text out of an image to show the background, or pasting the selected text into a new image. All this is possible with the Horizontal or Vertical Type Mask tool.

1   Switch to the Organizer.

2   In the Keyword Tags palette, click the Find box next to the Lesson 9 keyword tag, and then click to select the file 09_07.jpg, an image of two zebras.

3   Click the Editor button, and then choose Full Edit from the menu that appears.

Working with the Type Mask tool

The Type Mask tool (T) enables you to fill letter shapes with parts of an image. This can create a much more interesting effect than using plain text with a solid color.

1   In the tool box, select the Horizontal Type Mask tool (⊤).

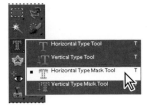

2   In the tool options bar, set the following text attributes:

• Stencil as font family (or any sans serif font like Impact or Arial bold is good)

• Bold as font style

• 100 pt as font size

Leave left aligned selected as text alignment. Don't worry about the color attributes as the mask will contain the colors and details of the image.

3 Click near the top of the left zebra's belly and type **ZOO**.

4 The background pattern of zebra stripes shows through the shapes of the letters you just typed, while the rest of the picture is hidden. Select Edit > Copy, and then Edit > Paste. In the Layers palette, notice that the type has been placed onto a new layer. *(See illustration on the next page.)*

5   Hide the background layer by clicking the eye icon (👁).

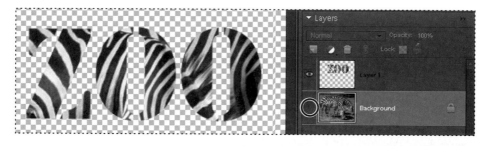

Although the text cannot be edited anymore, you can still apply a layer style or effect to make it more prominent.

6   Make the Layers 1 your active layer by selecting it, and then open the Effects palette.

7   At the top of the Effects palette, select Layer style (■), and then select Drop Shadows from the menu to the right.

8   In the Drop Shadows palette, select the shadow called Noisy, the second shadow in the second row of effects.

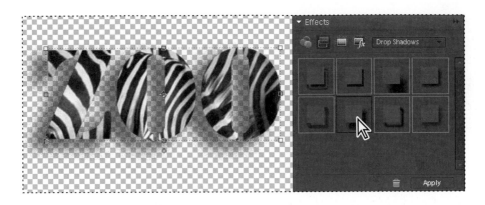

9 Since you don't need the background layer with the zebras, delete it by clicking Flatten Image in the Layers menu. Click OK in the upcoming dialog box asking whether to discard the hidden layers.

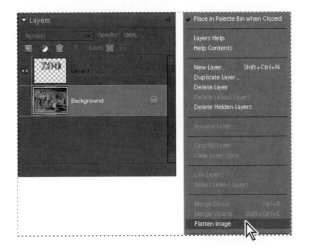

10 Choose File > Save As and in the Save As dialog box, name the file **09_07_Work**. Choose PSD as file format. Navigate to the My CIB Work folder.

Wonderful! You can add this project to your list of accomplishments for the day. In this part you've learned how to mask type and use it

Review

Review questions

1   What is the advantage of having text on a separate layer?

2   How do you hide a layer without removing it?

3   In the Layers palette, what do the lock icons do and how do they work?

4   What's the difference between point type and paragraph type?

Review answers

1   Because the text remains separate from the image, Photoshop Elements text layers can be edited in later work sessions, just like editable text in other documents.

2   You can hide a layer by clicking the eye icon (👁) next to that layer on the Layers palette. To make the layer visible again, click the empty box where the eye icon should be to restore it.

3   Lock icons prevent changes to a layer. You can click Lock All (🔒) to lock all the pixels on the selected layer, or you can click Lock Transparent Pixels to protect specific areas. To remove a lock, select the locked layer and click the active lock icon to toggle it off. (This does not work for the Background layer, which can be unlocked only by renaming and converting it into an ordinary layer.)

4   Point type is ideal for headlines, logos and other small blocks of text where each line is independent and does not wrap to the next line. Paragraph text is used where you want larger amounts of text to wrap automatically to the next line. The size of the paragraph text bounding box can be easily changed to fit your text perfectly to the job in hand.

10 | Combining Multiple Images

If you're ready to go beyond fixing individual pictures in conventional ways, this lesson is for you. In it you'll venture into the world of multiple images to add an effect, or move a person or object from one photo into another. In this lesson, you will do the following:

- Merge photos into a panorama.

- Use the Photomerge Group Shot tool to create the perfect group shot.

- Crop images.

- Combine images using multiple layers.

- Resize and reposition selections.

- Create a gradient clipping path.

- Remove the halo that may occur when copying and pasting selections of images.

Before you begin, make sure that you have correctly copied the Lessons folder from the CD in the back of this book onto your computer's hard disk. See "Copying the Classroom in a Book files" on page 3.

Getting started

For this lesson, you will be using the CIB Catalog you created at the start of the book. To open the CIB Catalog, follow these steps:

1   Start Photoshop Elements. In the Welcome Screen, click Organize in the row of shortcut buttons across the lower part of the Welcome Screen. If the CIB Catalog is open, skip to "Merging photos into a panorama" on the next page. If the CIB Catalog is not open, complete the following steps.

2   Choose File > Catalog.

3   In the Catalog Manager dialog box, select the CIB Catalog under Catalogs, and then click Open.

If you do not see the CIB Catalog file, review the procedures found in "Getting Started." See "Copying the Lessons files from the CD" on page 3, and "Creating a catalog" on page 4.

Merging photos into a panorama

The images you'll use for this first exercise are two slightly overlapping photos taken of Mont Saint Michel in France. The camera lens used for these shots did not have a wide enough angle to capture the entire scene. These pictures provide an ideal opportunity for learning how to create panoramas, having Photoshop Elements do most of the work for you.

1   If the Organizer is not currently active, switch to it now.

2   In the Keyword Tags palette, click the Find box next to the Lesson 10 keyword tag.

3   Ctrl-click to select the two pictures of Mont Saint Michel, named 10_01_a.jpg and 10_02_b.jpg.

Note: If you don't see the file names in the Photo Browser, choose View > Show File Names.

4   Choose File > New > Photomerge Panorama.

Photoshop Elements will load the Editor workspace in Full Edit mode and open the Photomerge dialog box.

5   Under Source Files in the Photomerge dialog box, select Files from the Use menu, and then click the Add Open Files button.

Note: You can select more than two files to create a Photomerge Panorama composition.

💡 *Select Folder from the Use menu, and then click Browse to add all photos from a specific folder on your hard disk. To remove photos from the selection, click to select them in the source file list, and then click Remove.*

6   Under Layout, select Auto, and then click OK.

Choosing a Photomerge layout option

Auto Photoshop analyzes the source images and applies either a Perspective or Cylindrical layout, depending on which produces a better photomerge.

Perspective Creates a consistent composition by designating one of the source images (by default, the middle image) as the reference image. The other images are then transformed (repositioned, stretched or skewed as necessary) so that overlapping content across layers is matched.

Cylindrical Reduces the "bow-tie" distortion that can occur with the Perspective layout by displaying individual images as on an unfolded cylinder. Overlapping content across layers is still matched. The reference image is placed at the center. Best suited for creating wide panoramas.

Reposition Only Aligns the layers and matches overlapping content, but does not transform (stretch or skew) any of the source layers.

Interactive Layout Choose this option to open the source images in a dialog and position them manually for the best result. See Create a photomerge interactively.

—From Photoshop Elements Help

7   Wait while Photoshop Elements creates the panorama and opens it in a new window.

That's it! You're basically done creating your panorama. All that remains to do is to crop the image and save your work. You'll do this in a moment. But first, let's have a closer look at how well Photoshop Elements did in merging the two images. (Depending on your source files, you may sometimes spot little problem areas and would then need to try a different layout option to merge you photos.)

8   In the Layers panel, click the eye icon (👁) for the top layer to hide it.

In the edit window, you can now see which part of the image in the second layer was used to create the panorama. The unused part is hidden by a layer mask. You can see a thumbnail of the layer mask in the Layers palette (with white representing the visible area and black the masked area).

9   Choose View > Actual Pixels. Then, use the Hand tool to drag the pictures so you can focus on the edge of the layer mask in the edit window. Repeatedly click the eye icon for the top layer to show either the complete panorama or just the part from the image in the second layer. When the complete panorama is shown, try to find any irregularities apparent along the edge of the layer mask (which you can only see when the top layer is hidden). Such irregularities could occur where some pixels along the edge of one layer mask appear misaligned with pixels along the edge of the adjoining layer mask. Use the Hand tool to drag to another area of the image along the edge of the layer mask and repeat your inspection.

Hide the top layer to reveal the edge of the image mask.

Show the top layer and check for irregularities along the edge of the image mask (now invisible).

10 If your inspection does not reveal any problem areas, make the top layer visible and you're ready to crop the picture and save it, as shown next. Should you find problems in your merged panorama, close the file without saving it, and then repeat the procedure trying a different Photomerge layout option in step 6. Using the interactive layout option, which gives you the most control when creating a panorama, is explained later in this lesson under "Creating a Photomerge Panorama interactively."

Cropping images

The Crop tool removes part of an image outside a selected area. Cropping is useful when you want to focus on a certain area of your photo. When you crop a photo, the resolution remains the same as in the original photo.

Since the photos that you just merged now have an irregular outline, you'll use the Crop tool to create a uniform edge.

1   Choose View > Fit on Screen.

2   Choose Image > Crop. A selection rectangle appears in the middle of your image, which you will adjust in step 3. You can also select the crop tool (🛗) from the toolbox and drag a cropping selection inside the image.

Note: You can crop images in Quick Fix mode the same way as in Full Edit mode. In Guided Edit mode you'll find a Crop Photo entry under Basic Photo Edits. If you are working in the Organizer, you can use the Crop tool in the Fix panel.

3   Drag the handles of the selection rectangle to make it as large as possible, being careful not to include any of the checkerboard areas where the image is transparent. Then, click the Commit button in the lower right corner of the selection rectangle.

4   Choose File > Save and save the merged image in the My CIB Work folder as **10_01_Work**, leaving Photoshop (*.PSD,*PDD) selected as the Format. Saving your file in Photoshop format enables you to later adjust individual layers, if necessary. When you convert to JPEG format, the layer information will be lost. You can export a JPEG version from the Photoshop file, for example, by using the Save for Web command.

Though it's not required for this image, when cropping you can specify any of the following settings in the options bar:

- The Aspect Ratio setting enables you to specify a preset crop. No Restriction lets you resize the image to any dimension. Use Photo Ratio retains the aspect ratio of the photo when you crop.

- The sizes listed specify preset sizes for the cropped photo. If you want your final output to be a specific size, such as 4 x 6 to fit a picture frame, choose that preset size.

- The Width and Height fields enable you to specify the physical dimensions of the image.

5   Choose File > Close to close the file 10_01_Work.psd, keeping the files 10_01_a.jpg and 10_02_b.jpg open in the Editor.

Creating a Photomerge Panorama interactively

If you need to manually rearrange your source images to create a panorama, select the interactive layout option in the Photomerge dialog box.

1   With the files 10_01_a.jpg and 10_02_b.jpg still open in the Editor, choose File > New > Photomerge Panorama.

2   Under Source Files in the Photomerge dialog box, select Files from the Use menu, and then click the Add Open Files button. Under Layout, select Interactive Layout, and then click OK.

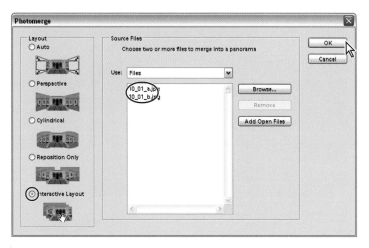

3   Wait while Photoshop Elements opens the interactive Photomerge dialog box.

Note: If the composition can't be automatically assembled, a message appears on-screen. You can assemble the composition manually in the Photomerge dialog box by dragging photos from the photo bin into the work area, and arranging the images where you want.

4 You can fine-tune the panorama in the large Photomerge dialog box by doing the following:

• Under Navigator, use the controls to zoom in or out of the image. When zoomed in, drag the red view box to navigate within the image.

• Use the Select Image tool (✎) and click to select any of the photos in the large work area. Drag with the pointer or use the arrow keys on the keyboard to reposition.

• To remove a photo from the composition, drag it from the large work area onto the light box above. To add it again, drag it from the light box onto the work area.

• Select the Rotate Image tool (✎) and drag to rotate the selected photo.

• Choose between Reposition Only and Perspective under Settings.

• With Perspective selected under Settings, select the Set Vanishing Point tool (✎) and click in the image to set a new vanishing point.

5   When you're satisfied with your result, click OK to close the Photomerge dialog box.

The Photomerge dialog box closes, and Photoshop Elements goes to work. You'll see windows open and close as you wait for Photoshop Elements to create the panorama.

6   If you like your new composition better than the one you created in the previous exercise, crop the image and save your work in the My CIB Work folder.

7   Choose File > Close All to close all open windows. When asked whether you want to save your changes, click No.

8   Switch back to the Organizer.

Vanishing Point

A vanishing point is the point at which receding parallel lines seem to meet when seen in perspective. For example, as a road stretches out in front of you, it will seem to grow thinner the farther away it is, until it is almost nonexistent on the horizon. This is the vanishing point.

You can change the perspective of the Photomerge Panorama composition by specifying the location of the vanishing point. Select Perspective under Setting in the Photomerge dialog box, and then select the Vanishing Point tool and click in the image to reset the vanishing point location.

Panorama perspective with approximate location of the vanishing point, using the street curb as guidelines.

Creating group composites

Making the perfect group shot is a difficult task, especially if you have a large family with squirmy kids. For this purpose, Photoshop Elements offers a powerful photo-blending tool, called Photomerge Group Shot. Going through the following exercise will show you how multiple photos can be blended together to create one image with amazing perfection. Gone are the family photos where the eyes of one person are closed or another one has an odder than usual facial expression—with this new tool you can pick and choose the best parts of several pictures taken successively, and merge them together to form one perfect picture.

1   If the Organizer is not currently active, switch to it now.

2   In the Keyword Tags palette, click the Find box next to the Lesson 10 keyword tag.

3   Ctrl-click to select the three pictures named 10_02_a.psd, 10_02_b.psd, and 10_02_c.psd.

Note: Although this exercise uses three quite obviously different source images for demonstrational purpose, you would normally use the Photomerge Group Shot command to create a merged image from several very similar source images.

4   Choose File > New > Photomerge Group Shot.

The Photomerge Faces tool is similar to the Photomerge Group Shot tool, only specialized for work with individual faces. You can have a lot of fun merging different faces to one, e.g. merge parts of a picture of your face with the one of your spouse to predict the possible appearance of future offspring. In Guided Edit, select Faces under Photomerge to create your favorite Frankenface.

Photoshop Elements will load the Editor workspace in Guided Edit mode and start the Photomerge Group Shot task.

5   (Optional) If you want to work with photos not currently in the Organizer (or you want to avoid switching to the Organizer first), you can also open the photos directly in the Editor. Then, select the image thumbnails in the Project Bin, switch to Guided Edit mode, and select Group Shot under Photomerge.

6   From the Project Bin, drag the green framed image (10_02_c.psd) and drop it onto the Final image area on the right. Double-click the yellow framed image (10_02_b.psd) in the Project Bin to open it in the Source image area on the left.

7   Select the Zoom tool (🔍), and then zoom in on the image so you can see all of the girl in the Source image area and at least part of the girl in the Final image area. Use the Hand tool (✋) to reposition the image if necessary.

8   In the Guided Edit panel, select the Pencil Tool.

9   With the Pencil tool selected, draw one stroke from head to toe of the girl in the source image, as shown in the illustration on the next page. When you release the pointer, Photoshop will merge the entire girl from the source image (including her shadow on the stone!) into the final image. Seeing this tool's magic in action should give you some healthy mistrust whenever you come across an unbelievable photo in the future. If necessary, use the Pencil tool to add additional image areas from the source. Or, use the Eraser tool (🖌) to delete a stroke—or parts thereof—drawn accidentally with the Pencil tool. The image area copied to the final image will adjust accordingly.

Note: Sometimes it can be tricky to make the perfect selection. If you end up switching several times between Pencil tool and Eraser tool but can't get the selection right, using the Undo button (↺) and starting again from scratch is probably the best choice.

10 Double-click the blue framed image (10_02_a.psd) in the Project Bin to open it in the Source image area. Reposition the image in the source image area with the Hand tool, and then use the Pencil tool to add a third girl to the final image.

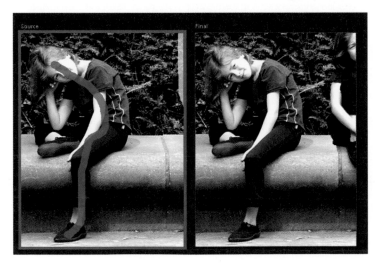

11   To see which parts of the three source images were used for the composition, click the Fit Screen button above the edit pane to see the entire image, and then select Show Regions in the Guided Edit panel.

12   Click the Actual Pixels button above the edit pane, and then use the Hand tool to position the image at a region boundary in the final image. Turn Show Regions off and on to look for imperfections along the region boundaries in the merged image. If necessary, use the Pencil or Eraser tool to add or remove areas from the respective source images in the final image. When you are satisfied with the result, click Done.

13   If necessary, use the Crop Photo tool (under Basic Photo Edits in the Guided Edit pane) to crop away distorted areas at the edges of the image. Select Use Photo Ratio from the Crop Box Size menu to keep the aspect ratio of the original photo. Then, click Done.

14 Choose File > Save and save the merged image in the My CIB Work folder as **10_02_Work**, leaving Photoshop (*.PSD,*.PDD) selected as the Format. Switch to the Full Edit mode, choose File > Close All, and return to the Organizer.

Note: The File > Close All command is only available in the Full Edit mode. In Quick Fix and Guided Edit mode you can only close one file at a time using the File > Close command.

Combining multiple photographs in one file

In this project, you'll combine three photos in one. For the first image, you'll apply a clipping path to blend it into the background image. Then, you'll add a selection from the second image and learn about removing the fringe that may be visible in the combined image. Your final work file will contain all the original pixel information, so that you can go back and make adjustments whenever needed.

Arranging the image layers

In this first part of the project, you're going to combine two images. You'll make the photo of an airplane gradually fade into the sky of the background image.

As background image you'll use a picture of King Ludwig's castle in Bavaria, the masterpiece that inspired the design of Disney's Sleeping Beauty castle.

1   In the Keyword Tags palette of the Organizer, click the Find box next to the Lesson 10 keyword tag.

2   Ctrl-click to select the two pictures named 10_03_a.jpg and 10_03_b.jpg.

3   With both images selected in the Photo Browser, click the Editor button located near the top right corner of the Organizer window, and then choose Full Edit from the menu that appears.

4   In the Editor, choose Window > Images > Tile to view both images at the same time.

5   Click the title bar of the 10_03_b.jpg document window to make it the active window. Select the Move tool (▸⊕). While holding down the Shift key, click and drag the airplane image (10_03_b.jpg) into the castle picture (10_03_a.jpg). Release the pointer when you see a selection outline around the castle picture, and then release the Shift key.

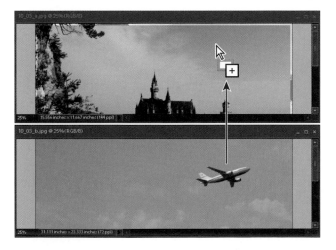

6   Close the 10_03_b.jpg image window (the one you copied from).

7 In the Layers palette, select Layer 1 (airplane). Then, choose Image > Resize > Scale.

8 In the tool options bar, make sure Constrain Proportions is selected, and then type **50%** in the W (width) field. This scales the height and width by the same percentage.

9 Click the Commit button (✔) near the lower right corner of the selection rectangle to accept the changes.

10 With the Move tool still selected, click and drag the airplane on Layer 1 to the upper right corner of the background image. Then, click and drag the lower left handle of the selection rectangle to further reduce the size of the airplane image, as shown in the illustration below.

11 Release the pointer, and then click the Commit button (✔) to accept the changes.

Creating a gradient clipping path

A clipping path serves as a kind of template that allows part of an image to show while hiding the rest by making it transparent.

In the next steps you'll create a gradient that changes from fully opaque to fully transparent, and then use this gradient as a clipping path to blend the castle and aircraft layers together.

1   In the Layers palette, click the New Layer button (▣) to create and select a new, blank layer, named Layer 2.

2   In the toolbox, select the Gradient tool (▬), and then select the Default Foreground and Background Colors icon, or press the D key on your keyboard.

3   In the tool options bar, click the arrow to open the gradient selection menu. Locate the Foreground to Transparent thumbnail. Its name appears in a tooltip when you roll the cursor over it.

4   Double-click the Foreground to Transparent thumbnail to select that gradient and to close the gradient selection menu.

5   Make sure that the other settings in the tool options bar are as follows:

- Radial Gradient (■)

- Mode: Normal

- Opacity: 100%

- Reverse is deselected

- Transparency is selected

6 With the Gradient tool selected, click in the center of the airplane in Layer 1 and draw a short line downwards. Then, release the pointer.

When you release the pointer, you'll see a black spot that is opaque where it covers the airplane, gradually becoming transparent towards the edges of the image. Next, you will use this gradient as clipping path for the image of the airplane in Layer 1, making the airplane visible while its surrounding sky gradually fades into the sky of the background castle image.

Applying the clipping path to a layer

With your gradient layer completed, it's time to put it to work.

1 In the Layers palette, drag the new gradient layer, Layer 2, under Layer 1.

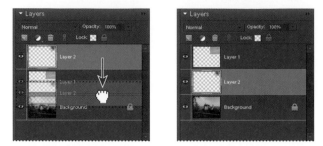

2 Select Layer 1, now the top layer, and then choose Layer > Group with Previous.

This action defines Layer 2 as the clipping path for Layer 1. In the Layers palette, Layer 1 is indented and shows an arrow pointing down to Layer 2. In the document window, the airplane image now blends nicely with the castle picture.

3 Choose File > Save As.

4 In the Save As dialog box, name the file **10_03_Work** and save it in the My CIB Work folder, with Photoshop (PSD) as Format and the Layers option selected. If Save in Version Set with Original is selected, deselect it before you click Save. If the Photoshop Elements Format Options dialog box appears, keep Maximize Compatibility selected and click OK.

Creating a clean edge with defringing

Defringing is used to remove those annoying bits of color that come along when copying and pasting a part of an image or deleting a selected background. When the copied area is pasted onto another background color, or the selected background is deleted, you can often see a fine halo around your selection. Defringe blends the halo away so you won't see a hard line.

Now you'll composite an image of a family so that they appear to be standing in front of the fence in the castle picture by selecting and deleting the background and using the defringe feature.

1   Switch to the Organizer, select the file 10_03_c.jpg, the picture of the family, and then open it in Full Edit mode.

2   With the family image (10_03_c.jpg) as the active window in the Editor, choose Select > All, then Edit > Copy, and then File > Close. Select the Background layer of the 10_03_Work.psd image, and then choose Edit > Paste. The image of the family is placed on a new layer, named Layer 3, just above the background layer.

3   With Layer 3, the family image, still selected in the Layers palette, choose Image > Resize > Scale.

4   In the tool options bar, make sure Constrain Proportions is selected, and then type **80%** in the W (width) field.

5   Click the Commit button (✔) near the lower right corner of the selection rectangle to accept the changes.

6   If necessary, scroll to see the lower left corner of the image in the document window. Select the Move tool. Click and drag the image in Layer 3, the family, to position it in the lower left corner of the castle image.

7   In the toolbox, select the Magic Wand tool (✎). In the tool options bar, enter **25** as Tolerance, select Anti-alias, and deselect Contiguous as well as All Layers. Then, click on the pink-colored background of the family picture. If necessary, hold down the Shift key and click to select any remaining unselected pink areas of the background.

8 Then, press the Delete key to delete the pink-colored background. Press Ctrl+D, or choose Select > Deselect to clear the selection.

9 Select the Zoom tool and zoom in on the lower left corner of the image to the area between the man's right hand and his sweater. The halo around that area, or fringe, is clearly visible.

10 Choose Enhance > Adjust Color > Defringe Layer. In the Defringe dialog box, enter **1** pixel for the width and click OK.

Notice how the fringe is eliminated.

Before applying the Defringe Layer command   *After applying the Defringe Layer command*

11   Double-click the Hand tool in the toolbox, or click the Fit Screen button in the tool options bar, to fit the image in the window and see your completed work.

12   (Optional) With the Layer 3 still selected in the Layers palette, select the Move tool in the toolbox. Then, drag the top right handle of the selection rectangle to enlarge the image of the family to become more the focus of the composition.

13   Click the Commit button (✔) near the lower right corner of the selection rectangle to accept the changes.

14   Choose File > Save to save your changes to the file. Then close the document and return to the Organizer.

Congratulations, you've completed the last exercise in this lesson. You've learned how to create a composite image by arranging layers and using a gradient layer as a clipping path. You also used the Defringe option, which eliminates the halo of edge pixels that remain from a deleted background.

Review

▶ ## Review questions

1 In the Photomerge dialog box, which tools can be used to fine-tune a panorama created from multiple images, and how do they work?

2 What does the Photomerge Group Shot tool do?

3 Why is it when you think you're finished with a transformation you cannot select another tool or perform other actions?

4 What is a fringe and how can you remove it?

▶ ## Review answers

1 The Select Image tool is used to select a specific image from within the merged panorama. This tool can also be used to drag an image so that it lines up more closely with the other images in the panorama. The Rotate Image tool is used to rotate merged images so that their content aligns seamlessly.

2 With the Photomerge Group Shot tool you can pick and choose the best parts of several pictures taken successively, and merge them together to form one perfect picture.

3 Photoshop Elements is waiting for you to confirm the transformation by clicking the Commit button, or by double-clicking inside the transformation boundary.

4 A fringe is that annoying bit of color that comes along when copying and pasting a part of an image or deleting a selected background. When the copied area is pasted onto another background color, or the selected background is deleted, you can see a fine halo around your selection. The Defringe Layer command (Enhance > Adjust Color > Defringe Layer) blends the halo away so you won't see a hard line.

11 | Advanced Editing Techniques

In this lesson, you will discover advanced editing techniques in Adobe Photoshop Elements. Using innovative tools that enable you to improve the quality and clarity of your images, you will learn to do the following:

- Use camera raw images from your digital camera.
- Save conversions in the DNG format.
- Use histograms to understand the characteristics of an image.
- Improving the quality of highlights and shadows.
- Resize and sharpen an image.
- Create effects with the filter gallery.
- Use the Cookie Cutter tool.

This lesson assumes that you are already familiar with the overall features of the Photoshop Elements work area, and recognize the two ways in which you can use Photoshop Elements: the Editor and the Organizer. If you need to learn more about these items, see Photoshop Elements Help and the Adobe Photoshop Elements Getting Started Guide. This lesson also builds on the skills and concepts covered in the earlier lessons.

Before you begin, make sure that you have correctly copied the Lessons folder from the CD in the back of this book onto your computer's hard disk. See "Copying the Classroom in a Book files" on page 3.

In this lesson, you will use the CIB Catalog you created earlier in the book. If necessary, open this catalog by choosing File > Catalog in Organizer mode, and then click Open.

What is a raw image?

Raw files are referred to as such because they are unprocessed by the digital camera or image scanner, unlike many of the other image file formats that you may recognize, such as JPEG or GIF.

Whether you are a professional or amateur photographer, it can be difficult to understand all the process settings on your digital camera. Processing images may degrade the quality of an image. One solution is to use the camera's raw setting. Raw images are derived directly from the camera's sensors, prior to any camera processing. Not all digital cameras offer the ability to shoot raw images, but many of the newer and more advanced cameras have this option.

Note: Depending upon the camera used to take the picture, raw file names have different extensions. Examples are Canon's .CRW and .CR2, Epson's .ERF, Fuji's .RAF, Kodak's .KDE and .DER, Minolta's .MRW, Olympus'.ORF, Pentax's .PTX and .PEF, Panasonic's .RAW, and the various flavors of Nikon's .NEF.
You can open a raw file in Photoshop Elements, process it, and save it—instead of relying on the camera to process the file. Working with camera raw files lets you adjust proper white balance, tonal range, contrast, color saturation, and sharpening, even after the image has been taken.

The benefits of a raw image

Raw images are high-quality image files that contain the maximum amount of original image data in a relatively small file size. Though larger than a compressed file, such as JPEG, raw images contain more data and use less space than a TIFF image.

Flexibility is another benefit, since many of the camera settings like sharpening, white balance, levels, and color adjustments can be undone when using Photoshop Elements. For instance, adjustments to exposure can be undone and recalculated based on the raw data. Also, because raw has 12 bits of available data, you are able to extract shadow and highlight detail that would have been lost in the 8 bits/channel JPEG or TIFF format.

Raw files provide an archival image format, much like a digital negative, but one that outlasts the usefulness and longevity of film. You can reprocess the file repeatedly to achieve the results you want. Photoshop Elements doesn't save your changes to the original raw file; rather, it saves the last setting you used to process it.

Workflow overview

To use raw files, you need to set your camera to save files in its own raw file format. Photoshop Elements can open raw files only from supported cameras. For an up-to-date list of supported cameras, please visit: http://www.adobe.com/products/photoshop/cameraraw.html.

After processing the raw image file with the Camera Raw window, you open the image in Photoshop Elements, where you can work with it in the same way as any other photo. Then, you can save the file in any format supported by Photoshop Elements, such as PSD.

Note: The RAW plug-in, which is used to open files from a digital camera, is updated over time as new cameras are supported. It may be necessary to replace your plug-in with the latest version from the www.adobe.com Web site.

Getting started

Before you start working, take a few moments to make sure that your work area is set up for these projects.

1   Start Adobe Photoshop Elements, and choose Edit in the Welcome screen.

2   Select the Full Edit mode.

3   Choose File > Open. Navigate to the Lesson11 folder and open the file 11_01.ORF, a raw image of a coastline generated from an Olympus digital camera.

4   Make sure that Preview is selected in the Camera Raw dialog box that comes up. *(See illustration on the next page.)*

The camera raw window provides the tools that you need to make adjustments to your image.
A. Zoom tool. **B.** Hand tool. **C.** White Balance tool. **D.** Crop tool. **E.** Straighten tool. **F.** Red Eye Removal.
G. Open Preferences dialog. **H.** Rotate counter-clockwise. **I.** Rotate clockwise. **J.** Histogram. **K.** White Balance
L. Zoom level. **M.** Bit Depth.

When you open a camera raw file, Photoshop Elements reads information in the file to see which model of camera created it, and then applies the appropriate camera settings to the image. You can save the current settings as the default for the camera that created the image, by clicking the palette menu—located in the top right corner of the palette—and selecting Save New Camera Raw Defaults. There you can also use the Photoshop Elements default settings for your camera by selecting Reset Camera Raw Defaults.

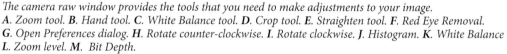

White balance controls for camera raw

A digital camera records the white balance at the time of exposure as metadata, which you can see when you open the file in the Camera Raw dialog box. This setting usually yields the correct color temperature. You can adjust it if the white balance is not quite right. The Adjust tab in the Photoshop Camera Raw dialog box includes the following three controls for correcting a color cast in your image:

White Balance

Sets the color balance of the image to reflect the lighting conditions under which the photo was taken. In some cases, choosing a white balance from the White Balance menu provides satisfactory results. In many cases, you may want to customize the white balance using the Temperature and Tint adjustments.

Temperature

Fine-tunes the white balance to a custom color temperature. Set the color temperature using the Kelvin color temperature scale. Move the slider to the left to correct a photo taken with light of a lower color temperature; the plug-in makes the image colors bluer to compensate for the lower color temperature (yellowish) of the ambient light. Conversely, move the slider to the right to correct a photo taken with a light of higher color temperature; the plug-in makes the image colors warmer (yellowish) to compensate for the higher color temperature (bluish) of the ambient light.

Tint

Fine-tunes the white balance to compensate for a green or magenta tint. Move the slider to the left (negative values) to add green to the photo; move it to the right (positive values) to add magenta.

To adjust the white balance quickly, select the White Balance tool, and then click an area in the preview image that should be a neutral gray or white. The Temperature and Tint sliders automatically adjust to make the selected color exactly neutral (if possible). If you're clicking whites, choose a highlight area that contains significant white detail rather than a specular highlight.

—From Photoshop Elements Help

Improving a camera raw image

There are two palettes in the Camera Raw window: Basic and Detail. The Basic palette gives you the controls to fine-tune options not available within the standard edit tools in Photoshop Elements. The Detail palette gives you controls to adjust sharpening and noise. You will use the controls on the Basic palette.

Note: Any correction you make to an image removes data from that image. Because you are working with much more information in a RAW file, any changes you make to the settings, such as exposure and white balance, will have less impact on the image than if you made drastic changes in a .PSD, TIFF, or JPEG file.

Adjusting the white balance

Presets are helpful if you need to accommodate for color casts introduced by poor lighting conditions when the image was taken. For example, if your camera was not set up correctly to deal with a sunny day, you can fix resulting problems in the image here by selecting Daylight from the White Balance menu.

1   In the White Balance menu, experiment by trying some of the presets available in the White Balance menu. Notice the change in the preview window as you select various White Balance presets. In the next section, you will discover why selecting the correct white balance is very important to the overall look of the image.

2   Select Cloudy as setting.

3   Before moving to the next part of this lesson where you'll use another way to improve the color balance, select As Shot from the White Balance menu.

By understanding what a neutral color is and how it works, you can easily remove color tints from an image in the Raw window. For this you need to locate a neutral color with the White Balance tool. Neutral colors include black, white, and gray.

4   Let's first zoom into the image by selecting the zoom level of 100% in the lower left corner of your Camera Raw dialog box.

5   Select the Hand tool (✋) from the tools at the top of the Camera Raw dialog box, and move into the center of the image where you see parts of the blue sky as well as the green of the grass.

6   Select the White Balance tool (✐) right next to the Hand tool.

7   Locate a neutral color in the image—a good example is a white or gray cloud—then use the White balance tool to click on it.

The White Balance is now at Custom, and the image is better balanced.

Working with tint control

Using the White Balance tool accurately removes any color cast, or tint, from an image. Depending upon the subject matter, you might want a slight, controlled color tint. In this instance, while the color temperature seems fine, you will fine-tune the green/ magenta balance of the image using the Tint controls.

1   Zoom out to view the entire picture by either clicking the Zoom tool or by selecting the zoom level of 33% (depending of the size of your computer screen) in the lower left corner of your Camera Raw dialog box.

2   Check out the Temperature slider in the Basic palette by dragging it to the left and to the right. You'll see how the colors of the image turn cooler (more blue), or warmer (more orange). While the original temperature of the image seems fine in this case, this slider could help you on other occasions, for toning down the warm glow in tungsten lighting, for example.

3   Go back to the original color temperature setting of 5350 by either dragging the slider or typing **5350** into the white box next to the Temperature slider.

4   Click the Tint slider. Either click and drag the slider slightly to the right, or type **+20** into the box.

Using the tone controls on a raw image

The Tonal controls are located under the White Balance controls in the raw window. In this next section, you'll find out how to use these controls to adjust for incorrect exposure, as well as check shadows, adjust brightness, contrast, and saturation.

Before you make adjustments, it is important that you understand these essential items:

Exposure is a measure of the amount of light in which a photo was taken. Underexposed digital photos are too dark; overexposed ones, too light. Use this control to recover the lighter, or blown-out information from overexposed images.

Recovery attempts to recover details from highlights. Camera Raw can reconstruct some details from areas in which one or two color channels are clipped to white or black. Clipping occurs when a pixel's color values are higher than the highest value or lower than the lowest value that can be represented in the image; overbright values are clipped to output white, and overdark values are clipped to output black.

Fill Light recovers details from shadows, without brightening blacks. Using Fill Light is similar to using the shadows portion of the Photoshop Shadow/Highlight filter.

Blacks specifies which input levels are mapped to black in the final image. Increasing Blacks expands the areas that are mapped to black. This sometimes creates the appearance of increased contrast in the image.

Brightness adjusts the brightness of the image, much as the Exposure slider does. However, instead of clipping the image in the highlights (areas that are completely white, no detail) or shadows (areas that are completely black, no detail), Brightness compresses the highlights and expands the shadows when you move the slider to the right. In general, use the Brightness slider to adjust the overall brightness after you set the white and black clipping points with the Exposure and Shadow sliders.

Contrast is the difference in brightness between light and dark areas of an image. Contrast determines the number of shades in the image. An image without contrast can appear "washed out." Use the Contrast slider to adjust the contrast of the midtones after setting the Exposure, Shadow, and Brightness values.

Clarity sharpens the definition of edges in the image. This process helps restore detail and sharpness that tonal adjustments may reduce.

Saturation is the purity, or strength, of a color. Also called chroma. A fully saturated color contains no gray. Saturation controls make colors more vivid (less black or white added) or more muted (more black or white added).

Vibrance adjusts the saturation so that clipping is minimized as colors approach full saturation, acting on all lower saturated colors but having less impact on higher saturated colors. Vibrance also prevents skin tones from becoming oversaturated.

You will check the Exposure of this image, and make adjustments based upon the lightness values in this image.

1   Hold down the Alt key while moving the Exposure slider. This shows the clipping (what parts of the image will be forced towards white) as you adjust the exposure. We moved the slider to +0.25.

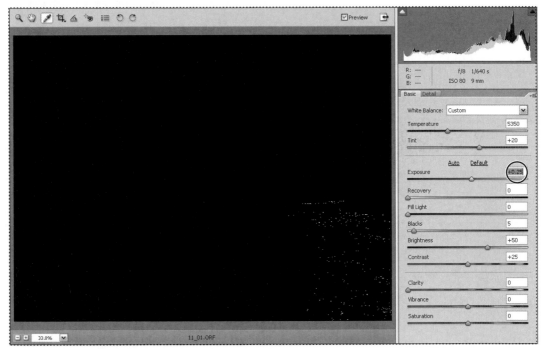

Hold down the Alt key while sliding the Exposure to see highlight clipping.

Now you will adjust the shadow.

2   Click and drag the Recovery slider to 60.

3 Hold down the Alt key and click and drag the Black slider. Any areas that appear in the clipping preview will be forced to a solid black. Release when only the deep areas of shadow in the image appear as black. We moved the slider to 10.

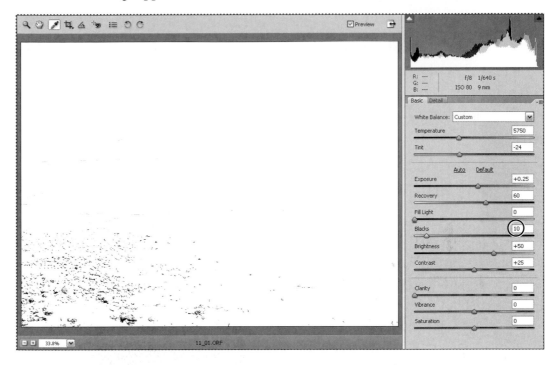

4 Select the Brightness slider and press the up arrow on the keyboard to increase the value to 64.

5 Select the Contrast slider and press the up arrow key on the keyboard to increase the value to +50.

6 Drag the Clarity slider to 28.

💡 *For an interesting effect, you can drag the Saturation slider all the way to the left to neutralize your image, essentially creating a three-color grayscale.*

The image, which was shot at a cloudy day and looked a little dull, now shows a larger range of detail and is more vivid in colors. *(See illustration on the next page.)*

Saving the image

You can reprocess this raw file repeatedly to achieve the results you want by saving in the DNG format. Photoshop Elements doesn't save your changes to the original raw file, but it saves the last settings you used to process it.

About the DNG format

Raw file formats are becoming common in digital photography. However, each camera manufacturer has its own proprietary raw format. This means that not every raw file can be read by software other than that provided with the camera. This may make it difficult to use these images in the future, as the camera manufacturers might not support these file formats indefinitely. Proprietary formats are also a problem if you want to use software other than that supplied by the camera manufacturers.

To help alleviate these problems, you can save raw images from Photoshop Elements in the DNG format, a publicly available archival format for raw files generated by digital cameras. The DNG format provides an open standard for files created by different camera models, and helps to ensure that you will be able to access your files in the future.

1 To convert and save the image, click Save Image In the 11_01.ORF raw dialog box. The Save Options dialog box appears.

2 Click the Select Folder button under Destination. In the Select Destination Folder dialog box, select your My CIB Work folder, and then click Select to return to the Save Options dialog box.

3 Under File Naming, leave Document Name selected in the menu on the left. Click the menu on the right and select 1 Digit Serial Number. This adds the number 1 following the name.

4   Click Save. The file, along with the present settings, will be saved in DNG format, which you can reprocess repeatedly.

5   Click Open Image in the right lower corner of the camera raw dialog box. Your image will open in the Editor window of Photoshop Elements Editor.

6   Choose File > Save. Navigate to the My CIB Work folder. Name the file **11_011_ Work.psd**. Make sure the selection in the Format menu is Photoshop, and then click Save.

7   Choose File > Close.

You've now experienced some of the pros of using camera raw formats. However, even though this format gives you more control and lets you edit your image in a non-destructive way, a lot of professionals choose not to use raw format. Raw files are usually considerably bigger than high-quality JPEGs and take much longer to be saved in your camera—quite a disadvantage for action shots or when you're taking a lot of pictures.

About histograms

Many of your images may be saved using a variety of formats, including JPEG, TIFF, or PSD. For these images, you will make your adjustments in the Full Editor. In this part of the lesson, you will discover how to use the histogram to understand what changes can be made to your images to improve their quality.

In this section, you will open an image that was shot with poor lighting and also has a slight magenta cast to it. Many digital cameras introduce a slight cast into images.

Using histograms

A histogram is a chart displaying the tonal ranges present in an image. The Histogram palette, located under Window > Histogram, shows whether the image contains enough detail in the shadows, midtones, and highlights. A histogram also helps you recognize where changes need to be made in the image.

Tonal corrections, such as lightening an image, remove information from the image. Excessive correction causes posterization, or banding in the image.

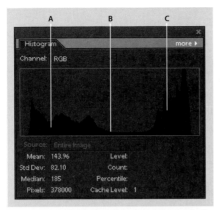

Histograms show detail and tonal range of an image.
A. Shadows. B. Midtones. C. Highlights.

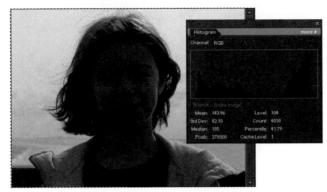

In this histogram low midtone levels are apparent.

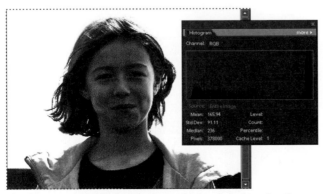

This histogram reveals that the image is already lacking detail.
Further corrections will degrade the image even more.

Understanding highlights and shadows

In the next part of this lesson, you will open an image and adjust the highlight and shadow. You will also make additional tonal corrections while keeping an eye on the Histogram palette.

1　In the Editor choose File > Open, then choose the file 11_02.psd in your Lesson 11 folder. It's the image of the girls from the previous page.

2　Choose File > Save As and navigate to the My CIB Work folder. Save the image as **11_02_Work.psd**. Click Save.

3　Make sure the Full Edit button is selected.

4　If it is not already visible, choose Window > Histogram.

5　In order to see your adjustments more directly, you can drag the Histogram palette out of the Palette bin and place it next to the face of the girl. Notice that the face is a little dark.

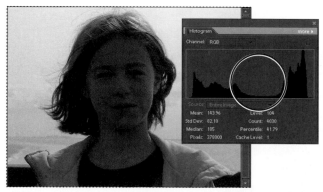

This image needs more information in the middle areas
and less information in the highlights and shadows.

According to the Histogram, there is a lack of data in the middle (midtones) of the image. You will adjust the tonal range of this image using Levels.

Adjusting levels

1   Choose Enhance > Adjust Lighting > Levels. The Levels dialog box appears.

You will use the shadow, midtone, and highlight sliders, as well as the Set Black Point, Set Gray Point, and Set White Point eyedroppers in this exercise. Although the range of midtones is the most problematic area of this image, it is important to first adjust the highlights and shadows.

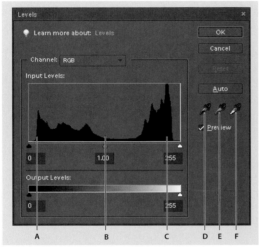

The Levels dialog box.
A. *Shadow.* **B**. *Midtone.* **C**. *Highlight.* **D**. *Set Black Point.*
E. *Set Gray Point.* **F**. *Set White Point.*

2   Double-click the Set White Point eyedropper.

This opens the Color Picker dialog box. In this dialog box, you will choose the highlight of your image. You will designate the lightest, non-specular point in the image as being the highlight.

Note: Specular highlights are the reflections of light on the surface of an object. The shiny spots on chrome or jewelry are typical examples. Pure white on an image is generally reserved for such specular highlights.

3 In the Color Picker dialog box, type **240** in the R (Red), G (Green), and B (Blue) text fields. This defines the light point of your image as a light gray, not pure white. Pure white is reserved for specular highlights in an image. Click OK in the Color Picker dialog box.

Double-click the Set White Point eyedropper to change the highlight value in the Color Picker.

4 Hold down the Alt key and click (don't drag!) the Highlight slider. The clipping preview for the highlight appears. The visible areas are the lightest areas of the image. Release the Alt key to see you've located the lightest portion of the sky in the image.

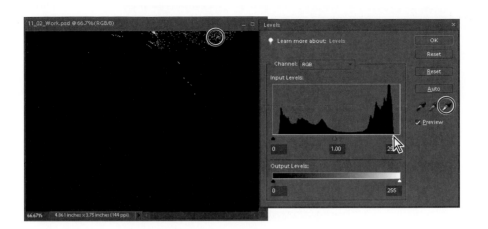

5   Select the Set White Point eyedropper and click the portion of your image that appeared in the clipping preview (the light part of the sky in the upper right corner). Notice how the image becomes slightly lighter, and small changes occur in the histogram.

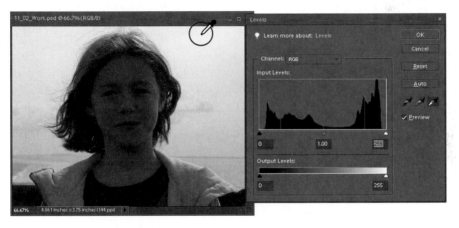

You will now set the Shadow area, using a slightly different technique.

6   Hold down the Alt key and click then drag the shadow slider to the right until the area below the left ear and the darkest areas of the image appear as dark spots in the shadow clipping preview. Then release the pointer and the Alt key. We adjusted the shadow input value to 16. *(See illustration on next page.)*

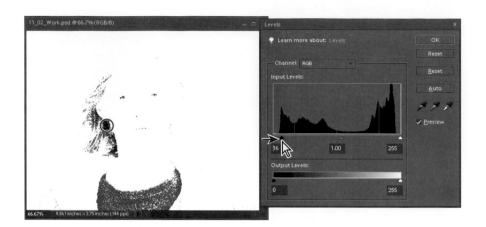

7   Visually lighten the midtone by selecting the midtone slider (the gray triangle in the center) and dragging it to the left. We adjusted our midtone to 1.50.

8   Notice the change in the Histogram as you make this change. Compare the old data (displayed in gray) to the data showing the correction that you are now making (displayed in black). Some gaps will be created, but you want to avoid creating very large gaps. Even if the image still looks fine on screen, large gaps may cause a loss of data that is visible when printed.

💡 *If you have easily identified neutrals in your image, you can remove a color cast quickly using the Set Gray Point dropper. Neutrals are areas in the image that contain only a gray tone, or an area containing as few colors as possible.*

9   Click OK to close the Levels dialog box. When the Adobe Photoshop Elements alert dialog box appears, click Yes. You should save the new target colors so you do not have to set the white point every time you use the Levels dialog box to make adjustments.

10   Select Edit > Undo Levels, or press Ctrl+Z to see how the image looked prior to changing the highlights and shadows. Choose Edit > Redo Levels, or Press Ctrl+Y to bring back the correction you made.

Before and after adjusting the levels.

Leave this image open for the next part of this lesson.

About unsharp mask

In this exercise, you will add some crispness to the image, and make it look much better when printed. Using the sharpening tools correctly can significantly improve an image.

You'll use the Unsharp mask feature in Photoshop Elements. How can something be unsharp and yet sharpen an image? The term unsharp mask has it roots in the print production industry: the technique was implemented by making an out-of-focus negative film—the unsharp mask—and then printing the original in a sandwich with this unsharp mask. This produced a halo around the edges of objects—optically giving them more definition.

💡 *If you are planning to resize an image, resize first, and then apply the Unsharp mask filter.*

1   With the 11_02_Work.psd image still open, choose Image > Resize > Image Size. This image needs to be made smaller, but with a higher resolution (pixels per inch).

2   If necessary, deselect the Resample Image check box at the bottom of the dialog box, and then type **300** in the Resolution text field. Notice that the width and height increments adjust. This method increases the resolution in the image without losing information.

Resolution means the fineness of detail you can see in an image. Measured in pixels per inch (ppi): the more pixels per inch, the greater the resolution. Generally, the higher the resolution of your image, the better the printed image.

3   Now select Resample Image, to reduce the height and width of the image and not affect the resolution. Click OK.

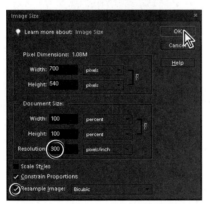

Always resize before sharpening an image.

4   Choose File > Save. Keep the file open for the next part of this lesson.

Applying the Unsharp Mask filter

Before applying any filter in Adobe Photoshop Elements, it is best to be at 100% view.

1   With the 11_face_work.psd image still open, choose View > Actual pixels.

2   Choose Enhance > Unsharp Mask. The Unsharp Mask dialog box appears.

The amount of unsharp masking you apply is determined by the subject matter. A portrait, such as this image, should be softer than an image of an object such as an automobile. The adjustments range from 100 to 500, with 500 being the sharpest.

3   Slide the Amount adjustment or type **100** in the Adjustment text field. Leave the Radius at 1 pixel.

4   Increase the Threshold only slightly to 2 pixels. Threshold is a key control in this dialog box, as it tells the filter what not to sharpen, In this case the value 2 tells it to not sharpen a pixel if it is within 2 shades of the pixel next to it.

💡 *Disable the preview in the Unsharp Mask window by clicking and holding down on the preview pane. When you release the mouse, the preview is enabled again. To reveal other portions of the image, click and drag in the preview pane.*

5   Click OK to close the Unsharp Mask dialog box.

Image with no sharpening.   *Image with unsharp mask applied.*

6   Choose File > Save, and then choose File > Close.

As you've seen, the Unsharp Mask filter does not mysteriously correct the focus of your image. It only gives the impression of crispness by increasing the contrast of the pixels. As a rule of thumb, the Unsharp Mask filter should be used only once as final step of your enhancements. When using it more often, you'll run into the risk of over sharpening your image and giving it a flaky, grainy look.

Note: *There are additional ways to adjust the sharpness of your photos: Choose Enhance > Auto Sharpen, or for even control Enhance > Adjust Sharpness.*

Creating effects using the filter gallery

You can experiment and apply interesting filter effects using the Filter Gallery, which enables you to apply multiple filters at the same time, as well as to re-arrange the order in which they affect the image. This gives you a lot of control over the way you want each filter to affect your image. Obviously, it's up to you to make the most out of these filters and to utilize them with intelligence. Have a look at "About Filters" in Photoshop Help to find out more about the different filters.

💡 *Not all filters are available from the Filter Gallery. Some are available only as individual commands from the Filter menu. Also, you cannot apply effects and layer styles from the Filter Gallery, as you can from the Effects palette.*

1   Select the file named 11_03.psd in your Lesson 11 folder, and then choose Edit > Go to Full Edit from the shortcuts bar.

2   Choose File > Save As, and navigate to the My CIB Work folder. Name the file **11_03_Work**. With Photoshop (*.PSD,*.PDD) selected as Format, click Save.

Because many filters use the active foreground and background colors to create effects, take a moment and set them now.

3   Click the Default Foreground and Background Color swatches at the bottom of the toolbar. This resets the default black foreground and white background colors.

4   Choose Filter > Filter Gallery. The Filter Gallery dialog box appears.

5   If necessary, use the menu in the lower left corner of the dialog box to set the magnification level at 100%. This view brings the image much closer so that the effects of the filters you apply are more obvious.

6 In the preview pane, click and hold the pointer to temporarily change the cursor into the hand tool (✋). While holding down the pointer, drag the image so that you can see the faces and hats of the two kids on the left in the preview pane.

Listed in the Filter Gallery are several categories of filters from which you can choose.

7 Expand the Brush Strokes category by clicking the arrow to the left of Brush Strokes.

8 Play around with the different sliders—the filter is applied in the preview image.

9   Click the New Effect layer (⬛) on the bottom right, and then select Film Grain from the Artistic filters. Both the Brush Strokes and Film Grain filters are applied simultaneously.

10   Using the Grain slider, change the value to 10, and then change the Highlight Area to 11 with the Highlight Area slider.

The Filter Gallery enables you to apply multiple filters simultaneously.

11   Click the New Effects layer again. If necessary, scroll down in the list of filters to be able to see the Stylize category. Expand the Stylize filters and select Glowing Edges. Again, your image has changed totally. *(See illustration on the next page.)*

   💡 *It's a good idea to apply filters to a duplicate layer of your image, as it is not possible to undo filters after you've saved your file. Press Ctrl+J to duplicate a layer.*

Experimenting with filters in the gallery

The Possibilities are endless for the effects that you might create in your image by combining different filters at different settings.

1   Experiment with the three filters that you have applied, turning them off or on by clicking the eye icon (👁) to the left of the filters.

2   Re-arrange the filters, for example by clicking and dragging the Film Grain filter to the top of the list.

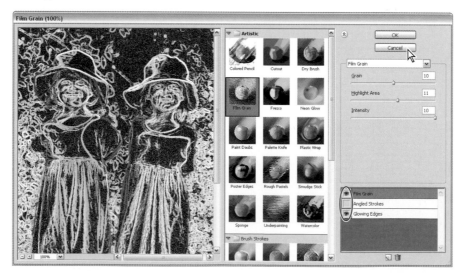

3   There is no need to apply the changes to the image. Click Cancel to close the Filter Gallery dialog box.

4   Keep the file open for the next part of the lesson.

Using the Cookie Cutter tool

The Cookie Cutter tool enables you to crop an image into a shape that you choose. Use the Cookie Cutter tool to clip a photo into a fun or interesting shape. In this part of the lesson, you'll add a heart shape to the image.

1   Select the Cookie Cutter tool from the toolbox.

2   Click the Shapes menu on the tool options bar to view a library of shapes from which you can choose. The visible selections are the default shapes.

💡 *There are many more cutout shapes available. Click the double-arrow in the upper right corner of the default shape selection to see a menu of 22 different categories from which you can choose.*

3   Double-click to select the shape named Heart Card (the shape of a heart), which fits well to the image.

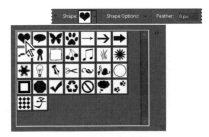

Note: The assigned name for each shape appears as a tooltip when you move the pointer over its thumbnail image.

4   Under Set Shape Options, select From Center.

Set Shape Options:

Unconstrained—Draws the shape to any size or dimension you'd like.

Defined Proportions—Keeps the height and width of the cropped shape in proportion.

Defined Size—Crops the photo to the exact size of the shape you choose.

Fixed Size—Specifies exact measurements for the finished shape.

From Center—Draws the shape from the center.

Enter a value for **Feather** to soften the edges of the finished shape.

Note: Feathering softens the edges of the cropped image so that the edges fade out and blend in with the background.

—From Adobe Photoshop Elements Help

5   Click and drag across the document window to create the shape on the image. While dragging, you can press the Shift key to keep the original aspect ratio of the shape, or press the Space key to reposition the shape. After releasing the pointer, you can use the handles on the selection rectangle to scale the object. Click inside the selection rectangle and drag to reposition it.

6   Click the Commit button (✔) near the lower right corner of the selection rectangle, or press Enter to finish cropping. If you want to cancel the cropping operation, click the Cancel button (✖), or press the Esc key.

7   Choose File > Save. Then, choose File > Close.

Congratulations, you have finished the lesson on advanced editing techniques in Adobe Photoshop Elements. You discovered how to take advantage of the raw features and adjust images using the histogram as a reference. You also found out how to create effects using the filter gallery and make cropping frames using the Cookie Cutter tool.

Learning more

We hope you've gained confidence, skill, and knowledge about using Photoshop Elements to bring out the best in your photographs. But this book is just the start. You can learn even more by studying the Photoshop Elements Help system, which is built into the application, by choosing Help > Photoshop Elements Help. Also, don't forget to look for tutorials, tips, and expert advice on the Adobe Web site, www.adobe.com.

Review

▶ Review questions

1   What is a camera raw image, and what are three benefits to using it?

2   What different methods can you use to control the white balance in the raw window?

3   What tools can you use in the Levels control to set highlight and shadow?

4   What is the Cookie Cutter tool used for?

▶ Review answers

1   A raw file is one that is unprocessed by a digital camera. Not all cameras create raw files.

Benefits include the following:

Flexibility—many of the camera settings, such as sharpening, white balance, levels and color adjustments can be undone when using Photoshop Elements.

Quality—because RAW has 12 bits of available data, you are able to extract shadow and highlight detail that would have been lost in an 8 bits/channel JPEG or TIFF format.

Archive—RAW files provide an archival image format, much like a digital negative, but one that outlasts the usefulness and longevity of film. You can reprocess the file repeatedly to achieve the results you want.

2   Three methods to control the White balance in the Raw window include:

•   Setting the white balance in an image automatically by using the White Balance eyedropper tool in the raw window. Selecting the White Balance eyedropper and clicking on a neutral automatically adjusts the Temperature and Tint sliders.

•   Selecting a preset white balance from the White Balance menu. Here you can choose from options that include corrections based upon variable such as whether the flash was used, it was a cloudy day, or the image was shot in fluorescent light, to name but a few.

•   Manually changing the Temperature and Tint adjustments by using the appropriate sliders under White Balance.

3   Use the Set Black Point and Set White Point eyedropper tools in the Levels dialog box.

• In the Levels dialog box you can double-click the Set Black Point and Set White Point tools to enter the desired values.

• To find the light point, you can Alt+drag the shadow or highlight sliders. This turns on the clipping preview.

• Select the darkest point with the Set Black Point tool by selecting the tool and clicking the darkest part of the image.

• Select the lightest point by using the Set White Point tool to click on the lightest part of the image.

4   The Cookie Cutter tool is used to clip an image in a variety of shapes. Use the default shapes in the Shape menu, or select from a variety of shape libraries available in the Shape dialog box palette.

Index

Production Notes

The *Adobe Photoshop Elements 6.0 Classroom in a Book* was created electronically using Adobe InDesign CS2. Additional art was produced using Adobe Illustrator CS2, Adobe Photoshop CS2, and Adobe Photoshop Elements 6.0.

Team credits

The following individuals contributed to the development of new and updated lessons for this edition of the *Adobe Photoshop Elements Classroom in a Book*:

Project coordinators, technical writers: Torsten Buck & Katrin Straub

Production: Manneken Pis Productions (www.manneken.com)

Copyediting & Proofreading: Ross Evans

Designer: Katrin Straub

Special thanks to Christine Yarrow.

Typefaces used

Set in the Adobe Minion Pro and Adobe Myriad Pro OpenType families of typefaces. More information about OpenType and Adobe fonts is available at Adobe.com.

Photo Credits

Photographic images and illustrations supplied by Katrin Straub, Torsten Buck, Marianne Barcellona, and Adobe Systems Incorporated. Photos are for use only with the lessons in the book.

Premiere Elements 4 Classroom in a Book

Premiere Elements 4 Classroom in a Book

ADOBE®
Premiere® Elements 4

CLASSROOM IN A BOOK®

www.adobepress.com

Contents

Getting Started

1   The World of Digital Video

2   A Quick Tour of Premiere Elements

3   Navigating the Workspace

4   Editing Video

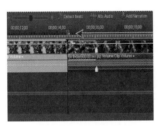

5 **Transitions**

6 **Working with Effects**

7 Working with Sound

8 Titles and Credits

9 Working with Movie Themes

10 Creating Menus

11   Sharing Movies

12 Working with Photoshop Elements

Getting Started

Adobe® Premiere® Elements 4.0 delivers video editing tools that balance power and versatility with ease of use. Premiere Elements 4.0 is ideal for home users, hobbyists, business users, and professional videographers—anyone who wants to produce high-quality movies and DVDs.

If you've used earlier versions of Premiere Elements, you'll find that this Classroom in a Book® covers the many new advanced skills and innovative features that Adobe Systems introduces in this version. If you're new to Adobe Premiere Elements, you'll learn the fundamental concepts and techniques that help you master this application.

About Classroom in a Book

Adobe Premiere Elements 4.0 Classroom in a Book is part of the official training series for Adobe graphics and publishing software developed by Adobe product experts. Each lesson in this book is made up of a series of self-paced projects that give you hands-on experience using Premiere Elements 4.0.

The *Adobe Premiere Elements 4.0 Classroom in a Book* includes a DVD attached to the inside back cover of this book. On the DVD you'll find all the files used for the lessons in this book.

Prerequisites

Before you begin working on the lessons in this book, make sure that you and your computer are ready.

Requirements on your computer

You'll need about 4.7 GB (4,700 MB) of free space on your hard disk for the lesson files and the work files you'll create.

Required skills

The lessons in this *Adobe Premiere Elements 4.0 Classroom in a Book* assume that you have a working knowledge of your computer and its operating system. This book does not teach the most basic and generic computer skills. If you can answer yes to the following questions, then you're probably well qualified to start working on the projects in these lessons. You will probably get most benefit from working on the lessons in the order in which they occur in the book.

• Do you know how to use the Microsoft Windows Start button and the Windows task bar? Can you open menus and submenus, and choose items from those menus?

• Do you know how to use My Computer, Windows Explorer, or Internet Explorer to find items stored in folders on your computer, or to browse the Internet?

• Are you comfortable using the mouse to move the cursor, select items, drag, and deselect? Have you used context menus, which open when you right-click items?

• When you have two or more open applications, do you know how to switch from one to another? Do you know how to switch to the Windows Desktop?

• Do you know how to open, close, and minimize individual windows? Can you move them to different locations on your screen? Can you resize a window by dragging?

• Can you scroll (vertically and horizontally) within a window to see contents that may not be visible in the displayed area?

• Are you familiar with the menus across the top of an application and how to use those menus?

• Have you used dialog boxes, such as the Print dialog box? Do you know how to click arrow icons to open a menu within a dialog box?

• Can you open, save, and close a file? Are you familiar with word processing tasks, such as typing, selecting words, backspacing, deleting, copying, pasting, and changing text?

• Do you know how to open and find information in Microsoft Windows Help?

If there are gaps in your mastery of these skills, see the Microsoft documentation for your version of Windows. Or, ask a computer-savvy friend or instructor for help.

Installing Adobe Premiere Elements 4.0

Adobe Premiere Elements 4.0 software (sold separately) is intended for installation on a computer running Windows Vista® or Windows® XP. For system requirements and complete instructions on installing the software, see the Premiere Elements 4.0 application CD and documentation.

Copying the Classroom in a Book files

The DVD attached to the inside back cover of this book includes a Lessons folder containing all the electronic files for the lessons in this book. Follow the instructions to copy the files from the DVD, and then keep all the lesson files on your computer until after you have finished all the lessons.

Note: *The videos on the DVD are practice files provided for your personal use in these lessons. You are not authorized to use these videos commercially, or to publish or distribute them in any form without written permission from Adobe Systems, Inc., or other copyright holders.*

Copying the Lessons files from the DVD

1   Insert the *Adobe Premiere Elements 4.0 Classroom in a Book* DVD into your DVD-ROM drive. If a message appears asking what you want Windows to do, select Open folder to view files using Windows Explorer, and click OK.

If no message appears, open My Computer and double-click the DVD icon to open it.

2   Locate the Lessons folder on the DVD and copy it to the My Documents folder on your computer. Inside the Lessons folder you will find individual folders containing project files needed for the completion of each lesson.

3   When your computer finishes copying the Lessons folder, remove the DVD from your DVD-ROM drive and put it away.

Additional resources

Adobe Premiere Elements 4.0 Classroom in a Book is not meant to replace documentation that comes with the program, nor is it designed to be a comprehensive reference for every feature in Premiere Elements 4.0. For additional information about program features, refer to any of these resources:

• Premiere Elements Help, which is built into the Adobe Premiere Elements 4.0 application. You can view it by choosing Help > Premiere Elements Help.

• Visit Adobe Elements Training Resources Web page (www.adobe.com/go/learn_pre_training), which you can view by choosing Help > Premiere Elements Help, and then following the link Adobe Premiere Elements Web site. You can also choose Help > Online Support for access to the support pages on the Adobe Web site. Both of these options require that you have Internet access.

• The Adobe Premiere Elements 4.0 User Guide, which is included either in the box with your copy of Adobe Premiere Elements 4.0 or in PDF format on the installation DVD for the application software. If you don't already have Adobe Reader (or if you don't have the latest version of Adobe Reader, formerly called Acrobat Reader) installed on your computer, you can download a free copy from the Adobe Web site (www.adobe.com).

Adobe certification

The Adobe Training and Certification Programs are designed to help Adobe customers improve and promote their product-proficiency skills. The Adobe Certified Expert (ACE) program is designed to recognize the high-level skills of expert users. Adobe Certified Training Providers (ACTP) use only Adobe Certified Experts to teach Adobe software classes. Available in either ACTP classrooms or on-site, the ACE program is the best way to master Adobe products. For Adobe Certified Training Programs information, visit the Partnering with Adobe Web site at http://partners.adobe.com.

1 | The World of Digital Video

This lesson describes the role of Premiere Elements in video production and introduces the following key concepts:

- Connecting a camera to your PC.
- Capturing video from a camera.
- Using USB 2.0 DV capture.
- Using the Media Downloader.
- Using audio in a video.
- Creating final video.

How Premiere Elements fits into video production

Adobe Premiere Elements includes all the tools necessary to acquire the footage from your Digital Video (DV) camera so that you can begin assembling movies. You import the source clips to your computer through a process called video capture. The process is simple: connect your DV camera to your computer, and then enable the Capture command in Adobe Premiere Elements. You can initiate a capture immediately after the program starts, or at any time while you are working. While Adobe Premiere Elements captures video, it also detects all the video's stops and pauses. Each separate recording sequence is captured as an individual scene. Each scene becomes a separate file, or clip, on your computer. Once you finish capturing video, the clips are added directly to your project, ready for editing.

The rest of this lesson describes fundamental concepts that affect video editing and other post-production tasks in Premiere Elements. All the concepts in this section and the specific Premiere Elements features that support them are described in more detail in the Adobe Premiere Elements User Guide.

Capturing video

Before you can edit your movie in Premiere Elements, all source clips must be instantly accessible from a hard disk, not from videotape. The files are transferred from your camera to the hard disk by video capture. You must have enough room on your hard disk to store all the clips you want to edit. To conserve space, capture only the clips you know you want to use.

Source clips exist in two main forms: Digital Media and Analog Media. Digital Media is already in a digital file format that a computer can read and process directly. Most newer camcorders digitize and save video in a digital format right inside the camera. Audio can also be recorded digitally; sound tracks are often provided digitally as well—on CD-ROM, for example. If the source video is analog, the capture process converts the video to digital format before storing the media on your hard disk.

The simplest way to capture DV is to connect a DV device, such as a camcorder or deck, to a computer with an Institute of Electrical and Electronic Engineers (IEEE, pronounced *I-triple-E*) 1394 port (also known as *FireWire* or *i.Link*). For more sophisticated capture tasks, a specialized DV capture card might be required. Premiere Elements supports a wide range of DV devices and capture cards, making it easy to capture DV source files.

Adobe Premiere Elements lets you add video, audio, graphics, and still images to your project from numerous sources. In addition to capturing footage, you can import image, video, and audio files stored on your computer's hard disk, card readers, mobile phones, DVDs, Blu-ray discs, CDs, digital cameras, other devices, or the Internet.

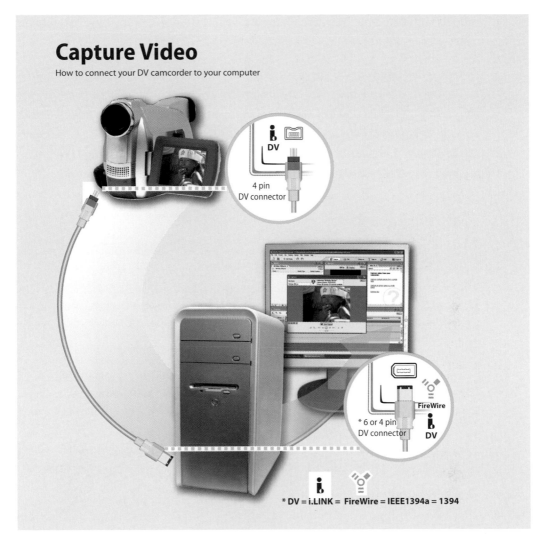

Capture Video

How to connect your DV camcorder to your computer

DV

4 pin
DV connector

FireWire

* 6 or 4 pin
DV connector

DV

* DV = i.LINK = FireWire = IEEE1394a = 1394

Firewire and USB 2.0 DV Capture

Traditionally, digital video has been imported from the camera to the PC using a
FireWire connection. In addition, Premiere Elements 4.0 enables you to import
full-quality video via a USB 2.0 cable. USB (Universal Serial Bus) products are often
peripherals such as printers, mice, and digital cameras. USB 2.0 is a high-speed transfer
protocol similar to IEEE 1394. Only certain cameras have USB 2.0 connections,
allowing you to transfer footage using a USB 2.0 cable. For an up-to-date list of camera

models supported by Premiere Elements, visit the Adobe Premiere Elements product page.

Note: Connecting your DV device using the IEEE 1394 port is recommended, and should be used whenever possible. Not all camcorders will work with USB. If you have problems connecting a USB 2.0 device, make sure that you are connecting to a USB 2.0 port and not a USB 1.0 port. Device control might not be available if you connect your device using the USB port. You cannot capture HDV (High Definition Video) using USB ports. See the Support Knowledgebase on www.adobe.com/support for more information.

System setup

Before you attempt video capture, make sure that your system is set up appropriately for working with digital video. Following are some general guidelines for ensuring a DV-capable system:

• Make sure that your computer has an IEEE 1394 (also known as *FireWire* or *i.Link*) port. This port may either be built into your computer, or available on a PCI or PC card (often referred to as *capture cards*) that you install yourself. The majority of computers manufactured now include onboard IEEE 1394 cards.

• Make sure that your hard disk is fast enough to capture and play back digital video. The speed at which digital video files transfer information, called the data transfer rate (often shortened to data rate), is 3.6 MB-per-second. The sustained (not peak) data transfer rate of your hard disk should meet or exceed this rate. To confirm the data transfer rate of your hard disk, see your computer or hard disk documentation.

• Make sure that you have sufficient disk space for the captured footage. Five minutes of digital video occupies about one gigabyte (1 GB) of hard disk space. The Capture panel in Adobe Premiere Elements indicates the duration of footage that you can capture based on the remaining space on your hard disk. Be certain beforehand that you will have sufficient space for the intended length of video capture. Also, some capture cards have size limits on digital video files from 2 GB and up. See your capture card documentation for information on file size limitations.

• Make sure that you periodically defragment your hard disk. Writing to a fragmented disk can cause disruptions in your hard disk's write speed, causing you to lose, or drop, frames as you capture. You can use the defragmentation utility included with Windows or purchase a third-party utility.

• The state of high-end video hardware changes rapidly; consult the manufacturer of your video-capture card for suggestions about appropriate video storage hardware.

Using the Capture panel

You use the Capture panel to capture DV and analog video and audio. To open and familiarize yourself with the Capture panel, you must create a new project.

Note: This exercise assumes that a DV camera has been successfully connected to your computer and that you have footage available to capture. If this is not the case, you can still open the Capture panel in order to review the interface; however, you will not be able to access all the controls.

1   Connect the DV camera to your computer.

2   Turn the camera on and set it to the playback mode, which may be labeled either VTR, VCR, or Play.

3   Launch Premiere Elements.

4   In the Welcome Screen, click the camera icon marked Capture Video.

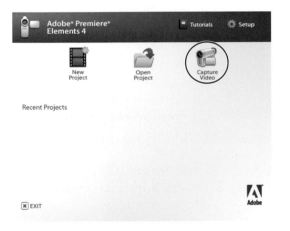

5   The New Project dialog box opens. In the Name field, enter the text **Test**. Click the Browse button and in the Browse For Folder dialog box, navigate to the Lessons folder. Select the Lesson01 folder as location to save your project file and the accompanying video files, and then click OK to close the Browse For Folder dialog box.

6   (Optional) To create a project using a different DV preset than specified when you installed the program, click the Change Settings button, and then select an appropriate preset in the Setup dialog box. You need to select a different preset to create projects in a different format (such as HDV), television standard (such as PAL), or frame aspect ration (such as widescreen).

7   Click OK to close the New Project dialog box.

Note: For best performance, you should consider using an additional internal or external hard disk dedicated solely for storage of your video projects and files.

The Capture workspace appears with the Capture panel open.

Note: If Premiere Elements is already open and you don't see the Welcome Screen, you can open the Capture dialog box by choosing File > Get Media from > Capture. Or, select Media (🖼) in the Edit tab of the Tasks panel, click Get Media, and then click the DV Camcorder, HDV Camcorder, Webcam button (🎥).

8   At the bottom of the Capture panel, click the Play button (▶) to begin playing your video footage in the preview area. Click the Stop button (■) to stop playback.

Premiere Elements uses a feature called device control, which lets you control your camera's basic functions (such as play, stop, and rewind) from within the Premiere Elements Capture panel, instead of using the controls on the device. You can use device control with devices connected through the IEEE 1394 port (recommended) or the USB port. If you connect using the USB port and do not get device control, use the IEEE 1394 port instead.

Note: *If your DV camera is connected but not turned on, your Capture panel will display Capture Device Offline in the status area. Although it is preferable to turn on your camera before launching Premiere Elements, in most cases turning on your camera at any point will bring it online.*

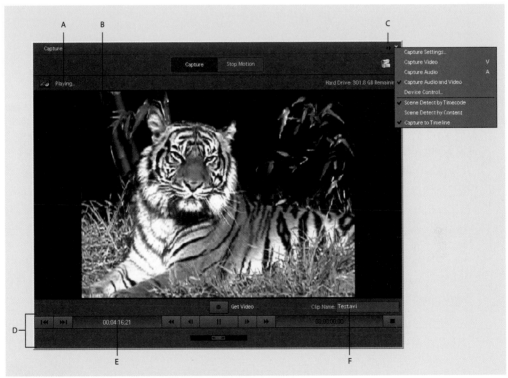

A. *Status area—Displays status information about your camera.*
B. *Preview area—Displays your current video as played through your camera.*
C. *Capture panel menu—Enables you to change the capture settings.*
D. *Device controls—Contains buttons used to directly control your camera.*
E. *Current position—Timecode display. Shows you the current frame of your video, measured in the format of hours;minutes;seconds;frames.*
F. *Clip name—Premiere uses the name of the project to name the AVI movie clips.*

Capturing video clips with Scene Detect

Some professional video programs require you to manually mark the area of your video that you would like to capture. Premiere Elements uses a feature called Scene Detect to capture a separate clip every time it detects a scene break in your original video. When you record digital video, your camera automatically lays down a time/date stamp. Every time you press Stop or Record, you create a new time/date stamp, which Premiere Elements marks as a new scene.

1   In the top right corner of the Capture panel, click the two black triangles to access the capture panel menu. Scene Detect by Timecode should be checked by default; if it is not, select it now.

Note: We suggest keeping Scene Detect—by Timecode or by Content—turned on. Turning off Scene Detect means you will have to manually capture each clip you wish to import into your project, using the device controls in the Capture panel. Scene Detect by Timecode, the default for DV, detects scene breaks using the tape's time/date stamp. Scene Detect by Content, the default for HDV (High Definition Video) and WDM (Windows Driver Model), detects breaks using changes in movie image content.

2   Using the device controls at the bottom of the Capture panel, locate the point in the video at which you would like to start capturing. For most new projects, this is often the beginning of the video.

3   Click the Get Video button (●) and Premiere Elements automatically captures each scene as an individual movie clip and adds it to your project.

Note: Footage must be captured in real time, thus a one-hour video will take one hour to capture. With Scene Detect enabled, you can capture an entire tape's worth of content into individual clips unattended, assuming you have sufficient free hard disk capacity. Remember that one hour of DV requires approximately 13 Gigabytes of storage space. Additionally, if you wish to stop capturing video at any point, you can click the Stop button to end the capture process. Any clips you have captured already remain in your project.

4   After you have captured three or four clips, click the Stop button (■) to stop capture.

Note: If you receive the error message "Recorder Error - frames are dropped during capture," or if you are having problems with the device control, it is likely that your hard disk is not keeping up with the transfer of video. Make sure you are capturing your video to the fastest hard disk available; for example, an external FireWire drive rather than a hard disk inside a laptop computer. For more information on this behavior, read "Components that affect video capture quality" on page 22.

5   After you have completed capturing your video, close the Capture panel by clicking the Close button (▨) in the upper right corner of the dialog box. Your captured clips appear in the Project view of the Tasks panel, as well as the Organizer. If necessary, click the Show All button at the top of the Organizer view to see all captured clips.

By default, Premiere Elements also places each clip in order into your Sceneline. You will learn more about the Sceneline (and its cousin, the Timeline) in Lesson 3, "Navigating the Workspace."

Capturing clips with device control

When capturing clips, device control refers to controlling the operation of a connected video deck or camera using the Premiere Elements interface, rather than using the controls on the connected device. You can use device control to capture video from frame-accurate analog or digital video decks, or cameras that support external device control. It's more convenient to simply use device control within Premiere Elements rather than alternating between the video editing software on your computer and the controls on your device.

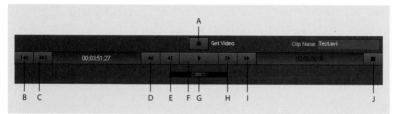

Capture panel controls:
A. *Get Video.* **B.** *Previous Scene.* **C.** *Next Scene.* **D.** *Rewind.* **E.** *Step Back (Left).*
F. *Play/Pause.* **G.** *Shuttle.* **H.** *Step Forward (Right).* **I.** *Fast Forward.* **J.** *Stop.*

Capturing clips with a noncontrollable device

If you don't have a controllable playback device, you can capture video from analog or DV camcorders or decks using the Capture panel. You can use this method to facilitate capture from an inexpensive consumer VCR or camcorder, for example.

1 Make sure that the deck or camera is properly connected to your computer. See your camera or deck documentation for more details on this process.

2 Choose File > Get Media from > Capture.

3 Use the controls on the deck or camcorder to move the video to a point several seconds before the frame where you want to begin capturing.

4 Click the Play button on the deck or camcorder, and then click the Get Video button (●) in the Capture panel.

5 When you reach the point where you want to stop recording, wait a few seconds to provide room for editing, and then click the Stop button (■) in the Capture panel to stop the capture process. You can also press the Escape (Esc) key to stop recording. Finally, press the Stop button on your deck or camcorder.

Capturing stop-motion and time-lapse video

Using stop-motion and time-lapse video, you can make inanimate objects appear to move, or show a flower grow and bloom in seconds. In this mode, you capture single video frames at widely spaced time intervals for later playback at normal frame rates.

You create stop-motion animations or time-lapse videos by using the Stop Motion button in the Capture panel. You can capture frames either from prerecorded tape or from a live camera feed. Stop-motion capture lets you manually select the frames you want to capture; Time Lapse capture automatically captures frames at set intervals. Using Time Lapse mode you can reduce a lengthy event, such as a sunset or a flower blooming, to a very short span.

Note: You cannot capture stop-motion video from an HDV source.

—From Premiere Elements Help

To capture stop-motion from a tape-based device

1 Connect your tape device to your computer and turn it on. Do one of the following:

• If capturing live from a camcorder, place the camcorder in Camera mode.

• If capturing from videotape, place the device in Play, VTR, or VCR mode.

2 In the Capture panel, click the Stop Motion button.

3 Click the Create New Stop Motion button in the middle of the Capture panel preview pane.

4 Click Grab Frame whenever the Capture panel displays a frame that you want to save to the hard disk. Each frame you grab will appear as a bmp file in the Project view with a sequential number in its filename.

5 Close the Capture panel and in the dialog box that appears, choose to save the still images as movie file:

See "Capture stop-motion and time-lapse video" in Premiere Elements Help for more information.

Capturing video or audio only

By default, Premiere Elements always captures the Video and Audio tracks of every clip. There may be times when you would like to capture only the video portion of your footage, or only the audio portion. This saves space on your hard disk. An example might be a musical performance in which the video portion is poorly lit, or for other reasons unusable. Or, perhaps you have a slide show from which you want to use only the video portion.

1   In the top right corner of the Capture panel (File > Get Media From > Capture), click the two black triangles to access the capture panel menu. From the list of options, select Capture Video if you want only the Video track. If you want just the Audio track, select the Capture Audio option. The Capture Audio and Video option is selected by default.

2   Click the Capture button and Premiere Elements captures only the Video or Audio, depending on which option you have chosen.

Converting analog video to digital video

Before DV camcorders were widely manufactured, most people used camcorders that recorded analog video onto VHS or 8-mm tapes, or other analog tape formats. To use video from analog sources in your Adobe Premiere Elements project, you must first convert (digitize) the footage to digital data, because Adobe Premiere Elements only accepts direct input from digital sources. To digitize your footage, you can use either your digital camcorder or a stand-alone device that performs analog-to-digital (AV DV) conversion.

You can perform a successful conversion using the following methods:

• Use your digital camcorder to output a digital signal from an analog input. Connect the analog source to input jacks on your digital camcorder and connect the digital camcorder to the computer. Not all digital camcorders support this method. See your camcorder documentation for more information.

• Use your digital camcorder to record footage from your analog source. Connect your analog source's output to the analog inputs on your digital camcorder. Then, record your analog footage to digital tape. When you are finished recording, Adobe Premiere Elements can then capture the footage from the digital camcorder. This is a very common procedure. See your camcorder documentation for more details on recording from analog sources.

• Use your computer's sound card, if it has a microphone input, to capture sound from a microphone.

• Use an AV DV converter to bridge the connection between your analog source and the computer. Connect the analog source to the converter and connect the converter to your computer. Adobe Premiere Elements then captures the digitized footage. AV DV converters are available in many larger consumer electronics stores.

Note: If you capture using an AV DV converter, you might need to capture without using device control.

—From Premiere Elements Help

Using the Media Downloader

The technology of digital video has come a long way in a short amount of time. Devices such as set-top recorders, mobile phones, digital cameras, DVDs, memory cards, and memory sticks are all potential sources for video. Premiere Elements provides a consistent method for importing video clips from these devices and media, allowing you to edit them in the Sceneline.

Most of the exercises in this book will use lessons and video clips found on the DVD in the back of this book. But for this exercise, you can use video that has been saved to your own DVD or another storage device, if you prefer.

Note: Premiere Elements will not import video from DVDs that are encrypted, such as most Hollywood DVD titles.

1 Place a DVD in your computer's DVD drive, or connect the DVD camcorder, mobile phone, or other device to your computer using the USB 2.0 port or IEEE 1394 port on your computer.

Note: To get files from a DV camcorder tape, use the Capture command.

2 Choose File > Get Media from > Media Downloader. Or, select Media (▣) in the Edit tab of the Tasks panel, click Get Media, and then click the DVD, Digital Camera, Mobile Phone, Hard Drive Camcorder, Card Reader button (▪).

The Media Downloader dialog box opens.

3 Under Source, choose the drive or device from the Get Media from menu. Then, click the Advanced Dialog button to switch to the advanced version of the Medial Downloader dialog box.

Adobe Premiere Elements Media Downloader (Standard Dialog):
A. Thumbnail image of first media file. B. Available drives and devices.
C. Location for saved files. D. Naming convention.
E. Advanced Dialog button. F. Get Media button. G. Cancel button.

The advanced version of the The Media Downloader dialog box opens. Thumbnails of all available files appear in the dialog box.

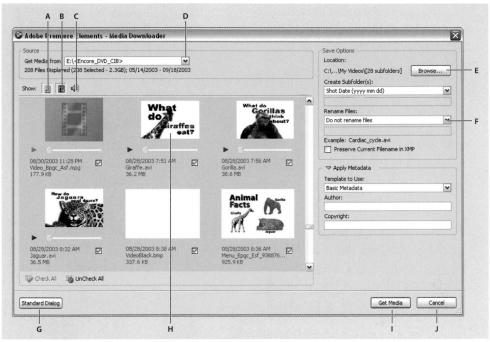

Adobe Premiere Elements Media Downloader (Advanced Dialog):
A. Show/hide image files. B. Show/hide video files. C. Show/hide audio files. D. Available drives and devices. E. Location for saved files. F. Naming convention. G. Standard Dialog button. H. Importable files. I. Get Media button. J. Cancel button.

Note: When you import a DVD using the Media Downloader, files for menus are distinguished from video files by the word Menu, as in Menu_Epgc_Esf_938876809.psd.

4   To show or hide specific file types, click the Show/Hide Images button (▣), Show/Hide Video button (▣), or Show/Hide Audio button (◀») located above the thumbnail area.

5   To preview a video file, click the black triangle in the lower left corner of the video thumbnail image.

6   To specify a location for the saved files, do one of the following:

•   To save files to the default location—inside the My Videos folder on our computer—leave the location unchanged.

•   To specify a new location for saving the files, click Browse and choose a folder, or click Make New Folder to create a new folder.

- Optionally, Premiere Elements saves imported files to one or more subfolders. Select Today's Date (yyyy mm dd) from the Create Subfolder(s) menu to save imported files in a subfolder—using today's date as name—in the location you have chosen.

- To create a single folder with a name of your choice, select Custom Name from the Create Subfolder(s) menu and enter the name of the folder in the text box that appears.

7 To rename the files to a consistent name within the folder, select an option other than Do not rename files from the Rename Files menu. When the files are added to the folder and to the Media panel, the file numbers are incremented by 001. For example, if you enter **animals** as Custom Name under Rename Files, the file names are changed to animals001.vob, animals002.vob, and so on.

8 In the thumbnail area, select individual files to add to the Media panel. A check mark below a file's thumbnail indicates that the file is selected. By default, all files are selected. Only selected files are imported. Click a check box to deselect it, thus excluding the related file from being imported.

9 Click Get Media. This transfers the media to the destination location, which is typically your hard disk. You can click Stop in the Progress dialog box at any time to stop the process.

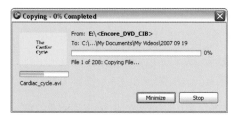

Files that you import using the Media Downloader are placed into the Media panel, and are accessible in the Project panel.

Note: If you don't intend to use all the files you add, you can delete them from the Project view. Deleting files from the Tasks panel doesn't delete them from your hard disk.

Using audio in a video

Audio can play an equally important role to imagery in telling your story. In Adobe Premiere Elements, you can adjust audio qualities. For example, you might combine dialogue clips with ambient background sounds and a musical sound track. Mixing audio in Premiere Elements can include any combination of the following tasks:

- Fading (increasing or decreasing) the volume levels of audio clips over time.

- Panning/balancing monophonic audio clips between the left and right stereo channels.

- Using audio effects to remove noise, enhance frequency response and dynamic range, sweeten the sound, or create interesting audio distortions such as reverb.

- Combining multiple audio tracks into a rich array of music, dialogue, and sound effects.

- Using the Audio Mixer to adjust the volume, balance, or both for the different audit tracks in your project.

- Adding narration directly in Premiere Elements using your computer's microphone.

When you import a video clip that contains audio, the audio track is linked to its video track so that they move together. Premiere Elements enables you to adjust and mix audio while you watch the corresponding video in real time.

Understanding digital audio

You hear sounds because your ear recognizes the variations in air pressure that create them. Analog audio reproduces sound variations by creating or reading variations in an electrical signal. Digital audio reproduces sound by sampling the sound pressure or signal level at a specified rate and converting that to a number.

The quality of digital audio depends on the sample rate and bit depth. The sample rate is how often the audio level is digitized. A 44.1 kHz sample rate is audio-CD quality, while CD-ROM or Internet audio often uses a sample rate of 22 kHz or below. The bit depth is the range of numbers used to describe an audio sample; 16 bits is audio-CD quality. Lower bit depths and sample rates are not suitable for high-fidelity audio, but may be acceptable (though noisy) for dialogue. The file size of an audio clip increases or decreases as you increase or decrease the sample rate or bit depth.

Creating final video

When you have finished editing and assembling your video project, Adobe Premiere Elements offers a variety of flexible output options.

You can record your production directly to DV or analog videotape by connecting your computer to a video camcorder or tape deck. If your camera or deck supports device control, you can automate the recording process, using timecode indications to selectively record portions of your program.

Export a digital video file for playback from a computer hard disk, removable cartridge, CD-ROM, or DVD. Adobe Premiere Elements exports Advanced Windows Media, RealMedia, AVI, QuickTime, and MPEG files; additional file formats may be available in Premiere Elements if they are provided with your video-capture card or third-party plug-in software.

About video and audio standards for DVDs

DVDs follow two basic television standards, NTSC or PAL. The standard varies from country to country. If you captured your video from a DV camera using the default settings for frame size and frame rate, it most likely conforms to one of the DVD TV standards. Although Adobe Premiere Elements can scale your video and adjust the frame rate if necessary, you will get the best results if your video matches the DVD TV standard to which you plan to export:

Television Standard	Areas commonly used	Frame Size	Frame Rate
NTSC	North America, parts of South America, Japan, Philippines, Taiwan, S. Korea, Guam, Myanmar, and others.	720 x 480	29.97 fps
PAL	Europe; Mid-East; parts of Asia, Africa, and South America, Australia, and others.	720 x 576	25 fps

Adobe Premiere Elements converts all imported audio to the bit depth and sample rate required by DVDs. If possible, it is best to record your audio using the DVD specifications:

- Audio bit depth: 16 bits.
- Audio sample rate: 48,000 Hz (48 kHz).

—From Premiere Elements Help

Components that affect video capture quality

Video capture requires a higher and more consistent level of computer performance—far more than you need to run general office software, and even more than you need to work with image editing software. Getting professional results depends upon the performance and capacity of all the components of your system working together to move frames from the video-capture card to the processor and hard disk. The ability of your computer to capture video depends upon the combined performance of the following components: video-capture card, hard disk, central processing unit, Codec, processing time, and data bus.

Video-capture card

You need to have a video-capture card installed—or the equivalent capability such as an IEEE 1394 port, built into your computer—to transfer video from a video camcorder, tape deck, or other video source to your computer's hard disk. A video-capture card is not the same as the video card that drives your computer monitor.

Hard disk

The hard disk stores the video clips you capture. The hard disk must be fast enough to store captured video frames as quickly as they arrive from the video card; otherwise, frames will be dropped as the disk falls behind. For capturing at the NTSC video standard of just under 30 frames per second, your hard disk should have an average (not minimum) access time of 10 milliseconds (ms) or less, and a sustained (not peak) data transfer rate of at least 3 MB per second—preferably around 6 MB per second. The access time is how fast a hard disk can retrieve specific data.

The key to optimal performance is to have as much contiguous defragmented free space as possible on your hard disk. Fragmented disks greatly inhibit access for real time preview, capture, or playback.

The data transfer rate is how fast the hard disk can move data to and from the rest of the computer. Due to factors such as system overhead, the actual data transfer rate for video capture is about half the data transfer rate of the drive. For best results, capture to a separate high-performance hard disk intended for use with video capture and editing.

Central processing unit (CPU)

Your computer's processor—such as an Intel® Core™ 2 Duo chip—handles general processing tasks in your computer. The CPU must be fast enough to process captured frames at the capture frame rate. A faster CPU—or multiple CPUs in one computer (multiprocessing)—is better. However, other system components must be fast enough to handle the CPU speed. Using a fast CPU with slow components is like driving a sports car in a traffic jam.

Codec (compressor/decompressor)

Most video-capture cards come with a compression chip that keeps the data rate within a level your computer can handle. If your video-capture hardware doesn't have a compression chip, you should perform capture using a fast, high-quality codec such as Motion JPEG. If you capture using a slow-compressing or lossy codec such as Cinepak, you'll drop frames or lose quality.

Processing time required by other software

If you capture video while several other programs are running (such as network connections, nonessential system enhancers, and screen savers), the other programs will probably interrupt the video capture with requests for processing time, causing dropped frames. Capture video while running as few drivers, extensions, and other programs as possible.

Data bus

Every computer has a data bus that connects system components and handles data transfer between them. Its speed determines how fast the computer can move video frames between the video-capture card, the processor, and the hard disk. If you purchased a high-end computer or a computer designed for video editing, the data bus speed is likely to be well matched to the other components. However, if you've upgraded an older computer with a video-capture card, a faster processor, or a hard disk, an older data bus may limit the speed benefits of the new components. Before upgrading components, review the documentation provided by the manufacturer of your computer to determine whether your data bus can take advantage of the speed of a component you want to add.

Review

▶ Review questions

1   How do you access the Capture panel in Premiere Elements?

2   Why is having a separate hard disk dedicated to video a good idea?

3   What is Scene Detect and how would you turn it on or off if you wanted to?

4   What is the Media Downloader and when would you use it?

5   What is device control?

▶ Review answers

1   In the Welcome Screen, click Capture Video. Or, choose File > Get Media from > Capture. Or, select Media in the Edit tab of the Tasks panel, click Get Media, and then click the DV Camcorder, HDV Camcorder, Webcam button.

2   Video files take up large amounts of space compared to standard office and image files. A hard disk stores the video clips you capture and must be fast enough to store your video frames. Additionally, the more free defragmented space you have on a hard disk, the better the performance of real time capture will be.

3   Scene Detect is Premiere Elements' ability during video capture to detect scene changes in your video (based on timecode or by content) and save each scene as an individual clip in your project. You can select or deselect Scene Detect by Timecode and Scene Detect by Content in the Capture panel menu.

4   The Media Downloader is a feature of Premiere Elements that enables you to access media from alternative sources of storage, such as non-commercial DVDs, memory cards, and certain electronic devices such as mobile phones. You can use this media in your Sceneline (or Timeline) as if it were captured directly from a camera.

5   Device control is the ability of Premiere Elements to control the basic functions of your digital video camera (such as play, stop, and rewind) through the interface in the Capture panel.

2 | A Quick Tour of Premiere Elements

Over the course of this tour, you will work on a very short home movie using video and audio clips provided on the DVD included with this *Adobe Premiere Elements 4.0 Classroom in a Book*. If you were producing this project with your own clips, you would be importing the video and audio from a digital video camera using the Capture function.

For more information on capturing video and audio, see the previous lesson, "The World of Digital Video."

Setting up a new project

To begin, you'll launch Adobe Premiere Elements and open the project file used for this lesson. Then, you'll review a final version of the movie you'll be creating.

1   Before you begin, make sure that you have correctly copied the Lesson02 folder from the DVD in the back of this book onto your computer's hard disk. See "Copying the Classroom in a Book files" on page 3.

2   Start Premiere Elements.

3 In the Welcome Screen, click the Open Project button.

4 In the Open Project dialog box, navigate to the Lesson02 folder you have copied to your hard disk, select the file Lesson02_Start.prel, and then click Open. If a dialog appears asking for the location of rendered files, click the Skip Previews button.

5 Your project file opens. Choose Window > Restore Workspace to ensure that you start the lesson with the default window layout. Choose Window > Show Docking Headers to see the docking headers of the Monitor, Tasks, and My Project panels.

Navigating the Premiere Elements workspace

If you are new to the program, a more complete introduction to the Adobe Premiere Elements Workspace can be found in the next lesson, Lesson 3, "Navigating the Workspace."

Viewing the completed movie before you start

To see what you'll be creating, you can take a look at the completed movie.

1   Select Media (🔳) in the Edit tab of the Tasks panel, click Project, and then double-click the file Lesson02_Movie.wmv to open the video in the Preview window.

2   In the Preview window, click the Play button (▶) to review the video you'll be building in this lesson. You can press the spacebar to stop the video at any time.

3   To close the Preview window when done previewing, click the Close button (▣) in the upper right corner of the Preview window.

💡 *To save space on your screen, you can make the docking headers disappear by choosing Window > Hide Docking Headers.*

Navigating in the Monitor panel

You can preview all or part of your movie in the Monitor panel. With a click of a button, jump to the beginning or end of the movie, or from one clip to the other.

1 In the Monitor panel, click the Play button (▶) to begin playing your project. Unlike the Lesson02_Movie.wmv movie you played in the Preview window, you are now viewing a Premiere Elements project made up of individual video clips. As the project is playing, notice the current-time indicator (♥) moving through the clip representations in the mini-timeline, located above the Play/Pause button in the Monitor panel.

2 Press the spacebar on your keyboard to stop the playback of the video. In the Monitor panel, click and drag the current-time indicator (♥) to reposition it.

3   Press the Home key on your keyboard to return the current-time indicator in the mini-timeline to the beginning of the project. Pressing the Home key is a keyboard shortcut you will be using often throughout this book.

Note: If pressing the Home key to jump to the beginning of the project doesn't work, make sure the Monitor panel is active by clicking its docking header.

4   Click the Go to Next Edit Point button (⏩) or press the Page Down key on your keyboard, to jump to the beginning of the second clip. Press the Page Down key a few more times until you reach the end of the movie. Click the Go to Previous Edit Point button (⏪) or press the Page Up key to navigate backwards one clip at the time. Finally, press the Home key to return to the beginning of the movie.

Deleting clips from the movie

When you shoot footage with your camera, you almost always produce much more material than you'll actually use in your video program. Premiere Elements allows you to easily remove unwanted clips, and shorten any clips that are too long.

1   Press the Home key to jump to the beginning of the project in the Monitor panel, and then click the Go to Next Edit Point button (⏩) three times to position the current-time indicator at the beginning of the peacock.avi clip. You are now going to delete this clip from the movie.

2   Press the spacebar on your keyboard to start playback of the clip. After a few seconds, press the spacebar again to stop playback. If Sceneline view is not currently selected in the My Project panel, click the Sceneline button now. The clip currently visible in the Monitor panel is highlighted in the Sceneline, indicated by a blue frame around the clip thumbnail.

3 In the Monitor panel, right-click the peacock.avi clip representation in the mini-timeline, and then choose Delete from the context menu. Or, make sure the Monitor panel is active, and then choose Edit > Delete and Close Gap.

The peacock.avi clip will be deleted from the movie. In the Sceneline, notice how the clips following the deleted clip move to the left to close the gap. This is called *ripple deletion*.

Note: Deleting a clip from the movie does not delete it from the project. The clip is still available in the Project view for reuse.

Trimming clips

Although Premiere Elements conveniently places the video clips into your Sceneline when you import video, you will most likely want to shorten clips in order to remove uninteresting portions, and to make your video more engaging. To create scenes, cuts, and transitions, you'll need to trim your clips to remove the parts you don't need. When Sceneline view is selected in the My Project panel, you can trim clips in the mini-timeline of the Monitor panel. Alternatively, you can trim clips in the Timeline view of the My Projects panel. You will use both techniques in the following exercise.

1   In the Sceneline view of the My Project panel, click the second clip from the start—the tiger 2.avi clip—to select it. The first frame of the clip is displayed in the Monitor panel and the clip representation is centered in the mini-timeline underneath. You are going to trim a few seconds from the beginning of the clip.

2   In the Monitor panel, click the In point handle (▶), located on the left side of the clip representation in the mini-timeline, and then drag it to the right. While dragging, notice how the Monitor panel displays the last frame of the previous clip next to the new first frame of the current clip. Release the pointer when the current time in the lower left corner of the Monitor panel reads +00;00;03;20 (give or take a frame).

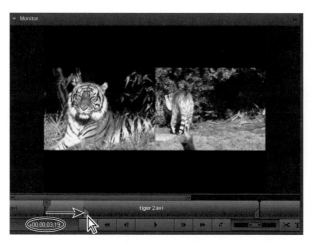

3   Press the Home key, and then press the spacebar to start playback of the video from the start. At the end of the first clip, notice how the second clip now starts at the newly defined In point. Press the spacebar again to stop playback.

You've successfully trimmed the start of the second clip in the Monitor panel. Next, you'll trim the end of the third clip in the Timeline view of the My Project panel.

4　In the Sceneline view of the My Project panel, click the third clip from the start—the rhino.avi clip—to select it. Then, click the Timeline button in the upper left corner of the My Project panel to switch to Timeline view. If necessary, use the scrollbar at the right side of the Timeline view to scroll to the Video 1 track.

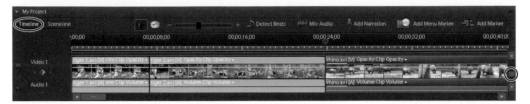

5　In the Timeline of the My Project panel, drag the current-time indicator all the way to the end of the rhino.avi clip, and then slowly backwards to the point just before the rhinoceros disappears from view. Then, release the pointer. Use the left and right arrow keys on your keyboard and the current time information in the lower left corner of the Monitor panel to position the current-time indicator at 00;01;10;00.

6　If necessary, scroll the Timeline view using the scrollbar at the bottom so that you can see the location of the current-time indicator and the end the rhino.avi clip at the same time. Place your cursor at the end of the rhino.avi clip in the Video 1 track. Your cursor should change to the Trim Out tool, a double black arrow with a red bracket pointing to the left (⬌). Pay close attention to your cursor; it needs to be on the left side of the edit line.

7　Making sure the red bracket is pointing to the left, click and then drag the end of the clip to the left, allowing the end of the clip to snap to your current-time indicator. Then, release the pointer. The clip is trimmed and the following clips automatically shift to the left to fill the gap.

8　Move the current-time indicator a few seconds to the left, and then press the spacebar to view the edited clip. You trimmed the final seconds of the clip, so now the scene ends before the rhinoceros disappears from view.

Deleting sections of a clip

In addition to trimming clips by shortening them, you can also split a clip and cut out sections of your video. In this exercise, you will delete a large section in the middle of the rhino.avi clip.

1   Click the Sceneline button in the upper left corner of the My Project panel to switch to Sceneline view.

2   In the Sceneline view of the My Project panel, click the third clip from the start—the rhino.avi clip—to select it.

3   In the Monitor panel, move the current-time indicator to the 31 second point (00;00;31;00). This is the starting point of the section to be cut.

4   In the Monitor panel, click the Split Clip button (✄) to split the clip into two sections.

Notice that there are now two rhino.avi clips in the Sceneline and each one has its own clip representations in the mini-timeline of the Monitor panel. You can work with these two segments as if they were two completely independent clips.

> 💡 *Splitting a clip into sections can also be used to apply different effects to different parts of a clip. One example would be speeding up the first part of a clip while leaving the second part at normal speed. You will learn more about applying effects later in this lesson.*

5   Position the current-time indicator at 51 seconds, 10 frames (00;00;51;10). This is the end point of the section to be cut. Choose Timeline > Split Clip, the menu command equivalent to clicking the Split Clip button in the Monitor panel. This command also has a keyboard shortcut, Ctrl-K.

6   In the Sceneline of the My Project panel, click the middle clip of the now three rhino.avi clips to select it. In the Monitor panel, right-click its clip representation in the mini-timeline, and then choose Delete from the context menu.

💡 *With the clip to be deleted selected in the Sceneline, you can press the Backspace key as the keyboard shortcut to delete the clip and close the gap.*

7   Press the Home key, and then press the spacebar to review your edited movie. Wait until the movie ends or press the spacebar to stop playback when you're done reviewing.

8   Choose File > Save to save your changes.

Note: *With the Auto Save option enabled in the Preference panel (Edit > Preferences > Auto Save), Premiere Elements will automatically produce a series of backup copies at specified time intervals in the Adobe Premiere Elements Auto-Save folder.*

Adding sound to the Soundtrack

Sound is an important part of video projects. Premiere Elements supports multiple audio tracks, allowing you to add music and sound effects to enhance your videos.

1   The sound track for this video has already been added to the Project view for you. To view the file, select Media (🖼) in the Edit tab of the Tasks panel, click Project, and then scroll down in the Project view, if necessary, to locate the file soundtrack.wav.

2   If not already selected, select Sceneline view in the My Project panel. The Soundtrack (♪) is the lower of the two audio tracks visible in the My Project panel.

3   Click and drag the soundtrack.wav file from the Project view into the Soundtrack of the Sceneline. Align the beginning of the soundtrack clip with the beginning of the first video clip. If you accidentally place the soundtrack clip too far to the right, you can click and drag it into position after it has been placed in the Soundtrack.

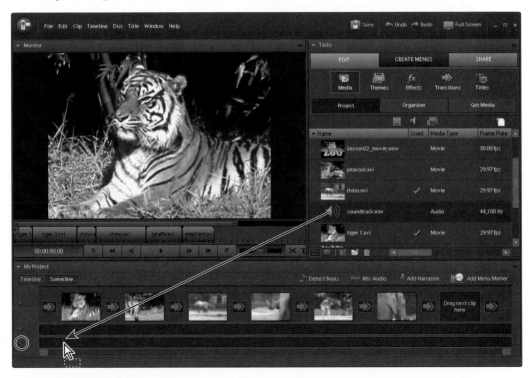

4   Press the Home key, and then press the spacebar to play your video with the music.

5   Choose File > Save to save your changes.

Applying and customizing transitions

Adding effects and transitions in Premiere Elements is as simple as dragging and dropping. In the following steps you will be adding a fancy 3D Motion transition between the two tiger clips and a basic dissolve between the two rhino clips.

1 Select Transitions (➡) in the Edit tab of the Tasks panel. Click the search box next to the magnifying glass icon (🔍), and then type the words **cube spin**. As you type, Premiere Elements automatically searches for and finds the Cube Spin transition in the 3D Motion category of the Video Transitions folder.

2 To add the transition, click and drag the Cube Spin transition from the Transitions view onto the transition rectangle (➡) between the tiger 1.avi and the tiger 2.avi clip in the Sceneline.

3 To view the transition, select the tiger 1.avi clip in the Sceneline, and then press the spacebar to play the video. Press the spacebar again to stop playback after viewing the transition.

The second clip comes from the left side into the picture, pushing the first clip out to the right. For these two clips it would look better if the cube spin went the other direction.

4 To customize the transition, click to select the Cube Spin transition in the Sceneline, and then click the Edit Transition button in the lower left corner of the Transitions view, or choose Window > Properties. To reverse the direction of the Cube Spin effect, scroll down in the Properties panel, if necessary, and then click to select the Reverse check box. Click Done to close the Properties panel.

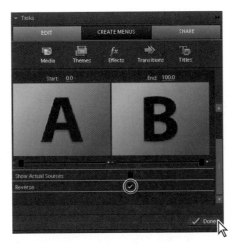

5 Review the new transition effect, as you did in step 3.

The customized transition works better for the flow of the movie.

6   With Transitions selected in the Edit tab of the Tasks panel, select the cube spin text in the search box next to the magnifying glass icon, and then type **cross dissolve**.

7   Click and drag the Cross Dissolve transition from the Transitions view onto the transition rectangle between the two rhino.avi clip sections in the Sceneline.

8   Select the first rhino.avi clip in the Sceneline, move the current-time indicator towards the end of the clip in the Monitor panel, and then press the spacebar to play the video. Press the spacebar again to stop playback after viewing the transition.

9   Choose File > Save to save your changes.

Using the Auto Levels effect

In addition to transitions, Premiere Elements offers numerous effects to improve or stylize your video. In this particular example, you will use the Auto Levels effect to improve the image quality of the elephant.avi clip.

1   If necessary, scroll to the end of the Sceneline in the My Project panel to be able to see the elephant.avi clip. Click to select the clip.

2   Select Effects (*fx*) in the Edit tab of the Tasks panel.

3 In the Effects view, select Video Effects from the effect type menu and Adjust from the effect category menu.

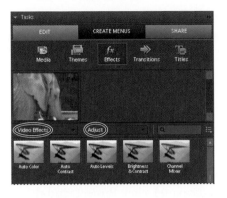

4 With the elephant.avi clip visible in the Monitor panel, click and drag the Auto Levels effect from the Effects view to the Monitor. Or, select the Auto Levels effect, and then click the Apply button (✔) in the lower right corner of the Effects view. This will apply the effect to the clip. You should notice an immediate change in the image in the Monitor panel.

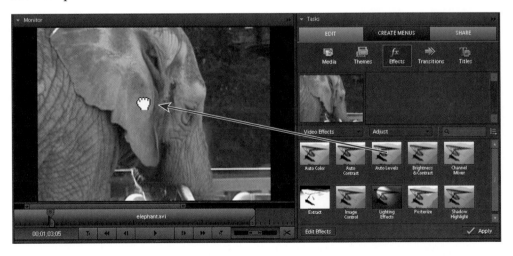

5 Choose Edit > Undo to view the original image. Choose Edit > Redo to reapply the Auto Levels effect.

6 Choose File > Save to save your changes.

Superimposing a title and an image

You will now add a title graphic and text to your video. The title graphic contains transparent areas enabling you to see parts of the video beneath the image. The Type tool in the Monitor panel enables you to create beginning and end titles, along with scrolling credits. In this exercise, you will add a simple, non-moving line of text to the title graphic.

1   In the My Project panel, click to select the first clip from the beginning in the Sceneline. This will reset the current-time indicator to the beginning of the movie. The time display in the lower left corner of the Monitor panel should read 00;00;00;00. This ensures that your title appears at the very beginning of your video.

2   Select Media (🖼) in the Edit tab of the Tasks panel, click Project, and then click to select the Show Still Images button (🖼) to only display media of type Still Image. Click to select the file title_frame.tif.

This particular title_frame.tif image contains transparent areas (defined by an image mask in the alpha channel), which will allow video beneath it to show through.

3   To place the title graphic over the video clip (as opposed to placing it sequentially before or after the video clip), hold down the Shift key on your keyboard, and then drag and drop the title_frame.tif image from the Project view onto the Monitor. When you release the pointer, choose Place on Top from the menu that appears.

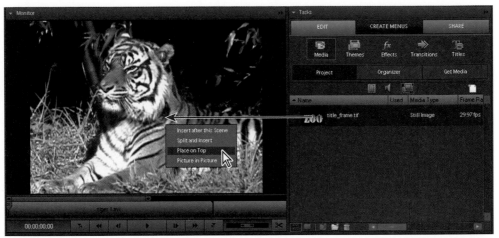

Hold down the Shift key while dragging the title image onto the Monitor, and then choose Place on Top.

4 Click the Play button in the Monitor panel to watch the beginning of the movie with the added title image. When done reviewing, press the spacebar followed by the Home key to stop playback and to return to the beginning of the movie.

The tiger 1.avi video clip can be seen through the transparent areas in the title graphic. After 5 seconds (or the Still Image Default Duration, which can be defined in the Preferences > General panel) the placed title graphic will disappear, leaving only the tiger 1.avi video clip playing.

In the next steps, you'll add a line of text across the top of the title graphic. With Adobe Elements' powerful titling tools you can use any font installed on your computer when creating your video titles. You can have your text run horizontally or vertically, add color or drop shadows, or stretch and shrink the text to your liking. Just be careful not to get too carried away. For a quick start, choose from the included templates and preset text styles. In this exercise, you'll add a simple line of text, using the default text style.

5 Make sure the current-time indicator is located at the beginning of the movie. Then, choose Title > New Title > Default Still.

Adobe Premiere Elements places default text in the Monitor panel and puts it in title-editing mode. *(See illustration on the next page.)*

6 Using the Horizontal Type tool (**T**), highlight the default text in the Monitor panel, and then type **Presenting:**.

7 Select the Selection tool (▲), and then click and drag the text towards the upper left corner of the Monitor.

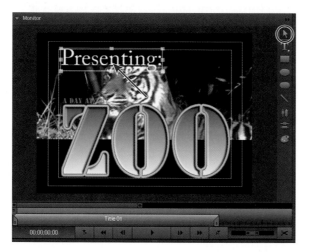

8 (Optional) Select a different Style or change the Style Properties in the Properties palette. You might have to reposition the text after changing the type style.

Note: You will be learning more about creating titles—including using title templates—in Lesson 8, "Titles and Credits."

9 Click Done (✓) in the lower right corner of the Project view to exit the Monitor's title-editing mode. Choose File > Save to save your changes.

Creating menus for DVDs or Blu-ray discs

Once you have finished your movie, Premiere Elements offers several ways to share it. One of the most powerful features is the ability to create DVDs or Blu-ray discs complete with disc menus directly in Premiere Elements.

1 In the Tasks panel, select the Create Menus tab, and then select Templates (⚇).

The Create Menus workspace appears with the Templates view open in the Tasks panel on the right and the Disk Layout panel replacing the Monitor panel on the left. You can select a disk menu template for your movie simply by dragging and dropping it from the Templates view onto the Disk Layout panel. Usually you add menu markers before you select a template, but you don't have to do it in this order. You can add, move, or delete menu markers even after choosing a template. Adobe Premiere Elements dynamically adjusts the disk menus to match the markers, adding or deleting buttons as necessary.

2 In the Templates view, choose Entertainment from the category menu, and then select the Countdown template from the menu next to it. Drag and drop the Main Menu template onto the Disc Layout panel.

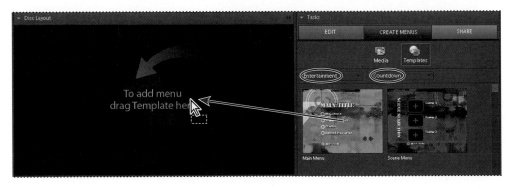

3 Click No in the Missing Menu Markers dialog box to not create menu markers automatically. You'll be adding menu markers manually in the following steps.

4 In the Sceneline, click to select the first video clip. Then, click the Add Menu Marker button (▣) to open the Menu Marker dialog box.

5 Type **Tiger** in the Name field of the Menu Marker dialog box, and then click OK.

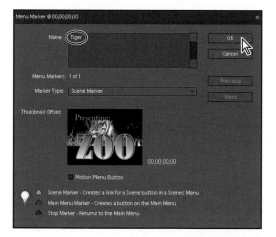

This creates the first chapter point that allows people to jump to this section using their remote control.

6 Create three more DVD markers: At the beginnings of the first rhino.avi clip, the giraffe.avi clip, and the elephant.avi clip, naming the menu markers **Rhinoceros**,

Giraffe, and **Elephant**, respectively. As you add menu markers, Premiere Elements automatically adds images, buttons, links and pages to the Disc Layout as needed.

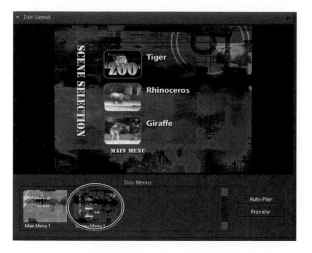

7   Under Disk Menus in the Disc Layout panel, select the Main Menu 1 thumbnail. If necessary, use the scroll bar to scroll to the thumbnail you want to view, or resize the panel so that the thumbnails are displayed side by side.

8   In the Disc Layout panel, double-click the main title to open the Change Text dialog box. In the Change Text dialog box, type **A day at the Zoo** under Change Text, and then click OK.

9   (Optional) Click and drag the main title text to reposition it. Resize the text by changing the text size in the Properties panel.

10 Under Disc Menus in the Disc Layout panel, select the Scenes Menu 1 thumbnail. Double-click the first scene thumbnail, the Tiger scene, to open the Menu Marker dialog box.

11 In the Menu Marker dialog box, change the Thumbnail Offset by clicking the current-time display to the lower right of the thumbnail image and dragging to the right. Release the pointer when the current-time display reads 00;00;05;00 (just after the superimposed title graphic disappears in the video clip). This thumbnail is more suitable as the scene selection button image.

12 Click OK to close the Menu Marker dialog box. In the Disc Layout panel, the thumbnail has been updated to the new image.

13 (Optional) Change the Thumbnail Offset for the remaining scene thumbnails to select more suitable images from within each clip.

Note: *With the scene marker button selected in the Disk Layout panel, you can also change the Thumbnail Offset (In Point) in the Properties panel under Menu.*

Previewing a disc menu

Premiere Elements allows you to preview your disc menu before burning a DVD or Blu-ray disc. You want to make sure all your buttons work and that the image thumbnails are accurate.

1   In the Disc Layout panel, click the Preview button.

2   In the main menu, place your cursor over the menu name for Scene Selection, and then click once to jump to the first Scene Selection page.

3   Use the controls at the bottom of the Preview Disc window to imitate pushing the controls on a standard remote control. Navigate to the **Rhinoceros** scene.

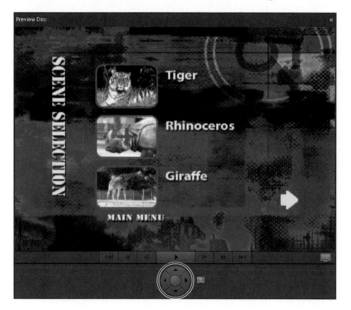

4   Press the Play button (▶) and the Rhinoceros scene begins to play. To return to the main menu, press the Main Menu button (▦).

5   Close the Disc Preview window by clicking the Close button (✖).

6   Choose File > Save to save your changes.

If you want to burn a DVD or Blu-ray disc you must have both an appropriate recorder attached to your PC and blank media onto which you can record your movies. It is recommended that you use rewriteable media for test projects. You will learn more about creating menus and burning DVDs and Blu-ray discs in Lesson 10, "Creating Menus."

Output to Web

In addition to burning DVDs or Blu-ray discs, Premiere Elements enables you to output your project in a format suitable for display on the Internet. You can have Premiere Elements convert the movie and upload it directly to a file server such as YouTube. Or, export the movie in a file format of you choice to your computer's hard disk, and then share the movie on the Web or send it as an E-Mail attachment. A movie exported in a format to be sent over the Internet is much lower in resolution and smaller in file size than a movie placed on a DVD or Blu-ray disc. Premiere Elements makes it easy to select an appropriate file size using presets.

1   Click the Share tab in the Tasks panel, and then click the Personal Computer button (▥).

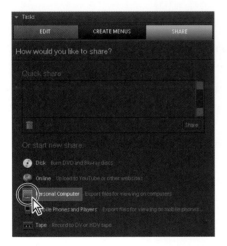

2   In the PC: Choose location and settings panel, choose Windows Media from the list of available output formats, and then select 128K Dual ISDN from the Preset menu. This will create a file with dimensions of 320 x 240, a size suitable for downloading over a fast Internet connection and for playback on other PCs. Enter **Lesson02_Export.wmv** as File Name. Click the Browse button next to Save in, and in the Browser for Folder dialog box, navigate to and select the Lesson02 folder. Then, click Save.

Premiere Elements starts making the movie, displaying a status bar that provides an estimate for the amount of time it will take to render the movie. The render or output time depends on the capabilities of your computer. On most systems, Premiere Elements should finish making the movie within a few minutes. You can cancel the process at any time by clicking the Cancel button. Otherwise, click Done when you see the Save Complete message.

3   Your movie will be saved in the location you chose in step 2. Double-clicking this file opens it in the program you have previously chosen to display movie files.

4   When you are done viewing the movie, switch back to Premiere Elements, and then choose File > Save and File > Close to save and close your project.

Congratulations, you have finished the Tour! You have learned how open projects and preview video clips. You edited clips in various ways, using the Monitor and the My Project panel. You know now how to delete entire clips from the movie and how to split a clip into sections. You've added sound, transitions, and effects to the movie. You created a disc menu starting from a template and customizing it to suit your needs. And finally, you exported the movie in the Windows Media format, suitable for presenting on a Web page. This lesson provided just an overview of Premiere Elements; the remaining lessons will go into more detail.

Review

▶ **Review questions**

1   What is the current-time indicator and where is it located?

2   How can you delete an entire clip from your movie, and how can you delete just a section of a clip?

3   What does *trimming* a clip mean and how do you do it?

4   How do you place an image above a video clip as opposed to placing it sequentially before or after it (for example to display a title graphic or text at the beginning of the movie)?

5   Do you have to set menu markers before selecting a template?

▶ **Review answers**

1   The current-time indicator shows which frame you are viewing in the Monitor panel. When the My Project panel displays the Sceneline, the current-time indicator is located in the mini-timeline in the Monitor panel, otherwise in the Timeline in the My Project panel. In either location, it can be clicked and dragged to locate a specific time in your project.

2   To delete an entire clip from the movie, select that clip in the Sceneline. Then, right-click the blue clip representation in the mini-timeline of the Monitor panel, and choose Delete from the context menu. The clips following the deleted clip in the Sceneline will move up to close the gap. To delete a section of a clip, you first have to cut the clip using the Split tool, and then delete the section.

3   You will rarely want to use an imported clip in its full length. Trimming is the process of defining the first and last frame of the portion of the clip that should be included in your movie. The preceding and trailing sections of the clip are not actually deleted from your hard disk, but will be skipped in playback. When the My Project panel displays the Sceneline, you can trim clips directly in the Monitor panel. Simply drag the In point and Out point handles in the mini-timeline to trim off sections of the clip. In the Timeline view of the My Projects panel, position the cursor at the end of a clip until the cursor changes to the Trim

Out tool, and then click and drag to trim off the ending of the clip. Changing the In point works in the same way.

4   Hold down the Shift key on your keyboard while dragging and dropping the image from the Available Media panel onto the Monitor, and then choose Place on Top from the menu that appears. If the graphic contains transparent areas you can see parts of the video playing beneath the image.

5   Usually you add menu markers before you select a menu template, but that isn't essential. You can add, move, or delete menu markers after choosing a template. If you select a template before setting menu markers, you can choose in the Missing Menu Markers dialog box to have Premiere Elements automatically add markers for you or to add them yourself later. As you add Menu Markers, Premiere Elements automatically adds images, buttons, links and pages as needed to the Disc Layout.

3 | Navigating the Workspace

In this lesson, you'll gain an understanding of the Premiere Elements workspace. You'll learn how to do the following:

- Customize your workspace.
- Navigate the Tasks panel.
- Manage assets in the Project view and the Organizer view.
- Work with the Monitor panel and the Preview window.
- Edit movies in Sceneline and Timeline view.
- Use the Info and History panels.

The workspace in Premiere Elements

All movies in Premiere Elements start as projects. A project is a single Premiere Elements file that combines everything you need to create a movie, including video, audio, effects, and titles. These assets are assembled on a Sceneline to create a final video. In this lesson you'll explore Premiere Elements' workspaces and panels optimized for the three major phases of a project: editing a movie, creating menus for DVDs and Blu-ray discs, and sharing movies.

Before you begin, make sure that you have correctly copied the Lesson03 folder from the DVD in the back of this book onto your computer's hard disk. See "Copying the Classroom in a Book files" on page 3.

Starting Premiere Elements

When you start Premiere Elements, a Welcome Screen appears. From here you can choose to start a new project, open an existing project, or capture video. Any recent projects you have worked on will be listed in the lower part of the screen.

1 Start Adobe Premiere Elements and click the Open Project button in the Welcome Screen. If Premiere Elements is already open, choose File > Open Project.

2 Navigate to your Lesson03 folder and select the project file Lesson03_Start.prel. Click the Open button to open your project. If a dialog appears asking for the location of rendered files, click the Skip Previews button. The Premiere Elements work area appears, with the Edit workspace selected in the Tasks panel.

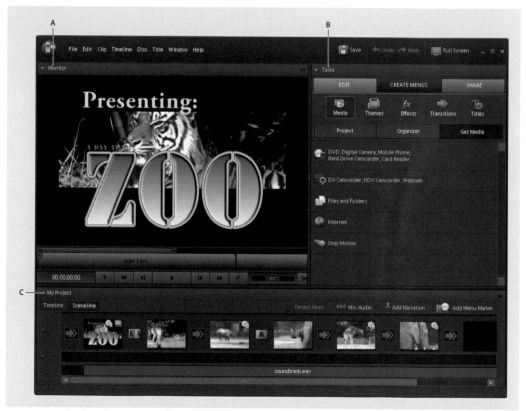

*A. Monitor panel. **B.** Tasks panel (Edit workspace selected). **C.** My Project panel (Sceneline view selected).*

The Adobe Premiere Elements workspace is arranged in three main panels: the Monitor panel, the Tasks panel, and the My Project panel. The following gives you an overview of these panels and the role they play when you are working on a movie project.

Monitor panel

This panel serves multiple purposes. It enables you to edit as well as to view your movie in one convenient place. You can navigate to any position in the movie and preview a section or the entire movie. It offers tools to trim unwanted footage and split clips. You can drag one scene onto another to create picture-in-picture effects, and add titles and other text directly in the Monitor panel. The Monitor panel adjusts its appearance for some edit tasks. When creating menus, the Monitor panel switches to become the Disk Layout panel and in title-editing mode the Monitor panel displays additional tools to create and edit text.

Tasks panel

The Tasks panel is the central location for adding and organizing media, finding, applying, and adjusting effects and transitions, creating DVD and Blu-ray disc menus, and sharing your finished projects. It is organized into three main task workspaces: Edit, Create Menus, and Share. Within each workspace are all the tools you need to accomplish your tasks.

My Project panel

This panel lets you assemble your media into the desired order and edit clips. The My Project panel has two different views:

- **Sceneline**: Enables you quickly to arrange your media, adding titles, transitions and effects.

- **Timeline**: Helps you trim, layer, and synchronize your media.

Edit workspace

The Edit workspace is divided into five views to access media, select movie themes, apply effects and transitions, and to create movie titles from templates.

- **Media (🖼):** Lets you view, sort, and select media you have captured or imported into your project, access media using the Organizer, and acquire new media. The Media view itself has three views:

- **Project:** Lets you view, sort, and select media you have captured or imported into your project. Media can be presented in List view or Icon view, selected by buttons at the lower left corner of the Project view.

- **Organizer:** Displays all the media currently stored and organized in the shared Photoshop Elements/Adobe Premiere Elements Organizer. You can use keyword tags to organize photos into groups and share directly between the two applications.

- **Get Media:** Shows buttons to access all the different methods for acquiring media for your movie: DVD, Digital Camera, Mobile Phone, Hard Drive Camcorder, Card Reader (📇), DV Camcorder, HDV Camcorder, Webcam (📷), Files and Folders (📁), Internet (🌐), and Stop Motion (🔄).

- **Themes (🎬):** Displays movie themes that you can use to instantly and dramatically enhance your movies. Using Themes enables you to create professional-looking movies quickly and easily. Themes come pre-configured with effects, transitions, overlays, title and closing credit sequences, intros, sound effects, and more. You can choose to simply apply all the available options in a theme, or select just the options you want.

- **Effects (*fx*):** Shows video and audio effects and presets you can use in your movie. You can search for effects by typing all or part of the name into the search box, browse through all available effects, or filter the view by type and category. The menu in the top right corner of the panel lets you choose between List view and Thumbnail view. You can apply video effects to adjust exposure or color problems, apply perspective or pixelate, or add other special effects. Audio effects help you improve the sound quality, add special effects like delay and reverb, and alter volume or balance.

- **Transitions (➡):** Shows video and audio transitions you can use in your movie. You can search for transitions by typing all or part of the name into the search box, browse through all available transitions, or filter the view by type and category. The menu in the top right corner of the panel lets you choose between List view and Thumbnail view. Transitions between clips can be as subtle as a cross dissolve, or quite emphatic, such as a page turn or spinning pinwheel.

- **Titles** (): Shows groups of pre-formatted title templates you can use in your movie. You can browse all available templates, or filter the view by categories such as Entertainment, Travel, and Wedding. Title templates include graphic images and placeholder text that you can modify freely, delete from or add to, without affecting the template itself.

Create Menus workspace

Use the Create Menus workspace to add menus to your movies before burning them onto DVDs or Blu-ray discs. The Create Menus workspace is divided into two views to access media and to create menus for your movies based on pre-configured menu templates.

- **Media** (): Gives access to the same three views you see when choosing Media from the Edit workspace. You can view, sort, and select media you have captured or imported into your project in the Project view, access additional media in the Organizer view, and acquire new media using the Get Media view.

- **Templates** (): Lets you preview and choose pre-formatted menu templates you can use for your movie. You can browse the available templates by categories such as Entertainment, Happy Birthday, and New Baby.

When the Create Menus workspace is selected, the Monitor panel switches to the Disc Layout panel.

Share workspace

Shows buttons to access all the different methods for exporting and sharing your movie: Disk (⬤), Online (⬤), Personal Computer (▯), Mobile Phones and Players (▮), and Tape (▭). Quick Share lets you create and reuse sharing options.

Properties panel

The Properties panel (Window > Properties) lets you view and adjust parameters of items—such as video or audio clips, transitions, effects, or menus—when selected in the Monitor or My Project panel.

Customizing the workspace

Premiere Elements uses a docking system to fit all the panels into the available space of the application window. However, panels can be moved and resized so that you can create a workspace that best fits your needs. Through this exercise, you will learn how to arrange panels on your screen in Premiere Elements.

When you first open a Premiere Elements project, the Edit workspace is displayed. You will notice that the Monitor panel, the Tasks panel and the My Project panel are separated by solid vertical and horizontal dividing lines. These dividers can be quickly repositioned to give you more space to work in on of the panels when you need it.

1 To increase the height of the My Project panel, click the horizontal dividing line between the bottom of the Monitor panel and the top of the My Project panel, and then drag it up toward the Monitor panel.

Dragging the horizontal divider was helpful for increasing the amount of space you have to work with in the My Project panel, but it has severely reduced the space you have for the Monitor panel and the Tasks panel. When you no longer need the My Project panel to be so large, you can drag the dividing line down again. Or, choose the reset workspace menu command to arrange the panels in their default workspace layout.

2   Choose Window > Restore Workspace. Notice how everything snaps back to its original position. You should consider restoring your workspace if you find your screen becomes cluttered.

To save some space on your screen, the docking headers of the panels—containing title, and sometimes palette menu and Close buttons—are hidden by default in Premiere Elements.

3   To show the docking headers, choose Window > Show Docking Headers. To hide them again, choose Windows > Hide Docking Headers.

While the default workspace layout has every panel docked into a specific position, you may find it helpful from time to time to have a more flexible environment. To do this, you can undock or float your panels.

4   If the docking headers are not currently visible, choose Window > Show Docking Headers. Then, click the docking header of the My Project panel and drag it a short distance in any direction. As you drag, the panel becomes transparent. When you release the pointer, the My Project panel becomes a floating window, allowing the Monitor panel and the Tasks panel to expand towards the bottom of the main window.

Note: The Tasks panel is the only panel that cannot be undocked into a floating window.

When you work with multiple monitors, you can choose to display the application window on the main monitor, and place floating windows on the second monitor.

5 Close the My Project panel by clicking its Close button (✖) in the top right corner. Reopen the panel by choosing Window > My Project. Notice that the panel opens where you have previously placed it. This is because Premiere Elements remembers the location of the panels, and retains it as part of the customized workspace.

Note: The Tasks panel is the only panel that cannot be closed.

6 Drag the My Project panel by its docking header. While dragging, press—and continue to hold down—the Ctrl key on your keyboard. When you hover with the pointer over the other panels you will see gray drop zones appear as shown in the illustration below. Releasing the pointer over a drop zone will dock the panel adjacent to the target panel in the main window. There are drop zones on all four sides of the target panel. To dock the panel above or below two panels which are positioned next to each other—like the Monitor panel and the Tasks panel in the illustration below—hover near the dividing line between the two panels until you see a drop zone which spans across both panels. Then, release the pointer.

7 Choose Window > Restore Workspace to return to the default workspace layout.

Note: To learn more about customizing your workspace, choose Help > Premiere Elements Help, and then search for "Customizing the workspace" in the Adobe Help Center window.

Working with the Project view

The Project view is where you import, organize, and store references to assets used in your project. When you import video from a DV camera, all the individual clips are listed in the Project view.

The filenames in the Project view identify the files imported into the project. It is important to note that files listed in the Project view are simply references to the clips you import, not the clips themselves. The original clips you import are on your hard disk and are untouched by Premiere Elements. Cutting or editing a clip in Premiere Elements does not affect the original file. Premiere Elements records your modifications along with the reference to the original file in the Project view. This means that a 20 MB clip takes up 20 MB of space on your hard disk whether you use only a portion of the clip—by trimming away unwanted sections—or whether you use this clip in its full length—or even two or more times—in a project.

1 To show the Project view, select either the Edit tab or the Create Menus tab in the Tasks panel, select Media (🖻), and then click Project. Or, choose Window > Available Media. The Project view lists all the source clips imported to your Premiere Elements project. When you capture video or import files, the individual clips are automatically placed in the Project view in alphabetical order, as shown here.

💡 By clicking the column headers, you can choose to sort by other attributes, or toggle between ascending and descending order. Which columns are shown in the Project view can be customized by choosing Edit Columns from the palette menu in docking header of the Tasks panel.

2   If necessary, use the scroll bar on the right side of the Project view to scroll down towards the bottom of the list. The soundtrack.wav file, halfway down the list, is an audio track, and the two items listed at the bottom of the list, called Title 01 and title_frame.tif, are still images used as superimposed title graphic and text at the beginning of the movie.

3   If the docking headers are not currently visible, choose Window > Show Docking Headers. Then, choose View > Icon from the palette menu located at the right end of the Tasks panels docking header. This will change your view from the default List view to the Icon view, which offers a slightly larger thumbnail preview.

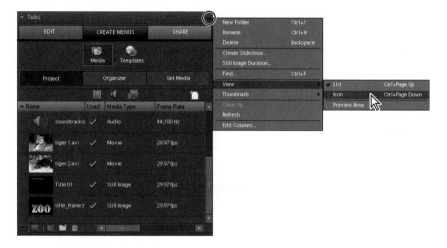

4   Change back to List view by choosing View > List from the palette menu, or by clicking the List view button (≡) in the lower left corner of the Project view.

5   Choose View > Preview Area from the palette menu. The Preview Area opens at the top of the Project view. Click the clip labeled tiger 2.avi in the Project view to select it. Important information about the clip appears in the preview area, including the duration of the clip and how many times it is used in the project.

Note: You may need to expand the size of the Tasks panel to be able to see all the information provided.

6   Click the Play button (▶) located to the left of the thumbnail to begin playing the clip in the Preview area. Click the Play button again after about five or six seconds into the clip. You should be able to clearly see the tiger walking to the left. Use the slider below the thumbnail to move forwards or backwards in the clip, if necessary.

7   Press the Poster Frame button (▣) just above the Play button to assign the current frame as new poster frame for this clip.

A poster frame is the image used to identify a video clip in the Project view. By default, Premiere Elements assigns the first frame of a video clip as the poster frame. Oftentimes, the first frame is not a good indicator of the clip's content. In such a case, selecting a different poster frame can make the clip easier to recognize.

8   Choose View > Preview Area from the palette menu to close the Preview Area. In the Project view, notice the new poster frame that you assigned for the tiger 2.avi clip.

9   Click the New Folder button (▣) at the bottom of the Project view to create a new folder; the name field should be active and the default name selected. Type **Titles**, and then press the Enter key on your keyboard to assign the folder name.

10   Click the file title_frame.tif, and then control-click the file Title 01 to select them both. Then, drag and drop the selected files onto the new Titles folder to place them inside that folder.

You can use folders to organize assets in the Project view, enabling you to save screen space as well as to better keep track of related clips.

Using the Organizer view

The Organizer view in Adobe Premiere Elements is a customized view of the Organizer used in Adobe Photoshop Elements. If you are familiar with the Organizer in Photoshop Elements, you will feel right at home using the Organizer view in Premiere Elements. The Organizer uses a catalog that lists media files available on your computer—similar to the Project view listing media files used in your project—and offers powerful tools to help you find and sort through material you might want to add to your project.

1   To show the Organizer view, switch to either the Edit workspace or the Create Menus workspace in the Tasks panel, select Media (🔲), and then click Organizer. Or, choose Window > Organizer. The Organizer view shows the contents of the catalog you have last opened in Photoshop Elements.

Note: To view the content of a different catalog in the Organizer view of Premiere Elements, you must first open that catalog in Photoshop Elements.

2   The Organizer view helps you find files in the catalog by numerous methods. Do any or all of the following:

• Browse through the entire catalog by using the scroll bar at the right side of the Organizer view.

• Select either Newest First or Oldest First from the Media Arrangement according to date menu located in the top right corner of the Organizer View, to sort the files in chronological or reverse chronological order.

• Select which media type to show—or not to show—from the Set Date Range / Media Type menu located near the top left corner of the Organizer view.

• Click the Show All button at the top of the Organizer view to clear any search criteria restricting the number of files displayed in the Organizer view—and to show the entire content of the catalog again.

• Restrict your search to files created within a period of time by choosing Set Date Range from the Set Date Range / Media Type menu, and then entering a start and end date in the Set Date Range dialog box.

• To show only files that have a certain star rating applied, click to select the number of stars in the star rating field, and then select one of the options from the menu next to it.

3   If the Show All button is visible at the top of the Organizer view, click it now.

4   To assign star ratings to files in the Organizer view, do the following:

•   Right-click any of the files in the Organizer view, and then choose Show Details from the context menu. This will show star ratings, filenames, and other details in the Organizer view.

•   Click to select the number of stars you want to assign to a file in the star rating field below the thumbnail image.

You can use keyword tags to organize your files in categories such as people, places, and events. Once keyword tags are applied, you can use them as search criteria to find files tagged with a specific keyword tag or any combination of keyword tags. Albums automatically keep track of which clips you used in a project so you can quickly find assets used in a previous project.

5   To open the Albums and Keyword Tags palette, click the Show / Hide Album-Tag View button (▣).

6 To assign a keyword tag to a file, drag the keyword tag from the Keyword Tags palette onto the thumbnail image in the Organizer view.

💡 Select multiple files in the Organizer view, and then drag a keyword tag onto one of the selected files. The keyword tag will be applied to all of the selected files at the same time.

7 To show only files in the Organizer view that have certain keyword tags applied, click to select the box next to the keyword tags.

Note: To learn more about working with keyword tags, choose Help > Premiere Elements Help, and then search for "keyword tags" in the Adobe Help Center window.

8   To add a still image, video, or audio file from the Organizer view to your project, drag the file from the Organizer view onto the Timeline or Sceneline view of the My Project panel. This will also automatically add the file to the Project view.

9   To show in the Organizer view only files that have been used in a specific project, click to select that project in the Albums palette.

10   Click the Show / Hide Album-Tag View button (⬛) to close the Albums and Keyword Tags palette, and then click the Show All button in the Organizer view.

Working with the Monitor panel

The Monitor panel is where you preview all or part of your movie. It offers various controls to navigate to specific points in your movie. When Sceneline view is selected in the My Project panel, the Monitor panel also features a mini-timeline just below the preview area, enabling you to do most of the clip editing directly in the Monitor panel.

*A. Docking header. **B.** Preview area. **C.** Palette menu.*
*D. Current Time. **E.** Clip Representation in Mini-Timeline. **F.** Playback controls.*

1   Select the first clip in the Sceneline, and then click the Play button (▶) in the Monitor panel to begin playback. As the movie is playing, notice that the timecode in the lower left corner of the Monitor panel is advancing. To pause playback, press the spacebar. Or, once again click the Play button, which becomes the Pause button (**Ⅱ**) during playback.

2   You can locate a specific frame in your movie by changing your position in time. Place your cursor over the timecode in the lower left corner of the Monitor panel, and your Selection tool (ᐃ) will change to a hand with two arrows (ᗒᗕ). Click and drag to the right, advancing your video. As long as you keep the mouse button held down, you can move backwards and forwards through the video. This is referred to as *scrubbing* through your video.

About timecode

Timecode represents the location of the frames in a video. Cameras record timecode onto the video. The timecode is based on the number of frames per second (fps) that the camera records, and the number of frames per second that the video displays upon playback. Digital video has a standard frame rate that is either 29.97 fps for NTSC video (the U.S. broadcast video standard) or 25 fps (the European broadcast video standard known as PAL). Timecode describes location in the format of hours;minutes;seconds;frames. For example, 01;20;15;10 specifies that the displayed frame is located 1 hour, 20 minutes, 15 seconds, and 10 frames into the scene.

—From Premiere Elements Help

3   The Shuttle control located in the lower right corner of the Monitor panel lets you navigate through the movie in a similar fashion. To move forward through your video, click, and then drag the Shuttle control to the right. The further to the right you move the Shuttle control, the faster you move through the video. This method is useful for quickly scanning a project for edit points.

A. Go to Previous Edit Point. B. Rewind. C. Step Back. D. Play/Pause. E. Step Forward. F. Fast Forward. G. Go to Next Edit Point. H. Shuttle.

4   You can move to a specific point in your movie by entering the time in the timecode control. Click the timecode in the lower left corner of the Monitor panel and it will change to an editable text field. Type the number **900**, and then press Enter to move to the 9 second point of your project.

5   Click the Step Forward button (I▶) repeatedly to advance your video one frame at a time. Video is simply a series of frames shown at a rate of approximately thirty frames per second. Using the Step Forward (I▶) or Step Back (◀I) buttons enables you to locate moments in time very precisely.

💡 *You can export a single frame of video as a still image using the File > Export > Frame menu command. To avoid video interlace artifacts in the still image, click Settings in the Export Frame dialog box, and then choose Deinterlace Video Footage in the Keyframe and Rendering section.*

6   Click the Go to Next Edit Point button (⁅) to jump to the first frame of the next clip. Notice in your mini-timeline that a gray playback head with a black line pointing downwards (⁆) jumps to the beginning of the next clip representation. This is called the current-time indicator and it is important to note that the point in the mini-timeline at which the current-time indicator is located is the frame displayed in the Monitor panel.

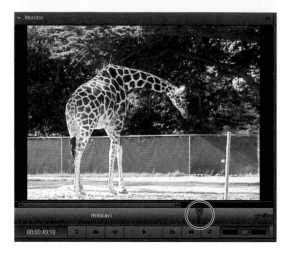

7   Reposition the current-time indicator in the mini-timeline by clicking and dragging it to the left or to the right.

8   The Zoom control, located just above the mini-timeline in the Monitor panel, lets you zoom in, to get a more detailed view of the clips, zoom out, to see more of the entire movie in the mini-timeline, or scroll through the mini-timeline to find a clip. Do any of the following:

• To zoom in, drag the left Zoom Claw (⬛) to the right, or drag the right Zoom Claw to the left.

• To zoom out, drag the left Zoom Claw to the left, or drag the right Zoom Claw to the right.

• Scroll through the mini-timeline by clicking and dragging the gray center bar of the Zoom control.

9 Press the Home key on your keyboard to position the current-time indicator at the beginning of the movie. The tiger 1.avi clip used for the first scene has two clips superimposed as title graphic and text. To select the title text clip in the Monitor panel, right-click the image in the preview area, and then choose Select > Title 01 from the context menu.

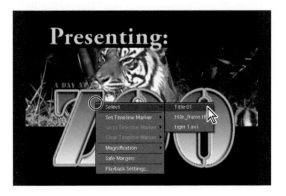

In the mini-timeline, a bluish-gray colored clip representation for the Title 01 clip appears above the lavender colored clip representation for the tiger 1.avi clip.

10 (Optional) With the superimposed Title 01 clip now selected, you can choose to reposition it in the Monitor panel, set new In and Out points using the Set In point handle (▶) or the Set Out point handle (◀), or delete the clip altogether by right-clicking the bluish-gray colored clip representation, and then selecting Delete from the context menu.

11 Choose Edit > Undo if you made any changes to the movie in the last step.

Working in the Preview window

The Preview window enables you to preview and trim individual clips. You can, for example, preview clips to decide whether to include them in your movie or trim off unwanted parts before adding the clip to the Sceneline.

Note: Trimming a clip in the Preview window does not change the In and Out points of instances of that clip already included in the My Project panel. It only sets the In and Out points for all subsequent instances of that clip placed in the My Project panel.

1 Select the Edit workspace or the Create Menus workspace in the Tasks panel, select Media (), and then click Project. Then, locate the peacock.avi clip in the Project view. Double-click the clip to open it in the Preview window. Note that the name of the clip is displayed in the title bar of the Preview window.

2 Click the Play button (▶) and play this clip from beginning to end.

The timecode in the lower left corner of the Preview window displays the current time in the movie, the timecode in the lower right corner of the Preview window tells you that this clip is 11 seconds and 21 frames long. You can navigate through this clip—as in the Monitor panel—by clicking the timecode in the lower left corner of the Preview window, and then dragging left or right.

3 Place your cursor over the current-time indicator in the lower left corner of the Preview window, and then click and drag to scrub through the clip.

4 Drag the current-time indicator in the mini-timeline to reposition it:

5 (Optional) Trim the clip by doing any of the following:

- To set a new In point, click and drag the In point handle (**▶**) to the desired location on the mini-timeline in the Preview window. Or, position the current-time indicator (**▼**) at the desired position, and then click the Set In Point button (⬛Set In).

- To set a new Out point, click and drag the Out point handle (**◀**) to the desired location on the mini-timeline in the Preview window. Or, position the current-time indicator (**▼**) at the desired position, and then click the Set Out Point button (⬛Set Out).

Note: In and Out points specified in the Preview window are automatically applied to all instances of the clip subsequently added to the Sceneline. Use the Monitor panel to change the In and Out points of specific instances of clips already included in the Sceneline.

6   Click the Close button (⬛) to close the Preview window.

Working with the My Project panel in Sceneline view

The My Project panel has two views: A Sceneline for basic movie editing, and a Timeline for more advanced techniques. You can switch between the two views by clicking either the Sceneline or the Timeline button in the top left corner of the My Project panel.

Adding clips in the Sceneline

In the Sceneline, each clip is represented by its first frame. This display makes it easy to arrange clips into coherent sequences without regard for clip length. This technique is referred to as *storyboard-style editing*.

1   If the My Project panel is not already in Sceneline view, click the Sceneline button.

The Sceneline:
A. Switch to Timeline. B. Sceneline (selected). C. Detect Beats in Music. D. Mix Audio.
E. Add Audio Narration. F. Set Marker for Disc Menu. G. Change Track Volume (Scenes).
H. Change Track Volume (Narration). I. Change Track Volume (Soundtrack).

2   Do any of the following:

• To add a clip at the end of the movie: Use the scroll bar at the bottom of the My Project panel to scroll to the end of the movie. In the Project view, click a clip, and then drag and drop it onto the empty clip target at the end of the movie.

• To add a clip before another in the Sceneline: In the Project view, click a clip, and then drag and drop it onto an existing clip in the Sceneline. The new clip will be inserted before the clip it was dropped onto.

• To add a clip after another in the Sceneline: In the Sceneline, select the clip after which you want to add the new clip. In the Project view, click a clip, and then drag and drop it onto the Monitor panel. The new clip will be inserted after the clip currently selected in the Sceneline.

💡 *Press the Shift key while dropping to get more options.*

Moving clips in the Sceneline

1 To move a clip to a new position in the movie, click the clip in the Sceneline view, and then drag it before or after another clip. Release the pointer when a vertical blue line appears at the desired position.

2 To move several adjacent clips to a new position in the movie, control-click to select multiple clips in the Sceneline view, and then drag them before or after another clip. Release the pointer when a vertical blue line appears at the desired position.

3   If a scene consists of multiple objects, like the first scene in this movie with the superimposed title images, you can choose to move just the scene, or the scene and all its objects. Shift-drag the first scene and position the vertical blue line after the second scene, and then release the pointer. Choose Move just Scene from the menu that appears.

Note: A transition following a scene moves with the scene.

4   Choose Edit > Undo to undo the changes you made in the last step.

Deleting clips in the Sceneline

1   To delete a scene, right-click it in the Sceneline view, and then choose one of the following from the context menu:

- Delete Scene and its objects: to delete the clip and any overlays it might have.

- Delete just Scene: to delete the clip but leave the overlays in place.

The clips following the deleted clip move to the left to close the gap.

2   Choose Edit > Undo to undo the changes you made in the last step.

Working with the My Project panel in Timeline view

While most editing tasks can be performed in the Sceneline view together with the Monitor panel, you'll use the Timeline view for some advanced editing tasks. The Timeline view of the My Project panel graphically represents your movie project as video and audio clips arranged in vertically stacked tracks.

1   In the My Project panel, click the Timeline button to switch to Timeline view. Depending on your monitor size, you might want to increase the height of the My Project panel to have more space to display additional video and audio tracks.

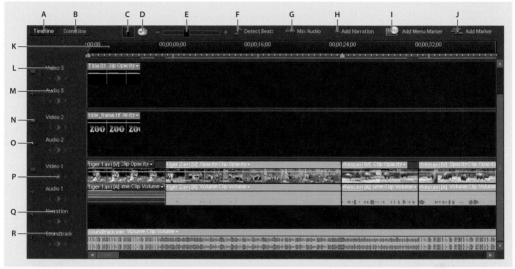

The Timeline:
A. Timeline (selected). B. Switch to Sceneline. C. Selection tool. D. Time Stretch tool. E. Zoom slider.
F. Detect Beats in Music. G. Mix Audio. H. Add Audio Narration. I. Set Marker for Disc Menu.
J. Set Unnumbered Marker. K. Time ruler. L. Video track. M. Audio track. N. Set Video Track Display Style.
O. Set Audio Track Display Style. P. Add/Remove Keyframe. Q. Narration. R. Soundtrack.

The Timeline displays time horizontally. Clips earlier in time appear to the left, and clips later in time appear to the right. Time is indicated by the time ruler near the top of the Timeline view.

The Zoom controls in the Timeline view let you change the time scale, allowing you to zoom out to see your entire video or zoom in to see time in more detail.

2   Click the Zoom In button (▊) once to zoom into the Timeline. Click and drag the Zoom slider to the right to zoom in further. Zooming in enables you to make precise edits in the Timeline. In doing so, however, you cannot see the entire Timeline at once.

3   Click and drag the scroll bar at the bottom of the Timeline to scroll through the Timeline. At a highly magnified time scale, scrolling through the Timeline might take longer than viewing the video in real-time.

4   Premiere Elements has keyboard shortcuts that enable you to quickly zoom in and out. Press the equal sign (=) to zoom in one step per keystroke; press the minus sign (-) to zoom out one step per keystroke. Press the backward slash (\) to fit the entire video into the Timeline.

Working with tracks

The Timeline consists of tracks where you arrange media clips. Tracks are stacked vertically.

Most of your editing will be done in the Video 1 and the Audio 1 tracks, the main movie. Directly above the Video 1 and Audio 1 tracks are the Video 2 and Audio 2 tracks. The stacking order of video tracks is important: any opaque areas of the clip in the Video 2 track will cover the view on the clip in the Video 1 track. Below the Video 1 and Audio 1 tracks are two more audio tracks: Narration and Soundtrack. Audio tracks are combined in playback and their stacking order is not relevant. Tracks let you layer video or audio and add compositing effects, picture-in-picture effects, overlay titles, soundtracks, and more. With multiple audio tracks, you can add a narration to one track and background music to another track. The final movie combines all the video and audio tracks. If necessary, you can choose Timeline > Add Tracks or Timeline > Delete Empty Tracks to increase or decrease the number of tracks displayed in your Timeline.

1   Drag the current-time indicator in the Time ruler of the Timeline as far to the left as it will go. Or, press the Home key to position the current-time indicator at the beginning of the movie.

2   Depending on the height chosen for the My Project view, you may need to scroll up using the scroll bar at the right end of the Timeline view to locate the Video 2 track.

3 There is a Title image in the Video 2 track. Titles usually have some form of transparency, allowing you to view parts of video in the track below them.

4 Click the Zoom In button (▮) at the top of the Timeline to magnify your view. As you zoom into the Timeline, you will see the full name of the title image, title_frame.tif.

5 Place your cursor over the yellow line running horizontally through the clip, the clip's Opacity graph. Your cursor will change to a white arrow with small double black arrows (⇕). Click and drag the Opacity graph all the way to the bottom. This changes the Opacity of this clip to 0% and enables you to see more of the clip in Video 1. Notice the effect in the Monitor panel. Click and drag the Opacity graph back up to 100% to restore the clip's opacity.

Note: Located next to the name of each video clip in Premiere Elements, the Opacity property is always enabled by default. There are additional properties you can control by clicking the Opacity menu and choosing a different option. You will be learning these techniques in Lesson 6, "Working with Effects."

Changing the height of tracks

You can change the height of each track in the Timeline view for better viewing and easier editing of your projects. As a track enlarges, it displays more information. You will now adjust the height of the Video 1 track.

1 If necessary, scroll down in the Timeline view to see the Video 1 track.

2 At the left side of the Timeline view, place your cursor between the Audio 2 and the Video 1 tracks; your cursor should change to two parallel lines with two arrows (⇕). Click and drag up to expand the height of this track.

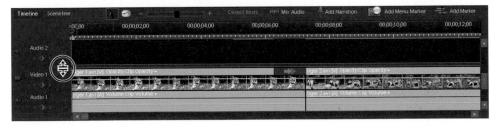

3   Choose Window > Show Docking Headers, if the docking headers are not currently visible. From the My Project panel menu, choose Track Size > Small, Track Size > Medium, or Track Size > Large, to change the track size for all tracks in the Timeline view at the same time.

Customizing track views

You can display clips in the Timeline in different ways, depending on your preference or the task at hand. You can choose to display a thumbnail image at just the beginning of the clip, or at the head and tail of the clip, or along the entire duration of the clip as seen in the previous illustration. For an audio track, you can choose to display or hide the audio waveform of the audio contents.

1   By default, Premiere Elements displays all the frames in a video clip. However, at times you may find you would like to work with fewer visual distractions in your clip. Click the Set Display Style button (■) to the left of the Video 1 track to set the display style to Show Head and Tail. This will show you the first frame and last frame of all the clips in Video 1.

2   Click the Display Style button again to view the Head Only of the clip.

3   Click the Display Style button again to view the clip by the Name Only. No thumbnails will be displayed on the clip.

4   Click the Display Style button one more time to view the default style all of the frames.

Using the Info and History panels

Premiere Elements offers advanced features to help you in your editing. The Info panel displays information about a selected clip in the Timeline. This panel can be helpful in identifying the duration of a clip, amongst other things. The History panel records the changes you make to a project. Each time you perform an action, the History panel adds that action to the bottom of its list.

1 Choose Window > Info. Drag the Info palette by its title bar to reposition it on the screen, if necessary. Then, click to select a clip in the Project view or the My Project panel. The Info panel displays the clip's name, type, duration, video and audio attributes, its location in the Timeline, and the position of the cursor.

Note: The Info panel is dynamic, and the fields can vary slightly depending on what is selected. For clips selected in the Timeline, the Info palette lists a start and end point, while for clips selected in the Project view it lists their In and Out points.

2 If necessary, scroll down in the Timeline view to be able to see the Soundtrack. Click the soundtrack.wav audio clip. The Info panel identifies this clip as an audio file 1;20;29;00 in duration with a Start point of 00;00;00;00.

3 Click and drag the soundtrack.wav clip to the right. As you drag, the Info panel updates the position information displayed. Move the clip until the Start point is at 00;00;02;00, and then release the pointer. Now the soundtrack will begin at 2 seconds rather than the beginning of the Timeline.

4   Open the History panel by choosing Window > History.

5   Click the list entry just above the bottom most Lift & Insert Selection command to undo the clip change you made in step 3.

Premiere Elements records each action you make and enables you to revert to a previous state of your project by clicking an entry higher up in the History palette. The most recent actions are at the bottom of the history list, so as you move up the list, you move back in history.

> *In addition to the History panel, Premiere Elements supports multiple undos by choosing Edit > Undo, or typing Ctrl+Z. Each time you press Ctrl+Z, you are undoing another step. You can also redo a step by choosing Edit > Redo, or typing Ctrl+ Shift+Z.*

6   Close the History and Info panels by clicking the Close button (☒) in the top right corner of each panel. Then, choose File > Close and close the project without saving any changes.

You've reached the end of this lesson. You were introduced to workspaces and learned how to customize them. You edited clips in the Monitor panel as well as the Sceneline and Timeline views of the My Project panel. Finally, you used the Info palette to call up additional information about the selected clip, and the History panel to undo changes made to your project. You should be well prepared to answer the review questions on the next page.

Review

▶ ## Review questions

1 What is a workspace and how can you change and reset workspaces?

2 What is the Monitor panel and what does it do?

3 What is the current-time indicator and where is it located?

4 Name at least two ways to see your Timeline view in more refined increments of time.

▶ ## Review answers

1 A workspace is the layout of the windows and panels in Premiere Elements, optimized for one of the three major phases of a project: editing a movie, creating menus for DVDs and Blu-ray discs, and sharing movies. Click the Edit, Create Menus, or Share tab in the Tasks panel to change to the respective workspace. To restore a workspaces to its default layout, choose Window > Restore Workspace.

2 The Monitor panel is used to play and review parts or all of your movie. Additionally, you can perform some clip editing directly in the Monitor panel.

3 The current-time indicator shows which frame you are viewing in the Monitor panel. With the My Project panel in Sceneline view, the current-time indicator is located in the mini-timeline of the Monitor panel, otherwise it's located in the Timeline view of the My Projects panel. In either location it can be clicked and dragged to locate a specific time in your project.

4 With the My Project panel in Timeline view, you can click the Zoom In button to get a closer look at the clips in your Timeline. Alternatively, you can drag the Zoom slider to the right or press the equal sign (=) on your keyboard to zoom in. There is also a menu command: Timeline > Zoom In.

4 Editing Video

In this lesson, you'll learn how to take uncut footage imported from a DV camera and shape it into a refined final version. You'll use these basic editing techniques:

- Insert, delete, and rearrange clips in the Sceneline.

- Import clips from another project.

- Trim and split clips.

- Use clip and Timeline markers.

- Add a frame hold to your movie.

Over the course of this lesson, you will work on a 1-minute home movie. You'll be working with video and audio clips provided on the DVD-ROM included with this *Adobe Premiere Elements Classroom in a Book*. If you were producing an actual film, you would be importing the video from a digital video camera using the Capture panel. For more information on capturing video and audio, see Lesson 1, "The World of Digital Video."

Getting started

To begin, you'll launch Adobe Premiere Elements, open the project used for this lesson, and review a final version of the movie you'll be creating.

1 Before you begin, make sure that you have correctly copied the Lesson04 folder from the DVD in the back of this book onto your computer's hard disk. See "Copying the Classroom in a Book files" on page 3.

2 Start Premiere Elements.

3 In the Welcome Screen, click the Open Project button. In the Open Project dialog box, navigate to the Lesson04 folder you copied to your hard disk. Within that folder, select the file Lesson04_Start.prel, and then click Open. If a dialog appears asking for the location of rendered files, click the Skip Previews button.

Your project file opens with the Monitor, Tasks, and My Project panels open.

4   Choose Window > Restore Workspace to ensure that you start the lesson with the default window layout.

Viewing the completed movie before you start

To see what you'll be creating in this lesson, you can take a look at the completed movie.

1   In the Edit tab of the Tasks panel, select Media (▣), and then click the Project button. In the Project view, locate the file Lesson04_Movie.wmv, and then double-click it to open the video into the Preview window.

2   In the Preview window, click the Play button (▶) to watch the video about a birthday race, which you'll be building in this lesson.

3   When done, close the Preview window by clicking the Close button (▣) in the top right corner of the window.

Setting up your hardware

This procedure is optional and is not required to complete any of the lessons in this Classroom in a Book. Arranging video/audio output from Premiere Elements to an external monitor takes a bit of setup, but is often worthwhile. Computer monitors and television monitors use two different methods for displaying video; therefore, the color and brightness levels you see on your computer monitor often do not match those on a standard television set. Previewing your video on a television will allow you to spot earlier in a project potential issues such as the length of shots, transitions, titles, etc.

To connect your computer to your VCR & TV:

1 *Connect your DV camcorder to the IEEE 1394 port (also known as FireWire or i.Link) or an USB (Universal Serial Bus) port on your PC.*

2 *Using an AV connector (which should have come with your DV camcorder), connect your camcorder to your TV set.*

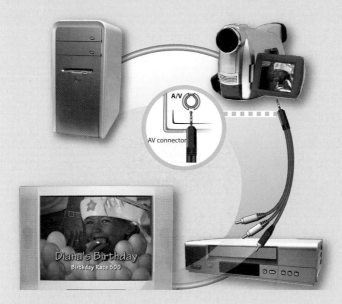

3 *Turn on your camcorder and set it to the VCR Setting.*

4 *Depending on your television, you will most likely have to change the Video input to "Video 1" or "Line 1."*

5 *Play a project in Premiere Elements to make sure you are viewing the output on your television set or video monitor.*

The real-time editing experience

The process of editing involves taking your initial series of clips and placing them in some sort of order, a process sometimes referred to as a *rough cut*. Once you are familiar with your footage you will want to make changes such as deleting, rearranging, or trimming clips. Additionally, you will add transitions, titles, and effects to create a *final cut*. Premiere Elements plays back full-resolution frames in the Monitor panel without waiting for your Sceneline to render. Rendering calculates all the frames needed to be played, stores them, and then streams them from RAM for smooth playback. It is also possible (although not required) to preview your project on an external video monitor, such as your TV.

Real-time preview

Throughout the lessons in this book, you'll preview your projects using real-time preview. All lesson files are full-frame digital video format, which is 720 x 480. (The 720 refers to horizontal resolution; the 480 refers to vertical resolution.) Real-time preview is an advancement in computer-based video technology. Previews are played instantly in fully rendered final quality. With render-free editing, you can review editing decisions as you make them, and experiment more freely.

Note: For best playback frame rates, use Pentium® 4 systems, 3GHZ or better. Playback frame rates and quality may degrade on less-powerful systems.

Importing files into the Media panel

In a sense, Premiere Elements creates a rough cut when you import video from your DV camera. Clips are automatically assembled in the Sceneline from beginning to end. However, there may be times when you would like to import footage from one project into another. For example, you may be making a compilation video of a child's first year and would like to use different clips from different projects. Or perhaps you have two tapes of footage from the same event. In this case, you would need to add these additional clips to your current project.

1   Select Media (🖼) in the Edit tab of the Tasks panel, click the Get Media button, and then click the Files and Folders button (🖾).

2   In the Add Media dialog box, navigate to the Tape_2 folder inside your Lesson04 folder. Ctrl+click to select the files Tape2_01.avi and Tape2_02.avi, and then click Open to import them into your project.

Note: *While Premiere Elements automatically places clips into the Sceneline when capturing DV footage from a camcorder, you'll need to manually place clips imported using the Add Media dialog box.*

💡 *You can also open the Add Media dialog box to import clips by using the keyboard shortcut Ctrl+I.*

Navigating the Sceneline

As you become familiar with your project, you will want to jump to certain sections of your footage. Be sure you have reviewed the "Working with the My Project panel in Sceneline view" section of Lesson 3 to make sure you understand how to navigate through your Sceneline. In this exercise, you will navigate to the end of your project in order to add the two clips you imported from the Tape_2 folder.

1   Click the timecode control located in the lower left corner of the Monitor panel and enter a value of **32;00** (32 seconds, zero frames). Then, press the Enter key to position your current-time indicator at that point in the movie. This is an effective way to jump to a specific time in your footage. However, this only works if you happen to know the exact time of a scene you want to edit—which you normally don't.

2   Press the Page Up key on your keyboard and your current-time indicator will move to the last edit point at 29;18. Page Up is the keyboard shortcut for Go to the Previous Edit Point. Alternatively, you can click the Go to Previous Edit Point button in the Monitor panel.

3   Press the Page Down key on your keyboard and your current-time indicator will move to the next edit point. Page Down is the keyboard shortcut for Go to the Next Edit Point. Press the Page Down key five more times to move your current-time indicator to the end of the project.

4   Press the Home key to move the current-time indicator to the first frame of the project.

5   Press the End key to move the current-time indicator to the last frame of the project. Using these keyboard shortcuts will significantly improve the efficiency of your editing.

Working with clips in the Sceneline

You will now add one of the two clips you imported from the Tape_2 folder.

1   In the Project view of the Tasks panel, double-click the file Tape2_01.avi to open it in the Preview window. Click the Play button to preview this clip of a boy on a tricycle. After viewing the clip, close the Preview window.

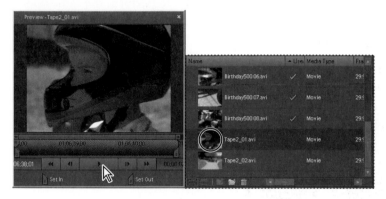

2   Place your cursor over the clip in the Project view, and then drag it to the empty clip target at the end of your project in the Sceneline. The Sceneline view will automatically scroll, if necessary, when you drag towards the end. When you release the pointer, the clip will snap to the end of the last clip.

3   In the Monitor panel, position the current-time indicator at roughly the 16 second mark (00;00;16;00), and then press the spacebar. The clip following the first clip in the project is obviously footage recorded by accident and needs to be deleted.

4   In the Sceneline, select the second clip, the Birthday500 02.avi clip, and then press the Delete key to remove it. Notice how all the subsequent clips automatically shift to the left to fill the space left by the deleted clip. This is the default behavior when deleting clips in Premiere Elements and is called a *ripple deletion.*

Note: *When a clip is deleted from the Sceneline, the transition following the clip is also deleted; when a clip is deleted from the Timeline, the preceding and following transitions are deleted.*

5   Choose Edit > Undo to undo the last step. Right-click the same clip in the Sceneline and choose Delete just Scene from the context menu to perform the same operation as in step 4. Premiere Elements provides many shortcuts to common operations from the context menu that appears when right-clicking an object.

Note: *The Delete Scene and its objects command deletes a scene and any overlays it might have—such as a superimposed title clip. The Delete just Scene command deletes the scene but keeps the overlays. If a clip has no overlays, both commands perform identically.*

Rearranging the order of clips

Premiere Elements allows you to rearrange the order of clips in your Sceneline by clicking and dragging.

1   Place your current-time indicator near the beginning of the second clip and press the spacebar. Play the project until the end. In the Birthday500 03 clip of the children lined up, notice that the girl in red is closest to the camera, yet the next shot is a close-up of a boy. To make the changing scenes flow more smoothly, you will place a close-up of the girl in red directly after the second clip, the Birthday500 03 clip.

2   Locate the Birthday500 08.avi clip in your Sceneline, the second to last clip, starting at the 39;22 second mark. Place your cursor over the clip and drag it to the left. Do not yet release the pointer.

3   Release the pointer when the vertical blue line appears between the second and third clip in the Sceneline. The view will automatically scroll, if necessary, when you drag towards the left edge of the Sceneline view.

Trimming clips in the Sceneline

Although deleting unnecessary clips and thoughtfully rearranging the order of clips will make a better video, you will inevitably want to shorten the length of some clips to create a more compelling movie.

Every clip must have a beginning and an end. In editing terminology these are referred to as the *In points* and *Out points*. Setting In and Out points does not actually delete frames from the hard disk, but instead isolates a portion of the clip for use in your movie. When you trim a clip in Premiere Elements you are simply changing the In and Out points.

1   Press the Home key, and then press the spacebar to play your movie from the start. When the first clip is finished, press the spacebar to stop playback. This first clip has extraneous footage at the beginning and the end; you will be trimming both.

2   Press the Home key and press the spacebar to play the first clip again, stopping playback when the clip ends. Note that the phrase "Today is a perfect day for racing" gets cut off at the second half, most likely because the camera operator turned off the camera.

3   Drag the current-time indicator to the 10 second mark; as you drag you should hear the audio. By slowly dragging the current-time indicator back and forth, locate the time where the first phrase "The season's smallest racing event" ends. We positioned the current-time indicator at 10;22.

4   Click the Out point handle (◀), located on the right side of the current clip representation in the mini-timeline, and then drag it to the left. Look at your Monitor panel and notice that it has changed to a split screen. This is a Premiere Elements behavior worth understanding. The left side of the screen is showing the last frame of the clip you are shortening. Continue dragging to the left and notice how the image changes as the man talks. The right side of the split screen shows the first frame of the next clip. This frame will not change because this clip is not being trimmed. Essentially, this split screen is a preview of what your edit line will look like.

Note: If necessary, you can adjust the magnification level of the mini-timeline in the Monitor panel. To zoom in, drag the claw at either end of the zoom control towards the center. To zoom out, drag the claw at either end of the zoom control away from the center.

5   Release the pointer when the Out point handle you are dragging is aligned with the current-time indicator at 10;22. Press the Home key to return the current-time indicator to the beginning of the movie, and then press the spacebar to play. Notice your new edit point at the end of the first clip, and then stop playback by pressing the spacebar.

Using the Split Clip tool

The Split Clip tool allows you to cut single clips into multiple clips. This can come in handy when you want to apply different effects to different parts of a clip. Or, as in this exercise, you can split a clip into two clips, and then delete the unnecessary part.

1   Press the Home key to return the current-time indicator to the beginning of the movie, and then press the spacebar. Notice how the man hesitates and takes a few breaths before speaking. You will be cutting this first portion out.

2   Position the current-time indicator at the 2 second mark. You can scrub your current-time indicator back and forth in the mini-timeline to find the point right before the man starts talking. We used 02;06.

Note: This technique of scrubbing the current-time indicator back and forth to view your video and hear the audio can take some getting used to, but the more you practice it, the easier your editing will become.

3   To split the clip at the position of the current-time indicator, click the Split Clip button (✂), located near the right end of the Monitor panel just below the mini-timeline. You might have to resize the Monitor panel to its full width in order to see this icon. Or, choose Timeline > Split Clip.

4   Click to select the short first clip section, and then right-click the clip representation and choose Delete from the context menu to delete it. Press the Home key, and then press the spacebar to play the movie. Notice how your first clip looks and sounds better with the extra footage removed.

5   When you are done reviewing the movie, choose File > Save As.

6   In the Save Project dialog box, name the file **Lesson04_Work** and save it in your Lesson 04 folder.

Using Clip and Timeline markers

As the video projects you work on become longer and longer, you will find the need to identify various sections of your movies. Premiere Elements provides two main methods of marking important points in a project. Clip markers are used within an individual clip—to identify a particular action or sound, for example. Timeline markers are placed on the time ruler in the Timeline to mark scenes, locations for titles, or other significant points within the entire movie. Timeline markers can include comments and even URLs to link to Web pages.

Markers can be numbered or unnumbered. You should use numbered markers if you plan to use many markers, allowing you to quickly jump to a specific marker number. In this exercise, you will add an unnumbered Clip marker to identify a specific point in a clip, and Timeline markers to identify where you would like to add titles.

Adding a Clip marker

1   Make sure you're still in Sceneline view by clicking the Sceneline button in the My Project panel.

2   In the Project view of the Tasks panel, double-click the Birthday500 08.avi clip to open it in the Preview window.

3   In the Preview window, click and drag the current-time indicator to the 01:06:05:00 mark. This marks the point in the scene where the girl is looking into the camera.

Note: If you are having trouble positioning the current-time indicator at the exact timecode that you are looking for, you can always use the left and right arrow keys on your keyboard to move backwards or forwards one frame at a time.

4   Choose Clip > Set Clip Marker > Unnumbered. This adds a Clip marker to the Birthday500 08.avi clip, identified by a little triangle in the mini-timeline.

5 In the Preview window, drag the current-time indicator towards the beginning of the clip.

6 Right-click the mini-timeline in the Preview window, and then choose Go to Clip Marker > Next from the context menu. This will position the current-time indicator at the next clip marker, in this case the 01:06:05:00 mark within the clip, where the girl is looking into the camera.

Note: Markers you add to a source clip (opened from the Project view of the Tasks panel) appear in each instance of the clip that you subsequently add to the movie. You need to switch to Timeline view to work with clip markers in your movie.

7 Click the Close button to close the Preview window.

Adding a Timeline marker

Unlike a Clip marker, which is attached to an individual clip, Timeline markers are placed in the Timeline and are used to mark specific points in your movie. Additionally, you can add comments to a Timeline marker to help yourself or others identify the purpose of a marker.

1 Click the Timeline button in the My Project panel. Press the Home key on your keyboard to place the current-time indicator at the beginning of your Timeline.

2 Press the Page Down key on your keyboard to advance to the beginning of the second clip in your Timeline, the Birthday500 03.avi clip.

3 Click the Add Marker button (🔻) at the top of the Timeline view to add a Timeline marker at the position of your current-time indicator. Timeline markers appear at the top of the Timeline in the time ruler. The newly added marker may be difficult to see, as it is partly hidden beneath the current-time indicator handle.

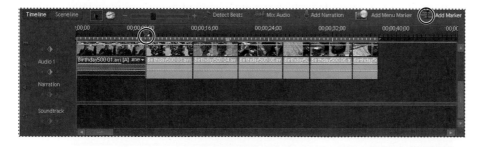

4   Press the Page Down key two times to advance the current-time indicator to the beginning of the Birthday500 04.avi clip. You should now be able to clearly see the first marker you added. If necessary, reduce the Timeline magnification by clicking the Zoom Out button.

5   Click the Add Marker button again to add another marker at the position of your current-time indicator. The two markers you have added can be used to indicate where you would like to later add titles.

6   Double-click the first marker you added to the Timeline at the beginning of the Birthday500 03.avi clip to open the Marker dialog box. Under Comments, type **Add first title here**. Click OK to close the Marker dialog box.

7   Move your current-time indicator to the left so that you can see the second marker you added to the Timeline (at the beginning of the Birthday500 04.avi clip). Double-click the marker to open the Marker dialog box. In the Comments field, type **Add second title here**. Click OK to close the Marker dialog box.

8   Double-click the first marker you added to review the comments in the Marker dialog box. Think of marker comments as notes to yourself to help you in your editing projects. Click OK to close the Marker dialog box.

9   Save your project.

Using Timeline markers for comments and Web links in a movie

If you intend to import your movie into Adobe Encore™ DVD, you can use Timeline markers to specify chapter links. Adobe Encore DVD automatically converts Timeline markers with text or numbers in the Chapter field to chapter points. It also places the contents of the Comment field into the Description field of the chapter point.

If your movie is intended for the Web, and you are comfortable designing frame-based Web pages, you can use Timeline markers to change what appears in other parts of the Web page. Timeline markers can specify a URL and Web page frame. When you include the movie in a frame-based Web page, the browser displays each specified link in the specified frame. So, as the movie plays, your Web page can change as each marker is reached. For example, in a family Web page, as your vacation movie plays, you can populate the other frames of the Web page with commentary and still images about the vacation. This advanced technique requires careful planning to coordinate the frames and content. You must export the movie using a file type that supports Web markers: QuickTime or Windows Media.

You can set the markers to be longer than one frame in duration. In the Timeline, the right side of a Timeline marker's icon extends to indicate its duration.

• To create a chapter point for Adobe Encore DVD, enter the chapter name or number in the Chapter field.

• To create a Web link, enter a URL and Frame Target. The frame number must match a frame in the Web page containing the movie.

—From Premiere Elements Help

Navigating, moving, and clearing markers

After you have added markers, you can then navigate from one marker to another. You can also remove markers once they are no longer needed in your project.

1   With the My Project panel in Timeline view, right-click anywhere in the Timeline ruler and choose Go to Timeline Marker > Previous from the context menu. Your current-time indicator will jump to the first Timeline marker you added.

2   Move the second marker by clicking and dragging it to the left until a black line snaps to the beginning of the Birthday500 08.avi clip. Then, release the pointer.

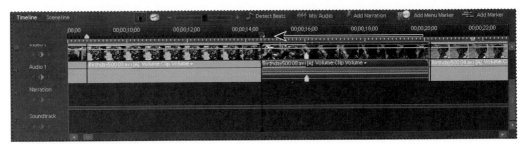

3   Right-click the Timeline ruler and choose Go to Timeline Marker > Next to jump to the marker you just moved.

Note: Timeline markers are not attached in any way to the frames they mark. When inserting, removing, or trimming clips, the existing Timeline markers do not shift, but remain where originally placed in the time ruler. However, clip markers within a clip shift with the clip.

4   To delete a Timeline marker, right-click the marker, and then choose Clear Timeline Marker from the context menu.

5   Save your work.

Adding a Frame Hold

Occasionally during a video, there may be a moment that you would like to freeze or hold the video. An example might be during a football game when a player catches the ball. Premiere Elements gives you the ability to display a single frame for the duration of a clip, while letting its sound track play unaltered. To do this, use the Frame Hold feature.

1   In Timeline view, drag your current-time indicator a few seconds into the Birthday500 08.avi clip where the girl with the blue helmet looks into the camera.

2   In the Monitor panel, click the Split Clip button.

3   In the Timeline, right-click the second clip section and choose Frame Hold from the context menu to open the Frame Hold Options dialog box.

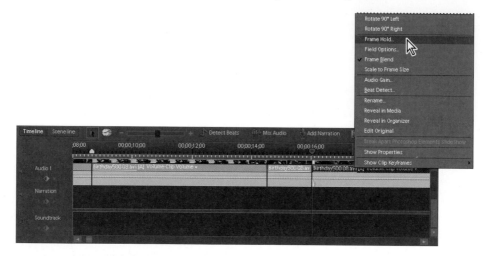

4   In the Frame Hold Options dialog box, select the Hold On check box and choose In Point from the menu next to it. Click OK.

Note: To use a frame other than the in and out point, you first need to define a numbered clip marker 0 for the clip.

5   Drag the current-time indicator to the beginning of the first Birthday500 08.avi clip section, and then press the spacebar to play the movie. When the current-time indicator reaches the second Birthday500 08.avi clip section, the image freezes for the duration of this clip section, although the sound continues normally.

6   When done reviewing, save your project as **Lesson04_End.prel**.

Wonderful! You've finished another lesson and learned about editing you movie (by trimming, splitting, deleting and rearranging clips) in Sceneline and Timeline view as well as in the Monitor and the Preview panels. You worked with clip and Timeline markers and added a frame hold to your movie.

Review

▶ Review questions

1   How can you import video files from one project into another?

2   What is an In point and an Out point, and what can you do with each?

3   What are two methods of shortening your video clips?

▶ Review answers

1   Select Media in the Edit tab of the Tasks panel, click the Get Media button, and then click the Files and Folders button to open the Add Media dialog box. Here you can add pre-existing video files on your hard disk to your current project. You can also choose File > Get Media from > Files and Folders, or use the keyboard shortcut Ctrl+I to open the Add Media dialog box.

2   The In point is the first frame of your clip as seen in the Scene or Timeline, and the Out point is the last frame. Both the In and Out points can be moved to create a shorter or longer clip.

3   One method of trimming your clips in the Sceneline is by dragging the In point handle at the beginning of your clip to the right, or the Out point handle at the end of your clip to the left. Another method is to use the Split Clip tool and split a clip into two or more pieces, thereby allowing you to remove the unneeded clip sections. Clips can also be trimmed in the Timeline and the Preview window.

5 Transitions

If you have followed the lessons in order, you should now feel comfortable with adding and deleting footage in your project, and trimming clips to improve the pace of your project. In this lesson, you'll learn how to take a final cut project and add nuance and dimension using transitions between clips. You'll learn how to do the following:

- Apply a transition using the Transitions panel.
- Preview transitions.
- Modify transition settings.
- Create fade-ins and fade-outs.
- Render transitions.

Getting started

You will affect scenes in this lesson's project by adding transitions in stages. But first you'll review a final version of the project you'll be creating.

1   Before you begin, make sure that you have correctly copied the Lesson05 folder from the DVD in the back of this book onto your computer's hard disk. See "Copying the Classroom in a Book files" on page 3.

2   Start Premiere Elements.

3   In the Welcome Screen, click the Open Project button. In the Open Project dialog box, navigate to the Lesson05 folder you copied to your hard disk. Within that folder, select the file

Lesson05_Start.prel, and then click Open. If a dialog appears asking for the location of rendered files, click the Skip Previews button.

Your project file opens with the Monitor, Tasks, and My Project panels open.

4 Choose Window > Restore Workspace to ensure that you start the lesson with the default window layout.

Viewing the completed movie before you start

To see what you'll be creating, you can take a look at the completed movie.

1 In the Edit tab of the Tasks panel, select Media (🖼), and then click the Project button. In the Project view, find the file Lesson05_Movie.wmv (you might have to scroll down to see it), and then double-click it to open the video in the Preview window.

2 Press the Play button (▶) to review the video you'll be building in this lesson. Notice the transitions from one clip to the next.

3 Close the Preview window.

About Transitions

Transitions assist you to phase out one clip while phasing in the next. The simplest form of a transition is the cut. A cut is when the last frame of one clip is followed by the first frame of the next. The cut is the most often used transition on video and film, and the one you will be using most of the time. However, you can also use other types of transitions to achieve effects between scenes.

Transitions

Using transitions, you can phase out one clip while phasing in the next. A transition can be as subtle as a cross fade or dissolve, or quite emphatic, such as a page turn or spinning pinwheel. While you generally place a transition on a cut to include clips on either side: a *double-sided* transition, you can also apply a transition to just the beginning or end of a clip: a *single-sided* transition.

For a transition to shift from one clip to the next, the transition must overlap frames from both clips. To achieve the overlap, transitions either use frames previously trimmed from the clips, if any exist (frames just past the In or Out point at the cut), or they repeat the frames on either side of the cut. It's important to remember that when you trim a clip, you don't delete frames. The resulting In and Out points simply serve as a window over the original clip. A transition either uses the trimmed frames to create the transition effect, or, if the clips don't have trimmed frames, the transition repeats frames.

—From Premiere Elements Help

The Transitions view in the Tasks panel

Adobe Premiere Elements includes a wide range of transitions, including 3D motion, dissolves, wipes, and zooms. The animated thumbnail view when clicking on a specific transition gives you a good idea of how it might be applied to your project. Transitions are grouped into two main folders in the Transitions panel: Audio Transitions and Video Transitions.

1   Transition can be accessed by clicking the Transitions button (➡) in the Edit tab of the Tasks panel. Select a transition to see an animated preview.

2   Select Video Transitions from the category menu in the top left corner of the Transitions view. Then select Stretch from the menu next to it to only see the different types of stretch transitions in the Transitions view.

💡 *You can also search for transitions by typing all of part of the name in the search box.*

3   Premiere Elements 4.0 includes a Favorites category where you can add your often-used transitions. Right-click the Stretch In transition in the Transitions view, and then select Add to Favorites from the context menu.

4   To view the content of your Favorites category, select Favorites from the category menu in the top left corner of the Transitions view. You'll see the Stretch In transition added to the Favorites category.

Applying a transition

Understanding how transitions work is essential in order to use them successfully. For a transition to shift from one clip to another, the transition must overlap frames from both clips for a certain amount of time.

1   In the Monitor panel, position your current-time indicator at the 08;12 second mark, the edit point between the Birthday500 01 clip and the Birthday500 03 clip. You will be placing a transition between these two clips.

Note: You do not have to reposition the current-time indicator to place transitions between clips. However, it is often helpful in locating the correct point in your project.

2   If Sceneline view is not already selected in the My Project panel, switch to it now.

3   From the Transitions view, which should still be showing the content of the Favorites category, drag the Stretch In transition and drop it onto the rectangle between the Birthday500 01 clip and the Birthday500 03 clip in the Sceneline. You will see the transition has been added, as its icon is visible in the rectangle between the two clips in the Sceneline.

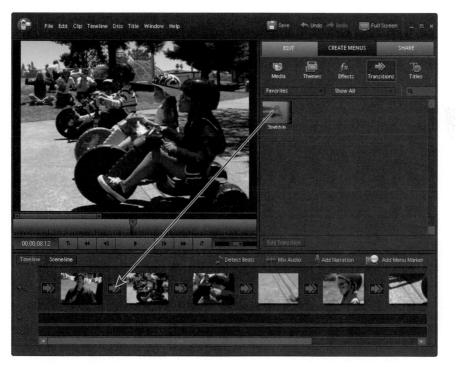

4   In the Sceneline, double-click the rectangle between the two clips to preview the Stretch In transition. After the transition ends, press the spacebar to stop playback.

Viewing transition properties

When you add a transition to a clip, the default length of the transition is determined by your preferences. You can change the length of transitions after applying them. Additionally, there are other attributes to transitions that you can adjust, such as alignment, start and end values, border, and softness. In this exercise, you will add a Push transition that pushes one image off screen to replace it with the next clip. You will then modify the various attributes of the transition in the Properties panel.

1   In the Transitions view of the Edit tab, choose Video Transitions from the category menu. Make sure Show All is selected in the menu next to it. Then, click in the text search box to the right of the magnifying glass icon (🔍) and type the word **push**. This automatically searches the list of video transitions and locates the Push transition.

2   If necessary, scroll to the right in the My Projects panel to be able to see the second and third clip of the movie, Birthday500 03 and Birthday500 08. Drag the Push transition from the Transitions view and drop it onto the rectangle between these two clips in the Sceneline.

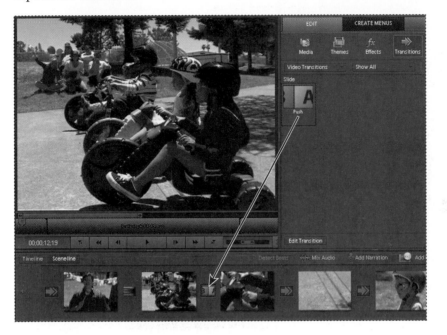

3   In the Monitor panel, position the current-time indicator a few frames before the transition. Press the spacebar to view the transition. The Push transition will push the first clip off to the side. After the transition ends, press the spacebar to stop playback.

4   Select the Push transition in the Sceneline, and then click the Edit Transition button in the lower left corner of the Transitions view. This will load the transition's parameters into the Properties panel where you can edit them.

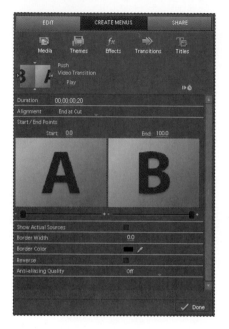

5   Click the Show Timeline button (🎞) at the top of the Properties panel to view a magnified version of your Timeline. This enables you to view the transition as it is applied between your two clips. If necessary, resize the Properties palette or just its Timeline view to better see this Timeline.

6   In the Timeline view of the Properties panel, drag the current-time indicator back and forth over the transition to preview your transition effect.

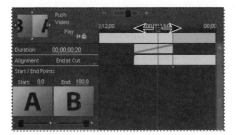

You will now modify the settings of the transition.

Modifying transition settings

All transitions have default settings. To achieve specific results, you can customize the settings in the Properties panel. Modifying the length of the transition is easy, as you will see in this exercise.

1   To change the length of a transition in the Properties panel, place your cursor over the Duration value, and then click and drag to the left to change the Duration to 00;00;00;15 (15 frames). Remember that there are 30 frames in one second of NTSC video; therefore, 15 frames represents a half-second of time.

2   Drag the current-time indicator—in either the Monitor or the Properties panel—to a position before the Push transition and press the spacebar to preview the transition. After the transition ends, press the spacebar to stop playback. If you should accidentally click the track area of your Sceneline, you will deselect the transition and its parameters will vanish from the Properties panel. Don't worry, just click the transition in your Sceneline to select it again and display its parameters in the Properties panel.

3   In the Properties panel, select the check box marked Reverse. This reverses the transition so that the second clip now pushes the first clip to the left. Depending on the size of your monitor, you may need to scroll down and resize the Properties panel or its Timeline view to be able to see this check box.

4   Drag your current-time indicator to approximately halfway through the transition; we used the 13;01 mark. Because you are in the middle of the transition, your screen will be split in half. This makes it easier to preview the modifications you are about to apply in the next steps.

5   If necessary, scroll down the Properties panel to view the additional controls. Click the value for Border Width, type the number **10**, and then press Enter. This creates a 10-pixel border on the edge of your transition. The default color of the border is black; but you can modify this as well.

6   Click the black color swatch, next to the Border Color. This opens the Color Picker dialog box.

7   In the color slider, which displays the spectrum of colors in a vertical strip, click in the blue hues. Then, inside the larger color spectrum, click in the bottom right corner to select a medium blue.

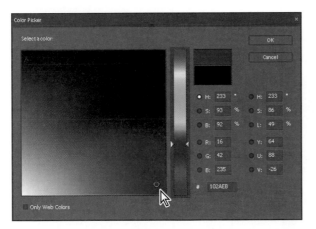

8   Click OK to close the Color Picker dialog box. The border of your transition is now 10 pixels wide and blue.

9 Drag your current-time indicator to a position before the transition, and then press the spacebar to play your modified transition. After the transition ends, press the spacebar to stop playback.

10 Choose File > Save As, name the file **Lesson05_Work** in the Save Project dialog box, and then click Save to save it in your Lesson05 folder.

Replacing a transition instance

Replacing an existing transition between two clips is done in essentially the same way as adding a new transition; simply drag the transition from the Media panel onto the existing transition in the Sceneline. You can do this repeatedly to check the effect of different transitions.

To practice adding and replacing transitions—this time using the Timeline view—you will now apply an Iris Box transition between the third and fourth clips of the movie, Birthday500 08 and Birthday500 05, and then replace it by an Iris Round transition.

1 In the My Project panel, click the Timeline button to switch to Timeline view. If necessary, use the zoom controls and scroll your view so that both the Birthday500 08 clip and the Birthday500 05 clip are visible in the Timeline. Use the Page Up and Page Down keys to position the current-time indicator at the edit line between the two clips. You might want to click the Zoom In tool (◻) to magnify the view at this edit line.

2 In the Transitions view of the Edit tab, click in the text search box to the right of the magnifying glass icon (🔍), select the word push, and then type **iris** to automatically list all of the Iris transitions.

3 In the following, do not release the pointer until instructed. Drag the Iris Box transition over the Edit line between the Birthday500 08 clip and the Birthday500 05 clip in the Timeline; do not release the pointer. Pay careful attention to the appearance of your cursor.

4 Move your cursor on top of the edit line between the two clips. Notice how your cursor changes to the Center at Cut icon (⯗), and then release the pointer. This will center the transition over the cut. For more information about alignment of transitions search for "transition alignment options" in Premiere Elements Help.

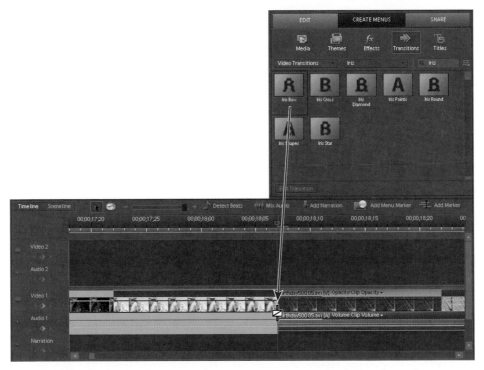

5 Preview the Iris Box transition by dragging your current-time indicator before the transition, and then pressing the spacebar. When the transition is over, press the spacebar to stop playback. Notice how transitions are represented by gray boxes above the cut between the clips in Timeline view.

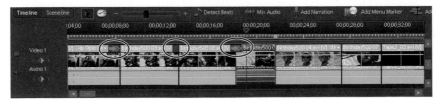

6   In the Transitions panel, click the Iris Round transition and drag it on top of the Iris Box transition in the Timeline to replace it. You may only have one transition between clips at a time.

7   Preview the new transition by dragging the current-time indicator before the transition and pressing the spacebar to start playback. After the transition ends, press the spacebar to stop playback.

Adding a single-sided transition to create a fade-in

Transitions do not necessarily need to be located between two clips. For example, you can quickly add a fade-in and fade-out to the beginning and end of your movie.

1   In the My Project panel, click the Sceneline button to switch back to Sceneline view. If necessary, use the scroll bar to scroll to the beginning of the movie. Press the Home key to position the current-time indicator at the beginning of the first clip.

2   In the Transitions view of the Edit tab, select the word iris in the text search box to the right of the magnifying glass icon (🔍), and then type the word **dip**. Two Dip transitions will automatically be located in the Dissolve folder.

3   Drag the Dip to Black transition from the Transitions view and drop it onto the rectangle to the left of the first clip, Birthday500 01.avi.

4   Press the spacebar to play the transition. The beginning of the transition starts at black, and then fades in to the video. After the transition ends, press the spacebar to stop playback.

5   To extend the duration of this transition for a half-second, select the transition in the Sceneline, and then click Edit Transition in the Transitions view.

6   Place your cursor over the Duration value in the Properties panel, and then click and drag to the right to change the Duration to 00;00;01;15 (1 second, 15 frames).

7   Press the Home key, and then press the spacebar to play the video from the start. When the fade-in is over, press the spacebar to stop playback.

Rendering transitions

Throughout this lesson you have been viewing transitions in real time. In other words, when you add a transition, you can play it back immediately to see if you like the effect. Depending on the performance capabilities of your system, or with more processor-intensive effects, you may notice that the previews are not as smooth as you would want. This is often resolved by a process called rendering, which enables Premiere Elements to calculate each frame of your transition before starting playback.

1   Switch to Timeline view in the My Project panel by clicking the Timeline button. Look at each transition you have added in the Timeline. Directly above each transition is a small red bar corresponding exactly to the length of the transition. This bar signals that the transition has not been rendered.

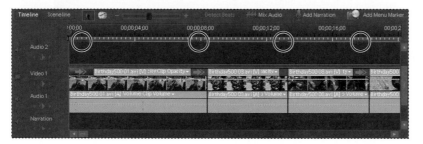

2   Press the Enter key or choose Timeline > Render Work Area, and Premiere will begin to render the video preview of each transition. When the program is done rendering, it will automatically begin playing the project from the beginning.

3   Notice the bar above each transition is no longer red, but has changed to green. This is a visual cue that the transitions in this project have been rendered. Once a transition has been rendered, you do not need to render it again unless you change any of its properties.

If you were to save and close this file, and then reopen it, the green bar would still be there.

Note: You are not required to render your transitions. Rendering is an optional process useful for previewing your transitions as they will appear in the final exported movie.

4   Save your project as **Lesson05_End.prel**.

GPU (Graphics Processing Unit) transition effects

Adobe Premiere Elements comes with many GPU-accelerated transitions including Card Flip, Center Peel, Page Curl, Page Roll, and Sphere. These transitions take advantage of the added video processing capabilities offered by video display cards that have Graphics Processing Unit (GPU) chips. These display cards help with graphics acceleration, so transitions can be previewed and rendered more quickly than by the CPU alone. If you have a display card that supports DirectX 9.x, Pixel Shader (PS) 1.3 or later, and Vertex Shader 1.1 or later, you can use the GPU-accelerated transitions. They are visible only if you have a card with a GPU and they reside in the Video Transitions view.

—From Premiere Elements Help

Our compliments, that's another lesson well done! You've discovered how transitions can make your projects more professional looking by adding continuity between the separate clips. You've learned about placing, previewing, modifying, and rendering different transitions.

Exploring on your own

1 Add cross dissolves to all the remaining clips in your Sceneline to get used to the process of quickly adding transitions to your clips.

2 Experiment with different transitions, preview their animated icons in the Transitions view. Remember that dragging a transition onto an existing transition will replace it.

3 Be sure that you are comfortable with modifying the default effect of your transitions. One by one, select the new transitions you have added and explore their settings in the Properties panel.

Review

▶ **Review questions**

1   Where are Video Transitions located and what are two ways to locate specific transitions?

2   Why might you want to render transitions and how do you go about doing this?

3   How can you extend the duration of a transition?

▶ **Review answers**

1   Video transitions are located inside the Transitions view, which can be accessed at any time from your Edit workspace. You can browse for individual transitions, which are organized in categories and by transition type. Additionally, you can find a specific transition by typing its name or part of its name into the search field in the Transitions view.

2   While Premiere Elements can display many transitions in real-time, the amount of calculations that this requires might cause an unnecessary load on your system. Rendering transitions eliminates that load. You can render your transitions by pressing the Enter key when the Timeline is active.

3   One method of extending the duration of a transition is to change the length in the Properties panel. Select the transition in the Sceneline to access its properties in the Properties panel. You can also change the duration of a transition by dragging its edges in the Timeline view of the My Project panel.

6 | Working with Effects

In this lesson, you'll learn how to apply effects to the Birthday500 racing clip that you already know from Lesson 4 and 5. You will use effects to improve your video, add color tints, create a picture-in-picture effect, work with an image pan, and control your effects with keyframes. Specifically, you'll learn how to do the following:

- Apply video effects.

- Change effects and settings.

- Copy effects and settings from one clip to another.

- Create a pan over a still image with preset effects.

- Control visual effects with keyframes.

Getting started

To begin, you'll launch Adobe Premiere Elements, open the project used for this lesson, and review a final version of the movie you'll be creating.

1   Before you begin, make sure that you have correctly copied the Lesson06 folder from the DVD in the back of this book onto your computer's hard disk. See "Copying the Classroom in a Book files" on page 3.

2   Start Premiere Elements.

3   In the Welcome Screen, click the Open Project button.
In the Open Project dialog box, navigate to the Lesson06 folder you copied to your hard disk. Within that folder, select the file Lesson06_Start.prel, and then click Open. If a dialog appears asking for the location of rendered files, click the Skip Previews button.

Your project file opens with the Monitor, Tasks, and My Project panels open.

4   Choose Window > Restore Workspace to ensure that you start the lesson with the default window layout.

Viewing the completed movie before you start

To see what you'll be creating, you can take a look at the completed movie.

1   In the Edit tab of the Tasks panel, select Media (▣) and then click the Project button. In the Project view, find the file Lesson06_Movie.wmv, and then double-click it to open the video in the Preview window.

2   Press the Play button (▶) to review the video you'll be building in this lesson.

3   When you're done reviewing, close the Preview window.

Using effects

Video and audio effects are extremely useful functions in Premiere Elements. For example, you can use certain effects to correct footage that is too dark or has an incorrect color balance. Additionally, you can use Premiere Elements' effects to create qualities not present in the original video. These include creating a blur or adding a color tint.

You can add an effect to any clip in the Sceneline, and even apply the same effect numerous times to the same clip, but with different settings. By default, when you add an effect to a clip, it is active for the duration of the clip.

Getting to know the Effects view

Effects (*fx*) are located in the Edit tab of the Tasks panel. All effects are stored in either the Audio Effects folder or the Video Effects folder, and are organized by type. For example, all video effects that create a blur are grouped within the Blur & Sharpen folder inside the Video Effects folder.

💡 *Premiere Elements offers a large selection of diversified effects. It's a good idea to look up the gallery of video effects in your Premiere Help file, which gives you a quick overview of all those effects actually applied to an image.*

Applying effects

Effects can be added to—or removed from—clips at any time. In this exercise, you will apply an effect to a clip to create an old film look. This effect is quite intriguing, as it makes your video look like an aged video including scratches and graininess, which can be fine-tuned to suit your project perfectly.

To apply an effect to a clip in the Sceneline

1   Make sure you are in Sceneline by clicking the Sceneline button.

2   Select Effects (fx) in the Edit tab of the Tasks panel.

3   In the Effects view, click the search box next to the magnifying glass icon (🔍), and then type the word **old**. This automatically searches the list of effects and locates the Old Film effect.

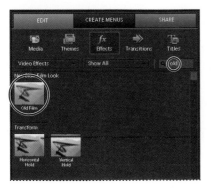

4   You will be applying the Old Film effect to the first clip in your Sceneline, the Birthday500 01.avi clip. Select this first clip in your Sceneline and drag the current-time indicator past the Dip to Black transition at the beginning. Notice the video is in color.

5   To apply the effect, drag the Old Film effect from the Effects view and drop it onto the first clip in your Sceneline. The effect is applied immediately, with the color of the clip shifted from full color to sepia color.

6   Press the spacebar to see how the Old Film effect is enabled for the entire length of the clip. When the clip has finished playing, press the spacebar to stop playback. Note that the next clip is in color. This illustrates that effects are enabled for only one clip at a time.

Working with effect controls

After an effect has been applied, you can modify it using the Properties panel.

1   With the Old Film Look effect still selected in the Effects view, click the Edit Effects button.

The Properties panel shows you the thumbnail of the current clip you have selected in the Sceneline, as well as the Motion, Opacity, Old Film, Volume and Balance parameters. These parameters are fixed effects that can be controlled by default on every single clip in Premiere Elements. In other words, they do not have to be added manually as you did with the Old Film effect.

2   In the Properties panel, just next to the Old Film parameter, you can see the eyeball icon (👁) for the Old Film effect. The eyeball acts as a toggle to turn the effect on or off. The original color image returns when you toggle the effect off by clicking the eyeball icon. This control helps you when fine-tuning effects by enabling you to easily compare the film after an effect has been applied with the look of the original clip.

3   Click the eyeball icon again to toggle the effect on.

4   You will now modify the Old Film look in an upcoming exercise. Click the triangle to the left of Old Film to open the parameter settings.

5   Increase Damage by dragging the slider to or typing **70**, reduce the Color-Sepia-B&W to **30**, augment the Jitters to **3**, and choose Cracky from the Wear Pattern submenu. It's amazing how much more control the parameter settings enable over the final look of the effect.

6   Choose File > Save As, name the file **Lesson06_Work** in the Save As dialog box, and then save it in your Lesson 06 folder.

Using effects to improve video quality

Often when you are shooting video, the lighting conditions are not ideal. The resulting video can be too dark. Although there is no magic effect to make poor quality video look perfect, you can improve your video with Premiere Elements' Shadow/Highlight effect.

1   Use the Page Down key to advance to the beginning of the Birthday500 08.avi clip, the third clip in the movie, and press the spacebar to play the clip. The face of the girl with the purple helmet is too dark.

2   In the Monitor panel, move the current-time indicator to approximately the 14;12 second mark to see the underexposed foreground. If the Birthday500 08.avi clip is not already selected in the Sceneline, click it now to select it.

3   In the Effects view, locate the Adjust folder in the category menu. You need to scroll down to locate it. If the text box still features the word old, delete the word. Click the arrow next to the Adjust folder to reveal the effects.

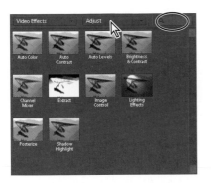

4   Click and drag the Shadow/Highlight effect from the Adjust folder and drop it onto the Monitor panel to apply the effect. This is an alternative to dropping the effect onto the clip in the Sceneline. As soon as you add the effect, the screen will brighten and the details in the shadow area are revealed.

Before applying Shadow/Highlight effect.

After applying Shadow/Highlight effect.

Copying effects from one clip to another

Because effects are added to a single clip at a time, it would be quite time-consuming to place the same effect across numerous clips, especially if you had to drag and drop the effect on each clip. Fortunately, Premiere Elements provides a simple way to copy effects and their settings from one clip to another.

1   Click the first clip, Birthday500 01.avi, in your Sceneline to select it, and then click the Old Film effect in your Properties panel. *(See illustration on the next page.)*

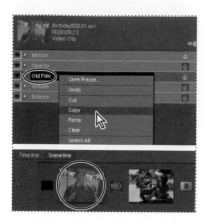

2   Choose Edit > Copy.

Note: You could also have right-clicked in the Properties panel and chosen Copy, or used the keyboard command Ctrl+C to copy the selected effects.

3   In the Sceneline, click to select the Birthday500 04.avi clip, the third clip from the end of the movie, starting with the close-up of the little boy. Click the title bar of the Properties panel to make this panel active, and then choose Edit > Paste. The two effects are applied to this clip in the same order and with the same properties.

4   Click the top of the Sceneline to make it active. Press the Home key to place the current-time indicator at the beginning of the project, and then press the spacebar to begin playback. When reviewing the movie, note the effects you have applied to the clips.

Note: Just like transitions, Premiere Elements creates a real-time preview, letting you see your effect immediately. Multiple effects require more processing and should be used sparingly. If you begin to notice a stuttering of playback or similar problems, remember that effects and transitions can be rendered by pressing the Enter key. In Timeline view, a red bar above a clip signifies that an effect can be rendered if playback is being affected. If you decide you don't like the parameters of the effect you set up, you can reset the effect to its default state, or you can click the effect and press the Delete key to remove it.

Creating a Picture-in-Picture overlay

Premiere Elements has the ability to superimpose multiple tracks of video. In this exercise, you will be superimposing one video clip in a small frame over your pre-existing background clip that covers the entire screen. This effect is called a Picture in Picture overlay.

1   In Sceneline, select the last clip, called Tape2_01.avi. The selected clip appears in your Monitor panel.

2   In the Edit tab of the Tasks panel, select Media (🖼) and then click the Project button.

3   In the Project view, locate the Birthday500 04.avi clip, the close-up of the little boy, which you refined earlier in this lesson. Click once to select the clip, then hold down the Shift key and drag the clip towards the lower right corner of Tape2_01.avi clip in the Monitor panel. Release the pointer and choose Picture in Picture from the menu that appears. Click to select the superimposed clip and notice that the clip changes appearance. There are now handles on the edges, indicating that the clip is active.

Note: If the superimposed clip is longer than the background clip, it appears over successive clips in the Sceneline for its entire duration, and appears superimposed over those clips during playback.

4   Select Window > Properties to open the Properties panel.

5   In the Properties panel, click the arrow to the left of Motion to reveal its properties. Make sure the Constrain proportions check box is selected. Place your cursor over the value for Scale, and then click and drag to change the value to 40. As you change the scale, the Birthday500 04 clip shrinks to 40% of its original size.

6   If necessary, you can reposition the clip using the Position controls. Or, simply click and drag the clip to the desired position in the Monitor panel.

7   Click the Home button on your keyboard to go to the start of your project, and then press the Play button (▶) to review your work. Note that the Birthday500 04.avi clip appears twice: once as the full sized clip you colored with a tint, and also as the Picture in Picture overlay. You will now delete one of those clips.

8   In the Sceneline, delete the Birthday500 04.avi clip with the Old Movie look by right-clicking it and selecting Delete Just Scene from the context menu.

9 Save your project as **Lesson06_Work.prel**.

Creating an image pan with a still image

Premiere Elements includes several frequently used effect presets, preconfigured effects that you can apply to clips. Typically, presets provide good results without you having to adjust their properties. You can also create your own presets.

The image pan is a popular device in many documentaries and films. An image pan is defined as a movement of the camera, usually from left to right, although it can be from top to bottom. A traditional pan would actually involve the physical movement of a camera over an image; however, in Premiere Elements you can simulate the movement of the camera with the Image Pan preset effect.

You'll use a vertical image pan with a happy birthday message to end your Birthday 500 project.

1 Choose File > Get Media from > Files and Folders. Navigate to the Lesson06 folder and select the 06_imagepan.jpg image. Then, click Open to import it.

2   In the Project view, right-click the 06_imagepan.jpg image and choose Properties. The upcoming Properties window enables you to—amongst other things—identify the size of the digital image you have imported.

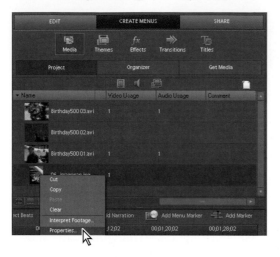

3   In the Properties window, note that this image is 960 pixels wide and 1,280 pixels high. You will need this information when creating the image pan in the steps that follow.

Still image resolution

It is important to determine the size of the still image you are using in this project. Successfully using image pan requires a basic understanding of image resolution. The standard dimensions of Digital Video are 720 pixels wide by 480 pixels high. In order to create a pan or zoom effect with a still image, the resolution (and therefore the dimensions) of the image must be larger than required to fit the video frame. For example, a typical resolution for digital still images is 960 pixels wide by 1,280 pixels high (although this number can be much higher or lower). A still image of this size gives you room to work with, as you can pan the image from left to right, or top to bottom, and reveal additional detail.

4   Click the Timeline button to switch to Timeline view in the My Project panel.

5   Click and drag the 06_imagepan.jpg image and drop it onto Video 2 track in your Timeline so that it extends slightly over the end of the last clip in Video 1 track. Position the current-time indicator so that you can see the superimposed image in the Monitor panel.

ADOBE PREMIERE ELEMENTS 4 **143**
Classroom in a Book

The image has been automatically scaled to fit entirely into the Monitor panel. Although the original image was 1,280 pixels high, Premiere Elements automatically scaled the image down to 480 pixels high. The default behavior of Premiere Elements is to scale still images to fit the screen. Keep the image selected.

6 Select Effects (fx) in the Edit tab of the Tasks panel, and then scroll down to the Presets folder to view the available presets.

7 Scroll down the Presets menu to Vertical Image Pans, and then click the 960x1280 Image Pan Down preset. *(See illustration on the next page.)*

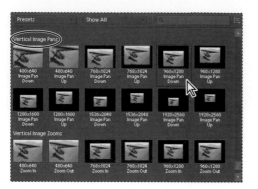

8   Drag the 960x1280 Image Pan Down preset from the Effects view and drop it onto the 06_imagepan.jpg clip in your Timeline. This automatically creates a vertical pan.

9   In the Monitor panel, click the 06_imagepan.jpg image to select it. Click the top right corner handle of the image, and then drag up and to the right. Release the pointer when the image fills the width of the Monitor panel. Premiere Elements maintains the aspect ratio of the image as it is enlarged.

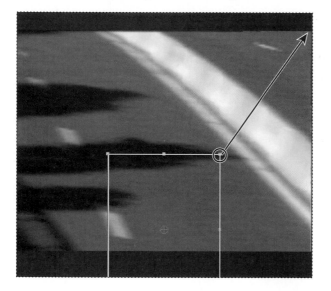

10 To view the pan effect, drag the current-time indicator in the Timeline to the left of the 06_imagepan.jpg clip, and then press the spacebar to play the movie. The image pan completely covers the underlying clip as soon as it starts, which does not seem ideal in this particular situation. One possible solution is to create a fade in, which you will learn more about later in this lesson.

Modifying the image pan

Although presets are useful for quick and easy effects, they often need modifying after they have been applied. For example, the movie stops rather abruptly just after the words Happy Birthday! appear on the screen. You will now extend the length of the clip to provide a smoother ending.

1 In the Timeline, place your cursor at the end of the 06_imagepan.jpg clip. When your cursor changes into the Trim Out tool (⬦), click and drag the clip to the right to extend the clip duration by about 5 seconds (while dragging you can check the timeline, which adds the seconds).

2 Drag the current-time indicator to the beginning of the 06_imagepan.jpg clip. Press the spacebar to begin playback. Notice that the pan stops halfway through the clip, but there are now five additional seconds of the still image at the end of the clip, enabling you, for example, to add a dip to black or fade out effect to end the movie gracefully.

Working with keyframes

Every clip in the Timeline has the ability to be modified over time. This involves a concept called keyframing. In the last step, when you added the image pan preset, Premiere Elements automatically created keyframes. The image started in one location, the first keyframe, and ended in a different location, the second keyframe. While progressing through the timeline, Premiere Elements moved the picture from one keyframe to the second keyframe, thereby creating the motion from bottom to top. By creating your own keyframes, you have much more control over the appearance and length of the effects used in your movie.

About animating effects

With each keyframe, you specify a value for an effect property at a specific point in time. Adobe Premiere Elements interpolates the values between keyframes, creating a transition from one keyframe to the next. For example, to create a blur effect that changes over time, you could set three keyframes—the first with no blur, the second with blur, and the third with no blur. Through interpolation, the blur gradually increases between the first and second keyframes, and then gradually decreases between the second and third keyframes.

—From Premiere Elements Help

Creating a fade-in using keyframes

You can control keyframes in two locations in Premiere Elements: the Timeline and the Properties panel. In this exercise, you will control the opacity keyframes of a video clip in the Timeline.

1   Click to select the 06_imagepan.jpg clip in Video Track 2. You may need to scroll to the right in the Timeline to fully see the clip.

2   Place the current-time indicator shortly before the end of the Tape2_01.avi clip (this is the last clip in the Video Track 1). Click the Zoom in tool (◘) in the Timeline to increase your view of the clip. When working with clip keyframes, it is often helpful to increase the magnification. The orange line spanning horizontally across the clip is the connector line (or graph) between keyframes. By default, all clips have the Opacity property enabled.

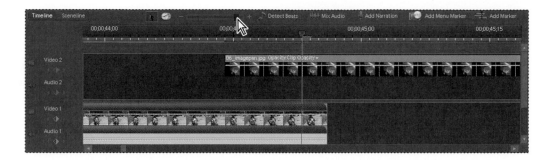

3   Place your cursor over the orange connector line at the location of the current-time indicator. The cursor changes to a double-arrow icon (↕). Click and drag the connector line down toward the bottom of the clip. As you drag, you will see a small window with changing numbers. The numbers represent the opacity values. Drag the connector line down to approximately the 50% level. Don't worry if you cannot get an exact number. When you release the pointer, you will see the clip is now semi-translucent, enabling you to catch a glimpse of the video clip below.

Note: If you do not see the opacity change, you may need to select the 06_imagepan.jpg clip inside the Monitor panel, and then try the opacity change again.

4   Click and drag the connector line back up towards the top of the clip to restore the clip's opacity to 100%. Now, you will create keyframes to have Premiere Elements automatically change the opacity levels from 0% to 100% over the length of the entire clip.

5   Position your pointer over the orange connector line at the beginning of the image pan clip. You need the cursor to change to the double-arrow icon (⇕). This can be a little tricky because your cursor changes to the Trim Out tool if you position the pointer too far to the left. With the double-arrow icon as cursor, hold down the Ctrl key on you keyboard, and then click the connector line once. You should see a small yellow diamond added to the orange connector line at the beginning of the clip, representing your first keyframe.

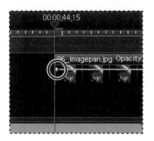

6   To use the current-time indicator as a guide, move it to the end of the Tape2_01.avi clip (we used the 00;00;44;26 mark). Position your cursor over the orange connector line at the current-time indicator. Hold down the Ctrl key, and then click to add a second keyframe.

7   You should now have two keyframes, as indicated by the two diamonds on the connector line. Place your cursor over the first keyframe at the beginning of the clip. Your cursor changes to an arrow with diamond icon (⬨) when it is correctly placed. Click and drag this first keyframe down to the bottom of the clip. This decreases the opacity of the first frame to 0%. The orange connector line runs now diagonally, connecting the first and second keyframes.

8 To create a fade-out, create another keyframe at the end of the 06_imagepan.jpg clip and drag its opacity value down to 0%.

9 To view the opacity fade-in and fade-out, move your current-time indicator to the beginning of the 06_imagepan.jpg clip, and then press the spacebar.

Modifying keyframes

You may have noticed that this effect resembles a Cross Dissolve transition. The visual effect is similar, but working with keyframes has certain advantages over transitions, including the ability to quickly change the duration of the effect and modify keyframes. You will now move the center keyframe further to the right, thereby lengthening the fade-in and shortening the fade-out you just created.

1 Position your cursor over the second keyframe in the 06_imagepan.jpg clip, making sure your cursor changes to an arrow with diamond icon ($\mathbb{R}_{\diamond}$). Click and drag the keyframe to the left to approximately the 00;00;44;21 mark. As you drag, a small yellow menu appears, displaying the current-time and the opacity value. Be careful as you drag the keyframe to the right not to drag it downwards, as that would change the opacity of the clip.

2 Review your modifications, and then save your project.

Using keyframes to animate effects

Adding keyframes to clips in the Timeline is perhaps the quickest way to work with advanced effects, but it is not the only way. Premiere Elements offers a more sophisticated set of keyframing tools in the Properties panel. One word of caution: this section is more advanced than some users of Premiere Elements may need, so feel free to skip to the next lesson if you wish. However, you should know that such keyframing is the basis of animation in programs such as Adobe Premiere Pro and Adobe After Effects, and this exercise is not difficult to complete. But, you can always revisit this lesson later if you wish.

In this section, you will be animating the blur effect to create a unique transition.

1 Select Effects (ƒ✲) in the Edit tab of the Tasks panel, and then type **gaussian blur** in the text box to the right of the magnifying glass icon (🔍) to locate the Gaussian Blur effect. This effect is located in the Blur & Sharpen folder inside the Video Effects folder.

2 Locate the Birthday500 03.avi clip, the second clip in the Timeline, and then click the clip to select it.

3 Place your current-time indicator on the first frame of the Birthday500 03.avi clip. Increase the magnification of the Timeline if needed.

4 Drag the Gaussian Blur effect from the Effects view and drop it onto the Birthday500 03.avi clip to apply it. You will see a slight change of blurriness.

5 Click the Edit Effects button in the Effects view, and then click the triangle next to Gaussian Blur to reveal the controls.

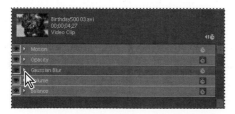

6 Place your cursor over the value for Blurriness and click and drag it to the right to change the value to 50. Leave the Blur Dimensions at Horizontal and Vertical. Note the image in the Monitor panel becoming more blurred.

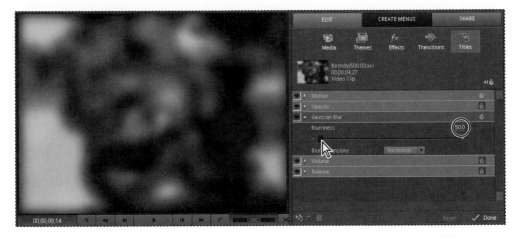

You can enter number values for effects directly by clicking once in the value field and then typing in the number you want.

7 At the top of the Properties panel, click the Show Keyframes button. You may need to expand the size of the Properties panel to better view the keyframes.

8 To the right of the Gaussian Blur property is a small stopwatch. Click this to turn on the animation for this property. After you click the stopwatch, a small diamond appears in the small Timeline within the Properties panel. This represents a keyframe.

9 In the Timeline view, click and drag the current-time indicator to 00;00;09;12 mark. Note that the current-time indicator in the Properties panel is also moving. Place your cursor over the value for Blurriness (it should be set to 50), and then click and drag to the left to change the value to 0.

Changing the value automatically adds a second keyframe, which is represented as a second diamond in the Timeline in the Properties panel. Once animation has been turned on, Premiere Elements will automatically animate between the two values. In this case you moved from a blurriness of 50 to a blurriness of 0 over a span of 1 second.

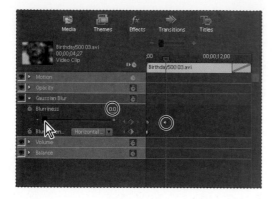

Note: The current-time indicators in the Properties panel and in the Timeline view of the My Project panel are actually the same. You can use either one to navigate through your clip. However, the Timeline in the Properties panel enables you only to navigate through the currently selected clip and is used primarily for working with keyframes.

10   Drag the current-time indicator to the beginning of the clip, and then press the spacebar to play the clip and the effect. The clip starts out blurry, and then quickly snaps into focus. Press the spacebar again to stop playback.

Extending the duration of an effect

Once you have added keyframes for an effect, you can control how quickly the effect changes over time. For example, in the last exercise you animated the blurriness of the clip from 50 to 0 over the time period of approximately one second. What if you would like to extend the duration of the effect? Premiere Elements offers a simple way to do this.

1   Be sure the Birthday500 03.avi clip is still selected and that you can see its values for Gaussian Blur in the Properties panel.

Located at the far right of the Blurriness property is a set of three buttons. The left-facing arrow is Go to Previous Keyframe; the center button is Add/Remove Keyframe, and the right-facing arrow is Go to Next Keyframe. You can hover over them to see the tool tips.

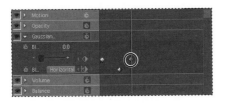

2	Click the left-facing arrow until you reach the first keyframe. Note the current-time in your Timeline. Ours was 8;12—don't be concerned if your value differs slightly. Also note that the blurriness value is 50.

3	Click the Go to Next Keyframe button, which is the right-facing arrow, to move to the second keyframe. Note that the current-time now reads 9;12 (or thereabout) and the Blurriness value is 0. Using these two arrows to navigate between keyframes enables you to quickly jump from keyframe to keyframe. In addition, when you make changes to properties, you need to be exactly on a keyframe.

4	Move the current-time indicator in the Properties panel to approximately the 10 second mark (00;00;10;00). Click and drag the second keyframe from its current location to the current-time indicator, and then release the pointer. This lengthens the animation. The blurriness values of 50 for the first keyframe and 0 for the second keyframe remain the same, except they now change over a longer period of time.

5	Press the Enter key on your keyboard to render the project. Remember that effects are viewable in real-time but the capabilities of the preview vary from system to system. Rendering your project will provide you with a more accurate representation of your final output.

6 View the rendered clip in the Monitor panel. Press the spacebar to stop or start playback; press the Home key to return the current-time indicator to the beginning of the Timeline.

7 Choose File > Save As and save your project as **Lesson06_End.prel**.

Congratulations! This exercise finished the lesson. Now you understand how to apply different visual effects on a video track as well as modifying them, and you learned how to create an image pan and control effects with keyframes.

Exploring on your own

1 Create a Picture-in-Picture effect using two or more clips on the same screen.

2 Experiment with alternative effects such as Adjust > Brightness & Contrast, or Distort > Bend. To get a sense of the different effects available in Premiere Elements, choose Help > Premiere Elements Help, or press F1 to access the Help guide. Listed in the Applying Effects section is a gallery of video effects.

3 Experiment with the various effects presets located in the Effect panel, specifically, the Horizontal and Vertical image pans.

4 Create two new Gaussian Blur keyframes on the 06_imagepan.jpg to create an effect that blurs out.

Review

▶ ## Review questions

1 How can you tell if an effect has been applied to a clip?

2 What is the quickest way to apply identical effects and settings to multiple clips?

3 What are fixed effects, and what is their purpose?

4 What is a keyframe and what does it contain?

5 How do you modify keyframes once they have been added to a clip?

Review answers

1 If the effect has not been rendered, a red bar is located at the top of the clip in the Timeline. If the effect has been rendered, you will see a blue-green bar. You can also see the effect listed in the Properties panel when the clip is selected.

2 After selecting the clip that contains the one or more effects that you wish to copy, click an effect to select it in the Properties panel, or shift-click to select multiple effects. Copy your selection by choosing Edit > Copy. Then, select the clip to which you wish to transfer the effects and choose Edit > Paste.

3 Fixed effects are the Property parameters that every clip in Premiere Elements has enabled by default. These effects are Motion, Opacity, and Volume. Within the Motion effect, Scale, Position, Rotation, and Anchor Point are all properties that can be adjusted to create, for example, a Picture-in-Picture effect.

4 A keyframe contains the values for all the controls in the effect and applies those values to the clip at the specific time.

5 Once keyframes have been added to a clip, they can be adjusted by clicking and dragging them along the connector line. If there are two keyframes, moving one keyframe farther away from the other extends the duration of the effect; moving a keyframe closer to another keyframe shortens the effect.

7 | Working with Sound

The sound you use has much impact on your movies. Adobe Premier Elements provides you with the tools to narrate clips while previewing them in real time, add and modify soundtracks and control the levels of volume within clips. The two little projects in this lesson cover the basics of working with audio. You will control the volume of an audio clip, add sound effects, modify the volume of the audio, and create a voiceover from a video clip. Specifically, you'll learn how to do the following:

- Add an audio track and match it to the length of the video.

- Use the audio mixer.

- Adjust the volume of an audio track with keyframes.

- Add narration.

- Create a voiceover from a video clip.

- Use audio effects.

Getting started

To begin, you'll launch Adobe Premiere Elements and open the project used for this lesson. Then you'll review a final version of the project you'll be creating.

1 Before you begin, make sure that you have correctly copied the Lesson07 folder from the DVD in the back of this book onto your computer's hard disk. See "Copying the Classroom in a Book files" on page 3.

2   Start Adobe Premiere Elements and click the Open Project button in the Welcome Screen. If Premiere Elements is already open, choose File > Open Project.

3   Navigate to your Lesson07 folder and select the project file Lesson07_Start.prel. Click the Open button to open your project. If a dialog appears asking for the location of rendered files, click the Skip Previews button. The Premiere Elements work area appears, with the Edit workspace selected in the Tasks panel.

4   The project file opens with the Media, Monitor, Properties and My Project panels. Choose Window > Restore Workspace to ensure that you start the lesson with the default window layout.

Viewing the completed movie for the first exercise

To see what you'll be creating as your first project of this lesson, a video about the zoo, you can take a look at the completed movie.

1   Select Media (▣) in the Edit tab, and then click the Project button. In the Project view, double-click the Lesson07_Movie.wmv file to open it in the Preview window.

2   Press the Play button (▶) to review the video. When done, click the Close button (✖) in the top right corner to close the Preview window.

Adding and adjusting audio files

Audio is a big part of all video projects, and is often what makes a good video great. Premiere Elements makes working with audio in your project very easy.

1   Choose File > Get Media from > Files and Folders. In the Lesson07 folder, select the file soundtrack.wav, and then click Open to import the file. The file will show up in the Organizer view.

2   If necessary, switch to Sceneline view by clicking the Sceneline button in the top right corner of the My Project panel.

3   Drag the soundtrack.wav file from the Imported Media view of the Media panel and drop it onto the Soundtrack of your Sceneline. Align the beginning of the soundtrack clip with the beginning of the first video clip. If you accidentally place the soundtrack clip too far to the right, you can click and drag it into position after it has been placed in the Soundtrack.

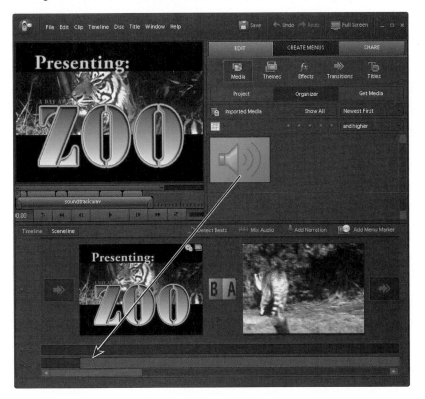

The music clip is longer than the video—Premiere Elements automatically added black video after the last video clip to compensate for the difference in length—but you can shorten the length of the audio clip to match the video.

4   Position your cursor at the end of the soundtrack.wav clip in the Sceneline; your cursor will change to the Trim Out tool (✦). Click and drag the end of the clip to the left until it coincides with the end of the last video clip in the Sceneline, the elephant.avi clip, and then release the pointer. *(See illustration on the next page.)*

5   Choose File > Save As, name the file **Lesson07_Work** in the Save As dialog box, and then save it in your Lesson 07 folder.

Adjusting the volume of an audio track

Mixing and refining your audio will result in sound that has a much greater impact. To control a clip's volume, you can either use the Volume graph—the yellow line running horizontally across the audio track of each clip in Timeline view (sometimes referred to as the volume rubberband), or the Audio Mixer. For the next exercise, you'll use the Audio Mixer to adjust the volume, balance, or both for the different audio tracks in your project.

Working with the Audio Mixer

When you have multiple tracks of audio playing at once, the audio you want to hear can get lost. Using the Audio Mixer, you can adjust the volume and balance of the different audio tracks as the audio plays, so you can make sure your audience hears what you want them to hear. For example, you can lower the volume for the Soundtrack while people are talking, and increase it again when they are silent.

1   Press the Home key to place the current-time indicator at the beginning of the movie. Press the spacebar to begin playing your video.

You will hear the drums of the soundtrack.wav clip, as well as the audio part of the video clips, background noise, and voices of visitors at the zoo. Next you'll mute the background noise.

2   When done, press the Home key again to set the current-time indicator right at the beginning of the video, which is where you want to start mixing audio.

3   Click the Mix Audio button (⋕⋕) or choose Window > Audio Mixer.

4   In the upcoming Audio Mixer window, choose Show/Hide Tracks from the Audio Mixer panel menu, and then deselect the Narration, Audio 2, Audio 3, and Audio 4 tracks.

Note: In Premiere Elements, volume is measured in decibels. A level of 0.0 dB can be thought of as the original volume (not silence). Changing the levels to a negative number reduces the volume, and changing the volume to a positive number increases the volume.

5   After you click OK your Audio mixer window shows only the 2 audio channels you are working with. Click the Mute box at the bottom of the Audio 1 channel, and experiment with the volume of the soundtrack by dragging the handle up and down. Once you're done, leave the Soundtrack at 0.0 dB.

6 Press the Home key to place the current-time indicator at the beginning of the project, and then press the spacebar to begin playback. You'll now hear only the drums of the soundtrack.

7 Select File > Save.

💡 *While listening to audio tracks and viewing video tracks, you can fine-tune the settings. As you change the volume of the audio, keyframes are added to the track. You can specify a default minimum interval for keyframes in the Audio preferences.*

Edit to the beat of your favorite song

Click Detect Beats in the Sceneline or Timeline to automatically add markers at the beats of your musical soundtrack. Beat detection makes it easy to synchronize slide shows or video edits to your music.

1 *Add an audio clip or a video clip that includes audio to the soundtrack in the Timeline or Sceneline.*

2 *Click the Detect Beats button (♪) at the top of the Timeline or Sceneline.*

3 *In the Beat Detect Settings dialog box, specify settings as desired and click OK.*

4 *Markers appear in the Timeline corresponding to the beats in the soundtrack.*

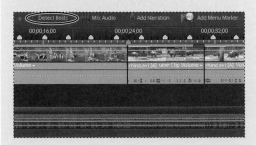

Raising and lowering volume with keyframes

Understanding how keyframes work is important if you want to increase the amount of control you have over the look and sound of your video projects. Keyframes can be used to change over time parameters of effects such as opacity, as well as to modulate the volume of your audio tracks. In this exercise, you will add keyframes to lower the volume of the music track at the end of your movie to create a fade out.

1   With the My Project panel in Timeline view, place the current-time indicator a few seconds before the end of the last clip, the elephant.avi—we used the 00;01;11;00 mark.

2   Click to select the soundtrack.wav clip in the Timeline's Soundtrack.

3   Select Window > Properties, and then click the Show Keyframes button (ⓞ) in the upper right corner of the Properties panel.

4   Click the Toggle Animation button (ⓞ) to activate keyframes for the effect properties; this will set the first keyframe at the current-time indicator.

The next keyframe you'll set in the Timeline.

💡 *You can adjust the volume of individual clips under Volume in the Properties panel.*

5   Press the Page Down key to move the current-time indicator to the end of the elephant.avi clip, which is also the end of the movie.

6   In the Timeline view of the My Project panel, position the cursor over the yellow Volume graph of the soundtrack.wav clip at the current-time indicator. Make sure not to position the cursor too far to the right. The cursor needs to change to a white arrow with double arrows (⬚) and not the Trim Out tool (⬚). Hold down the Control key on your keyboard, and then click the Volume graph to add a second keyframe.

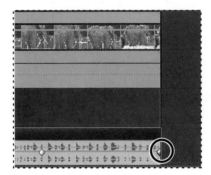

7   Drag the keyframe all the way down to create a fade out. You might want to use the Zoom tool to enlarge the view. You can check the Properties panel: the Clip Volume reads -oo to resemble the mathematical symbol $-\infty$ for minus infinity.

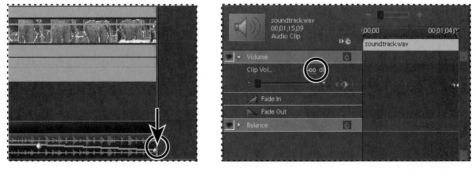

💡 *In the Timeline, adding keyframes and specifying precise values are separate tasks. In the Properties panel, you can combine both tasks in one step.*

8   To hear this change, press the Page Up key, and then press the spacebar to play. You should be able to hear the music track in the background. Towards the end of the elephant.avi clip, the volume of the music track decreases and fades out due to the keyframe adjustments you made.

9   Save your first project as **Lesson07_Zoo_End.prel**.

Creating a split edit

At times, you may want the audio to begin before the video or to extend after the video into the next clip (or vice versa). Trimming linked audio and video separately is called a split edit. Usually, when you split edit one clip, it requires that you split edit the adjacent clip so they don't overlap each other. You can create two kinds of split edits:

- A J-cut, or audio lead, in which audio starts before linked video, or video continues after the audio.

- An L-cut, or video lead, in which video starts before linked audio, or audio continues after the video.

—From Premiere Elements Help

Viewing the completed movie for the second exercise

To see what you'll be creating as your second project of this lesson, adding and refining the narration of the nursery rhyme Ring a Ring O'Roses to a video clip, take a look at the completed movie.

1   Choose File > Open Project. In the Open Project dialog box, navigate to the Lesson07 folder you copied to your hard disk. Within that folder, select the file Lesson07_Rosies.prel, and then click Open.

2   The project file opens with the Monitor, Tasks, and My Project panels open. Choose Window > Restore Workspace to ensure that you start the lesson with the default window layout.

3   In the Project view, double-click the Lesson07_Movie2.wmv file to open it in the Preview window.

4   Click the Play button (▶) to review the video you'll be building in this lesson. When done, click the Close button (✖) to close the Preview window.

Creating and adjusting a voiceover from a video clip

In Premiere Elements, the audio and video tracks of a clip are linked together by default. When you click and drag a clip in the Sceneline or the Timeline, the video and audio tracks will always move in tandem. This ensures that the sound is always synchronized with the picture. However, there may be times when you would like to remove either the video or the audio track of a particular clip, to create a voiceover, for example. In this exercise, you will drop a video clip into the Narration track of your sceneline to get just the voiceover.

1   Make sure you have Sceneline view selected in the My Project panel.

2   Choose File > Get Media from > Files and Folders, select the file 07_Voiceover.avi and click Open.

3   In the Project panel double-click the file 07_Voiceover.avi to open it in the Preview window, and then click the Play button. You'll watch a video of a man reciting the lines of the nursery rhyme.

4   Drag the 07_Voiceover.avi clip from the Project view and drop it onto the Narration track in the My Project panel.

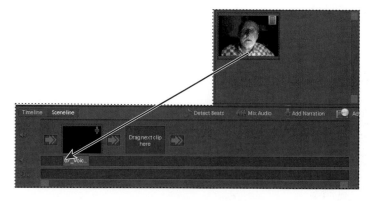

Note: Placing a video clip in the Narration track will only add the audio portion of that clip to the movie—a voiceover. You can work with the audio part of the clip in the same way that you would work with any other sound clip.

5   Click the Play button (▶) to hear the voiceover added to the project. Note that the background music needs to be toned down so that the narration is more audible.

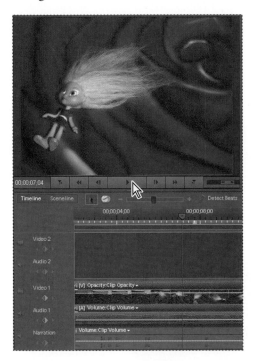

6   Click the Mix Audio button (♦♦♦) and in the upcoming Audio Mixer window drag the handle in the Audio 1 channel down to -6.0 dB.

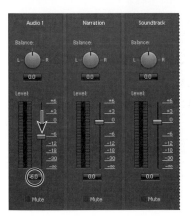

7   Click the Play button (▶) and listen to the improved audio mix.

By default, audio/video clips that you drag into the Timeline will try to snap to the position of the current-time indicator, the beginning or end of a clip, or the beginning of your Timeline. In this case, words would better fit the image if the voiceover started later. You'll adjust the starting position of the voiceover in the next steps.

8   Position the current-time indicator at about the 5 seconds mark, which is after the first movement of the piece of music. Notice the decreased sound volume visualized in the waveform of the Audio 1 track in the Timeline; if necessary use the Zoom In tool.

9   Select the 07_Voiceover.avi in the My Project panel and drag its starting point to the 5 seconds mark.

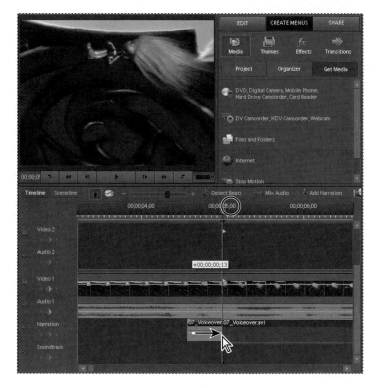

10   Press the Home key, and then press the spacebar to start playback. Notice how the voiceover now better corresponds with the video.

11   Save your file as **07_Rosies_Work.prel** in your Lessons07 folder.

Narrating a clip

For best results, confirm that your microphone is working correctly with your computer and Adobe Premiere Elements before narrating a clip.

Using your computer's microphone, you can narrate clips while previewing them in the Monitor panel. Your narration is then added to the Narration soundtrack visible in either the Timeline or Sceneline.

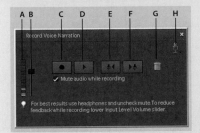

Record voice narration: **A.** Volume indicator **B.** Input Volume Level slider **C.** Record **D.** Play **E.** Go To Previous Narration Clip **F.** Go To Next Narration Clip **G.** Delete **H.** Microphone source

1 *In the Timeline, drag the current-time indicator in the Timeline to the point where you want the narration to begin. In the Sceneline, select the clip you want to narrate. Then, in the Monitor panel, drag the current-time indicator to the point where you want the narration to begin.*

2 *In the Timeline or Sceneline, click the Add Narration button ( ).*

3 *In the Record Voice Narration window, click the Mic Source button and select your sound device from the menu.*

4 *For best results, turn off your computer speakers to prevent feedback. To monitor sound while you narrate, plug headphones into your computer and deselect Mute Audio While Recording.*

5 *Speak into the microphone at a conversational volume, and raise or lower the Input Volume Level slider until your loudest words light up the orange part of the meters.*

6 *Click the Record Narration button.*

7 *Near the top of the Record Voice Narration window, a timer appears next to Start Recording In. When Start Recording In changes to Recording, speak your narration as the selected clip plays.*

8 *When you finish narrating, click the Stop button.*

An audio clip containing your narration is added to the Media panel and to the Narration track in the Timeline or Sceneline (below the selected clip). In the Sceneline, a microphone icon appears in the top-right corner of the clip you've narrated.

—From Premiere Elements Help

Adding a sound effect

With a wide variety of audio effects, you can improve or enhance the audio portion of your video projects. These effects range from controlling volumes and frequencies of the different channels, detecting and removing tape noise, or eliminating background noise, to inverting channels or adding the reverberation of sounds to give ambience and warmth to the audio clip. You can find the audio effects in the Effects view.

Audio playback controls are available only if the selected clip contains audio.

1   Click Edit in the Tasks panel, and then click Effects (*fx*) to open the Effects view.

2   Choose Audio Effects from the menu at the top of the panel.

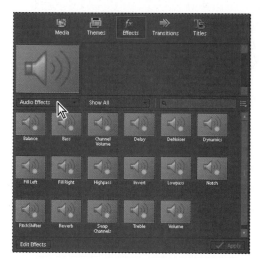

3   Scroll down in the Effects view to locate the Reverb effect, or type **reverb** in the search box.

The Reverb effect increases the ambience to an audio clip by adding the reverberation the sound might have had if recorded in a larger room. You can adjust parameters such as the Pre Delay, which specifies the time between the signal and the reverberation. In the example you're currently working on, this adds a mysterious echo to the voice, making it seem to come from far away.

4   In the Timeline, select the 07_Voiceover.avi clip, and then drag the reverb effect to the clip's soundtrack in the Timeline.

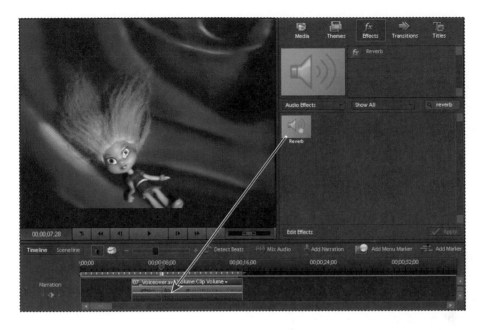

5 To refine the effect setting, click the Edit Effects button at the bottom of the Tasks panel, and expand the effect by clicking the triangle next to Reverb. You might need to scroll down in order to see all effect properties.

6 Make the following adjustments by either clicking a control and dragging up or down, or by clicking the text box below the control and entering the value directly: Pre Delay 55.00 ms, Size 36%, Density 88%, Lo Damp -8.00 dB, and Hi Damp -6.00 dB.

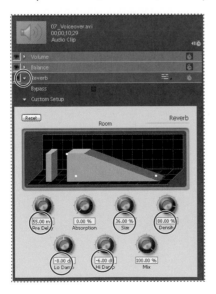

7   Press the Home key, and then press the spacebar to again play the video.

8   Choose File > Save As, and save the file as **Lesson07_Rosies_End.prel**.

Great, you've finished another lesson and learned the basics of working with sound. In the first exercise, you improved your project by eliminating unwanted noises and by matching the length of the audio to the video clip and creating a fade-out. In the second project, you created a voiceover from a video clip and applied a sound effect.

Exploring on your own

1   Experiment with various Audio effects such as Delay and Dynamics. You can also use the audio of the Birthday500 video clip from Lesson 4 and experiment with Audio effects like the PitchShifter. A description of Premiere Elements audio effects can be found in the Audio effects section of Adobe Premiere Elements Help.

2   As you did for the fade-out of the soundtrack, try to create a fade-in for the beginning of your project, the clip with the tiger.

3   Using the techniques described in "Creating a split edit," create an L-cut on two clips. An L-cut is when there are two clips side-by-side and the audio portion of the first clip extends into the video portion of the second clip.

Review

▶ **Review questions**

1   What is the Audio Mixer and how can you access it?

2   How would you change the volume of a clip over time using keyframes?

3   How do you change the presets of an audio effect?

4   What is a split edit?

▶ **Review answers**

1   Using the Audio Mixer, you can easily adjust the audio balance and volume for different tracks in your project. You can refine the settings while listening to audio tracks and viewing video tracks. Each track in the Audio Mixer corresponds to an audio track in the Timeline or Sceneline, and is named accordingly. You can access the Audio Mixer by clicking the Mix Audio button or choosing Window > Audio Mixer.

2   Each Premiere Elements clip in the Timeline has a yellow connector line that controls the keyframes of the clip. To add keyframes, you Ctrl+click the line. You must have at least two keyframes with different values to automatically change the level of the volume of an audio clip. You can also use the Audio Mixer to set keyframes to change the volume for your audio clip.

3   First, select the clip that contains the effect you want to adjust in the Timeline view. Then, in the Effects view, click the Edit Effects button. In the Properties view, expand the property by clicking the triangle next to the property name (if available), and then drag the slider or angle control.

4   A split edit is performed whenever you choose to independently edit the length of the audio and video tracks of a clip. Two common split edits are the L-cut and the J-cut.

8 | Titles and Credits

In this lesson, you'll learn how to create original titles and rolling credits for a home movie about a trip to the zoo. You'll be adding still titles and rolling titles, placing images, and using the drawing tools in the Monitor panel. Specifically, you'll learn how to do the following:

- Add and stylize text.
- Superimpose titles and graphics over video.
- Create and customize rolling titles.
- Use title templates.

About titles and the title-editing mode

Within Premiere Elements, you can create custom graphics and titles. When you add a title over one of your video clips, it is also added to your Project view as a new clip. As such, it is treated much like any other clip in your project. It can be edited, moved, deleted, and have transitions and effects applied to it. Premiere Elements allows you to create original titles using text, drawing tools, and imported graphics. However, for ease of use, Premiere Elements also provides a number of templates based on such common themes as Sports, Travel, and Weddings.

Getting started

To begin, you'll launch Adobe Premiere Elements, open the project used for this lesson, and review a final version of the movie you'll be creating.

1   Before you begin, make sure that you have correctly copied the Lesson08 folder from the DVD in the back of this book onto your computer's hard disk. See "Copying the Classroom in a Book files" on page 3.

2   Start Premiere Elements.

3   In the Welcome Screen, click the Open Project button. In the Open Project dialog box, navigate to the Lesson08 folder you copied to your hard disk. Within that folder, select the file Lesson08_Start.prel, and then click Open. If a dialog appears asking for the location of rendered files, click the Skip Previews button.

Your project file opens with the Monitor, Tasks, and My Project panels open.

4   Choose Window > Restore Workspace to ensure that you start the lesson with the default window layout.

Viewing the completed movie before you start

To see what you'll be creating, you can take a look at the completed movie.

1   In the Edit tab of the Tasks panel, select Media (▣) and then click the Project button. In the Project view, find the file Lesson08_Movie.wmv, and then double-click it to open the video in the Preview window.

2   Press the Play button (▶) to review the video you'll be building in this lesson.

3   When you're done, click the Close button (▣) to close the Preview window.

Creating a simple title

You can add titles to your movie—whether simple, still titles, advanced titles with added graphics, or styled text scrolling across the screen horizontally or vertically—directly in the Monitor panel of Premiere Elements. To begin, you will create a basic still title. You will work with a short project that has already been set up; all that you need to do is add the title clip at the beginning of the movie. First you will be adding a few seconds of black video over which you can then type the title text.

1   In the Sceneline of the My Projects panel, click the first clip to select it. In the top right corner of the Project view, click the New Item button (▣), and then choose Black Video from the menu that appears.

2   A five seconds long black video clip will be placed after the previously selected first clip in the Sceneline. To move the black video clip to the beginning of the movie, click and drag it to the left of the first clip in the Sceneline.

3   With the black video still selected in the Sceneline, choose Title > New Title > Default Still. Premiere Elements places default text over the black video in the Monitor panel, and switches to title-editing mode. In the mini-timeline of the Monitor panel, notice the bluish-gray colored clip representation for the new title clip that is placed on top of the lavender colored clip representation for the black video clip. Also notice the text and drawing tools now visible on the right side of the Monitor panel, and the text options, text styles, and text animation choices accessible in the Properties panel.

4   The Horizontal Type tool should be selected by default. If not, click the Horizontal Type tool button (T) in the Monitor panel to select it now.

Note: The Horizontal Type tool is grouped with the Vertical Type tool. To switch between the two, click and hold the tool button, and then choose from the menu that appears.

5   Click and drag to select the default text, type the words **A day at the**, and then press the Return key to create a new line. Next, type the word **ZOO**.

6   To reposition your text, click the Selection tool (↖) in the top right corner of the Monitor panel, and then click anywhere inside the text to select the text block. Click and drag to reposition the text so it appears centered in the upper half of your title window. There are two white margins in the title window; these are referred to as the title-safe and action-safe margins. Stay within the inner margin (title-safe) while repositioning your text. The exact position is not important at the moment. The text will need to be repositioned later in this lesson, after changing the text style and placing an image in the lower part of the frame.

7   Choose File > Save to save your work.

Basic titles like the one you just created are interpreted by Premiere Elements as still image files. Once you have created a title, an image file is automatically added to your Project view. In this case it was superimposed over the black video clip at the beginning of the movie, but you could just as well have placed it over any other clip in your movie. Even after a title has been added to the Sceneline, it is still possible to change its text or modify the look and view the changes immediately.

Title-safe and action-safe margins

The title-safe and action-safe margins visible in the Monitor panel when in title-editing mode designate the title's visible safe zones. These margins are on by default.

Safe zones are useful when editing for broadcast video and videotape. Most consumer television sets use a process called overscan, which cuts off a portion of the outer edges of the picture, allowing the center of the picture to be enlarged. The amount of overscan is not consistent across televisions, so to ensure that everything fits within the area that most televisions display, keep text within the title-safe margins and keep all other important elements within the action-safe margins. If you are creating content for computer screen viewing only, the title-safe and action-safe margins are irrelevant because computer screens display the entire image.

A. Safe action area. B. Safe title area.

To turn title-safe and action-safe margins on or off, choose Window > Show Docking Headers if the docking headers are not currently visible, and then choose Safe Title Margin, or Safe Action Margin from the Monitor palette menu. Or, right-click in the Monitor panel, and then choose View > Safe Title Margin or View > Safe Action Margin from the context menu. The margin is on if a check mark appears beside its name.

Modifying text

After you have entered you title text, you have full control over the appearance of your text, much like in a word processor or page layout program. In this exercise, you will learn how to adjust the alignment of your type as well as its style, size and color.

Changing the text alignment, style and size

1   In the Sceneline of the My Project panel, click the first scene—the black video with the title—to exit the title-editing mode of the Monitor panel. Click to select the superimposed title text image in the Monitor panel. The entire image is selected but the text itself cannot be selected or modified.

2   To be able to modify the text of your title, reenter the title-editing mode by first selecting and then double-clicking the superimposed title text image in the Monitor panel.

3   To center the text in its text box, use the Selection tool to select the title text box, and then click the Center Text button (≋) located under Text Options in the Properties panel.

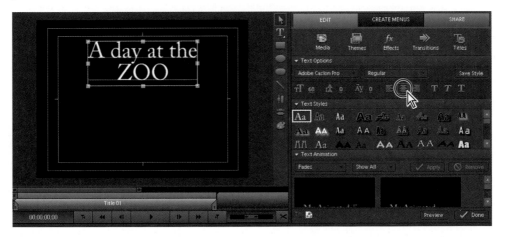

4   Use the Type tool to select the first line of text. Under Text Options in the Properties panel, choose Bell Gothic Std from the font menu and Black from the style menu next to it.

5   With the first line of text still selected, do the following to change the font size: Under Text Options in the Properties panel, place the cursor over the Size value. The cursor will change to a hand with two black arrows (🖐). Click and drag to change the Size value to 50. If you have difficulties getting a precise value by dragging, click the size value once, and then type **50** into the text field.

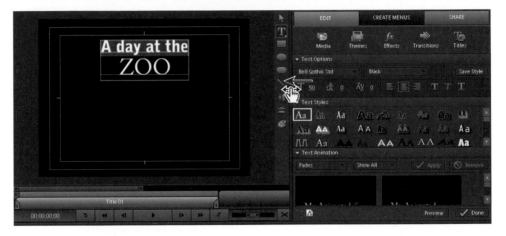

💡 *You can also change the size of text by selecting its text box, and then clicking and dragging one of the anchor points. Hold down the Shift key as you are dragging to maintain a proportional height and width of the text box and the type therein.*

6   Select the second line of text—the word ZOO—with the Type tool, and choose Lithos Pro White 94 from the list of predefined text styles under Text Styles in the Properties panel. This changes the text font and applies a drop shadow.

7   Change the text size to 105, so that the second line is about as wide as the first.

Changing the color of your type

As you have seen, changing the style and size of your type is easy. You can change all text within a text box equally, by first selecting the text box using the Selection tool, and then applying the change, or restrict the change to portions of the text by selecting them using the Type tool. You will now change the color of the word ZOO.

1   Select the Horizontal Type tool (T), and then click and drag over the word ZOO to highlight it. You will now change the color of the type from white to an orange-yellow. Any changes you make will apply only to the selected type.

2   Click the Color Properties button ( ) at the bottom of the tool buttons in the Monitor panel to open the Color Properties dialog box. Set the RGB values to R: 255, G: 175, B: 0. Notice that Drop Shadow is turned on for the selected text. This is part of the definition of the predefined style Lithos Pro White 94.

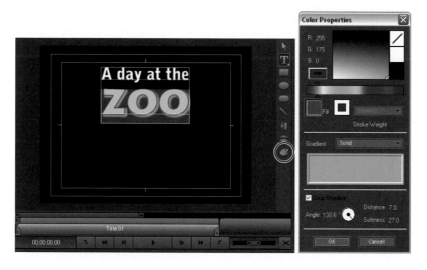

3   Click OK to close the Color Properties dialog box. Use the Selection tool and click outside the text box in the Monitor panel to deselect the text and review your work.

4   Save your project.

Centering elements in the Monitor panel

Now that the text formatting is done, you can manually reposition the text box with the Selection tool to be horizontally centered. Or, you can let Premiere Elements do the work for you.

1   Using the Selection tool, click the text box to select it.

2   Choose Title > Position > Horizontal Center. Or, right-click the text box, and then choose Position > Horizontal Center from the context menu. The text box will now be horizontally centered in the window. Depending on how you positioned the box earlier in this lesson, you might see little or no change.

3   Save your work.

Adding an image to your title files

To add an extra element of depth and fun to your titles, you can import images from any number of sources. For instance, photos you may have taken with your digital still camera can be used as elements in your title file. In this exercise, you will use an arrangement of still images taken from the video clips, and place it in the lower half of the title image.

1   With the Monitor panel still in title-editing mode, choose Title > Image > Add Image, or right-click the Monitor panel, and then choose Image > Add Image from the context menu. Or, click the Add Image button (🖼) located in the lower left corner of the Properties panel.

The Import Image as Logo dialog box appears. By default, the window may be pointing to the list of files in Premiere Elements Logos folder. These are the default images that were installed with the application. Feel free to use these in your other projects, whether from this book or otherwise.

2   In the Import Image as Logo dialog box, navigate to the Lesson08 folder. Within that folder, select the file title_zoo.psd, and then click Open to import the image into your title.

3   The image of three circles with animals inside appears stacked in front of the text box in your title. Use the Selection tool to drag the placed image towards the bottom of the title screen.

4   (Optional) Drag any anchor point to resize the placed image. Hold down the Shift key while dragging to maintain the height and width proportions of the image.

5   Right-click the image and choose Position > Horizontal Center from the context menu.

6   Save your work.

If you have overlapping frames, you can change the stacking order by right-clicking on a selected frame, and then using one of the Arrange commands from the context menu. To align multiple frames, select the frames you wish to align, and then right-click and choose any of the Align Objects commands from the context menu.

Creating fade-in and fade-out effects

Any transition that you use on video clips can also be added to title clips. In this exercise, you will add a fade-in and fade-out effect to the title clip.

1   In the Sceneline view of the My Project panel, click the first scene—the title over the black video—to select it.

2   In the Monitor panel, right-click the title image and choose Select > Title 01 from the context menu.

3   Choose Window > Properties and make sure the Properties panel shows the properties of the Title 01 clip. If necessary, click the triangle next to Opacity to see the Opacity controls.

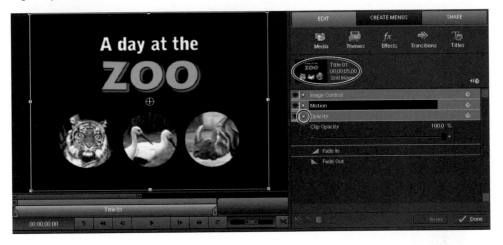

4   Under Opacity in the Properties panel, click the Fade In button once. The title image seems to disappear from the Monitor panel. Drag the current-time indicator in the mini-timeline to the right to see the image slowly fade in. After one second (30 frames for NTSC) the clip's opacity is at 100% and fully visible again.

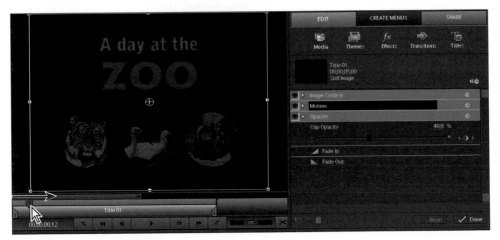

5   Click the Fade Out button once to add a fade-out effect for the clip.

6   Review your work by playing the movie from the beginning, and then choose File > Save to save your project.

Animate a still title

You can easily apply a preset animation to any still title. Text animation presets quickly and easily animate the characters in your title so that they fade or pop characters into view, or fly in from the top or bottom of the screen. For example, using the Fade In Characters preset instantly makes each separate character in your title fade into view until the title is complete.

To preview an animation, position the pointer on the animation thumbnail in the Text Animation section of the Tasks panel. (To see the Text Animation section, you must select a title so that the Tasks panel is in title-editing view.)

1 Do one of the following:

• Create a new still title.

• In the Timeline, double-click the title clip.

• In the Sceneline, select the superimposed clip. In the Monitor panel, click the clip, and then double-click the title text.

The Tasks panel changes to title editor view, displaying the text options.

2 Select an animation preset under Text Animation.

3 (Optional) Click the Preview button in the bottom-right corner of the Tasks panel to see how the animation looks on your title text.

4 Do one of the following to apply the animation to the title:

• Click the Apply button in the top-right corner of the Text Animation section in the Tasks panel.

• Drag the animation preset to the Monitor window and drop it on top of the title text.

5 Click Done at the bottom of the Tasks panel to close out of the title editor view.

Note: *To remove an animation from a title, select the title text and click the Remove button in the top right corner of the Text Animation section in the Tasks panel.*

—From Premiere Elements Help

Superimposing a title over video clips

When you place a title clip as a still image next to your video clips, you can work with it as with any other clip in the movie (such as adding effects and transitions or changing the playing order). Premiere Elements also enables you to superimpose titles directly over video clips to give them a more interesting look.

1 With Sceneline view selected in the My Project panel, click to select the first scene in your movie, the title clip. In the Monitor panel, click the Go to Next Edit Point button (▶) once, to jump to the beginning of the second scene, the first appearance of the tiger.

2 Choose Title > New Title > Default Still. With the Text tool, select the default text and type **Tiger**.

3 Use the Selection tool to position the title in the lower left corner of the safe title area.

To improve the readability of the text, you can try to change the text color or apply a style with a drop-shadow. Or, you can add a colored rectangle behind the text, as explained in the following steps.

4 Select the Rectangle tool (▭) from the tools on the right side of the Monitor panel. Click and drag to create a rectangle that will be covering your title—you will shortly be positioning the rectangle behind the text. *(See illustration on the next page.)*

5   Click the Color Properties button (⬤) at the bottom of the tool buttons in the Monitor panel to open the Color Properties dialog box. Set the color to black by clicking the large black rectangle near the upper right corner of the dialog box. Click OK to close the Color Properties dialog box and to apply the color to the rectangle you created.

6   Right-click the rectangle and choose Arrange > Send to Back from the context menu to place your black box behind your white type. The white text is now clearly visible over the black rectangle.

When you create any visual elements such as squares or circles, there is a stacking order that is created. The most recent items added (in this case, the rectangle) are placed at the top of the stacking order. You can control the stacking order—as you did here—using the Arrange commands from the context menu or the Title menu.

7 Select the black rectangle using the Selection tool, and then resize and reposition the rectangle as shown in the illustration below.

To quickly add titles at the same position in other clips you can use the copy and paste commands.

8 Using the Selection tool, click to select the black rectangle, and then shift-click to also select the text frame. Choose Edit > Copy.

9 In the Sceneline view of the My Project panel, click to select the first scene with the Rhinoceros.

10 Choose Title > New Title > Default Still to switch to title-edit mode. Use the Selection tool to select the default text which was added, and then choose Edit > Clear.

11 Choose Edit > Paste to add the black rectangle with the word Tiger at the same position as in the original clip. Use the Type tool, select the word Tiger and replace it by typing **Rhinoceros**. Use the Selection tool to select the black rectangle, and adjust its width to the new text length by dragging the right center anchor point to the right.

12 Review your movie, and then save your project.

💡 *You can add a fade-in or fade-out effect to the superimposed title clip in the same way as you did for the title over the black video at the beginning of the movie.*

Creating a rolling credit

The titles you have been creating up to this point have been static, but Premiere Elements can create animated titles as well. There are two types of animated titles: rolls and crawls. A rolling credit is defined as text moving vertically up the screen, like the end credits of a movie. A crawl is defined as text moving horizontally across the screen, like a news ticker. In this exercise you will create a rolling credit at the end of the project.

1 In the Sceneline of the My Projects panel, use the scrollbar at the bottom to scroll to the end of the movie. Click to select the last scene in the movie, the elephant.avi clip. In the Project view, click the New Item button (🖺), and then choose Black Video from the menu that appears. This will add a five seconds long black video at the end of the movie, serving as background for the rolling credit text.

2 With the newly added black video selected in the Sceneline, choose Title > New Title > Default Still. Premiere Elements switches to title-editing mode.

3   Using the Type tool, select the default text in the Monitor panel, and then type **The End**. Press the Return key twice to add vertical space before typing the text that will follow.

4   Type **Thanks to**, select this line of text, and then reduce the text size to 40 under Text Options in the Properties panel.

5   Place the cursor at the end of the "Thanks to" line, press return, and then type **(in order of appearance)**.

6   Use the Selection tool to move the text box towards the top of the Monitor panel, so you can continue to see the text you'll be adding at the bottom of the text box.

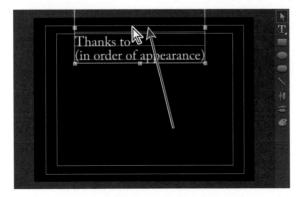

7   With the Text tool, place the cursor at the end of the "(in order of appearance)" line. Press return twice, and then type **The Tiger**, return, **The Rhinoceros**, return, **The Giraffe**, return, and **The Elephant**.

8   To center the text, click the Center Text button (≡) under Text Options in the Properties panel.

9   Right-click the text box and choose Position > Horizontal Center from the context menu.

10   Choose Title > Roll/Crawl Options.

💡 *The Roll/Crawls Options command is also accessible from the Monitor palette menu.*

11   In the Roll/Crawl Options dialog box, select Roll under Title Type, and then select both the Start Off Screen and the End Off Screen option under Timing (Frames). Click OK to close the dialog box.

When you play the clip, the text box with the credits will move—in the five seconds given by the length of the black video—from bottom to top across the monitor.

12   Play to review your rolling credits, and then save your project.

Changing the speed of a rolling title

When Premiere Elements creates a rolling title it is, in effect, creating an animation. The only way to change the speed of a rolling title is to increase or decrease the length of the title clip. The default duration for titles is 5 seconds. If you want to display more text or have the text move slower across the screen, you need to increase the clip length.

1   Switch to Timeline view in the My Project panel and scroll to the end of the movie. If necessary, increase the My Project panel so you can see Video tracks 1 and 2 at the same time.

2   Click to select the black video on Video track 1 at the end of the movie, and then hold down the Shift key and click the title clip in Video track 2 to select it as well.

3   Place your cursor over the end of the rolling title clip. When the cursor changes to a red bracket pointing to the left (⬌), click and drag the clip to the right. Note that as you drag there is a small yellow context menu that shows you how much time you are adding to the clip. Add two seconds to the length of the clip, and then release the pointer.

4   Place your current-time indicator just before the beginning of the rolling credits. Press the spacebar to play the rolling credits clip. Notice how your titles are now moving slower across the monitor.

Note: If you are having problems viewing your titles smoothly, they may need to be rendered. Pressing the Enter key on your keyboard will render all effects, transitions, and titles in a project.

5   Save your work.

Using title templates

Creating your own titles, as you have done in the exercises in this lesson, will give you the most flexibility and options when it comes to customized titles. However, this involves a considerable number of steps to be performed from start to finish. To help you get started designing your titles, Premiere Elements ships with numerous templates for different types of projects. All you need to do is customize the text, replace an image, or do both to create a great-looking title.

1   Select Titles ( ) in the Edit tab of the Tasks panel. Choose a category of title templates from the menu on the left, and then choose a template name from the menu on the right. If necessary, scroll down to see all available templates within the chosen theme, such as rolling titles and alternative title graphics.

2   To superimpose a title template over a video clip, select the clip in the Sceneline, and then drag and drop the template from the Titles view onto the Monitor panel. For rolling credits you can add some black video to your project first, or place the text directly over one of your movie clips.

3   Use the Type tool to select the default text and replace it with your own text. Use the Selection tool to reposition or resize text and image frames. Add or delete text and image frames as necessary.

4   Save your project as **Lesson08_End.prel**.

Exploring on your own

1   Experiment with the different templates Premiere Elements provides. Keep in mind that elements like the color of text and position of graphics can be modified.

2   Replace the custom title you created with a title created from a template.

3   Explore the drawing tools available to you when in title-editing mode.

4   Create an animated title choosing from the available options under Text Animation in the Properties panel.

5   Place different transitions between your title clips and your video clips to view the different effects you can achieve.

Congratulations, you have completed the lesson. You've learned how to create a simple still title with text and graphics. You changed the style, size, alignment and color of text. You positioned and aligned text and graphic frames in the Monitor panel, and you've used one of the Arrange commands to change the stacking order of overlapping frames. You added black video to your project and applied fade-in and fade-out effects to your title clip. You know now how to create rolling credits and how to use and customize title templates. It's time for a well-earned break. But before you stop, review the questions and answers on the next page.

Review

▶ **Review questions**

1 How do you create a new title?

2 How do you exit title-editing mode and how can you reenter it to make adjustments to the title clip?

3 How do you change the color of title text?

4 How do you add a fade-in or fade-out effect to a superimposed title clip?

5 What is a rolling credit and how do you make it run slower or faster?

▶ **Review answers**

1 With a video clip selected in the My Project panel, choose Title > New Title > Default Still. A title clip will be created and superimposed over the selected video clip.

2 To exit title-editing mode click Done in the lower right corner of the Properties panel, or click to select any clip in the My Project panel. To reenter title-editing mode, click to select the superimposed title text image in the Monitor panel, and then double-click it.

3 Switch to title-editing mode in the Monitor panel. Select the text using the Type tool. Then, click the Color Properties button, and pick a new color in the Color Properties dialog box.

4 In the Monitor panel, right-click the scene, and then select the title clip from the context menu. Under Opacity in the Properties panel, click the Fade In or Fade Out button.

5 A rolling credit is text that scrolls vertically across your screen. The only way to make a rolling credit change speed is by selecting the clip in the Timeline view of the My Project panel, and then extending the length of the clip to slow it down, or shorten the length of the clip to speed it up.

9 | Working with Movie Themes

Once you have arranged all the clips, transitions and effects for
your video project, Movie themes come in handy to quickly add
some flamboyance and a professional look. Movie themes include
a consistent appearance for the effects, transitions, overlays,
introductions, titles and even sound. To add pizzazz to your movie,
or maybe just give it a special film genre look, you can choose from
a wide variety of themes ranging from templates for birthdays and
weddings to road trips and more. What's particularly nice about
Movie themes is that they are flexible: you can apply an entire theme
or just parts of it to perfectly fit your creative concept. In this lesson,
you'll learn how to do the following:

- Select a Movie theme.

- Choose some Movie theme properties and apply them to your
clip.

- Change the title and apply a different text style, color, size and
leading to your rolling credits.

- Delete elements of a Movie theme.

- Add an image as logo.

Getting started

To begin, you'll launch Adobe Premiere Elements, open the project
used for this lesson, and review a final version of the movie you'll be
creating.

1   Before you begin, make sure that you have correctly copied the Lesson09 folder from the DVD in the back of this book onto your computer's hard disk. See "Copying the Classroom in a Book files" on page 3.

2   Start Premiere Elements.

3   In the Welcome Screen, click the Open Project button. In the Open Project dialog box, navigate to the Lesson09 folder, select the file Lesson09_Start.prel, and then click Open. If a dialog appears asking for the location of rendered files, click the Skip Previews button.

4   Choose Window > Restore Workspace to ensure that you start the lesson with the default window layout.

Viewing the completed movie before you start

To see what you'll be creating, you can take a look at the completed movie.

1   In the Edit tab of the Tasks panel, select Media (🖼), and then click the Project button. In the Project view, find the file Lesson09_Movie.wmv, and then double-click it to open the video in the Preview window.

2   Click the Play button (▶) to review the video you'll be building in this lesson. You might recognize the video from Lesson 7. Note the change of colors and the addition of some elements from a Movie theme: the introduction, transitions, effects and credits.

3   When you're done reviewing, click the Close button (▣) to close the Preview window.

About Movie themes

Movie themes enable you to quickly create videos with a specific look and feel. The Wedding Doves theme, as an example, adds an elegant, animated introduction, an overlay of flying white doves, wedding background music, and closing credits for a wedding video. In contrast, the Comic Book theme provides more funky effects and fonts along with picture-in-picture overlays that might be more appropriate for a kids' party video.

You can apply all of the properties in a theme, choose to add only a subset, or even just modify some parts. Likewise, in the Sceneline you can add a theme to an entire movie or to only a single clip.

Movie themes are accessible via the Themes button (▣) in the Edit tab of the Tasks panel. The different themes use animated thumbnails that give you a good idea of the overall feel of the theme.

Note: When you apply a theme, all of the effects and transitions that you've previously applied to a project are deleted and replaced by the theme.

💡 *Before applying a theme, choose File > Save to save your project. If you apply a theme, and then decide you don't like it, choose Edit > Undo to return to your original version.*

Applying and selecting parts of a Movie theme

A Movie theme can change the look of your project considerably. Let's first take a look at the little video—the one you worked on when experimenting with sound and voiceover in Lesson 7—before applying a theme.

1   Make sure you're in the Sceneline view by clicking the Sceneline button in the My Project panel.

2   From the Project view, drag the Rosies.avi movie onto the empty clip target in the Sceneline.

3   In the Monitor panel, click the Play button (▶) to start playback. When you're done reviewing, press the spacebar to stop playback.

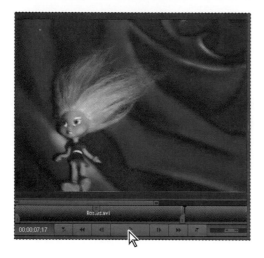

You'll now apply a movie theme to this movie.

4   Click the Themes button (▣) in the Edit tab of the Tasks panel.

5   Select Movie Genre from the theme category menu. Hover the pointer over the News Reel theme thumbnail in order to see an animated preview of the theme. Notice the intro and closing credits with piano music. In the next step you will choose not to include these parts before applying the theme to your movie.

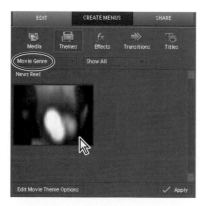

6 Click to select the News Reel movie theme thumbnail, and then click the Edit Movie Theme Options button. In the Movie Theme Options view, deselect the Intro Movie checkbox as well as the Closing Movie checkbox, and then click Done.

7 In the Movie Theme dialog box that appears, click OK to apply the theme.

8 Press the Home key, and then press the spacebar to review your edited movie. Wait until the movie ends, or press the spacebar to stop playback.

Working with titles in a Movie theme

Next, you will replace the placeholder text with your own text and change the type style, size and color. You'll start with entering the movie title.

1   In the Sceneline view, click to select the first clip. If necessary, press the Home key to position the current-time indicator at the beginning of the movie. Then, click to select the superimposed title image in the Monitor panel. The news_reel_title title image is selected but the text itself cannot yet be selected or modified.

2   Double-click the news_reel_title image to enter title-editing mode.

3   Using the Type tool, select the words Movie Title, and then type **Rosies** to replace the selected placeholder text. Done, your movie has a new title.

4   In the Monitor panel, click the Play button (▶) to review your edited movie until the Add text here title appears—at approximately 7 seconds into the movie. Then, press the spacebar to stop playback.

5 Click to select the superimposed news_reel_credits image in the Monitor panel. Then, double-click the image to reenter title-editing mode.

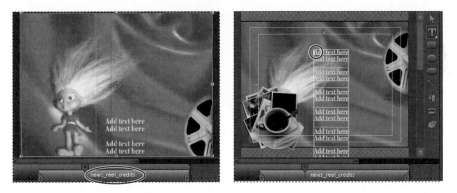

6 Use the Selection tool to select the text box. Then, click the Center Text button (⬇) located under Text Options in the Properties panel. You may not notice any difference in the text layout at the moment, but you've set the text justification control so that everything you're going to write in this text box will be centered.

7 Switch to the Type tool, click inside the text box, and then press Ctrl+A to select the entire text. Under Text Options in the Properties panel, set the text size to **80** pt. Under Text Styles, hover the pointer over the text styles to see their names displayed in a tool tip window. Click to select the Eccentric Std Gold 45 text style.

8   Using the type tool, again click inside the text box and press Ctrl-A to make the text box active and select the entire text. Type the words **RING AROUND THE ROSIES**, and then press the Return key to create a new line. Type the words **POCKETFUL OF POSIES**, and after pressing the Return key continue typing **ASHES, ASHES** followed by pressing the Return key and **WE ALL FALL DOWN**.

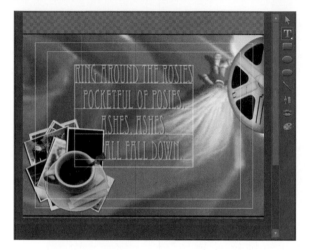

9   Increase the space between the text lines by entering **100** as Leading under Text Options. This will make the pace of the rolling titles work better with the voiceover.

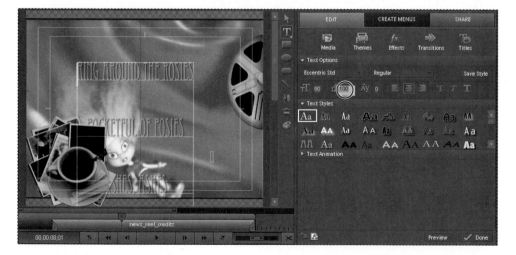

10   Click the first clip in the Sceneline to exit title-editing mode. Press the Home key, and then press the spacebar to review your movie.

Adapting elements of a Movie theme

As you've seen, it only takes a few moments to replace and adjust the placeholder text that comes with a movie theme. Next, you'll delete an image from the movie theme template and replace it with an image that was installed on your computer with your copy of Premiere Elements.

1   In the Monitor panel, position the current-time indicator so you can see the rolling title, with the coffee cup image on the left and the film reel image on the right. Click to select the title image, and then double-click it to enter title-editing mode. Choose the Selection tool (↖), click to select the image with the cup of coffee on the left, and then right-click the image and select Clear from the context menu.

2   In the Monitor panel, click the film reel image on the right, and then choose Edit > Clear to delete this image as well.

3   Click the Add Image button (🖻) located in the lower left corner of the Properties panel to open the Import Image as Logo dialog box. By default, the dialog box is pointing to the Premiere Elements Logos folder.

4   In the Premiere Elements Logos folder (inside the Presets folder of your Premiere Elements application folder), select the file album_butterfly, and then click Open. *(See illustration on the next page.)*

5   The logo of a blue butterfly appears in your Monitor window. Click the butterfly image and use the bounding box handles to reduce the size of the image. Press the Shift key while dragging any of the handles to scale the image proportionally. Click and drag the image to position it as show in the illustration below.

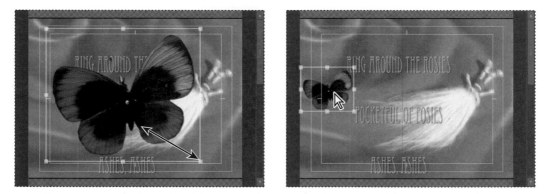

6   Click the first clip in the Sceneline to exit title-editing mode. Press the Home key, and then press the spacebar to review the entire video. The image of the butterfly moves upwards at the same pace as the rolling credits.

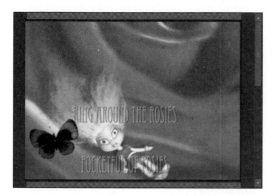

7   Save your project as **Lesson09_End.prel** in your Lessons09 folder.

8   Close your project.

Exploring on your own

1   Experiment with the different Movie themes provided with your copy of Premiere Elements. Keep in mind that you can apply an entire theme or pick and choose parts of it.

2   Change the appearance of the rolling credits by experimenting with different text styles, font sizes, and other text attributes.

3   Replace the butterfly image with another image from the Premiere Elements Logos folder or one of your own images.

Well done, you have completed this lesson. You've learned how to apply a Movie theme and how to customize its properties. You changed the title of the movie as well as the placeholder text of the rolling credit, including changing its text size, alignment, leading and style. If you don't like any of the images that come with a Movie theme, you now know how to delete them. Or, replace them with an image from the Premiere Elements Logos folder.

Review

▶ Review questions

1 What is a Movie theme?

2 How do you change the style of text?

3 What does leading mean?

4 How can you add an image to a rolling title?

▶ Review answers

1 Movie themes are templates that enable you to quickly turn your clips into a more professional looking movie. You can choose from event-based themes like Birthday or more style-based themes like Silent Film. A Movie theme includes coordinated transitions, effects, music, as well as layouts for titles and credits. You can apply an entire theme or choose to select only parts of it.

2 To enter title-editing mode, click to select the superimposed title text image in the Monitor panel, and then double-click it. Select the text box. Under Text Styles in the Properties panel, click to select any of the available text styles.

3 Leading is the spacing between lines of text. At times you may want to adjust the leading to make a block of text more pleasing to the eye, or to make it take up more or less space on the screen.

4 You can add an image to a title by first entering title-editing mode, and then clicking the Add Image button (⊞) located in the lower left corner of the Properties panel. In the Premiere Elements Logos folder you have a wide variety of images to choose from. When adding an image to a title, you can add it as a graphic element or place it in a box to become part of the text. Adobe Premiere Elements accepts both bitmapped images and vector-based artwork such as images created with Adobe Illustrator. By default, an inserted image appears at its original size. Once inserted into a title, you can modify the image properties such as its size in the usual manner.

10 | Creating Menus

In this lesson you'll be creating a menu for a collection of home movies to be used on a DVD or Blu-ray disc. You can follow along with most of this lesson even if your system does not have a DVD or Blu-ray disc burner, although it will be helpful if you do. You are about to learn how to work with menu markers in order to create menu chapters and how to customize disc menus based on the content of your project. You will also learn how to preview a menu and then burn a DVD or Blu-ray disc for playback on a standard DVD or Blu-ray disc player. Specifically, you'll learn how to do the following:

- Add menu markers to your movie.
- Create an auto-play disc.
- Use Templates to create disc menus.
- Customize the look of the menus.
- Preview a disc menu.
- Burn a DVD or Blu-ray disc.

Getting started

To begin, you'll launch Adobe Premiere Elements, open the project used for this lesson, and review a final version of the movie you'll be creating.

1   Before you begin, make sure that you have correctly copied the Lesson10 folder from the DVD in the back of this book onto your computer's hard disk. See "Copying the Classroom in a Book files" on page 3.

2   Start Premiere Elements.

3   In the Welcome Screen, click the Open Project button. In the Open Project dialog box, navigate to the Lesson10 folder, select the file Lesson10_End.prel, and then click Open. If a dialog appears asking for the location of rendered files, click the Skip Previews button.

A finished version of the project file you will be creating in this lesson opens with the Monitor, Tasks, and My Project panels open. You may review it now or at any point during the lesson to get a sense of what your project should look like.

4   Select Create Menus in the Tasks panel to switch to the Create Menus workspace. In the Disc Layout panel, click Preview to open the Preview Disc window.

The Preview Disc window allows you to view and test your menus as they will appear when played on a DVD or Blu-ray player.

5   In the Preview Disc window, click the Scenes button in the Main menu to switch to the Scene Selection menu. Click the Tiger button to begin playing this section.

6   Press the spacebar on your keyboard to stop the playback, and then close the Preview Disc window by clicking its Close button (✖) in the upper right corner.

7   After reviewing the finished file, choose File > Close. When asked, do not save any changes made to the project. Then, click the Open Project button, select the file Lesson10_Start.prel, and click Open. If a dialog appears asking for the location of rendered files, click the Skip Previews button.

8   Choose Window > Restore Workspace to ensure that you start the lesson with the default window layout.

Understanding DVDs and Blu-ray discs

DVD stands for Digital Video Disc and is an optical disc storage medium similar to a Compact Disc but capable of storing much more data. For example, a CD stores about 650 megabytes of data. A DVD stores up to 4.7 Gigabytes of data. DVD is actually a generic term that encompasses a few different formats. The format you will be working with in Premiere Elements is commonly referred to as DVD-Video. This is the same format of DVD that you can purchase or rent and play on a DVD player connected to your television set or on a computer fitted with the appropriate drive.

A Blu-ray disc—also called BD disc—is an optical disc format that has five times the storage capacity of DVDs. It can store 25GB on a single-layer disc or 50GB on a dual-layer disc. It gets its name from the blue-violet laser it uses (as opposed to the red laser used by other optical discs).

To make a DVD or Blu-ray disc in Premiere Elements, you must have a compatible DVD or Blu-ray disc burner. It is important to note that although your system may have a DVD or Blu-ray disc player it may not be a recordable drive, also known as a DVD or Blu-ray disc writer or burner. A disc drive will only play DVDs or Blu-ray discs, not record them. Check the system specifications of your computer to make sure which drive (if any) you have. Drives capable of recording DVDs and Blu-ray discs are also available as external hardware. Often such external recordable drives are connected through your system's FireWire or IEEE 1394 port, although some drives connect through the USB port.

Physical media

The type of disc onto which you will record your video is important. There are two basic formats you should be aware of: Recordable (DVD-R and DVD+R for DVDs, BD-R for Blu-ray discs) and Rewritable (DVD-RW and DVD+RW for DVDs, BD-RE for Blu-ray discs). Recordable discs are single use discs; once you record data onto a recordable disc you cannot erase the data. Rewritable discs can be used multiple times, much like the floppy disks of old.

So which format should you choose? Compatibility is of the major issues with the two formats. There are many older DVD players that may not recognize some rewritable discs created on a newer DVD burner, for example. Another issue is that, as of this writing, the media for recordable discs is less expensive than the media for rewritable discs. However, if you make a mistake with a recordable disc, you must use another disc, whereas with a rewritable disc you can erase the content and use the disc again. For this reason, we suggest using rewritable discs for making your test discs, and then using recordable discs for final or extra copies.

Manually adding Scene Markers

When watching a DVD or Blu-ray disc movie, you normally have the option to jump to the beginning of the next chapter by clicking a button on the remote control. To specify the start of chapters or sections in your project, you must add Scene markers.

1   Scroll through the entire movie in the Sceneline view of the My Project panel.

This project consists of three main sections, labeled Tiger, Rhinoceros, and Elephant. Each section has a title superimposed for the first 5 seconds. You will be placing Scene markers at the beginning of each section in order to include them on the disc menu. You'll start by adding the marker for the Tiger section.

Note: This project is only about 1 minute long due to necessary limitations on the file size. Most projects would likely be longer, but the basic principles remain the same.

2   Click to select the first clip in the Sceneline, the tiger 1.avi clip with the word Tiger superimposed as title. Click the Add Menu Marker button (◉) located near the top right corner of the My Project panel to open the Menu Marker dialog box. You will be working more with this dialog box later in this lesson; for now, just click OK. Notice the Scene Marker icon added to the tiger 1.avi clip in the Sceneline.

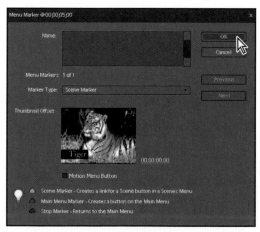

3   In the My Project panel, click the Timeline button to switch to Timeline view. Notice the green scene marker located on the Timeline under your current-time indicator.

Note: You may have to move the current-time indicator to better see the green scene marker beneath.

4   (Optional) If you prefer to work in Sceneline view, click the Sceneline button in the My Project panel.

5   Press the Page Down key a few times to advance to the Rhinoceros scene. The Page Down key is a shortcut for advancing to the next edit point and is extremely useful when creating markers because it ensures you are on the first frame of the clip. You could also have moved your current-time indicator to this position by clicking the Go to Next Edit Point button (🏴) a few times in the Monitor panel.

6   Again click the Add Menu Marker button (📷) in the My Project panel to add a second scene marker at the position of the current-time indicator, the first frame of the Rhinoceros scene. In the Menu Marker dialog box, click OK to confirm the creation of the scene marker and to close the dialog box.

7   Using the Page Down key, advance to the elephant.avi clip, and then add yet another scene marker. You should now have three markers in you project, one for each section of this short movie.

Creating an auto-play disc

Generally speaking, most professional DVDs or Blu-ray discs have a navigation system of some sort, commonly referred to as a menu. You will be working with menus shortly, but there is a quick and easy way to make a disc that does not involve menus: creating an auto-play disc. An auto-play disc is similar to a videotape; when you place the disc into a player it will begin playing automatically. There is no navigation, although there is the ability to jump from scene to scene—defined by the markers you just added—using a remote control.

1 Select Create Menus in the Tasks panel to switch to the Create Menus workspace. The Disc Layout panel replaces the Monitor panel and the Templates view opens in the Create Menus tab of the Task panel. If you want to see the panel names, choose Window > Show Docking Headers.

Note: The Auto-Play button should be dimmed and no template selected. Click the Auto-Play button if your Disc Layout panel looks different than in the illustration above.

2 In the Disc Layout panel, click the Preview button to open the Preview Disc window. The Preview Disc window allows you to view and test your disc as it will appear after creation when it is playing on a DVD or Blu-ray disc player.

3 In the Preview Disc window, click the Play button (▶) to begin playing your project. Once the first video clip begins playing, press the Next Scene button (▶▶❙) and the video jumps to the next scene. The scenes are defined by the scene markers you added to your project. When viewing this disc on a TV set, you could use a remote control to advance through the scenes.

4 Click the Close button (⊠) in the upper right corner of the Preview Disc window to close it.

5 Choose File > Save As and save this project file into your Lesson10 folder as **Lesson10_Work.prel**.

Automatically generating Scene Markers

Manually placing markers in the Timeline gives you ultimate control over the placement of your markers. For longer videos however, you may not wish to place all the markers by hand. To make the process of placing markers easier, Premiere Elements can create markers automatically based on clips boundaries or specified time intervals.

1 Choose File > Save As and save this project file into your Lesson10 folder as **Lesson10_Markers.prel**. You will be returning to the original project file after you are done exploring the automatic generation of scene markers.

2 Choose Auto-Generate Menu Markers from the palette menu. Or, right-click in the preview area of the Disc Layout panel, and then choose Auto-Generate Menu Markers from the context menu.

3 The Automatically Set Menu Scene Markers dialog box appears. Keep the default option selected to set a scene marker At Each Scene, which is to say at the beginning of every clip on the Video 1 track. Keep the Clear Existing Menu Markers check box unselected. Selecting this option would remove existing markers including marker names and thumbnail offsets associated with each one. If you already spent time to create some markers manually and don't want to lose any of your work, be careful not to select this option. Click OK to close the dialog box. Scene markers will be placed at the beginning of every clip.

4   Switch to Timeline view in the My Project panel to review the position of all the markers in your project.

5   Click the Preview button in the Disc Layout panel.

6   In the Preview Disc window, click the Play button (▶) to begin playing your project. Once the first video clip begins playing, click the Next Scene button (▶▶|) repeatedly and notice how the video jumps from scene to scene.

7   Click the Close button (⊠) in the upper right corner of the Preview Disc window to close it.

8   Right-click in the preview area of the Disc Layout panel, and then choose Auto-Generate Menu Markers from the context menu to again open the Automatically Set Menu Scene Markers dialog box. Choose the Total Markers option and type **4** into the number field. Select the Clear Existing Menu Markers check box, and then click OK.

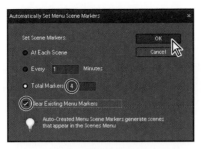

There are now four markers evenly spread out across the Timeline.

💡 *Markers can be repositioned in the Timeline by clicking and dragging them to the left or right.*

Using the Total Markers option may be preferable to creating a marker for every clip in order to cut down on the number of scenes in your movie. As you will see in the next exercise, when creating a disc with menus, Premiere Elements will automatically create buttons and menus based on the markers in your project. Too many markers might result in too many navigation buttons and screens for your movie.

9   Choose File > Save. Then choose File > Open Recent Project > Lesson10_Work.prel to return to the project file from the previous exercise.

Creating a disc with menus

The auto-play disc you created in the last exercise is perhaps the quickest way to go from a Premiere Elements project to a disc you can watch using a standard player, but auto-play discs lack the navigation structure that most users have come to expect when watching a DVD or Blu-ray disc. The ability to view the image thumbnails of a specific scene and then jump directly to that scene by pressing a button on the remote control is a feature found in almost all commercially available DVDs or Blu-ray discs. You can quickly create such navigation menus in Premiere Elements using a variety of templates designed for this purpose.

1   If you are not currently in the Create Menus workspace, select Create Menus in the Tasks panel to switch to it now.

2   Premiere Elements ships with several distinctive menu templates—predesigned and customizable menus that come in a variety of themes and styles. In the Templates view under the Create Menus tab, select Entertainment from the category menu, and then select the template called Countdown from the menu next to it.

3   To apply the Countdown template to your project, click to select the template in the Template view, and then click the Apply button (✔) in the lower right corner of the Template view. Or, drag the template from the Templates view and drop it onto the Disc Layout panel.

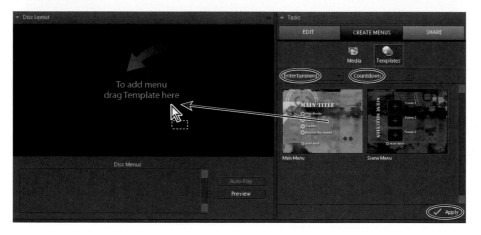

Each template contains a Main menu and a Scenes menu. The Main menu is the first screen that the viewer sees when the disc is played. The Scenes menu is a secondary window and is accessed only when the viewer clicks the Scene Selection button in the Main menu.

4   Under Disc Menus in the Disc Layout panel, click to select the Main Menu 1. There are two buttons currently visible in this menu, called Play Movie and Scene Selection. Additionally, there is a generic text button reading Main Title. You will now change the text of this generic button to something more appropriate for your project.

5   In the preview area of the Disc Layout panel, click the Main Title text once. A thin white rectangle appears around the button indicating that it is selected. Now double-click the Main Title text to open the Change Text dialog box. If the text under Change Text is not already highlighted, select it now, and then type **A day at the zoo**. Click the OK button to close the Change Text dialog box and to commit the change.

6   You can adjust the position of text boxes by clicking and dragging them. Click and drag the title box to reposition the title slightly to the right. Later in this lesson you will learn how to further customize the appearance of text in your menus.

Click and drag text boxes to reposition them.

7   Click the Preview button to preview the main menu. Place your cursor over the Play Movie and Scene Selection buttons, but do not click them yet. Notice the white circle to the left of the buttons when the pointer passes over them. This rollover effect is part of the menu template. Click the Play Movie button and the movie begins to play.

The preview menu feature is designed to make sure your menus are working correctly. The video quality of the image is not indicative of the final video. Because of the differences between computer monitors and television sets, you may see noticeable horizontal lines as the video is playing on the computer monitor. These lines are referred to as interlacing, and will not be visible in the final movie when played on a TV.

8   As the movie is playing, click the Main Menu button (▤) at the bottom of the Preview Disc window. Clicking this button at any point during playback returns you to the main menu, so you don't have to watch the whole movie if you're just testing your menus.

9   Click the Close button (▨) in the upper right corner of the Preview Disc window to close it.

Working with submenus

For many people, the previous exercises will fulfill most disc menu needs: applying a menu template to a project, modifying the menu appearance, and automatically generating markers. But Premiere Elements also offers more advanced menu creation features. For example, many Hollywood movies have a link on the main menu to bonus or deleted clips sections. Premiere Elements enables you to have a submenu button appear on your main menu by adding a special menu marker. In this exercise you will add a button on the main menu linking to a bonus video clip.

1   Under Disc Menus in the Disc Layout panel, click to select the Main Menu 1. There are currently two buttons in this menu: the Play Movie and Scene Selection buttons. The template design leaves space for more buttons below these two buttons, if needed.

2   Select Timeline view in the My Project panel. Press the End key on your keyboard to navigate to the end of the last clip.
You will now add a special marker to the end of your movie.

3   Click the Add Menu Marker button (▤) located near the top right corner of the My Project panel to open the Menu Marker dialog box. Choose Stop Marker from the Marker Type menu. When a stop marker is reached during playback you will be returned to the main menu.

4   Click OK to add the Stop Marker. In the Timeline, stop markers are colored red to help you differentiate them from the green scene markers and the blue main menu markers. You will learn more about main menu markers later in this lesson.

Three types of menu markers

Scene Markers (⌂) Adding a scene marker to your Timeline will automatically add a scene button to the scene menu of your disc. Scenes menus are secondary to the main menu and there should be a Scenes button on the main menu which links to the Scenes menu.

Main Menu Markers (⌂) Adding a main menu marker to your Timeline will automatically add a button to the main menu of your disc. Most templates have space for either three or four buttons on the first menu page. The Play Movie button and the Scenes button are often added by default. This will leave you with space for one or two more buttons, depending on the template you have chosen. If you add additional main menu markers to your movie, Premiere Elements will create a secondary main menu.

Stop Markers (⌂) Adding a stop marker to your Timeline will force Premiere Elements to stop the playback of your Timeline and return the viewer to the main menu. Stop markers are most often used when you want to add after the main movie additional clips such as bonus clips or deleted scenes. Using scene or main menu markers, you can link to additional clips in the Timeline that are placed after the main movie.

You will now add an additional clip to the end of your Timeline. This clip will be a bonus clip that users can access from the main menu, but is not part of the main movie. You will use a full-length version of the rhino.avi clip as a bonus clip.

5   Select Media (📷) in the Create Menus tab of the Tasks panel, and then click Project. From the Project view, click and drag the rhino.avi clip into the Video 1 track, after the Credit sequence at the end of your Timeline. Be sure to place the clip with a few seconds distance from the last clip. In other words, leave a gap between the clips.

6   Press the Page Down key to advance the current-time indicator to the beginning of the added rhino.avi clip, and then click the Add Menu Marker button (📷) to open the Menu Marker dialog box.

7   In the Menu Marker dialog box, choose Main Menu Marker from the Marker Type menu. In the name field, type **Bonus Clip**, and then click OK to close the Menu Marker dialog box.

A button named Bonus Clip, the name given to the main menu marker in the Menu Marker dialog box, has been added to the Main Menu 1 in the Disc Layout panel.

8   Click the Preview button, and then click the Bonus Clip button to play the video associated with it. When the bonus clip has finished playing, the main menu appears. If you play the main movie from start to finish, you will not see the bonus clip because of the stop marker you added at the end of the last clip in the main movie.

Note: You do not have to add a stop marker at the end of the bonus clip. When Premiere Elements reaches the end of the Timeline, it will automatically return the viewer to the main menu.

9   Close the Preview Disc window.

By using a combination of the three different menu markers you can create unique menus for your movies.

Using the Properties panel for the disc menu layout

Customizing your disc menu involves a combination of the Disc Layout panel, the Properties panel, and the Menu Marker dialog box. The Properties panel is visible in the Tasks panel when objects are selected in the Disc Layout panel and enables you to modify the settings of your menu. Its content depends on which object is selected.

For menus, the Properties panel displays two sections: Menu Background and Motion Menu Buttons. These two sections can be expanded or collapsed by clicking the arrows to the left of the section. In the Menu Background section there are subsections for Video or Still backgrounds, and Audio backgrounds. Video clips, photo stills, and audio clips can be added as menu background by dragging them from the Project view and dropping them onto the Media drop zones in the Properties panel.

A. Properties panel inside the Tasks panel. B. Menu thumbnail. C. Menu Background section. D. Media drop zones. E. Motion Menu Buttons section.

Customizing disc menus

Although Premiere Elements allows you to customize a disc menu, keep in mind that you are customizing only a template. Changes made will not be saved back to the template; they apply only to the current project. If you would like to create custom templates to be used in multiple projects, you can create one in Adobe Photoshop Elements, and then add the template to Premiere Elements.

In this exercise you will make changes to your menu appearance and buttons.

1 Make sure you are in the Create Menus workspace, and then choose Window > Restore Workspace to reset the location of your panels.

2 Under Disc Menus in the Disc Layout panel, click the Main Menu 1 thumbnail to make sure the main menu is loaded.

3   Click the Play Movie button to select it. The rectangle around the button is referred to as the bounding box. There are eight selection points around the box. Place your cursor on one of the corners, and then click and drag outward to enlarge the text box.

Scaling text boxes in this manner can be tricky because the width and height do not scale proportionally. Text can easily become distorted.

4   Press Ctrl+Z on your keyboard to undo the changes. Premiere Elements allows you to undo multiple steps, so you can backtrack through your changes.

5   With the Play Movie button still selected, press the equal sign (=) on your keyboard and the text box size increases proportionally. Press the minus key (-) on your keyboard to reduce the size of your text box proportionally. Using the keyboard commands to change the size avoids the risk of distorting the text.

6   Click the Scene Selection button in the Disc Layout panel to select it, and then press the left arrow key on your keyboard to move it. Pressing the arrow keys on your keyboard allows you to move a button one pixel at a time in the direction of the arrow. Press the right arrow key to move the button back to its original location.

7   Double-click the Scene Selection button text and change the label to **Scenes** in the Change Text dialog box. Click OK to close the Change Text dialog box and to commit the change.

Changing text properties of menu buttons

The Properties panel allows you to modify the font, size, color, and style of your menu buttons. Changes made to one type of button can be automatically applied to similar buttons.

You can modify the text attributes of five types of objects: Menu Titles, which are objects that are text only and are not linked to clips or movies, Play buttons, which link to the beginning of your main movie, Scene Marker buttons, which link to the Scenes menu, Marker buttons, which directly link to a menu marker on the Timeline, and Navigational buttons like the link back to the main menu on the Scenes Menu.

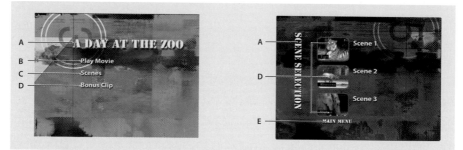

A. Menu Title. **B.** *Play button.* **C.** *Scene button.* **D.** *Marker button,* **E.** *Navigational button.*

1   Under Disc Menus in the Disc Layout panel, click the Scenes Menu 1 thumbnail.

2   Click the Scene 1 marker button. The Properties panel updates automatically and shows that this is a marker button, specifically a Scene Marker button. The Text subsection allows you to change the properties of the text. If necessary, scroll down in the Properties panel to see all of the Text subsection.

3   In the Text subsection, click the font menu, and then choose Arial from the list of available fonts. The marker text appearance changes.

4   Click the style menu, currently set at Regular, and change the style to Bold.

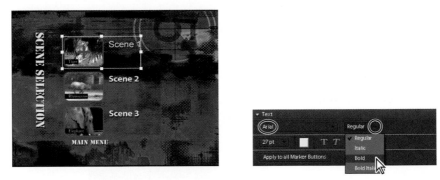

5   The next menu, the text size menu, allows you to change the text size to any of the preset sizes. Change the text size to 30 pt.

6   Click the white color swatch next to the text size menu to open the Color Picker dialog box. You will now change the color of your text to orange. Click once in the vertical color spectrum in the general range of orange. Then, click in the lower right corner of the large color field to choose a bright orange. We selected a color with R: 222, G: 159, B: 13. Click OK to apply the color.

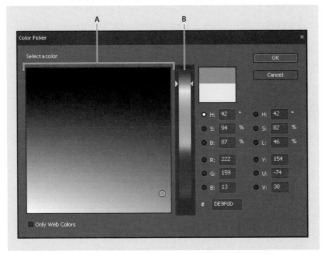

A. Click here to pick the specific shade within the selected range of colors
B. Click here to change the general range of colors.

7   Notice that the other scene marker buttons have retained their original formatting. Normally, changes only affect the selected object. But Premiere Elements also gives you the option to change the text attributes of all buttons of the same type simultaneously.

8   In the Text subsection of the Properties panel, click the Apply to all Marker Buttons button. This applies the same text attributes to all three Scenes Marker buttons.

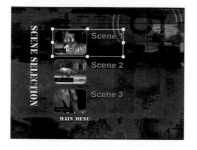

9   Under Disc Menus in the Disc Layout panel, click the Main Menu 1 thumbnail. Notice that the Bonus Clip marker has also changed its appearance. This is because the Marker button category encompasses both Scene Marker and Main Menu Maker buttons.

Note: You can override any single button by returning to the Properties panel and making changes for just the selected button.

10   Choose Edit > Undo, select the Bonus Clip marker button in the Main Menu 1, and then click the Apply to all Marker Buttons button in the Text subsection of the Properties panel. This first resets the text attributes of the Bonus Clip marker button, and then applies them to all three Scene Marker buttons as well.

Customizing menu backgrounds

You can customize your menus even further in Premiere Elements by adding sound, motion, or a still image to the menu background. You can use video to create a moving background, or have an audio clip play while the menu is visible. Clips can be taken from your movie or from other sources. You can also combine multiple items, such as a still photo for a background, and an audio clip. Alternatively, you can add a video clip and replace the audio track with a separate audio clip, if desired.

Adding a still clip to a background

You can browse for images and add them to the background, or you can drag image files from the Project view onto your Disc Layout panel.

1   Under Disc Menus in the Disc Layout panel, click to select the Main Menu 1. If the Bonus Clip marker is still selected from the previous exercise, right-click anywhere in the preview area of the Disc Layout panel, and then choose Select Menu Background from the context menu. The Properties panel should show the properties of the Main Menu 1.

2   Under Video or Still in the Menu Background section of the Properties panel, click the Browse button. Navigate to your Lesson10 folder, and then select and open the image file called Disc_menu_background.jpg.

The background of the Main menu is replaced by the selected image. Depending on the nature of your background image, you might need to change the text attributes or reposition the buttons—as described earlier in this lesson—to ensure good readability.

You will now load the same background image into the scenes menu, using a different technique.

3   Click the Scenes Menu 1 thumbnail in the Disc Menus section of your Disc Layout panel.

4   (Optional) Click the background image of the Scenes Menu 1 to show its properties in the Properties panel. For the following steps to function, it is of no importance whether any object on the menu page might still be selected from the previous exercise.

5   Select Media ( ) in the Create Menus tab of the Tasks panel, and then click Project. If necessary, scroll up or down in the Project view to locate the image named Disc_menu_background.jpg. Because you added this image to your project in step 2, Premiere Elements has added the image file into the Project panel.

6 Click and drag the Disc_menu_background.jpg image from the Project view and drop it onto the preview area of the Disc Layout panel.

The image becomes the new background for the Scene Menu 1.

Note: Certain menu templates in Premiere Elements feature frames or borders that are designed to show only a portion of the menu background. Not every menu has this feature.

For each menu page, you can select a different still image as background, or keep the background image that came with the menu template. In the next exercise, you will learn how to select a single image from a video clip, and use it as menu background.

Adding a video clip to the background

Video clips can also be added to your background. These are sometime referred to as motion menus because the entire menu can be made of a moving video clip. You can use any clip for a background. By default, both the video and the audio portion of a clip are used for the background.

1 Under Disc Menus in the Disc Layout panel, click to select the Main Menu 1.

2 Click and drag the tiger 1.avi video clip from the Project view onto the preview area of the Disc Layout panel, replacing the still image background added in the last exercise.

3 Under Disc Menus in the Disc Layout panel, click the Main Menu 1 thumbnail to load its properties in the Properties panel. In the Menu Background section of the Properties panel, click the green Play button to begin playing the thumbnail version of the video clip. You may need to scroll down to see this button.

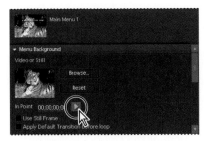

Click the button again after a few moments to pause the playback. A video sequence used as menu background may be as long as 30 seconds.

4 Place your cursor over the values for the In point, and then click and drag to change the In point to 00;00;01;00.

5 (Optional) Select the Use Still Frame check box. Premiere Elements will use this frame as a still image for the menu background.

Adding an audio clip to the background

Audio clips can also be added to a menu background. If you add an audio track after you've already added a video with audio track, it will replace the original audio track.

1 If necessary, scroll down the Properties panel to locate the Audio section. As there is no audio file yet specified as background sound, the Reset button is grayed out.

2 Click the Browse button, select the soundtrack.wav clip in the Lesson10 folder, and then click Open. Alternatively, you could have selected a video clip and only use its audio portion.

3 (Optional) Select the Apply Default Transition before loop check box. This adds a fade-out so the audio loops nicely.

4 In the Disc Layout panel, click the Preview button. You can see the video or video frame and hear the audio track you selected for the Main menu background.

5 Close the Preview window.

6 (Optional) Click the Reset button next to the speaker icon in the Audio section of the Properties panel. This removes the audio portion from the menu background.

7 Save your project.

Modifying scene marker buttons

One of the benefits of DVDs or Blu-ray discs is the ability to quickly jump to specific scenes in the movie. For each scene marker you add in the Timeline, Premiere Elements automatically generates a scene marker button on the scenes menu, and assigns an image thumbnail to it. If necessary due to the amount of scene markers, additional scenes menu pages are created and navigational buttons added to jump back and forth between the pages. You can customize the appearance of the scene marker buttons by providing a name for the label and changing the image thumbnail used to identify the scene.

Changing button labels

1 Click the Scenes Menu 1 thumbnail under Disc Menus in the Disc Layout panel to view the Scenes menu.

Premiere Elements has generated the three scene buttons and their image thumbnails based on the scene markers you added in the first exercise. By default, the image thumbnail is the first frame of the clip it links to. The names of the scene buttons are Scene 1, Scene 2, etc. These are the default names for scenes. You will now rename the scene buttons to relate them more specifically to your movie.

2 Double-click the Scene 1 button to open the Menu Marker dialog box for the first marker. In the Name field, type **Tiger**, and then click OK. The name of the button is updated accordingly. You will now change the names of the remaining two buttons.

Double-clicking a marker in the Timeline is an alternative way to open the Menu Marker dialog box, and is useful when you have many markers in the Timeline.

3 In the Timeline view of the My Project panel, double-click the second green scene marker, located at the beginning of the rhino.avi clip, to open the Menu Marker dialog box.

💡 *Double-clicking a marker in the Timeline will allow you to modify that marker even if you are not currently in the Create Menus workspace.*

4 In the Name field of the Menu Marker dialog box, type **Rhinoceros**. Then, click OK to commit the change.

5 Double-click the third green scene marker in the Timeline, and then type **Elephant** as name in the Menu Marker dialog box. Click OK to close the Menu Marker dialog box.

6 When finished renaming the scene buttons, click the Preview button to open the Preview Disc window. Click the Scenes button to navigate to the Scenes menu. Notice that the button names have been updated to reflect your changes.

7 At the bottom of the Preview Disc window you can see a group of navigation buttons. Click any of the arrows to advance through the Scene Menu buttons. The navigation arrows mimic the controls on a DVD remote control. Premiere Elements determines the navigation of the menu buttons automatically; therefore, it's a good idea to use the Preview Disc navigation controls to ensure that you placed your markers logically. When done, close the Preview Disc window.

A. Up. B. Right. C. Main Menu button.
D. Left. E. Enter. F. Down.

Changing image thumbnails

By default, the image thumbnail used for each scene button is the first video frame at the corresponding marker in the Timeline. Sometimes the first frame of the video clip is not the best choice to describe the scene. For example, in this project the image thumbnails show the superimposed title clips at the beginning of the clip, which are too small to be useful in a thumbnail image. You will now change the image thumbnails.

1   Double-click the Tiger scene button in the Disc Layout panel to open the Menu Marker dialog box. This corresponds to the first green scene marker in your Timeline.

2   In the Thumbnail Offset section, notice the time counter being set to 00:00;00;00. Place your cursor over the time counter, and then click and drag to the right. Navigate to the 5 second mark (00;00;05;00), and then release the pointer to freeze the movie at the first frame after the superimposed title disappears. Click OK. The image thumbnail is automatically updated in the scenes menu.

3   Click the Preview button, and then click the Scenes button. The image thumbnail you chose in the last step has automatically been placed in the Tiger scene button. Click the Tiger scene button to jump directly to that scene. Notice that the original start point for this scene is still the same, as changing the image thumbnail does not move the scene marker.

4   Click the Close button to close the Preview Disc window.

5   You can advance the Thumbnail Offset through several clips in order to find the most useful thumbnail in the scene. Double-click the Rhinoceros button—or the second green scene marker in the Timeline—to open the Menu Marker dialog box. Place your cursor over the Thumbnail Offset counter and click and drag to the right to navigate all the way to the 22 second, 16 frame mark (00;00;22;16). Or, click the counter and set the value by typing it into the text field that appears. Click OK to commit the change.

6 Select the Elephant scene button, and then, under Poster Frame in the Properties panel, set the In Point to the 9 second, 23 frame mark (00;00;09;23).

Animating buttons

Animated buttons take a few seconds of video from your Timeline and place them into your Scene and Main Menu buttons. To be able to do this, your template must include buttons that display a thumbnail. The main menu for this project does not include any buttons with image thumbnails. However, the scene menu does have image thumbnails. You will now assign video clips to them.

1 Select the Scenes Menu 1 thumbnail under Disc Menus in the Disc Layout panel.

2 Click the Tiger button to select it. Currently this button is displaying a still frame extracted from the video clip at the 5 second mark.

3 In the Properties panel, scroll down, if necessary, to see all of the Poster Frame section, and then select the Motion Menu Button check box.

4   (Optional) Click and drag the time counter (currently reading 00;00;05;00) to change the In point of the video clip.

Note: You cannot set the Out point or the end of clips in the Properties panel, but you can set all your motion menu buttons to be the same duration, as explained below.

5   Click an empty area of your background menu. This deselects the current scene button, and the Properties panel switches to the Menu Background properties. Scroll down to the bottom of the Properties panel, if necessary, to locate the Motion Menu Buttons section.

6   Change the Duration value for the Motion Menu Buttons to 00;00;05;00. This value (5 seconds) will now be the duration of all motion menu buttons. You cannot set the duration of motion menu buttons individually.

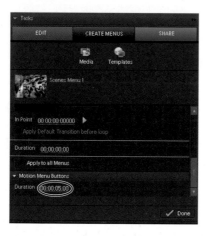

7   Click the Preview button in the Disc Layout panel. In the Main menu, click the Scenes button to access the Scenes menu. The Tiger button should now be animated.

8   Close the Preview Disc window.

9   (Optional) Select the Motion Menu Button option and choose suitable In Points for the two other scene buttons. You must individually activate scene buttons to animate them. All animated buttons share the same duration.

10   Choose File > Save As and save this project file into your Lesson10 folder as **Lesson10_Final.prel**.

Overlapping buttons

Buttons on a disc menu should not overlap each other. If two or more buttons overlap, there is a potential for confusion. Someone who is using a pointer to navigate and click the menu may not be able to access the correct button if another one is overlapping it. This can easily happen if button text is too long or if two buttons are placed too close to each other.

Overlapping buttons can sometimes be fixed by shortening the button name or, in general, by simply repositioning the buttons. By default, overlapping buttons in Premiere Elements are outlined in red in the Disc Layout panel. This feature can be turned off or on by choosing Show Overlapping Menu Buttons from the Disc Layout panel menu at the right side of the docking header.

Burning DVDs or Blu-ray discs

After you have previewed your disc and have checked the menus and button names, you are now ready to burn the project to a DVD or Blu-ray disc. As noted at the beginning of the chapter, you must have either a DVD or a Blu-ray writer to make a respective disc.

The process of making a DVD or Blu-ray disc involves the compression of your video. When making a DVD or Blu-ray disc, Premiere Elements converts your video and audio files into a compressed format. Compression is the process of shrinking your original video and audio files to take up less storage space. For example, a 60 minute video in Premiere Elements takes up approximately 13 Gigabytes of hard disk space. However, a DVD-video holds only 4.7 Gigabytes of space. So how do you fit 13 Gigabytes of video into a 4.7 Gigabyte disc? Through compression!

The process of compression can be quite lengthy. In essence, Premiere Elements is evaluating every frame of video in your project and attempting to lower the file size without sacrificing the image quality. You should allow quite a bit of time for this process. For example, a 60 minute video project may take 4 to 6 hours of time to burn on a DVD, and your computer will be tied up during this period. For this reason, it may be a good idea to start the burning of a disc at a time when you will not need your computer.

To maintain maximum quality, Adobe Premiere Elements compresses the movie only as much as necessary to fit it on the disc. The shorter your movie, the less compression required, and the higher the quality of the video on the disc.

Note: This exercise ends with the burning of a DVD. If you do not wish to create a DVD, you may follow the steps of the exercise up to the point of writing the disc. If you will be creating a DVD, we suggest using a DVD-RW (Rewritable) disc, if you have one available, so that you can reuse the disc later.

1   Select the Share workspace by clicking the Share tab in the Tasks panel.

2   Save your current project. It is always a good idea to save your Premiere Elements project file before burning a disc.

3   Click the Disk button (⊙) under How would you like to share? to open the Disk view. Choose DVD from the list at the top of the Disk view. To burn a Blu-ray disc you would select Blu-ray from that list.

4   Make sure Burn to Disc is selected in the Burn to menu. You would select the option to burn to a folder on your hard disk if you prefer to use an alternative program to burn your discs.

5   In the Disc Name field, type **A day at the zoo**. Software playing DVDs or Blu-ray discs on a personal computer may choose to display this disc name.

6   Select the desired DVD or Blu-ray disc burner from the Burner Location menu. If you don't have a compatible disc burner connected to your computer, the Burner Location menu is disabled and the Status line reads "No burner detected."

7   If you wish to create a DVD or Blu-ray disc, make sure that a compatible blank disc is inserted in the disc burner. If you insert a disc, click Rescan to have Adobe Premiere Elements recheck all connected burners for valid media.

Note: Adobe Premiere Elements detects only burners that are connected and turned on at the time you started Adobe Premiere Elements. If you connected and turned on any burners after that point, they are not recognized until you restart Adobe Premiere Elements.

8   Next to Copies, select the number of discs you want to burn during this session. For this exercise, choose 1. When you select multiple copies Premiere Elements asks you to insert another disc after writing of each disc is completed, until all the discs you specified have been burned.

9   Make sure Fit Contents to Available Space is selected. This will ensure that Premiere Elements maximizes the quality of your video based on the disc size.

10   From the Presets menu, select the NTSC_Dolby DVD option. Premiere Elements is also capable of burning a project to the PAL standard (used in Europe, parts of Africa, South America, and the Middle East, Australia, New Zealand, some Pacific Islands, and certain Asian countries), in both normal or widescreen format. For Blu-ray discs, you have the choice between H.264 1080i and MPEG2 1080i, for both NTSC Dolby and PAL Dolby.

11   If you wish to burn a disc at this point, click the Burn button. If you do not wish to burn a disc, click the Back button.

Congratulations, you have successfully completed this lesson. You learned how to manually and automatically add scene markers to your movie, and then created an auto-play disc and—by applying a menu template—a disc with menus. You added a submenu for a bonus clip and learned about stop and main menu makers. You customized the disc menus by changing text attributes, background images, button labels, and image thumbnails. You added sound and video clips to the menu background, and activated motion menu buttons. Finally, you learned how to burn your movie onto a DVD or Blu-ray disc.

Review

▶ **Review questions**

1   What is an auto-play disc? What is the benefit and disadvantage of an auto-play disc?

2   How would you identify separate scenes for use in your disc menu?

3   What is a submenu and how would you add one to your disc menu?

4   Which properties can you change for the text of your menu buttons, and how are these properties modified?

5   What are the five types of text objects you can modify in your disc menus, and how can changes made to one type be applied to others in the same category?

▶ **Review answers**

1   An auto-play disc allows you to quickly create a DVD or Blu-ray disc from the main movie of your project. The advantage of an auto-play disc is that it can be quickly and easily created, while the disadvantage is that it does not have a menu for navigation during playback.

2   Separate scenes can be defined by placing a scene marker on a specific frame in the Timeline. Scene markers are set in the Timeline using the Add Menu Marker button.

3   A submenu is a button on your main disc menu that points to a specific section of your project, such as a credit sequence or a bonus clip. Submenus are created by adding a main menu marker to your Timeline.

4   You can change the font, size, color, and style of your text buttons. Changing the properties of your text is done inside the Properties panel for objects selected in the Disc Layout panel.

5   The five types of text objects you can modify in your disc menus are Menu Titles, Play buttons, Scene buttons, Marker buttons, and Navigational buttons. If you want to change all the objects in a category to the same style, you can click the Apply to all button located in the Properties panel.

11 | Sharing Movies

This lesson is based on a finished project that you will export back to video and various formats suitable for display online. In this lesson, you'll learn how to send your completed video project to the digital media or device of choice, for example a DV camera. You will also learn the different ways you can export movies to view online or on a personal computer. Specifically, you'll learn how to do the following:

• Export directly to your DV camcorder or DV recording device as the movie plays in the Monitor or Timeline.

• Export a video file for subsequent viewing from a hard disk or CD-ROM.

• Export a single frame or a sequence of frames as still images.

• Export a video file for viewing over the Web, and upload it to a video sharing website such as YouTube.

• Use the Quick Share feature to save and reuse your favorite sharing methods.

Exporting movies

In the previous lesson, you learned how to create a DVD or Blu-ray disc from a Premiere Elements project. Technically speaking, exporting a movie is the same as creating a DVD or Blu-ray disc. The exported movie—including any menus you might have added—conforms to a specific format designed to play on dedicated set-top disc players or on a personal computer with the required hardware and software. You may also export your projects in other ways for different purposes, as we explore in this lesson.

About sharing and exporting

Apart from creating DVDs or Blu-ray discs, you can export and share movies, stills, and audio in a variety of file types to the Web, mobile devices, videotape, Video CDs, and Super Video CDs. You can also copy and save projects for remote editing or storage.

The Share workspace in the Tasks panel is your starting point for exporting your finished project. Here you can choose an export format suitable for the medium on which you want to share your movie.

Selecting any of the options listed under How would you like to share? opens a view in the Tasks panel that provides specific options and settings for sharing to the respective media type. The Share view simplifies sharing and exporting by providing presets of the most commonly used formats and settings. If you want to specify unique settings for any format, you can click Advanced options and make changes. Or, you can use the export commands in the File menu, where you can customize the settings by clicking Settings in the respective export dialog box.

When exporting using the Share workspace, you can create a Quick Share preset to save and reuse for future projects your favorite sharing method, along with all the settings. After you share your project, simply click Save As Quick Share and name the preset. The preset appears in the Share view of the Tasks panel in the Quick Share box. Whenever you want to share a project using those settings, just select that preset and click the Share button.

Exporting to digital video

The same camera that you use to record your original footage can also be used to record your final project. One advantage of recording to a digital video camera is that due to the nature of digital recordings, there is very little loss of quality when making a copy of your project. This makes it suitable for archiving your projects as well as presenting them.

Additionally, thanks to device control you can conveniently operate your digital video camera using the controls in Premiere Elements, just as you can during the capture process. For more information on device control and the relationship between Premiere Elements and your DV camera, review Lesson 1, "The World of Digital Video."

Exporting to analog video

Export of your movies to digital video may be the best way to archive your movies. However, you may also want to export your Premiere Elements project directly to a VHS or beta tape, for example. Based on your available system, this often requires an additional piece of equipment called an analog-to-digital converter (or AV DV converter).

Exporting for hard disk playback

Instead of playing your movie on a television set, you may wish to give someone a copy on a CD-ROM or other storage media, and allow them to copy the movie to their personal computer's hard disk and view it using standard software.

Exporting a movie for the Internet

Sharing your movies these days often means placing them on the World Wide Web or sending them as attachments in an e-mail. When this is your objective you will want to reduce the large files used in digital video projects to make it feasible to transfer of your movies over the Internet. However, reduction in file size of your movie will often result in a loss of quality.

Getting started

An important note before you get started: if you have access to a DV camera, you may want to make use of it for this exercise. We will proceed as if a digital video camera is connected to your system, but if this is not the case, you may follow this exercise anyway, or skip to the next exercise in this lesson, "Exporting to hard disk."

To begin, you'll connect your digital video camera to your personal computer. Note that in this exercise, you will be connecting and turning on your digital video camera before you open Premiere Elements. In most cases, if Premiere Elements is already open, it will recognize a DV camera as it is attached and turned on; however, we have found this happens more reliably if the DV camera is connected first.

1   Connect your DV camera to your computer. For help, refer to your owner's manual or the diagram located in Lesson 1, "The World of Digital Video."

2   Turn on your DV device and switch it to the VTR (or VCR) mode. If a Digital Video Device dialog box appears, click the Cancel button to close it.

3   Start Premiere Elements and open the project file Lesson11_Start.prel in the Lesson11 folder. If a dialog appears asking for the location of rendered files, click the Skip Previews button.

4   In Sceneline view of the My Project panel, click to select the first scene, the black video. What you can't see at the moment is that this scene also contains a title that fades in when the movie starts.

In general, you should add an additional black clip at the beginning of the project to provide your recording deck with a few seconds of extra time. This may prevent your recording device from accidentally cutting off the first seconds of your project.

5   In the top right corner of the Project view, click the New Item button (⬚), and then choose Black Video from the menu that appears.

A new item called Black Video appears in your Media panel and will be added to your Sceneline after the first scene.

6   In the Sceneline, click and drag the newly added Black Video to the beginning of the movie, to the left of the existing scene with the title. You can identify the Black Video containing the superimposed title by the title icon (⬚) visible in the top right corner of the clips thumbnail in the Sceneline.

The newly added Black Video now precedes the Black Video containing the title.

Note: Menu markers—e.g. the scene marker 5 seconds into the movie— remain in their original locations when you rearrange clips in the Timeline. By adding the black video at the start, all scene markers are now out of sync with their respective clips. This is of no consequence when exporting to a DV camera. For export to DVD or Blu-ray disc however, you would set markers only after you have finished editing your movie. If you make further changes, menu markers may become out of sync and need to be updated.

7   Choose File > Save As. Rename this file **Lesson11_DV.prel**.

Exporting to tape

A DV device is most often your camcorder. However, there are also dedicated DV decks that will record and play your DV tapes. One of these devices will save you wear and tear on your camcorder and will make playback of your tapes more convenient if the deck is connected to your television set. If you have connected an analog device such as a VCR to your computer, you may follow these steps as well.

1   Make sure your recording device is turned on and in VTR (or VCR) mode, and that you have enough blank tape to record your project.

2   Select the Share tab in the Tasks panel, and then click the Tape button () at the bottom of the Share view. Or, choose Window > My Project or click inside the My Project panel to make that panel active, and then choose File > Export > Export to Tape.

If your recording device is properly connected to your computer, the Export to Tape dialog box opens.

3   If you are recording to a DV device, make sure the Activate Recording Device check box is selected under Device Control. This ensures that Premiere Elements can communicate with the device. If you are recording to an analog device, you should deselect this option.

Note: If you are recording to a DV device and device control is unavailable, click Cancel, choose Edit > Preferences > Device Control, make sure that your device is set up properly in the Device Control options, and then try recording to tape again.

Export to Tape options

• **Activate Recording Device**—lets Adobe Premiere Elements control your DV device.

• **Assemble at timecode**—indicates the place on your DV tape that you want the recording to begin, if you have a tape that already has timecode recorded, or striped, on it. You stripe a tape by first recording only black video before you record your footage. You usually record black video by recording with the lens cap on. If your tape is not striped, leave this option unselected to have recording begin at the location where you have cued the tape.

• **Delay movie start by n frames**—specifies the number of frames that you want to delay the start of the movie so that you can synchronize it with the DV device recording start time. Some devices need a delay between the time they receive the record command and the time the movie starts playing from the computer. Experiment with this setting if you are experiencing delays between the time you enable record and the time your DV device begins recording.

• **Preroll by n frames**—specifies the number of frames that you want Adobe Premiere Elements to back up on the recording deck before the specified timecode. Specify enough frames for the deck to reach a constant tape speed. For many decks, 5 seconds or 150 frames is sufficient.

• **Abort after n dropped frames**—specifies the maximum number of dropped frames you want to allow before Adobe Premiere Elements aborts the recording. If you choose this option, you generally want to type a very low number because dropped frames will cause jerky playback, and are indicative of a hard disk or transfer problem.

• **Report dropped frames**—specifies that Adobe Premiere Elements displays the number of dropped frames.

—From Premiere Elements Help

4 If you are using a DV device, click the Record button. Your DV device will begin to record as Premiere Elements begins to play the Timeline from the beginning. If you are using an analog device, you must manually press the Record button on the device first (see your manual for instructions), and then click the Record button in the Export to Tape dialog box.

Note: If your project has any unrendered clips in the Timeline, Premiere Elements must first render them. Once all clips are rendered, export will begin. For more information on rendering, see Adobe Premiere Elements Help.

5 Once the end of the project has been reached, the recording will stop automatically if you are using a DV device. If you are using an analog device, you must manually press its Stop button to stop recording.

6 Click the Cancel button to close the Export to Tape dialog box.

Exporting to hard disk

In the previous exercise, you exported a Premiere Elements project to tape. In this exercise, you will export your project as a standalone video file. Once you have exported a movie file out of Premiere Elements, you could transfer it to a form of storage such as a CD-ROM, or an external hard disk. Or, you can simply keep the file on your own system as an archive.

Using the Share workspace

1   In the Sceneline, click the first clip, the extra Black Video added in the last exercise, and then press the Delete key to remove it. This clip is necessary only when exporting to tape, not when exporting as a file.

2   Choose File > Save As and rename the project **Lesson11_HardDisk.prel**.

3   In the Share view, click the Personal Computer button (▣).

4   Choose a file format from the list at the top of the Share view, and then choose a preset appropriate for the intended use of your exported video. Each file format comes with its own set of presets available from the Presets menu.

5   Enter **Lesson11_SharePC** next to File Name, and then click Browse to select your Lesson11 folder as the Save in folder.

6   Click the Advanced button to open the Export Settings dialog box. Here you can review the settings used for the chosen file format and preset. If necessary, you can make adjustments to the export settings, such as selecting a different video or audio codex, or changing the frame rate, pixel aspect ratio, or audio compression. Click Cancel to close the Export Settings dialog box without making any changes.

7   To start exporting your movie, click Save.

Premiere Elements will proceed to render the video frame by frame. This may take a few minutes or more, as the program's rendering speed is based on the capabilities of your system. You will see a progress bar in the Share view and an estimated time to complete each phase of the rendering process.

You can click Cancel at any time to stop the exporting process. Otherwise, you will see a Save Complete! message in the Share view, once the rendering is complete. Before you click Done in the lower right corner of the Share view, notice the Save As Quick Share button next to it.

8   (Optional) Click Save As Quick Share, provide a name and description for your quick share profile, and then click Save. Next time you want to export a movie with the same export settings, you only need to select your Quick Share profile, click Share, provide file name and folder location in the following view, and click Save.

Using the Export Movie menu command

Alternatively to using the Share view to export your movie, you can use the Export Movie command under the File menu.

1   Choose File > Export > Movie to open the Export Movie dialog box.

Note: If the File > Export menu is grayed out, make sure the My Project panel is active by either clicking on it, or choosing Window > My Project.

2   In the Export Movie dialog box, notice that Lesson11_HardDisk.avi has automatically been chosen as file name. Premiere Elements uses the AVI file format as the default video format for exporting movies. Click the Settings button to open the Export Movie Settings dialog box.

3   Click the File Type menu to view a list of available alternative export file formats. You will not be selecting an alternative file type in this step. Make sure Microsoft DV AVI is selected.

You can choose from the following file formats in the Export Movie Settings dialog box:		
Audio Interchange File Format	Windows Bitmap	Filmstrip
Animated GIF	GIF	JPEG
QuickTime	Targa	TIFF
Uncompressed Microsoft AVI	Microsoft AVI	Microsoft DV AVI
Windows Waveform	Windows Waveform	

Note: When you choose the file type, Premiere Elements will automatically set all the default export settings for that format.

4   Make sure the check box for Add to Project When Finished is selected. This will place the completed AVI file into your Project view.

5   (Optional) Review the settings in the Video, Keyframe and Rendering, and Audio sections of the dialog box. Click Save to save a profile of your chosen settings, including any adjustments you might have made. Click Load to load this profile next time you want to export a movie using the same settings.

6   Click OK to close the Export Movie Settings dialog box.

7   In the Export Movie dialog box, make sure you are saving to your Lesson11 folder, and then click Save. Premiere Elements will proceed to render the video frame by frame. Again, this may take a few minutes or more, as the program's rendering speed is based on the capabilities of your system. Once the rendering is complete, the clip has been exported and added to your Project view.

8   Switch to the Edit workspace in the Tasks panel, select Media, and then click Project. Scroll down, if necessary, to locate the file Lesson11_HardDisk.avi. Double-click the file to open it in the Preview window. The length of the clip is approximately one minute. Play the clip, and then close the Preview window.

All your clips from the original project have been consolidated into one single clip. You could now reuse this clip, as a single element in another project, for example.

Note: This technique, called pre-rendering, may be used to consolidate your video files. For example, your original project quite likely had footage trimmed from the individual clips. Although this footage is not present in your project, the original footage still resides on your hard disk and takes up storage space. Exporting your movie as you did in this exercise will give you one single video clip; you could conceivably delete the original video and project files, which would save you hard disk space. The downside of this is that your original project would no longer exist and you could not modify it. You could, however, archive the original project and video files on a separate storage system, such as an external hard disk or DVD.

Exporting a frame of video as a still image

Occasionally, you may wish to use your video footage as a source for still images. For example, if your video camera was the only device recording a special event, and you wanted a snapshot to share with friends and family, Premiere Elements enables you to export single frames of video as still images using the Export Frame command. In this exercise, you will create a preset allowing you to export images for the Web.

1   In the Monitor panel, position the current-time indicator at a frame you wish to export as a still image. If necessary, use the Step Forward (▶) or Step Back (◀) buttons to locate the exact frame.

2   Choose File > Export > Frame to open the Export Frame dialog box. You can also click the Freeze Frame button (📷) in the lower right corner of the Monitor panel, and then click Export in the Freeze Frame dialog box. You might have to enlarge the Monitor panel in order to see the Freeze Frame button.

3   In the Export Frame dialog box, click the Settings button to open the Export Frame Settings dialog box.

4   In the General section of the Export Frame Settings dialog box, choose JPEG from the File Type menu and select the Add to Project When Finished option.

5   Click Video in the left column to access the Video control settings. Choose Square Pixels (1.0) from the Pixel Aspect Ratio menu. The pixels for Digital Video are actually rectangular in nature; choosing Square Pixels ensures that your image will be converted for view on a computer monitor.

6   Click Keyframe and Rendering to access these controls. Select the Deinterlace Video Footage check box. Deinterlacing is a process used to remove the artifacts from a video image.

7   Click the Save button to open the Save Export Settings dialog box.

8   In the Name field of the Save Export Settings dialog box, type **Still images for the Web**. In the Description field, type **Setting used to export still images to be viewed on a computer monitor**.

9   Click OK to save your setting and to close the Save Export Settings dialog box, and then click OK to close the Export Frame Settings dialog box. Back in the Export Frame dialog box, locate the Lesson11 folder and name your file **Lesson11_Frame.jpg**. Click Save to save the still image onto your hard disk.

10   The still image was also placed in your Project view because in step 4 you selected the Add to Project When Finished option. Double-click the Lesson11_still.jpg image to view it in the Preview window, and then close the Preview window and save your project.

11   In the Monitor panel, position the current-time indicator at another frame you wish to export as a still image, and then choose File > Export > Export Frame.

12   Click Settings in the Export Frame dialog box, and then click Load in the Export Frame Settings dialog box. Select the Still images for the Web.prexport preset you have created in step 8, notice your description of the preset being displayed at the bottom of the dialog box, and then click Open.

13   Click OK to establish the same export settings for this frame as used for the previous frame. Name the file **Lesson11_Frame2.jpg**, and save it in the Lesson11 folder.

Exporting clips as a sequence of still images

If you want to export a whole scene or even just a few seconds of your movie as a sequence of still images, doing it one by one can be tiresome—even with the help of an export settings preset. In this case you would use a different technique to have Premiere Elements do most of the work for you. Exporting a sequence of still images is useful if you want to work with the images in an animation or 3D application that does not support video formats or requires a still-image sequence.

To define the range of still images to be exported, you have the following choices:

- An entire clip from the Project view.
- From the In point to the Out point of a clip in the Project view.
- The entire movie in the My Project panel.
- The part of the movie defined by the work area bar in the My Project panel.

In Lesson 3, "Navigating the Workspace," you've learned how to set In and Out points for clips in the Project panel (see "Working in the Preview window"). In this exercise you will be introduced to the work area bar in the My Project panel. With the work area bar you define a time period in the Timeline to restrict the extent of tasks such as rendering an area for preview or exporting a sequence of still images.

1   Select Timeline view in the My Project panel. Position the current-time indicator near the 17 second mark, and then drag the Zoom slider all the way to the right to zoom in as much as possible. Depending on your screen size, you should be able to see about one second of movie, or 30 frames, in the Timeline view.

2   Double-click the work area bar, the gray bar directly below the Time ruler, to set its range to the area currently visible in the Timeline view. Choose Timeline > Zoom Out to better see the handles on either side of the work area bar. You can use these handles to resize the work area bar, or use the gripper in the center to reposition it.

3   Choose File > Export > Movie, and then click Settings in the Export Movie dialog box.

4   From the File Type menu under General in the Export Movie Settings dialog box, choose a still-image sequence format, such as GIF, JPEG, Targa, or TIFF.

Note: If you select a movie format or Animated GIF, all frames will be exported into a single file, not a sequence of still images.

5   From the Range menu, select Work Area Bar. Select the Add to Project When Finished option.

6   (Optional) Specify additional export settings such as changing the Frame Size in the Video section, or choosing the Deinterlace Video Footage option in the Keyframe and Rendering section.

7   Click OK to close the Export Movie Settings dialog box. In the Export Movie dialog box, locate the Lesson11 folder and enter **Lesson11_Sequence.jpg** as file name.

8   Click Save to export the still-image sequence. The individual still image files will be saved to your Lesson11 folder and named Lesson11_Sequence01.jpg, Lesson11_Sequence02.jpg, Lesson11_Sequence03.jpg, etc.

To set the sequence numbering, type a numbered filename. To specify the number of digits in the filename, determine how many digits will be required to number the frames, and then add any additional zeroes you want. For example, if you want to export 20 frames and you want the filename to have five digits, type Car000 for the first filename. The remaining files will automatically be named Car00001, Car00002, ..., and Car00020. When exporting many files in this manner it is usually best to save them to an empty folder so that they don't become mixed with other files.

Exporting a movie for the Internet

Premiere Elements is not only designed to make DVDs, Blu-ray discs, and videotapes, but also to export movies as standalone files. In a previous exercise, you exported a movie for use on a hard disk or other media. The current project is only about 70 seconds long, yet the AVI file you exported was over 270 megabytes in size. A file of this size could take hours to download on a 56k modem! In order to reduce the size of a movie file, there are a few factors to take into consideration—in fact there are many factors, but we will focus on the most important.

Frame Size—The standard dimensions of a single frame of video used in DV projects is 720 pixels wide by 480 pixels high. These dimensions provide enough visual information for digital video to be displayed clearly on a television set. Due to the limitations of the medium, video displayed on the Web is much smaller. One multimedia standard for the Web is 320 pixels wide by 240 high. A smaller frame size means there are fewer pixels in each frame, which results in a smaller file size.

Frame Rate—Video is nothing but a series of still images displayed over time. The succession of images results in an illusion of motion. The number of frames displayed over a given period of time is referred to as the frame rate. The common frame rate for NTSC video is 30 frames per second, while the PAL frame rate is 25 frames per second. For the Web, you often can reduce the number of frames per second without losing the illusion of motion. Using 15 frames per second will reduce the size of your file by about half. Yet, the movie might still play relatively smoothly in a Web browser.

Audio format

The audio portion of your project can easily get overlooked when exporting to the Web. However, because a typical desktop or laptop computer may be playing audio through a small speaker, the rich stereo sound we expect on a home theater system may not be as important online. Therefore, when a movie is for playback on the Web, you can often reduce the quality of your audio in order to reduce file size.

Compression

Compression was discussed in the Lesson 10 section on making DVDs and Blu-ray discs, and the same principles apply here: compression is the process of using mathematical formulas to reduce the file size of your video. These compression formulas are called codecs, a name being derived from compression/decompression. In essence, compressing video discards enough data in your video files to make them smaller, yet ideally retains enough information to ensure the image is still of adequate quality. The more you compress your video, the smaller your file size becomes. If you compress it too much, your image quality will deteriorate, sometimes unacceptably. If you do not compress your video enough, the image may look great, but the file will be too large for users to download. In order for someone to decompress and view your video, they must have on their machine the same codec that you used to compress it.

Exporting your video file for the Web

When exporting you movie using the File > Export > Movie command or the Personal Computer option in the Share workspace, Premiere Elements enables you to choose your file format, such as QuickTime, and select from a range of compression codecs, such as MPEG-4 Video. Each format and codec has its advantages and disadvantages. One thing they have in common is that viewers of the movie must have the appropriate software on their computer to view the files. For example, the QuickTime format (.mov) is the native format for the Macintosh; if Windows users would like to view a QuickTime movie, they must have the QuickTime software installed on their systems.

If all this is getting too technical for you, or you just want to get your movie out there for all to enjoy, the Online option in the Share workspace is the way to go. From there you can export and upload your movie directly to the popular YouTube video sharing website, or any other website you can access via FTP. For your convenience, Premiere Elements provides a preset for Adobe Flash Video (.flv) format, covering the requirements of most servers and the bandwidth and player options available to most viewers.

1   In the Tasks panel, click the Share tab to switch to the Share workspace. Then, click the Online button (●).

2   Select YouTube from the list at the top of the Share view. The Flash preset for YouTube and the video Quality level is automatically selected for you. In the lower part

of the view, review the information about the resulting video file, such as frame size, frame rate, and file size, and then click Next.

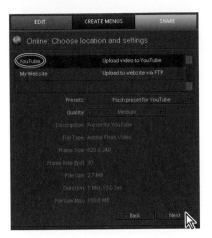

3   If you already have an account at YouTube, sign in using your username and password, Or, click Sign Up Now to first create a new account. Then, click Next.

4   Enter the required information about your project, including title, description, and tags. Choose a category and language, and then click Next.

5   Choose whether you want to allow the public to view your project, and then click Share. Premiere Elements will render and upload you movie. This may take a few moments depending on your computer hardware and your Internet connection speed.

When rendering and uploading is complete, the Web address to which the movie has been uploaded appears in the Share view. You can click on View My Shared Video to open YouTube and watch your video, or click Send an E-mail to tell friends about your new posting. If you are planning to upload frequently to YouTube, you can save the workflow by clicking the Save Workflow button.

6   Click Done, and then save and close your project.

Congratulations, you have finished this lesson. You've learned to export your movie to tape or as file on a hard disk or other media, using the Share workspace and the Export commands in the File menu. You exported a single frame as a still image and a sequence of still images from a scene of your movie. Finally, you used an export settings preset to optimize your movie to be viewed on the Web, and uploaded it to YouTube.

Review

▶ **Review questions**

1 What are the advantages of exporting your Premiere Elements project to DV tape?

2 What are two ways you can export your Premiere Elements project as a standalone file?

3 How do you export a frame of video as a still image? How do you export a sequence of still images from a video?

4 What is the easiest way to upload your movie to a website such as YouTube?

▶ **Review answers**

1 One advantage of exporting to DV tape is the ability to connect your DV device to your personal computer, in the same way you did to capture video. Additionally, there is less video quality loss when recording to DV tape than there is when recording to analog media such as a VCR tape. Exporting to a DV device also enables you to take advantage of device control within Premiere Elements to stop and start your DV device.

2 You can export your Premiere Elements project as a movie file by choosing File > Export > Movie. Or, click the Personal Computer button in the Share workspace.

3 You can export a single frame of video as a still image by choosing File > Export > Frame. To select a sequence of images from a clip or the movie in the Timeline, choose File > Export, Movie, and then choose a still-image sequence format, such as GIF, JPEG, Targa, or TIFF, as file type.

4 Switch to the Share view, and then click the Online button. Choose YouTube or My Website, and then follow the instructions in the Share view to render and upload your movie.

12 | Working with Photoshop Elements

Adobe Photoshop Elements and Adobe Premiere Elements are designed to work together and let you seamlessly combine digital photography and video editing. You can spice up your video projects with title images or customized menu templates created in Photoshop Elements, or build slideshow presentations in Photoshop Elements, and then use parts of them in Adobe Premier Elements for further editing.

To work on the following exercises, you must have Photoshop Elements installed on your system. In this lesson, you will learn how to integrate Photoshop Elements with Premiere Elements. Specifically, you will learn how to do the following:

- Use the Send To command in Photoshop to create a slide show in Premiere Elements.

- Drag photo images from Photoshop Elements into Premiere Elements.

- Paste images into Premiere Elements.

- Create a Photoshop file optimized for video.

- Edit a Photoshop image from Premiere Elements.

Viewing the completed movie before you start

To see what you'll be creating, you can take a look at the completed movie.

1   Before you begin, make sure that you have correctly copied the Lesson12 folder from the DVD in the back of this book onto your computer's hard disk. See "Copying the Classroom in a Book files" on page 3.

2   Within the Lesson12 folder, double-click the Lesson12_Movie.wmv to play the movie in your default application for watching Windows Media Video files.

Getting started

You will now open Photoshop Elements 6.0 and import the files needed for the Lesson12 project.

1   Start Photoshop Elements.

2   In the Welcome Screen, click the Organize button to open the Photoshop Elements Organizer.

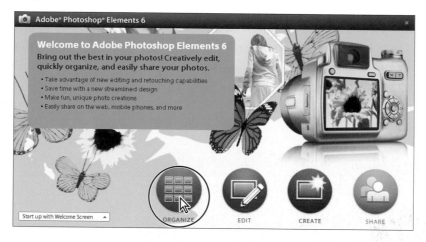

3   If you have previously been using Photoshop Elements, your Organizer may be displaying the photos in your current catalog. If this is the first time you are launching Photoshop Elements, you may receive a message asking if you would like to designate a location to look for your image files. Click No, starting with an empty Organizer window.

4   Choose File > Get Photos and Videos > From Files and Folders. Navigate to your Lesson12 folder and select—but do not open—the images subfolder. Then, click Get Photos.

All the photos in this folder will be imported into Photoshop Elements.

5   If a message appears telling you that only the newly imported files will appear, click OK. In the Organizer window, you should see six thumbnail images portraying a pair of twins at different stages of their lives. Thumbnail images are small versions of the full-size photos. You will be working with the full-size photos later in this lesson.

Using the Send To command in Photoshop Elements

You can add images to a Premiere Elements 4.0 project using the File > Send To command in Photoshop Elements 6.0. Photoshop Elements will create a new project in Premiere Elements if none is currently open. Or, if there is a project currently open, Photoshop Elements will place the photos at the end of the current Sceneline or Timeline. In the following exercise you will create a new project and add images to it.

To sort images in the Organizer, Photoshop Elements uses the date and time information embedded in the image file by the digital camera. In the Organizer menu, choosing to show the oldest files first by selecting Date (Oldest First) enables you to create a slideshow in chronological order when transferring the photos to Premiere Elements.

1 Right-click the first image and choose Show Properties from the context menu. The Properties panel opens. Under General Properties, this panel displays the name of the image and also gives you detailed information about the file size, the date the photo was taken, and its location on your hard disk. The date the picture was taken is also displayed below the image thumbnail in the Photo Browser if you select View > Details. With View > Details selected you can opt to display file names in the Photo Browser as well by choosing View > Show File Names.

2 Press and hold the Ctrl key on your keyboard, and then in the Photo Browser click the four images 12_2001.jpg, 12_2003.jpg, 12_2006.jpg, and 12_2007.jpg to select them, as shown in the following illustration. A blue outline around the thumbnail indicates a selected image. In the next step, Photoshop Elements will only process the selected images.

Note: Before performing the next step, make sure you do not have any project open in Premiere Elements, otherwise the images will be placed in the open file.

3   Choose File > Send to Premiere Elements. A dialog box may appear informing you that the files will be inserted at the end of your Timeline and that the Premiere Elements defaults will be used. Click OK. If Premiere Elements is not already open, it will launch automatically.

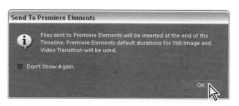

4   In the Premiere Elements New Project dialog box, type **Lesson12_Start** in the name field. Click the Browse button. In the Browse For Folder dialog box, navigate to the Lesson12 folder located on your hard disk. Click OK to close the Browse For Folder dialog box, and then click OK to close the New Project dialog box.

A Premiere Elements project is created, and the images you selected in Photoshop Elements are now visible in the Organizer view of the Tasks panel. They have also been added to the Project view and placed in the Sceneline (or Timeline) of the My Project panel. The first frame of the first clip is displayed in the Monitor panel. In Sceneline view of the My Project panel you'll see all images as individual scenes.

5   With all scenes selected in the Sceneline, choose Clip > Group to place the entire group onto one target that can be moved as a single clip. Then, choose Clip > Ungroup to treat each still image as its own scene in the Sceneline.

6   Press the spacebar to play your project. Premiere Elements has used the default duration of 5 seconds for each still image and applied a cross dissolve as the default transition between each clip.

Note: The total length of the slideshow is less than the number of images times the default duration for still images. This is because Premiere Elements renders the transition effect between the images by overlapping the clips by the default length of the transition effect.

Creating a slide show in Premiere Elements

You can create slide shows in Premiere Elements without stills being sent from Photoshop Elements.

1 *In the Edit tab of the Tasks panel, select Media, and then click Project.*

2 *Click the Show Still Images button at the top right of the Project view, and deselect the Show Video button and Show Audio button.*

3 *Ctrl-click still images in the order in which you want them to appear in the slide show. Drag the selected group to a target area in the Sceneline and choose one of the following:*

• *Add As Individual Stills (This option places each still image onto its own target area in the Sceneline).*

• *Add As Grouped Slideshow (This option places the entire group onto one target that can be moved as a single clip).*

4 *In the Create Slideshow dialog box, select the required options and click OK.*

A grouped slide show clip is created in the selected target area of the Sceneline. A slide show icon appears to the upper right of the grouped slide show clip.

Changing the default still image duration

You may wish to modify the default duration Premiere Elements uses when importing still images, if you want a faster-paced slide show for example. In this exercise, you will now shorten the default duration to increase the pace of the slide show.

1 Choose Edit > Preferences > General. The Still Image Default Duration should be 150 frames unless it has been modified by you or another user. Remember that NTSC video uses 30 frames per second; therefore 150 frames are equal to 5 seconds. Type **90** into the Still Images Default Duration field, to change the duration to 3 seconds. *(See illustration on the next page.)*

Also in the General section of the Preferences dialog box are the options for controlling the default length of video transitions. In the field for Video Transition Default Duration, the value should be 30 frames (which equals one second). If you wanted to change the length of the transition, you would do so here. Do not change this value now. Click OK to close the Preferences dialog box.

2   Return to Photoshop Elements by clicking the Photoshop Elements button at the bottom of your screen in the Windows task bar.

3   Click to select only one image, the one named 12_2004.jpg, and then choose File > Send to Premiere Elements. Your open application should switch to Premiere Elements and the image will be placed at the end of your Sceneline or Timeline.

Note: Because you are sending only a single image from Photoshop Elements to Premiere Elements, there was no transition placed on this image. In this case, if you wanted to add a transition, you would have to do so manually. See Lesson 5 for more information about adding transitions.

4   Choose Window > Info to open the Info panel. Click the image you added to the Timeline in the last step. Notice that the duration of this clip is 3 seconds because you changed the default duration of still images imported into Premiere Elements.

5   Click the Close button to close the Info panel.

6   Choose File > Save As and save this project file into your Lesson12 folder as **Lesson12_Work**.

Moving images manually into Premiere Elements

Using the Send To Premiere Elements command in Photoshop Elements will not only add the images to the Project view, but also place them in the Sceneline. At times you may prefer to only add the images to the Project view so that you can manually place them in the Sceneline. To do this, you can drag images from the Photo Browser in Photoshop Elements to the Project view in Premiere Elements. Or you can copy images from the Photo Browser in Photoshop Elements and paste them into Premiere Elements. You will now use both these methods to transfer images from Photoshop Elements to Premiere Elements. Finally, you will learn how you can add images from your Photoshop Elements catalog without even having to open Photoshop Elements.

Using drag and drop from Photoshop Elements

1   Switch to Photoshop Elements by clicking the Photoshop Elements button in the Windows task bar at the bottom of your screen. You will now drag an image from the Photo Browser into the Project view of Premiere Elements.

2   For the next step to work, you must be able to reposition the Photoshop Elements program window on your screen. If your Photoshop Elements program window is maximized, you must click the Restore button in the upper right corner of the Photoshop Elements window. Once your Photoshop Elements program window is restored, you're ready to take the next step.

When maximized, click the Restore button. When restored, the Maximize button is visible.

3   Place your cursor at the top of the Photoshop Elements Organizer window and click and drag it to the left until you can see the Tasks panel of the Premiere Elements window beneath.

4   In the Photoshop Elements Photo Browser, click the image named 12_2005.jpg and drag it over the Premiere Elements Tasks panel. Your cursor icon will change to a small hand with image thumbnail when correctly positioned and the Project view opens in the Tasks panel. Release the pointer and the image will be added to the Project view in Premiere Elements.

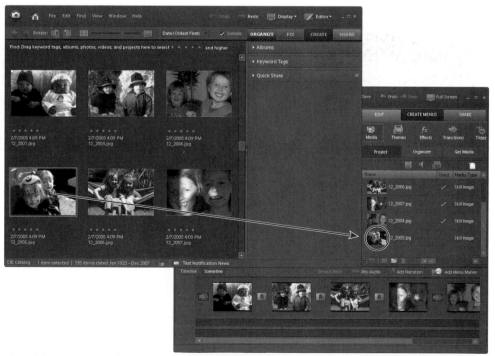

The Adobe Photoshop Elements Organizer window (left) and the Adobe Premiere Elements window (right).

After you released the pointer, Premiere Elements should automatically have become active. If not, switch to Premiere Elements. You can now use the image as a clip in your project.

5 In Premiere Elements, click and drag the newly added image from the Project view onto your Sceneline, placing it in between 12_2003.jpg, the photo of the twins wearing black hats, and 12_2006.jpg, the photo of the twins in the hammock. When you release the pointer, all subsequent clips will shift to the right.

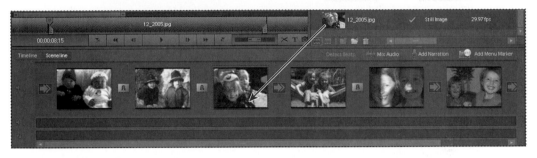

6 To get the stills back into a chronological order, click and drag the last image in the Sceneline, called 12_2004.jpg, between the images 12_2003.jpg and 12_2005.jpg. Notice the two transitions that have not yet had a cross dissolve transitions applied.

7 Click the Transitions button (➡) in the Edit tab of the Tasks panel, and then locate the Cross Dissolve transition in the video transitions category.

💡 *To make it easy to find transitions that you use frequently, add them to the Favorites category by right-clicking the transition and choosing Add To Favorites from the menu.*

8 Click and drag the Cross Dissolve transition onto the rectangle between still images 12_2004.jpg and 12_2005.jpg, as well as onto the rectangle between 12_2005.jpg and 12_2006.jpg. *(See illustration on the next page.)*

9   Review your project, and then save your work.

10   Switch back to Photoshop Elements and move the Photoshop Elements application window to its original location. Maximize the window if you prefer.

Using Copy and Paste to add images

Dragging images from Photoshop Elements to Premiere Elements requires fitting both windows on your screen, which may prove to be awkward, especially if you also have other windows open. It should help to close any unnecessary windows. To move images quickly between the two programs, you can use the copy and paste commands.

1   Make sure Photoshop Elements is your active application.

2   Click to select an image thumbnail in the Photo Browser, and then choose Edit > Copy. Alternatively, you could use the keyboard shortcut Ctrl+C, or right-click the image thumbnail and choose Edit > Copy from the context menu.

3   Switch to Premiere Elements by clicking the Adobe Premiere Elements button at the bottom of your screen in the Windows task bar.

4   Select Media in the Edit tab of the Tasks panel, and then click Project to open the Project view.

5   Choose Edit > Paste to add the image to the Project view. You can also use the keyboard shortcut Ctrl+V, or right-click inside the Project view and select Paste from the context menu. The file appears at the bottom of the Project view.

Using drag and drop from the Organizer view

If you found it cumbersome switching between the two applications and moving application windows around, you'll appreciate using the Organizer view in Premiere Elements. The Organizer view displays the content of the catalog last opened in Photoshop Elements, even if Photoshop Elements is not currently open.

From the Organizer view you can drag and drop assets directly onto the Sceneline or the Monitor panel to add them to your project. Assets added from the Organizer view will also be automatically added to the Project view and tagged with a project specific keyword tag. For more information on catalogs, keyword tags, and the Organizer view see "Using the Organizer view" in Lesson 3, "Navigating the workspace."

Creating a new Photoshop file optimized for video

The integration between Photoshop Elements and Premiere Elements works both ways. The first part of this lesson has focused on importing image files from a Photoshop Elements catalog into Premiere Elements. In this exercise, you will create a new still image in Premiere Elements, open it in Photoshop Elements to modify it, and then use it in your Premiere Elements project.

1 Make sure you are in Premiere Elements. Choose File > New > Photoshop File. In the Save Photoshop File As dialog box, navigate to your Lesson12 folder and name the file **Word_Balloon.psd**. Select the Add to Project (Merged Layers) check box, and then click Save. This will create a new Photoshop file in your Lesson12 folder and add a blank placeholder image in the Project view.

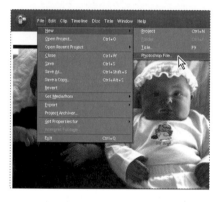

2 Your application will automatically switch to Photoshop Elements. Click OK if you see a dialog box notifying you that the file you are about to see was meant to be viewed on a television screen. The file Word_Balloon.psd opens in the Photoshop Elements Editor.

Note: If the file opens with a different application than Photoshop Elements, see Microsoft Windows File Associations at the end of this chapter. You might have to open the file manually from within Photoshop Elements.

Photoshop Elements has two primary components. The Organizer, which you have been using in the beginning of this lesson, enables you to sort and categorize your digital media files. The Editor, which you will be using now, enables you to enhance and modify your digital images using a series of image-editing tools.

3   In the Editor, make sure Full Edit mode is selected. If necessary, click the Full Edit button under the Edit tab.

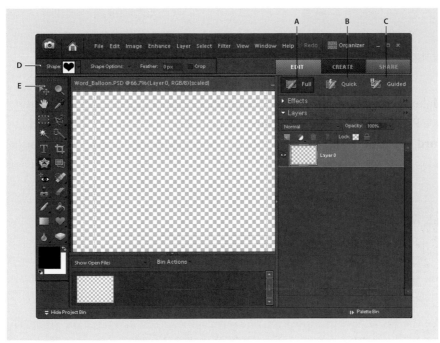

*A. Full Edit button. **B.** Quick Fix button. **C.** Guided Edit*
*D. Tool options bar. **E.** Toolbox.*

The Word_Balloon image was automatically formatted for your digital video project using the dimensions 720 pixels wide by 480 pixels high. The checkerboard that you see indicates that the image is on a transparent background.

4   In the toolbox, select the Custom Shape tool (♥) that is grouped with a range of other shape tools. The Custom shape menu offers a large selection of shapes ranging from ornaments, symbols and arrows to frames, titles, characters, and much more.

5   In the tool options bar, which changes depending on what tool is selected, click the color swatch to open the Select color dialog box. In the Select color dialog box, enter the values R: **255**, G: **255**, and B: **255** to set the color to white, and then click OK.

6   Click the Shape menu in the tool options bar, and then select the Talk Bubbles category from the menu in the top right corner of the palette that appears. *(See illustration on the next page.)*

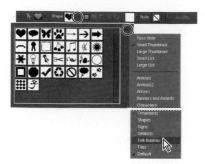

7   From within the Talk Bubbles category, double-click to select the Talk 4 shape.

8   Now, place your cursor near the top left corner of the Word_Balloon document window. Click, and then drag down and to the right to create a word balloon shape. Then, release the pointer. Don't worry about the exact placement and size yet.

9   Use the Move tool to reposition the talk balloon. You can have the shape slightly hang out of the image at the top edge. Resize the balloon using the handles of the bounding box. Try to resize and position the shape as shown in the illustration below, and then click the green Commit button or press Enter to apply the transformation.

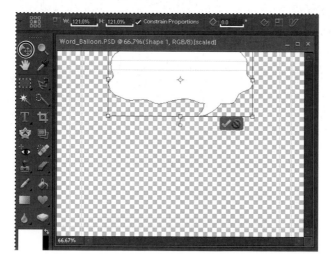

10 Choose File > Save. The Save As dialog box should be showing the Lesson12 folder. If not, navigate there now. The file name should default to Word_Balloon.psd. Click Save. When the alert dialog box appears notifying you that the file already exists, click OK. If a Photoshop Elements Format Options dialog box appears, click OK to close it using the default settings. Then choose File > Close.

11 Switch back to Premiere Elements by clicking the Premiere Elements button in your Windows task bar. The Word_Balloon.psd file has automatically been updated in your Project view. You can see a white word balloon over a black background. But don't worry, the background that appears as black in Premiere Elements, is—in effect— transparent.

12 In the Sceneline, select the first clip with the twins sitting on a blue couch, the image named 12_2001.jpg. Then, hold down the Shift key on your keyboard and drag and drop the Word_Balloon.psd file from the Project view onto the Monitor. When you release the pointer, choose Place on Top from the menu that appears. Because the word balloon was created on a transparent background, it is superimposed over the twins on the couch clip. In the next exercise, you will add text to the word balloon.

Hold down the Shift key while dragging and dropping the file from the Project view onto the Monitor panel, and then choose Place on Top from the menu that appears.

13 If you don't like the placement of the word balloon, you have two choices for changing it:

• Click to select the superimposed image in the Monitor panel, and then click and drag it to change its position relative to the image in the background.

Note: You can also use the Position parameters under Motion in the Properties panel (Window > Properties) to change the location of the superimposed clip.

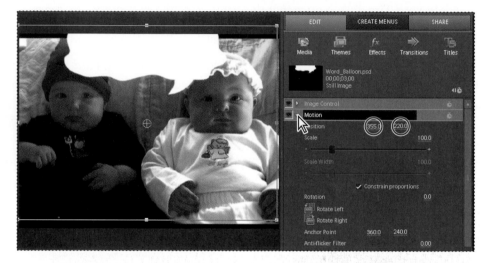

• Or, jump back to Photoshop Elements by right-clicking the image in the Project view and choosing Edit Original from the context menu. Adjust the position of the word balloon, and save the changes. The appearance of the image will automatically update when you switch back to Premiere Elements.

14 Save your work.

Editing a Photoshop image from Premiere Elements

You can edit a Photoshop Elements image while you're working in Premiere Elements, using the Edit Original command. Changes you make to the image will be updated automatically, even if the clip is already placed in your Sceneline or Timeline.

1   Switch to Timeline view in the My Project panel. If necessary, scroll to see the Video 2 track. Click to select the Word_Balloon.psd clip, superimposed on Video 2 track in your Timeline. Notice that the duration of the superimposed image is 3 seconds, the new default duration for still images you changed to earlier in this lesson.

When in Timeline view, pressing the equal sign (=) on your keyboard is a quick way to zoom in to better view the clips.

2   To adjust the duration of the superimposed balloon image, position the cursor at the end of the clip in the Video 2 track and when the cursor changes to Trim Out tool (✥), click and drag to the 00;00;03:15 mark where the transition to the next image starts. Then release the pointer.

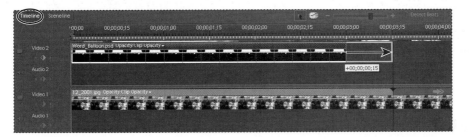

3   Right-click the clip in the Timeline and choose Edit in Adobe Photoshop Elements from the context menu. The Word_Balloon.psd file opens in Photoshop Elements.

Note: If Photoshop Elements is closed, it will automatically launch and open the file.

4   Select the Horizontal Type tool (T), which is grouped with the Vertical Type tool in the toolbox.

5   Position your cursor inside the word balloon near the left edge, and then click once to add an insertion point. Click the Default Foreground and Background Colors button in the toolbox. You will use the default black foreground color for your text.

6   In the tool options bar, click the Font Family menu and choose Arial Black from the list of fonts. In the font size menu, select 72 pt.

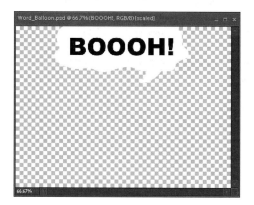

7   Using the Type tool, enter the following in the text layer: **BOOOH!**.

8   Select the Move tool (⬥) in the toolbox and click and drag the text layer to center it properly in the word balloon. If necessary, select the Shape 1 layer in the Layers palette, and then use the handles of the bounding box of the text balloon shape to adjust its size. When done, click the green Commit button to commit the changes.

9   Choose File > Save, overwriting the Word_Balloon.psd file in the Lessons12 folder. Close the file, and then switch to Premiere Elements by clicking the Premiere Elements button in your Windows task bar. The changes made to the Word_Balloon.psd file in Photoshop Elements have automatically been updated in the Premiere Elements project. This is very useful because it removes the need to re-import an image file every time a change is made.

10 If necessary, click the word balloon in the Monitor panel to select it, and then click and drag to reposition it. Because the image is on a transparent layer, it can be easily repositioned.

11 Click the top of the Timeline to select it, and then press the Home key to place the current-time indicator at the beginning of the Timeline. Press the spacebar to play your project. When done reviewing, save your work.

Creating a slide show using images from a folder

1 You can also set up a slide show relying only on Premiere Elements. Create a new project file and save it as **Lesson12_Slideshow.prel**.

2 Choose File > Get Media from > Files or Folders. Ctrl+click to select the six pictures from the images folder inside the Lesson12 folder, and then click OK.

3 Select all the imported image files in the Project view of the Tasks panel, and then drag and drop them collectively onto an empty clip placeholder in the Sceneline. Choose Add as grouped slideshow from the menu that appears when you release the pointer.

4 In the Create Slideshow dialog box, choose between Sort Order and Selection Order under Ordering. Keep the Image Duration at 90 Frames and leave the Apply Default Transition (Cross Dissolve) option selected. Then, click OK. This will place the selected images as a grouped scene, or slideshow, in the Sceneline. This method of creating a slide show can be used with any still images on your system, and does not require Photoshop Elements to be available.

Congratulations! You have finished the lesson on working with Photoshop Elements. You've discovered how to get photos from the Organizer and how to enhance them using the Editor. You also learned how to personalize a video clip with a speech bubble and text.

This is the last lesson in this book. We hope that you have gained confidence, skill, and knowledge about using Premiere Elements. But this book is just the start. You can learn more by studying the Premiere Elements 4.0 Help system that is built into the application, by choosing Help > Premiere Elements Help. Also, don't forget to look for tutorials, tips, and expert advice on the Adobe website, www.adobe.com.

Microsoft Windows® file associations

The Edit Original command can be very useful when there are changes to be made to an image. However, there are a few possible pitfalls to be aware of. When you use the Edit Original command on an image, Windows XP® opens the file in the application that is associated with the file name extension. For example, using the Edit Original command on the .jpg files used in this lesson may very well open them on your machine in another program such as a Web browser. You can force Windows XP® to use Photoshop Elements as the associated application for your image files using the following steps. Be aware that you will need to perform these steps each time for different file types, .jpg, .gif, .tiff, etc. Additionally, if you happen to have both Adobe Photoshop and Adobe Photoshop Elements on the same machine, you will need to choose which one you want to open image files.

Changing file associations in Windows XP®

1 *Choose Start > My Computer.*

2 *Double-click a drive or folder.*

3 *Right-click the selected image file and from the context menu that appears choose Open With > Choose Program.*

4 *In the Open With dialog box, select Photoshop Elements if it is in the list of Recommended Programs. If it is not in the list, click Browse and locate the Application in your hard drive.*

5 *In the Open With dialog box, make sure the check box Always Use the Selected Program to Open this Kind of File is selected.*

For more information, see the help documentation that came with your copy of Microsoft Windows®.

Review

▶ **Review questions**

1   Where can you find the command to place images from Photoshop Elements into Premiere Elements? Where are the images placed once they are sent to Premiere Elements?

2   What are additional ways to transfer images from Photoshop Elements into Premiere Elements?

3   How can you create a Photoshop file in Premiere Elements? What are the advantages of doing so?

▶ **Review answers**

1   In the Organizer of Photoshop Elements, choose the command File > Send to Premiere Elements. All files selected in the Photo Browser will be sent to Premiere Elements and added at the end of your Timeline. You can select individual images in the Photoshop Elements Photo Browser by Ctrl+clicking them.

2   You can transfer images from Photoshop Elements to Premiere Elements by dragging the desired files from the Photo Browser of Photoshop Elements into the Project view of Premiere Elements. The two windows must be visible on your screen for you to do this. You can also transfer images by selecting them in Photoshop Elements, choosing Edit > Copy, switching to Premiere Elements, and then choosing Edit > Paste. From the Organizer view in Premiere Elements you can add to your project assets organized in a Photoshop Elements catalog, without having to open Photoshop Elements itself.

3   The command File > New > Photoshop File will create a blank Photoshop file with dimensions of 720 pixels wide and 480 pixels high. The file is automatically optimized for use in Premiere Elements. This will enable you to use the various image editing tools in Photoshop Elements to modify or create images for use in your video project.

Index

Production Notes

The *Adobe Premiere Elements 4 Classroom in a Book* was created electronically using Adobe InDesign CS2. Additional art was produced using Adobe Illustrator CS2, and Adobe Photoshop CS2.

Team credits

The following individuals contributed to the development of new and updated lessons for this edition of the *Adobe Premiere Elements Classroom in a Book*:

Project coordinators, technical writers: Torsten Buck & Katrin Straub

Production: Manneken Pis Productions (www.manneken.com)

Copyediting & Proofreading: Ross Evans

Designer: Katrin Straub

Special thanks to Christine Yarrow & Jill Merlin.

Typefaces used

Set in the Adobe Minion Pro and Adobe Myriad Pro OpenType families of typefaces. More information about OpenType and Adobe fonts is available at Adobe.com.

6499

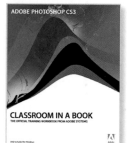